HISTORY OF
THE UNITED STATES

VOLUME VI

VOLUME VI
SECOND PART OF ANNUAL CHRONICLE

GENERAL DOUGLAS MacARTHUR

THE MARCH OF DEMOCRACY

A

HISTORY OF THE UNITED STATES

By

James Truslow Adams

Volume VI

SECOND PART OF ANNUAL CHRONICLE

NEW YORK

CHARLES SCRIBNER'S SONS

CONTENTS

vii

CONTENTS

ILLUSTRATIONS

ix

ILLUSTRATIONS

ILLUSTRATIONS

xi

ILLUSTRATIONS

END OF VOLUME

FRUITS OF AMERICAN INDUSTRIES

CHAPTER I

THE RECORD OF 1942

THE year 1942 started as one of the most sombre in the history of the United States, certainly the most sombre in the lives of living Americans. As a nation we have had little experience of war. Only in the American Revolution, ended about a hundred and sixty years ago, and the Civil War ended about eighty years ago, had the national existence been at stake or a large part of the people involved. The Mexican and Spanish Wars were "side shows" and menaced neither the nation as a whole nor any great number of its citizens. Even the first World War was fought far from our shores and the total number of lives lost in action or as a result of wounds was less than 50,000, whereas 40,000 were killed in automobile accidents in our own country in 1941. This war is different, and for the first time in the memory of most of us it is being brought home to every household in one way or another.

It began with the sickening disaster to our forces and our pride in the dastardly attack by the Japanese on Pearl Harbor on that December "Day of Infamy," as the President called it, which we mentioned at the end of the re-

I

view of 1941. It soon became obvious that the blow had been heavy, though just how heavy the people were not to learn until a year later. However, Mr. Knox, Secretary of the Navy, flew to Hawaii at once, and on December 18, 1941, the President despatched a commission of enquiry headed by Associate Justice Owen J. Roberts of the Supreme Court to make a report, which was given to the public on January 25, 1942. According to Knox the battleship *Arizona* and the target ship *Utah* had been sunk, the battleship *Oklahoma* capsized, a mine layer and three destroyers sunk, and heavy damage inflicted on our air fleet. In February the President broadcast the casualties as 2340 killed and 946 wounded.

The Roberts Report may be summed up in the words of an editorial in the *New York Times* which said that it was evident that "Prior to the attack almost every military mistake possible seems to have been made by those immediately in charge of the defense of Hawaii, while the evils of unlucky chance added to those of incompetence." The Report amply confirmed this estimate of the situation, as have later papers issued by the Government. Those responsible on the spot had received ample warning from Washington far in advance but had not taken the necessary precautions. Japan had spun out the negotiations ostensibly looking toward a peaceful solution but meanwhile had for weeks been making every military preparation for the attack. Washington was not unaware of what was going on and both the Secretaries of State and

War had informed the local commanders. The likelihood of an attack on the harbor had been foreseen by the government at least as early as the preceding January. Yet even in December the fleet was concentrated in its narrow waters and everyone locally was wholly unprepared.

The trouble, however, had been more than local. It stemmed in part from the old-time antagonism and jealousy between the two departments of the forces, military and naval, both in Washington and in the field. Even in spite of urgent cables from Washington, the two leaders at Hawaii, Major General Walter C. Short and Rear Admiral Husband E. Kimmel had not conferred together or taken any concerted steps to protect Hawaii from November 27 on, though the attack did not come until ten days later, December 7. The full truth was not revealed until the anniversary of the disaster, in December 1942, and we may note the final revelations here, well out of their chronological order, so as to complete the tale of what was perhaps the greatest blow ever struck against us owing to our own inefficiency. Knox's first report, a year earlier, had been quite inadequate. Even the Roberts Report did not tell the whole story. We did not know the whole truth until the Navy Department revealed the facts just a year later. A certain reticence at first was obviously necessary for military reasons, but the Japanese government had known what had happened many months before the American people learned it.

In brief the statement was that (although we had no

3

two-ocean navy), the backbone of our whole fleet, eighty-six of our larger vessels, had been concentrated in Pearl Harbor. The revised figures informed us that eight battleships, seven cruisers, twenty-eight destroyers and five submarines were gathered there. Of these, five battleships, three destroyers, a mine layer and target ship, and the large floating dry dock were sunk or damaged so severely as to be useless for a long time. Three other battleships, three cruisers, and other vessels were heavily injured. Of the 202 naval airplanes at the island base, 150 had been disabled at once by the Japanese; and of the 273 army planes, "very few were able to take off" when the attack occurred. The catastrophe was colossal. Our men had fought and suffered with the utmost courage and, as always, there had been conspicuous examples of gallantry, but none could stand before the treachery of the enemy and the inefficiency of our own command. In February the government accepted the requests of General Short and Admiral Kimmel to be retired, but it did so "without condonation of any offense or prejudice to any future disciplinary action," and with the additional notice that the officers would be court-martialled but not "until such time as the public interest and safety would permit." No action known to the public has as yet been taken.

The year was to be so crowded with military movements and events all over the globe that it will be impossible for us to treat them with anything like the same detail we have given in speaking of Pearl Harbor. We may note that the mere chronology of the events of the war, in its first twelve months, occupies fifty-four pages, double column, and very fine print, in the *World Almanac*. Even to mention all these, apart from discussing them and speaking of other factors in our history for the year, is impossible within the limits of a single chapter. Let us hope that there will never again in our annals be a Pearl Harbor. That attack was for us the beginning of the war, and so calls, perhaps, for more space than we can give to the innumerable engagements which were to follow.

As we noted at the end of the last chapter, Winston Churchill, the British Prime Minister, with a party of eighty-five high members of government and experts in various lines, had come to Washington, for a fortnight, just before Christmas. For the time being that city was the center of planning for the global war, and far-reaching decisions of the utmost importance had to be taken by the Premier and the President. There were two temptations for us as Americans yet untouched by war on our own continent. One was to wait until we felt every preparation had been made,—the "perfectionist theory"—and the other was to concentrate on licking Japan for what she had done to us. In a war, however, involving fields of operation and dangers in every quarter of the earth, high strategy involved problems never faced before by any belligerents.

It is reported that when Woodrow Wilson was leaving his home in Princeton to take up his duties as President in the White House, he remarked to a friend that "it would be the irony of fate if during his term he should have to transfer his attention from national to international affairs." Roosevelt, on the other hand, has shown great ability in the handling of international matters and understanding of the present world crisis. What decisions may have been arrived at by the President and Mr. Churchill cannot be known, but in his speech to Congress on the state of the nation on January 6, the President said that during the coming year our operations would have to be both defensive and offensive, and that American land, air and sea forces would be found in the Pacific, in the British Isles, "which constitute an essential fortress in this world struggle," and in bases elsewhere, in protecting this hemisphere.

By the end of the month a large contingent of our new "A.E.F." had landed in North Ireland, the first of an ever-increasing stream to go overseas. De Valera, on behalf of Eire, protested that this was an infringement of Irish neutrality, though it is difficult to understand why, and the protest had no effect on later events.

Meanwhile, on January 1, a Declaration by the United Nations had been signed in Washington, accepting the Atlantic Charter on behalf of all of them. Each government pledged itself to use its full strength against those members of the Tri-partite Pact with which it might be at war, and to make no separate armistice or peace with the enemy. The nations signing were the United States, the United Kingdom of Great Britain and Northern Ireland, the Union of Soviet Republics, China, Australia, Belgium, Canada, Costa Rica, Cuba, Czecho-Slovakia, the Dominican Republic, El Salvador, Greece, Guatemala, Haiti, Honduras, India, Luxembourg, the Netherlands, New Zealand, Nicaragua, Norway, Panama, Poland, South Africa and Yugoslavia. They all stated that they were "convinced that complete victory over their enemies is essential to defend life, liberty, independence and religious freedom, and to preserve human rights and justice in their own lands as well as in other lands, and that they are now engaged in a common struggle against savage and brutal forces seeking to subjugate the world." This was the New Year's greeting of the liberty-loving nations to the Germans, Italians and Japanese.

We may note the names of the South American Republics included in the list. During January an inter-American conference had been held at Rio Janeiro which ended on the 28th after adopting resolutions for the severance of diplomatic, commercial and financial relations with the Axis Powers by all the participants. Brazil immediately did so, and in the course of the year all the other South American nations did likewise, with the exception of Argentina.

In the Pacific the Japanese continued to push the initial advantage they had gained. Our forces were distributed in Hawaii, the Philippines and in smaller islands, such as Guam and Wake, which latter were unprepared for attack because Congress had never been willing to appropriate the necessary money. Moreover, all our troops were widely scattered over the great stretches of the Pacific Ocean and with our navy, on which we had counted heavily, temporarily out of commission, our situation seemed desperate. The enemy had been bombing the more than three-century-old city of Manila and on December 26 General MacArthur had not only declared it to be an open town but withdrew both his troops and the anti-aircraft installations so as to save the defenseless inhabitants from wanton slaughter. The Japanese, however, had no regard for international law and the following day blasted the city from the air, destroying among other buildings the ancient cathedral and the long demilitarized historic fort of Santiago built in 1591. Secretary Hull denounced this complete disregard of all long-accepted military law as "fiendish inhumanity." On January 2 the city fell and the American forces which had been located outside of it retreated to the Bataan Peninsula, finally withdrawing to Corregidor, one of the strongest armed fortresses in the Pacific area, located on a steep rock about four miles long and situated two miles south of Bataan in Manila Bay. The epic of Bataan-Corregidor had begun.

While the Japanese command was living in the luxurious Manila Hotel and using the former residence of the United States High Commissioner as their headquarters, General MacArthur and his men—and we must not forget the women army nurses—were carrying on a terrific struggle against the conquerors, among the peaks, ravines, jungle swamps and "fox-holes" of the strange landscape of Bataan.

Although it will carry us somewhat out of our chronological order we may here finish the story of this aspect of the war. Glorious as the defense of the peninsula was, it was to be hopeless in the absence of reinforcements or additional supplies. Meanwhile, the Japanese, as will be noted later, had been extending their conquests elsewhere in the Pacific. Australia feared that its own hour had struck, and had asked for General MacArthur to help in its defense. Nothing was known to the public of this, but three weeks later the world was electrified to learn by a laconic cable that MacArthur had escaped from Bataan by motor boat and plane and was in Australia as "supreme commander in that region, including the Philippine Islands." The men in Bataan and Corregidor continued to fight but Bataan fell to the enemy in mid-April and Corregidor on May 6.

We shall return to the Pacific theater of war presently but will consider first the civilians on the home front.

On January 7 the President presented to Congress the budget for the current year which amounted to over $59,000,000,000, which was $25,000,0000,000 more than was spent on the whole of the First World War. The deficit, even after an increase in taxation of $9,000,000,000, was estimated to be probably over $35,000,000,000, and the President asked to have the debt limit raised to $110,000,000,000. Such figures are as far beyond our realization

9

as are astronomical distances but they have to be recorded, and were to be greatly increased later. What the ordinary citizen could understand was that his taxes would be enormously enlarged, his future work mortgaged, and that prices and the cost of living would undoubtedly rise. Ominous from another angle of war's possible impacts, and more easily understood by the man in the street than the astronomical figures of finance, were the gradual disappearance of treasures from libraries and museums. The first week of January the Constitution of the United States, the Declaration of Independence, the Gutenberg Bible on vellum, and the British Magna Carta all disappeared from the Library of Congress, sent to an unknown hiding place for safe-keeping; and such disappearances became common.

On New Year's Day something else disappeared from American life with a startling suddenness—new cars. The government issued a decree that all retail sales of passenger cars or trucks would be absolutely prohibited until the 15th, when it would ration the 650,000 then on hand, or to be made during the month, as it saw fit. The motor industry, employing directly and indirectly nearly 7,000,-000 Americans, came to a halt as abruptly as though one of its own cars had run into a stone wall. As the year went on, the manufacturing part of the industry was to be completely transformed into the greatest mass production plant for instruments of war the world has ever seen. In 1942 General Motors alone produced $1,900,000,000 of

Harper in The Birmingham Age-Herald

THE HIGHWAY WILL BE PATROLLED: MR. HOARDER MEETS
GENERAL RATIONING

war matériel. But if the industry was set on its feet so also were most Americans. The bicycle business boomed, until bicycles also were prohibited and practically unobtainable. Later, on account of the rubber and gas shortages, came the rationing of gas and driving. The U-boats were beginning to sink our tankers (*e.g.,* the *Rochester* off the Virginia coast and many others in January), and we had built no pipe-lines from the oil fields of the West and Southwest to the great industrial areas of New England and the Middle States. Then we found that, with our sources of raw rubber cut off, we had no means of making any. Next we woke up to the fact that about one third of our sugar came from the Philippines, which were lost to us, and from Hawaii, where the crop would be cut in half, and that half of the whole came from Porto Rico and Cuba, involving the problem of shipping again. So sugar rationing came, and even chewing gum became scarce. Mr. and Mrs. Ordinary Citizen were beginning to feel the pinch and by February had started a vast hoarding spree, which helped to force rationing all along the line later. Another item which brought home to all a change in daily life was the adoption of nation-wide, year-round daylight saving, which was to be called "War Time" and not "Daylight Saving Time."

Meanwhile the country was becoming somewhat alarmed by the failure of the Civilian Defense program. This had been in the hands of Mrs. Roosevelt and Mayor LaGuardia but both were busy with other matters. Yet the possible safety of the entire population was at stake, and even by January investigation was still going on to devise some means of turning off the 31,000 street lights in New York City other than by hand in the case of each individual light, which required the service of 93,000 air

Hungerford in The Pittsburgh Post-Gazette

THE COUNTRY WAS BEING STIRRED TO NEW EFFORTS IN
THE CIVILIAN DEFENSE PROGRAM

wardens or substitutes. Finally the President appointed Dean James M. Landis of the Harvard Law School as

Executive Officer of the department, with LaGuardia still as nominal head and Mrs. Roosevelt as Assistant Director, although both the latter resigned later. The sinkings of ships along our coast were increasing but we may now turn again briefly to affairs in the Pacific so far as they directly concerned ourselves. In a sense, of course, every event of the world struggle has concerned us, whoever has been involved and wherever, so that the comparatively few events which are all that can be mentioned cannot possibly be made to offer a complete picture.

Following Pearl Harbor the Japanese appeared off Alaska in the Aleutian Islands and have not as yet been dislodged. It is unpleasant to have them on American soil, and in a later phase of the war, when Germany has been defeated and the death blow to Japan may be in view as the *finale* of the drama, these islands may take on a new importance. Meanwhile one of the results of their occupation has been the building of the great highway to Alaska from our own northern boundary across Canadian territory, a military road about 1600 miles long and completed toward the end of the year several months ahead of schedule in spite of the great difficulties encountered. Aside from the strategic importance in the present war of this long road through the wilderness, it may eventually prove of great value in the development of Alaska and of our friendly relations with our neighbor on the north, with whom we share almost the whole of the North American continent. Looking ahead to a post-war world it is a satisfaction to realize that this common struggle in which we have been engaged has immensely improved our relations with every other nation in the New World, with the possible exception as yet of the Argentine. Moreover, although we are—also "as yet"—the most powerful of them all, it is well to recall that we are only the third in size, Canada and Brazil both being larger than the United States, even though one is thought of as largely Arctic waste and the other as tropical jungle. Nevertheless, with new raw material discoveries or needs, altered trade routes, and so on, things change. When in 1763 England had to decide whether to take Canada from France, or the "rich sugar islands" of Guadelope and Martinique, the government was severely criticized for choosing Canada. Who today would swap that great Dominion for the two West India islands? In any case, and without travelling too far into the realm of the future, one of the encouraging things about the war has been the new relations and more friendly understandings it has fostered among the nations of the New World.

In the four months following the attack on Pearl Harbor the enemy scored a series of successes throughout the entire South Pacific area which would have been considered unbelievable when the war began. Roughly, the area formed a triangle each side of which was about two thousand miles long, and within it were sections of Asiatic mainland and innumerable islands, some of very large extent and some mere dots in the watery waste but of marked strategic importance. The distances were enormous, such as the three thousand miles from Yokohama to Singapore and the two thousand from Singapore to Port Darwin in Australia. Control of the air was to prove a deciding factor in the Japanese advance, which was amazing in its speed and completeness. We speak of speed but in each case the enemy advanced step by step and it is hard to set particular dates for their conquest of any particular spot, even naval battles sometimes lasting for a week or more.

In brief, during January the British Crown Colony of Hong Kong had been taken, and the Japs were in Borneo, the Celebes and New Guinea; also heading toward Singapore; advancing against the British through Malaya; and attacking the Dutch East Indies. In February they were fighting in Java and Burma, bombing Rangoon, threatening India and raiding the Indian Ocean with their submarines. On the 15th, to give a precise date, they received from the British local command the unconditional surrender of the supposedly "impregnable" naval base and fortress of Singapore, the strongest and most important point possessed by the Allies in the Far East. The blow not only to British prestige in the whole East but to the Allied cause was a terrific one. Churchill in London next day made no effort to minimize it. "Tonight," he said in Parliament, "the Japanese are triumphant. They shout their exultation 'round the world. We suffer. We are taken aback," but there was no yielding by either the Prime Minister or the British people, only a grimmer determination to win. Nor was there any weakening in America. In a radio broadcast February 23 President Roosevelt admitted that we had suffered serious reverses and would meet more but affirmed that we were wholly committed to the destruction of the power of the Axis aggressors and that we were gaining steadily in strength.

With the loss of the citadel the British also lost thirty-two warships and transports, and also at sea the only two capital ships the Allies had, H.M.S. *Repulse* and H.M.S. *Prince of Wales*. Another great disaster was soon to follow. In the Battle of the Java Sea, February 27–March 1, the United Nations lost most of their ships in that section, including British, American, Dutch and Australian, twelve warships being sunk against Japanese losses of only seven. In a report Admiral Hart admitted that our Asiatic fleet had lost a campaign.

During March the Japanese continued their successful advance. On the 7th the Netherlands Government in London received a laconic cable from Java which said, "We are shutting down. Good-bye till better days. Long live the Queen." Java had fallen; Timor was occupied; Australia attacked; and India threatened. Then came the fall of Sumatra, and the Japanese landing on the Solomons. Japanese occupation of Burma had cut off the Burma Road along which alone supplies had been able to reach the hard-pressed Chinese, who had put up a magnificent fight for over four years. At the beginning of April American planes began flying supplies to Chiang

Kai-shek from bases in India. That country, however, was in the throes of an imperial crisis, and the mission of Sir Stafford Cripps, which had offered every possible concession to the Nationalists under the circumstances of the time, had failed. The American Government also sent a mission to India the end of March but without result.

The Japs had also seized the Moluccas and the Marshall Islands, the latter being among those for which they had been given a mandate under the Versailles Treaty and the League of Nations. When Japan had withdrawn from the League she had refused to give up the mandated islands, in accordance with the terms under which they had been entrusted to her. Not only that, but in absolute violation of her pledge she had fortified them, and they had been useful as stepping stones in her march of conquest. We had declined to join the League ourselves, partly because we did not wish to assume responsibility for policing the world. We were now being forced to "police it" to an extent we had never dreamed of! The American Navy had taken more than one sound thrashing, and American troops had been captured in the Philippines, and were now being poured into remote places in the South Pacific of which most Americans had never before heard. American flyers were not only transporting supplies to China but—for the most part at this time volunteers—were fighting the Japanese from the Chinese lines.

On April 9 occurred the naval Battle of the Indian Ocean in which the Japanese sank two British heavy cruisers. It is, as I have said, simply impossible to note all the sinkings and engagements even in the Pacific area (where we were chiefly engaged in the early part of the year), much less what was happening to our Allies and enemies all over the globe, all of which was of either direct or indirect importance to us. Not merely are the facts too numerous and complex for a brief account but many of them were not made public until months later and many are even yet military secrets.

For example, good news at last came from the Pacific war area on April 18 when Americans read that American flyers had bombed Tokio and other Japanese cities. Official confirmation of any sort was slow in coming. A few days later, one U. S. bomber was reported as having been grounded in Siberia and its crew interned by the Russians. Where our planes had started from has always remained a mystery. When asked, Mr. Roosevelt merely smiled and said from "Shangri-la," obviously a false name. Some of the story was disclosed a month later when the leader of the raid, Brigadier General James H. Doolittle, was decorated in Washington. No mention was made of any loss until six months afterwards when it was announced that four of our planes had failed to return. At the time, the raid made a great impression both in Japan and America, but the mystery in which it was always shrouded has continued, and it was never repeated. This indicates some of the difficulties in trying to write in detail of military events so near to us and which for obvious reasons cannot as yet be authentically described. This is perhaps especially true of the numbers, types of forces, and locations of our troops in all theaters.

On April 25 our government announced that we had taken possession of the French island of New Caledonia in the Southwest Pacific with the consent of the local French authorities. This brings us to a fresh point regarding the Japanese conquests and threats. The small island, aside from its purely strategic importance, has always been a considerable producer of nickel and chrome, and the Japanese advance had already played havoc with the sources of many of the basic materials essential to both our peace and war economy. For example, all of the burlap we have used has come from India, and 99 per cent of that from the provinces most closely threatened by the Japs. We need about 500,000,000 pounds a year of it to pack and handle our farm produce and other products. Nothing else can take its place. Hemp for ropes and other purposes had largely been lost to us when the Philippines went. We are the greatest makers of steel in the world but almost wholly dependent for manganese, a most important factor in the industry, on imports from India and Soviet Russia. The war had stopped practically all imports from the latter. Mica does not sound important to the average man but it is essential as an insulator in almost all electrical apparatus. It is in your radios, your telephone, your motor engine, in almost everything connected with electricity. Eighty per cent of it comes from India. We have already spoken of the loss of rubber and sugar, and could continue the list—with the loss of tea from Java and Sumatra, oil from that island and Burma, shellac, and other things—but have already pointed to enough to indicate the seriousness of the damage which Japan was inflicting on us.

It must also be recalled that what we were losing for *our* war effort Japan was gaining for *hers*. Moreover, shipping was becoming scarce. The demands on it for transport of troops and supplies, for imports from wherever we could get them, all made the submarine the increasing peril which it was to remain increasingly to the end of the year. The British were also badly off in that regard. They, too, had heavy needs and had suffered heavy losses, and in addition, owing to the closing to them of the Mediterranean and the Suez route, all their ships to the Near and Far East had to ply the many thousands of miles extra involved in going round the Cape of Good Hope. All this added poignancy to the cry of chagrin and rage which went up when on February 9 the *Normandie* was burned at her dock in New York. This great ship, one of the finest, largest and latest afloat, which had been taken over by the government from the French and rechristened the *Lafayette,* was being refitted when fire broke out and almost completely destroyed her. rendering her useless for the duration of the war even if she may ever be salvaged. The giant ship was almost 80,000 tons, over 1000 feet long, and had originally cost $59,000.000

to build. Several courts of enquiry decided that there had been no sabotage but that there had been gross carelessness.

Before continuing with the story of military operations we may note other happenings at home during these months.

More and more America was turning to war as its sole interest. Industries were continually being shifted from the mass production of civilian goods at mass prices to the making of war supplies. As an instance, we may mention the $200,000,000 radio industry which was ordered on February 13 to convert its whole facilities to the production of arms. It may be noted here that although American industry was to make a wonderful showing and enormously increase its output, its earnings, contrary to the case in the previous war, were not to increase. In fact in many cases they were to be sharply curtailed, owing to taxation. There were no "war babies" in the stock market this time, and the great increase in national income was almost wholly given to labor and not to the owners of industries. It may also be noted at this point that not only was labor more careful, perhaps, of its spending than in the earlier war boom, but as goods grew scarcer and in many cases were strictly rationed or taken off the market entirely, labor had less on which to spend. The changes in all phases of our life related to automobiles were notable in this regard as were also new restrictions on instalment buying. One result was that, as the year advanced, the savings of the lower income classes increased by leaps and

Shoemaker in The Chicago Daily Sun

THE RACE FOR LIFE: THE FIGHT AGAINST THE SUBMARINE

bounds, in the form of savings bank and other deposits, government bonds and stamps, life insurance and paid-off mortgages. War for the first time in America had assumed a wholly new aspect, which may prove to be of great importance when peace comes and savings are released coincident with a return to civilian production.

Meanwhile we may note the growing war effort in other ways. Whereas in January the estimate that there would be 3,600,000 men eventually in the army was considered "huge" by some leading newspapers, by May Under-Secretary of War Patterson announced that the army goal had been raised to 8,000,000, and as it had been previously announced that the goals for the Air Force and Navy were 2,000,000 and 1,000,000 respectively, this meant a future possible stepping-up to a total in the armed forces of 11,000,000, or about three times the number then in service. A slight but interesting sidelight on what this meant in the way of providing for them was given in a Reuter despatch from aboard a large transport "in the Pacific" in April, which stated that 10,000 eggs were eaten for breakfast every morning, requiring the all-night service of four men to crack the shells. No soldiers in history have ever had such ample supplies of the best quality of food and clothing as have our troops in this war, whenever it was possible to get them to them. We may contrast the 10,000 eggs daily for breakfast on the transport with the one a week which is the ration of the British Prime Minister!

Without entering too deeply on the maze of government finance bills, we may glimpse another step-up in the war effort by one or two examples. On February 2 the Senate made a record in time and figures by passing the largest single appropriation made in our history, a $26,500,000,000 Navy Supply Bill, after only two hours of debate. A week later the President asked Congress for an additional $5,430,000,000 for the Lease-Lend program, which would bring our total for that purpose to almost $30,000,000,000. On the other hand, it was estimated that overtime pay was adding some $4,000,000,000 to the cost of naval contracts, and throughout the year there was much discussion of the unfairness of a forty-hour week for labor at home when our soldiers, sailors, marines and flyers were risking their lives in an "all round the clock" all over the world. March 17 the limit for the national debt was raised to $130,000,000,000, and estimates were made that before the end of the war it might reach $300,000,-000,000.

Apart from Lease-Lend operations we were far from limiting our activities to the Pacific, though that was the area in which the most spectacular news items were being made. In addition to what we already mentioned there were sinkings on both sides, Japanese warships by American submarines, even in the China Sea, and more attacks on ourselves, which would make only a bare catalogue of names and dates in the telling, and can be found elsewhere. For a moment we may turn to the Old World.

Throughout the year we were to have our difficulties in steering a tortuous course with the French government at Vichy, and the Free French, now called the Fighting

French, under the leadership of General de Gaulle with headquarters in London. The details of this diplomacy are too complex for this brief survey of the year, but we may note that on April 7 the Vichy government protested against our recognition of the Free French in Equatorial Africa and the Cameroons. The same day word was received of the arrival in London of General George C. Marshall, Chief of Staff of the U. S. Army, and of Mr. Harry Hopkins, Chief of the British-American Munitions Assignment Board. In view of future events the coincidence was interesting. It was evident that another and important step had been taken in joint planning of major strategy.

Meanwhile the traitor Laval had returned to power and influence at Vichy and was trying to provide "full collaboration" of France with the Nazis. What that meant was clear. The sinister SS-man, Prince Waldeck-Pyrmont, arrived in Paris, to be followed by Richard Heydrich, head of the dreaded Gestapo, known even to Germans as "the Hangman." Then came Göring and Hitler himself. Laval was also conferring with the Japanese Ambassador to Berlin, who had come from thence with Admiral Nomura, head of the Japanese Mixed Axis Commission in Germany and Admiral Abe who held a similar post at Rome. Far-reaching plans were being laid, but of immediate concern to the Allies was the fate of the great island of Madagascar, which was to be occupied by the Japanese, and would be a base from which the Axis could

26

attack British shipping to the Near East and India even when it took the long route around the Cape. The immediate answer was the beginning of the seizure of the island by the British, completed after a few weeks, and the announcement by the United States that it was firmly behind the British in their move. We had learned that the Vichy government had surrendered Indo-China, with all the important results of that move, to the Japs, and this time we were not to be caught napping. It is an added illustration, however, of how the foreign policy of the United States, backed by our forces, was gradually circling the entire globe.

At home, events were also moving fast, and we may note here the beginning of the organizing of women in the war effort. They were not, as some in Russia, to take up arms and form a "battalion of death" but were to perform most useful service, as well as to add to the alphabetical complexities of government departments and organizations. First there were the WAACS. Starting with 25,000 women, the Act authorizing this women's auxiliary army permitted an ultimate enrollment of 150,-000. Women between 21 and 45, married or unmarried, provided they did not have children under fourteen years of age, were eligible if they passed certain required tests. It was an army organization and its members served as typists, clerks, operators of office machines and telephone switchboards, drivers and repairers of cars, aircraft warners, dieticians, cooks, pharmacist's assistants, and in many other capacities, freeing men for the fighting line. They could go wherever the army went and were liable to overseas service.

The WAVES formed a branch of the Naval Reserve and their work was usually highly technical, including knowledge of such subjects as mathematics, aeronautical engineering, astronomy, accounts and business statistics, foreign languages, radio operating, and many others. Starting with only 10,000 the service proved so efficient that it was much enlarged.

Next came the WAFS. This was an auxiliary aviation unit made up of pilots with the necessary administrative members. Among other duties they flew planes from the point of manufacture to that of service, including trans-Atlantic flying.

Women in these organized services were, however, but a small proportion of the total who took part in the war effort, and in many lines men were rapidly replaced by women. Not only in such fields as hospital nursing and others already largely pre-empted by women, but in all forms of business and daily work women undertook their share of the national burden. To mention only one, we may note that after a year of war about 65,000 women were employed in banks, or one quarter of the total personnel. We should also include all those men and women, a large part of them teachers in the schools, who served without pay in the thankless and dull work of the rationing boards. There was no glamor about it, and no uniforms, with often unpopularity and sour looks as the only reward, but it was democracy at work and service freely given for the cause of the nation.

In the summer of 1942 the outlook was grim. More and more the war was becoming global and almost every nation had become involved. For example, on June 3 Hungary, Bulgaria and Rumania declared war on us, and on the same day Mexico declared war on the Axis. This was but a sample of what was gradually happening everywhere. The issues were so vast, so vital, so fundamental that no self-respecting nation could remain aloof. Hitler's record of broken pledges and lies, those lies on which he had intended, so he frankly told all peoples in his book *Mein Kampf,* to build his new world order, had shown the futility and inanity of trying to remain "neutral." Every man on earth had to be for or against him. To that extent he had come to dominate the entire human race as one had never done before him. Much as all of us who belong to the freedom-loving nations may hate him and all he stands for, there is no use in minimizing his influence and power. To do so is only to endure the fate of nation after nation which has thought it need not suffer from the strife but could carry on its life by the simple method of standing aside.

We may now turn again to the military events, fortunately as yet at long distance from our own shores, though distance, even if it saved us in our homes, entailed excessive difficulties. As one went about America it was hard to picture it in the condition of other countries, with bombed and pulverized cities and ruined countrysides. We had only the choice of that or of holding the enemy overseas, though both for the British and ourselves these military enterprises thousands of miles from bases was as exhausting, Churchill said, as holding a heavy "dumbbell at arm's length." Yet such efforts were also exhausting our enemies, whose resources were less than ours for a protracted struggle.

In the spring and early summer there was bad news for the Allies from many theaters of war, Egypt, Lybia, Russia and elsewhere, but the outlook was also brightened by successes. In the first week of May we won a decisive victory over the Japanese in the naval battle of the Coral Sea, in which our only loss was the sixteen-year-old aircraft *Lexington,* which went down gloriously, as against Japanese losses of a new aircraft carrier, three heavy cruisers, one light cruiser, two destroyers, four gunboats and four transports sunk, as well as nine other important war vessels damaged.

Exactly one month after the Coral Sea battle began the Japanese and Americans again met in that area of Midway, where we once more inflicted losses on the enemy far in excess of our own, losses, moreover, which their resources did not permit them to repair. Not only were we at last beginning to pay off scores for Pearl Harbor but our weight was also beginning to tell and we had learned valuable lessons. The chief was the importance of land-based airplanes to operate in conjunction with the fleets. This pointed the way to immensely increased production of planes and the need for seizing bases already occupied by the enemy. As to the first, we may note that orders were given for these, and other material, to automobile manufacturers equivalent to the production of 15,000,000 cars and trucks under normal conditions, or the output for the whole best three years of peace-time production. We shall mention later the bases we seized, and merely add here the statement made by the British Prime Minister before the House of Commons early in the year 1943, which lies just beyond this chapter, though the speech referred to events in 1942. Churchill said that the "ingenious use of aircraft to solve intricate tactical problems" as shown in MacArthur's generalship in the Pacific, should be carefully studied by all concerned with the technical problems of the war. We had at least gone a long way from that black seventh of December in Hawaii.

Nevertheless, general news was bad. The Nazis were pressing the Russians hard; Tobruk had fallen to the Axis after a long siege with 25,000 prisoners; and the Allies were slowly losing, for the time, the battle of shipping against the German submarines. Argentine reversed her policy in July and seemed to align herself in sympathy with the Axis, although in August Brazil openly declared war against Germany and Italy. In October Under-Secretary of State Sumner Welles was to issue a thinly veiled rebuke to both the Argentine and Chile for their complacency with regard to the activities of Axis agents within their borders.

Although we were sending large contingents of troops to Ulster and England, our military activities continued to be centered in the Pacific. In August we attacked the Japanese in the Aleutians simply with the idea of holding them, wearing them down, and preventing them from extending farther. We also, for quite different reasons, made an attack on Tulagi in the Solomon Islands and landed marines on Guadalcanal. The islands struck at formed perhaps the most vital key for operations in the Southwest Pacific. Our initial success was a major check to what had hitherto been the steady advance of the enemy, and when, after six months of hard fighting, we came into complete control, it meant that the tide had turned. Without minimizing the importance of other battles, probably the epics of Corregidor-Bataan and Guadalcanal will live longest in the annals of the heroism of American soldiers during the first year of our struggle for life against a nation which, nearly a century earlier, we had introduced to what we thought was civilization. In October, it may be noted, both Britain and the United States relinquished their extra-territorial rights so long held in China, an action deeply appreciated by the rising and nobly fighting Chinese nation.

The events of November were of the first importance. In the Far East we won another great victory over the Japanese in the naval battle of the Solomons, the heaviest "slugging match," as Admiral Nimitz called it, in which the American navy had been engaged since the Civil War. Irreparable losses were inflicted on the enemy, and their attempt to reinforce Guadalcanal was completely frustrated. Vice-Admiral Halsey was in command of our fleet. The victory was hailed by our Allies, and a statement was given out that including our losses at Pearl Harbor we had lost, all told, from our navy eight-six ships against a total of three hundred and twenty-one by the Japanese. On the evening of November 17, President Roosevelt on the radio said that the war had reached a turning point.

But we must now consider another field of operations. If, as we have already said, it is utterly impossible, because of lack of space, to treat even our own war actions in detail or to do more than mention those of our Allies, which nevertheless were of great importance to us, the reader must bear in mind that something was happening nearly every moment in every part of the world. The leaders, however, had been in touch, and as we have noted, far-reaching plans had been in the making. Roosevelt and Churchill were in constant communication. In September Churchill visited Stalin. Emissaries had gone hither and thither. Wendell Willkie, for example, had made a six weeks' tour round the world by plane, partly as a private citizen and partly as a representative of the President. Among others he had talked with Stalin and Generalissimo Chiang Kai-shek. Russia was doing mar-

33

vellously and driving back the Nazis but needed help in the form of a second front opened somewhere against the common enemy.

At last, at nine o'clock on the night of Saturday, November 7, the news broke on an expectant world. A very large force of American troops, partly from those gathered in Britain and partly sailing direct from the United States, all under command of Lieut. General Dwight D. Eisenhower, landed in North Africa, together with British troops and ships. Exact figures are not yet available but the great armada apparently included more than five hundred vessels, and the immense preparations made months in advance and the exact timing of all coordinated operations mark it as the most perfectly executed expedition in all military and naval history. It was equally successful, and as we learned that we had occupied Oran, Algiers and Casablanca, some of the sting was taken out of Pearl Harbor. The combination of army, navy and air forces, as well as the cooperation between British and Americans, had been perfect, and the occupation of most of the long coast line was accomplished with a surprisingly small amount of casualties.

We had, of course, landed on French territory, and the long and difficult maintenance of relations with the traitorous Vichy government bore fruit. In Africa itself there were French leaders who assisted the operation, but Vichy itself naturally rejected our explanations. The two governments broke off diplomatic relations, the French Ambassador, or rather the accredited representative of Vichy, M. Gaston Henri-Hay was handed his passport in Washington, and we seized the remaining French ships in American ports. Among the local French in Africa who helped us were Admiral Darlan of the French navy and General Giraud of the army.

The situation was complex in the extreme, and in addition to his purely military duties General Eisenhower had probably the most difficult diplomatic problems to solve with which any American general in the field has ever had to grapple. Darlan had been a turncoat more than once and was bitterly anti-British. No one knew whether to trust him or not, and he was hated by many French but seemed to have the support of the navy, the major part of which was lying in the harbor of Toulon. Giraud had been loyal as a strong anti-Nazi Frenchman, and had made two daring escapes from German prisons. On the other hand, in London, General de Gaulle, who had become the leader of the Free, or Fighting, French, was strongly opposed to both the men on the spot. It is utterly impossible to fathom the motives of these three men as they looked forward to the future of France and to that of their own careers.

In any case, Giraud appealed to all the French in Africa to welcome the American aid. We soon held also Dakar, the jumping-off place for planes and submarines from the African coast toward all the New World. Before the assassination of Darlan, and acting it is said under

35

his orders, almost the entire French fleet, instead of proceeding against us or falling into the hands of the Germans, was scuttled by its officers in Toulon harbor. At present writing the political situation of the French among themselves remains confusing to the foreigner. We had, however, gained a firm foothold on northern and western Africa with remarkably small loss of life, had opened a second front threatening Italy and Germany across a narrow stretch of water, and prepared a place from which to stab at the soft side of the Axis.

Meanwhile the British Eighth Army had been chasing the redoubtable German General Rommel and his Afrikan Corps out of Egypt, across all Libya and into Tunisia. It is only fair to say that the way had long been prepared by Churchill, who assumed heavy risks when the outlook was darkest. The Prime Minister, however, took occasion to say that the plan for the African campaign, which was an "American show," had been prepared by Roosevelt and that he himself was a willing lieutenant. Weather and other conditions prevented during the remainder of the year much land fighting and a clearing of the position, but the Mediterranean had once again been made safe for Allied shipping; the threat to Egypt and the Suez Canal had passed; and pressure on Russia relieved, enabling her to make her amazingly successful campaign against the German invaders. The fall of Stalingrad, with over 300,-000 German losses and the threat at the year's end to all the Nazi armies in the Ukraine and the Caucusus, were all part of the daring move on Vichy Africa. Germany had not only lost a large part of the supplies—wheat, oil, and so on—which she had thought within her grasp, but was becoming encircled, and Italy had become immediately and desperately threatened. Air raids by both British and American flyers became ever intensified over both the central European Axis powers, from Britain and Africa. The year, which had begun so inauspiciously and had held so many disappointments and catastrophes, ended with the almost certainty of ultimate victory, however much of cost and suffering yet remained to be borne. At the end of the year—December 12—the President stated that we had more than 1,000,000 men in overseas service.

We had not only to fight abroad. The Fifth Column was at work at home, and was well taken care of, although it is noteworthy that there was little of the anti-alien hysteria of the first World War. The ban on the teaching of German in the schools, the prohibition of German music in concerts and the opera, the discharging of German musicians and conductors, and other such manifestations, which had been so common in 1917 and 1918, were almost wholly, if not quite, absent. The fact marked, perhaps, an increased maturity and self-confidence in the American. In the autumn, in fact, we went so far as to announce that resident Italians even if not American citizens should not be considered as *enemy* aliens. This apparently greatly annoyed Mussolini.

Many arrests were made, however, particularly of Germans, and in such organizations as the blatant Bund, the Silver Shirts, and others. The most sensational case was that of the eight German saboteurs who had landed from submarines amply supplied with cash, implements and instructions for sabotaging our war effort. Four had been landed on the beach at Amagansett, Long Island, during the night of June 13, and the other four landed four nights later near Ponte Vedra, Florida. All were eventually captured, and tried.

As compared with the sudden executions and mass massacres of the Nazis who claim to be introducing a "New Order" into civilization, it is interesting to note how these men were treated by a democracy. They first were accorded a long and fair court martial, with seven generals on the bench, and the finding was handed over to the President as Commander-in-Chief. Six of the culprits had been condemned to death and two, who had turned state's evidence, were given long sentences in prison. However, to avoid the slightest possibility of their not having had a fair trial, the Supreme Court convened in the first special session it had held in twenty-two years, to hear their case. The Court upheld the judgment of the court martial and on August 8 the six met their end in the electric chair in the District of Columbia jail death-chamber.

At the end of November three naturalized American citizens of German birth were sentenced to death for treason in shielding and hiding one of the saboteurs, and the wives of the three to twenty-five years in prison and $10,000 fine each. With the exception of the conviction (with death penalty) of Max Stephan, a tavern keeper in Detroit, for aiding the escape of a German aviator who had been a prisoner in Canada, these were the first convictions for treason by the United States since 1791. John Brown, the pre-Civil War Abolitionist was hanged for treason at Harpers Ferry in 1859, but under the laws of the State of Virginia and not under a Federal statute. There were a good many other arrests, and prison terms were meted out, but the number was infinitesimal in proportion to the totals in our foreign groups, even if we include somewhat wholesale removals of Japanese from certain districts along the California coast. Two points having important bearing on the making of the American may be noted. One was the loyalty of the vast majority of those among us, aliens and new citizens alike; and the other was the willingness with which all, old Americans and new, accepted the draft and other wartime measures. We had had our "draft riots" in the Civil War, our anxieties over foreigners in the first World War. In this war the people stood together and behind the government.

There was considerable trouble with labor. The A. F. of L. and the C.I.O. failed to get together. A conference called early in the year by the President to enable a wartime pact to be made between employees and employers also failed, the stumbling-block being the demand by labor unions that employers force their men to join the union which might show a majority in the plant. There was also much bad feeling about the length of the work-week, mostly forty-hour with overtime up to the limit of forty-eight hours. Service men (and their wives, parents and others), who knew they were risking their lives and living hard twenty-four hours a day could not see why workers at home on high wages and in safety should demand such special treatment. Moreover, the people at large, staggering under terrific taxation and being urged to make every sacrifice felt that the burdens and sacrifices should be borne by all with some degree of equality. The A. F. of L. appear to have been more aware of the needs of the situation, and willing to consider themselves as American citizens first and union members second, than the C.I.O. Further, it was believed by many that even the "overtime pay week" was too short for a nation fighting for its life. President Roosevelt maintained that the worker began to slow down after 48 hours, yet the Co-ordinator of Empire and Allied Requirements of the British Supply Council, reported that after three years' experience it was decided that the maximum output for men was reached at between 60 and 65 hours a week, and for women at between 55 and 60 hours. We should hardly like to say that the Americans cannot stand as much as the British. Strikes were numerous but had the days been those of peace instead of the hardest war we have ever fought, they would have been of less importance. The loss of man-hours due to strikes was less than in 1940 or in 1938. (In 1937 there had been the steel and automobile strikes, in 1939 and 1941 the two great bituminous coal strikes of the C.I.O.) This does not, however, quite tell the story. The loss of

A PICTORIAL PRESENTATION OF THE FARMER'S PLIGHT

Seibel in The Richmond (Va.) Times-Dispatch

INCREASING NUMBERS IN THE ARMED FORCES LEAVE THE FARMER SHORTHANDED

man-hours in one plant might long delay the production of parts for most important war implements made in some other plant, and the loss of man-hours in the comfort and safety of America might mean the loss of many man-lives in far parts of the world.

In November came the Congressional elections. There had been grumbling for a long time. The shock to national pride given by the unnecessary disaster in Pearl Harbor had rankled. The administration had to bear the brunt of the resentment felt. It is true that the Secretary of the Navy was one of the two Republicans whom the President had added to his Cabinet, but Mr. Roosevelt had first come to national prominence as Assistant Secretary of the Navy, and that branch of the services was supposed to be his special "pet." There were many other grievances. Many persons felt that the war was being waged in favor of the New Deal and its experiments. Many were tired of these and of the red tape which tied so many rambunctious Americans to their chairs when they wanted to be "raring" on their hind legs. As a sample of the red tape and complexity of questionnaires, Congress was presented by a well-known firm with a questionnaire which demanded answers to "Form No. 1–1071–PLOF–5– NOBU–COS–WP." In connection with this, Senator Byrd told Congress that the instructions to farmers for filling out applications for the use of trucks was 24,000 words long. Business men were complaining that so much of their time was being taken in studying and filling out questionnaires that they had none left for war production. Moreover, the government's labor policy, or perhaps lack of policy, had disgruntled others. The plans for industrial mobilization so carefully worked out since the previous war had been discarded in favor of sudden opportunistic ideas. American life had come to be based on the car, not merely for pleasure but for every sort of business. The public was bewildered by the conflicting statements of members of the administration as to why they were so suddenly shut off from normal supplies of gas. One day they were told by X that it was to save oil, and the next by Y that it was not that but it was to save rubber. The confusion over rubber, not wholly cleared up by the Baruch-Conant Report, made a deep impression on the man in the street. We are not trying to appraise the essentials of the national situation but merely to suggest some of the straws in the wind which indicated that the ordinary turnover of a mid-term election might be more than normal.

It was. Briefly, as Senator George (Democrat) of Georgia said, the returns constituted "a 'Stop, Look, and Listen' sign painted in red." The Democratic majority in Congress, which for some years had been wholly abnormal, was reduced to a new low, with the House composed of 221 Democrats, 209 Republicans, and 5 of other parties. Moreover the Republicans had come into control of twenty-three states, including New York (for the first time in twenty years, where former District Attorney Thomas E. Dewey was elected Governor), Ohio and California. Their party made a clean sweep through a part of the country containing 75,000,000 people, and they controlled states with a large majority of the votes in the Electoral College, looking forward to 1944. There was a tremendous overturn in the farm states of the Middle West, where the veteran Senator Norris was defeated in

Nebraska. One of the odd features of the election was that the candidates whom President Roosevelt had backed were defeated and those whom he had opposed were elected, yet the result cannot be considered to have been a repudiation of either the President or his war policies. In so far as the President personally was concerned it seemed to be merely another underscoring of the fact that the American voter does not like, indeed distinctly resents, outside interference with his local choice. It was one of the smallest turnouts of voters in elections in recent years, only about 26,000,000 going to the polls as compared with twice that number in 1940. However, the result was emphatic, and developed three men who may well be considered as in the running for the Presidential candidacy in 1944, Governors Dewey of New York, Bricker of Ohio and Stassen of Minnesota.

One thing appeared certain, which was that even if the New Dealers were not to face a wholly hostile Congress during the ensuing two years, the people had demanded that the balance between the Executive and Congress be restored more nearly to normal and that Congress would hearken. One bone of contention would be the limitation of salaries to $25,000 after taxes, which Congress had previously declined to vote and which the President had decreed in an Executive order. This, as well as a limitation of all incomes to a net of $25,000, as was later to be asked by the President and sponsored by Mrs. Roosevelt, had been a plank in the Communist party platform of 1928

44

and demanded later by the C.I.O. It was to make trouble in the coming year. In December the President took action that wiped out the W.P.A. which also had long been the object of criticism. In a nation whose man power was urgently needed to the fullest extent either at the front or behind the lines, there had for some time been little need to expend public money in "making work" for unemployed.

An interesting and recurring item of news throughout the year was the number of split decisions in the Supreme Court and the way the different judges voted. As we noted in the preceding chapter, the Court had been largely appointed by the President, although he delayed several months in appointing a successor to Justice Byrnes who had resigned. The difficulty in which the Court began to find itself because recruited so much from political office instead of from the bench of other courts or from distinguished jurists in private life, was notable one day late in November when, with only eight members, the Chief Justice and three Associate Justices all had to disqualify themselves leaving only four out of a supposed nine in that august body to pass on a case.

Without attempting to detail all the cases of the year we may note that—although during the years that Mr. Hughes was Chief Justice there were from ten to twenty dissenting verdicts in a year—in the first six months of 1942 there were fifty-two, of which fourteen involved votes of five to four, the old bugbear to which the President had so greatly objected. It was remarked by one observer that if in the old days the Court was made up of "nine old men" (which it never was), it had got to be like the Quiz Kids! All that this indicated was, as has been shown over and over in our history and a fact to which we called attention in an earlier chapter, that, fortunately for the republic, judges on the bench develop an independence of the appointing power which placed them there, just as Chester A. Arthur wholly ceased to be the local spoilsman politician handing out Custom House jobs in New York when he suddenly found himself elevated to the White House.

One of the dramatic events of the year, so filled with drama, was the rescue of the celebrated flyer of two wars, Eddie Rickenbacker. The fifty-two-year-old ace and his seven companions had last been heard from about 1500 miles out from Hawaii, flying for an undisclosed Pacific area. Three days later the navy began a search, which criss-crossed hundreds of thousands of square miles of that vast ocean. It seemed hopeless. The traditional needle in the haystack was nothing compared with trying to locate eight men in a life raft or two in the illimitable stretches of the greatest ocean of the globe. All, except one, Staff Sergeant Alexander T. Kacmarczyk, who had succumbed and been buried at sea, were found after twenty-one days' search, and "Captain Eddie" was brought back to the United States to do good work.

At the end of the preceding chapter we spoke of the vastly important gift to the nation of his art collection, now in Washington, by the late Andrew W. Mellon. In 1942 the museum he founded was enhanced by the gift by Mr. Peter A. B. Widener of his noted collection, long known to collectors and connoisseurs all over the world. It was estimated to have cost Mr. Widener $50,000,000 and it was a free gift to the people but the peculiarities of our tax system were disclosed and the state of Pennsylvania charged a gift tax of 5 per cent. President Roosevelt estimated the value as $3,900,000 and the nation paid Pennsylvania a tax of $195,000.

The most notable among the deaths of the year was that of Brigadier General Hugh S. Johnson, who died at the age of fifty-nine. Known as "Old Ironpants," he had had a distinguished career in the army but had first become familiar to the entire nation as head of the N.I.R.A., or the "Blue Eagle," during the depression, and later as a columnist after he had turned against the New Deal. A man of tremendous energy, dynamic force, and vitriolic language, he was charming in his personal life and a force for clear thinking throughout the whole country.

The war's first year, and longer, though we cannot anticipate, was for America a year of defensive rather than aggressive action. It had begun with a colossal disaster, and although in the second half we won notable victories against the Japanese in the Far East the actions were all parts of a defensive delaying movement rather than of advances made against vital centers of the enemy's power and resources. In North Africa we initiated a carefully planned and most skillfully executed campaign against the Axis in Europe, in a real offensive, but it was, when the year ended, still only a beginning. At home, our industry had accomplished marvels in transforming civilian production into war production but that, again, was rather in the nature of preparing for future action. We had voted and spent tens and tens of billions of dollars. We had contributed heavily to the resources of our Allies. We had raised great forces, we had piled up long records of distinguished courage and ability shown by those forces, both as individuals and as units. As was said in a review of the year, we had done everything possible to prepare for victory, but we had yet to begin the march to victory. Our preparations were so vast and costly that they enhanced the sense of confidence and national pride, but the feeling of ultimate victory would have been less certain at the beginning of 1943 had it not been for the British Eighth Army's brilliant pursuit of the German forces under Rommel across a thousand miles of Africa, and the astounding successes of the Russians. It is well to consider this when some of our leaders are busy planning the post-war world according to their ideas. There will be others—the Chinese, the British and the Russians among them—who have borne the burden of the war far longer than we and who have contributed infinitely more in suffering, who may sit with us at the table of the post-war world. We shall all have to work together.

CHAPTER II

THE RECORD OF 1943

THE year 1943 is the most complex for any recorder to recount in the entire history of the United States. It marked a complete change-over from civilian life to total war. The war itself, not only total but global, reached, let us hope, a turning point in favor of the Allies and freedom, and for the whole human race. At home there were important events, political, economic and social, which may have permanent effects on the life of our nation.

As I have pointed out before, it is impossible to write *history* within a few weeks or months of such stupendous events. We are obliged to forego the chronological method and must devote ourselves to such major topics as the home front, the fighting front, and certain scattered matters, if we are to make the year intelligible at all. I may add that *all* the threads on all the fronts are, of course, inextricably intertwined and that events and acts have mutually influenced one another.

On the home front we may begin, as usual, with the messages of the President to Congress on the state of the nation and its needs, and we shall follow first the political aspects of the year, although politics, obviously, were closely intertwined with economics at home and war abroad.

During the entire preceding year, the President had not only been under terrific strain but he had been in a false position. Ever since the dastardly attack on Pearl Harbor by the Japanese, December 7, 1941, the President had had information about the extremely dangerous situation both of the United States and of its Allies. He *knew* but he could not *tell* all he knew. The public knew he knew and was not telling, so that a false and annoying relation was formed between him and the people. An enormous improvement in the Allied condition had come about by January 1943, and the President's message to Congress on the 7th of that month reflected his growing confidence. In the first part of that message he gave an admirable survey of the war to date. In the second, he reviewed the stupendous production of war materials by the nation. As the figures he gave out were, naturally, those for 1942, we shall reserve the figures for 1943 until later. In the third part, he looked to the future and our post-war aims. These included the permanent disarming of the Axis aggressors, as well as plans for employment and "assurance against the evils of all major economic hazards—assurance that will extend from the cradle to the grave." It was this part of the message which caused most criticism but, on the whole, both the tone and substance of the message afforded a happy contrast to some of his speeches the preceding year, and the way seemed open for better relations between the Chief Executive and Congress, as well as between him and the public.

That instead of this, Congress was to revolt more and

FULL SPEED AHEAD IN 1943

A cartoon by Harper in *The Birmingham Age Herald*.

more, as 1943 progressed, was apparently due to the fact that although the nation was practically wholly united on the questions of war it was greatly divided as to domestic issues. Both the fine qualities of Mr. Roosevelt, and his defects, were to add to this division. I am citing no personal opinion of my own but that generally held, I be-

51

lieve, even by his followers, when I say that although a fine leader in the war and as regards our foreign relations, the President is not good as an administrator. To the natural differences of opinion on domestic matters was added the confusion of mind caused by the overlapping authority and conflicting orders and opinions of the innumerable Boards and officials.

On January 11, the President submitted his message on the Budget, in the form of an 881-page book, most of which detailed only how $4,000,000,000 should be spent for the ordinary running of the government, though the total amount asked for was $109,000,000,000, of which $100,000,000,000 was for war. He estimated that by the end of the fiscal year, June 30, 1943, the national debt would be $210,000,000,000, but stated that the nation was "thoroughly solvent," and that "freedom from want for everybody, everywhere, is no longer a Utopian dream." The Secretary of the Treasury announced also that government expenses had risen $19,000,000,000 during the past year, and income taxes about 129.5 per cent. Methods of raising the huge new amounts needed were barely suggested and were left to Congress.

During the month the President made his journey to Casablanca to confer with Churchill but, for the sake of clarity, we may defer mention of his journeys abroad until we discuss the fighting front.

In spite of the conciliatory references to Congress in both the President's messages, trouble with that body began almost immediately, and wholly on domestic issues.

A Tammany leader from the Bronx, Edward J. Flynn, who had also been National Chairman of the Democratic Party, became the center of a scandal in New York City because the large courtyard of his country estate had been paved with paving blocks belonging to the city. Other charges, also, were made. Whatever their truth, the situation became embarrassing for the Democratic Party, and rumors spread that Flynn was to resign as Party Chairman and to be appointed Minister to Australia. On January 11, in an editorial the New York *Times* said: "Our prestige abroad, and our morale at home, would both be [so] harmed by an action so cynical" that it refused to believe the appointment would be made unless the President himself announced it. Unhappily, the President did. Public opinion, both at home and in Australia, was aroused against the appointment, and the Senate balked at confirmation. The fight was bitter and partisan but, also, it was felt by the public that in the world crisis only our best men should be sent as Ministers to the great Dominions, and that in the case of Canada, and now of Australia, domestic politics, none too savory, had played too great a part in foreign diplomacy. On January 31, within a few hours after the President's return from Casablanca, Flynn, after consultation with Democratic leaders, and less than twelve hours before final Senate action, withdrew his name. The withdrawal was immediately accepted by Mr. Roosevelt. It was a distinct rebuff to the

President by the Senate, and important as marking the first of a series of such rebuffs which the Houses of Congress were to deal him on domestic issues. Perhaps Flynn was, as Mrs. Roosevelt said, a good and honest man, and the paving-block incident one of "those things that are sometimes done by friends" and that "should not have been brought out," but there is no question but that the people and the Senate did not like the appointment. Mrs. Roosevelt added that the attack was engineered by enemies of the Administration, but the majority leader of the Democratic Senate said that the appointment might not pass and that, if it did, it would do so perhaps by only one vote.

The next rebuff came from the House. By a majority of six to one it provided for a committee of seven to investigate all the New Deal agencies and bureaus, to determine which might have exceeded their legal authority. In February, Congress decided that the President himself had exceeded his, and there occurred one of the bitterest fights since the President's effort to pack the Supreme Court. By an Executive Order, Mr. Roosevelt had proclaimed (October 3, 1942) that all salaries must be limited to $25,000, after taxes. In a Report, filed with the House, on the President's request for an increase in the limit of the national debt from $125,000,000,000 to $210,000,000,-000, it was recommended to add a rider to the Debt Bill which would substitute action by Congress on incomes for the fiat of the President. Representative Disney of

Oklahoma, who presented the amendment, stated that the Committee found not only that the President had not been given any authority for his action in the earlier anti-

OLD HENPECK WILL TAKE JUST SO MUCH

A cartoon on the growing rift between the President and the Congress, pictured in a cartoon by Hutton in *The Philadelphia Inquirer*.

inflation measures but that the intention of Congress had been "to the contrary."

In an historically remarkable communication between the Executive and the legislature, the President offered to withdraw his edict if Congress would pass a measure, dictated by him, limiting all incomes to $25,000 for a single person and $50,000 for a married couple. Owing to the high surtaxes, to keep $25,000 net meant an income, before taxes, of $67,500, and the President said it was inequitable that anyone should get that much while the men in the forces got only $600. The country immediately asked, if $25,000 was inequitable, how about $10,000, $5,000, or the wage scale of every miner, factory worker and laborer at home? Hospitals, small colleges, and other social institutions, felt that they might face extinction from loss of support. Many of the public felt that if the President, without and even against, consent of Congress, could fix the income of everyone, he could do anything. In a word, both the country and Congress were in turmoil. The opposition did not come from the small number of citizens affected directly but from the people at large. In March, the House accepted the Disney rider by a vote of 268 to 129, and ten days later, on the 23rd, the Senate killed the President's salary order by the phenomenal vote, on a domestic issue, of 74 to 3. It was, perhaps, the heaviest rebuke which Mr. Roosevelt had received during his three terms of office.

Another remarkable example of the rift between the President and Congress occurred toward the end of February. In the preceding October, Congress had given the President authority, under certain restrictions, to fix minimum prices for farm products. Mr. Roosevelt issued an order in which Congress considered he had again not only exceeded his authority but had gone contrary to the clearly expressed intention of the legislature. A new Bill which was a distinct rebuke to the Executive was introduced, and passed the Senate by the again remarkable majority, for a domestic issue, of 78 to 2. Not only that. Among the 78 rebuking the President were those who were numbered among his closest friends and advisers and who were regarded as the strongest New Dealers, such as Senators Barkley, Wagner, Guffey, and Senator Thomas of Utah.

In April, the Senate, by unanimous vote, deprived the President of the power, which he had held since 1934, further to devaluate the dollar. On May 26, the Senate wrote into a Bill a provision to prevent the Executive from using money for projects for which Congress had refused appropriations. On the other hand, on June 21, the House passed the requested $71,500,000,000 Army Appropriation by a unanimous vote of 345 to 0. Yet again, on the other hand, Congress, only a few days later, passed the Smith-Connally Bill, badly drawn and unsatisfactory as it was, over the President's veto. The overriding of the veto merely showed the intense dissatisfaction of Congress and the country with the Administration's labor policy or, rather, with its lack of one, just as all the instances above cited showed the complete willingness of the people and legislature to back the war policy in spite of their growing resentment against the handling of domestic affairs. It would seem impossible to read any other meaning into the record.

Meanwhile, and throughout the year, the threat of inflation, due to increased national income and a diminished amount of goods to be bought, evidently did not arise

"KEEP 'EM UP—WHILE I MAKE UP YOUR MIND!"

A cartoon published in *The Philadelphia Inquirer* during the so-called miners' "truce."

because of larger income for the rich, whose income had had been cut drastically—50 to 90 per cent—but because of the millions who were receiving larger incomes than they had ever known before, and who paid low taxes, or none. Nevertheless, the year was marked by a series of strikes in essential war industries. The number of man-hours lost in proportion to the total means nothing, since the effect depends on what the men involved were engaged in: making lip-sticks, steel, planes, ships, or providing fuel or steel, and so on.

Strikes occurred in motor works, ship-building plants, coal mines, steel works, rubber manufacture, rail transport, and other essential industries. On the whole the rank and file of labor were sound Americans, but the same cannot be said of many of their leaders. The Wagner Act, and certain decisions during the past few years by the Supreme Court, seemed to have put such leaders almost outside any possible legal control, either by government or their own union members. The most impertinently flagrant example was, perhaps, that of Petrillo, the head of the Musicians Union, who said he had nothing to negotiate because he intended to end entirely the business of transcriptions for radio. In other words, one individual labor leader stated bluntly that he planned to destroy an industry, and, thus far, he has been upheld by the law and the courts.

Throughout the year there were constant strikes and threats in the field of coal mining. On May 1, 530,000 miners struck, under the leadership of John L. Lewis, and the Government took over the mines. After an apparent settlement, the miners struck again, and Congress enacted the Smith-Connally anti-strike bill, passing it over the

President's veto, as already noted. Lewis consistently defied the President and Government, as well as public opinion, and when, toward the end of October, what he had called a "truce" expired, the miners went on strike again, following Lewis and not the President. The Government again took over the mines, but the war effort was seriously damaged and great numbers of innocent citizens suffered severely in their homes for lack of fuel.

The highly skilled rail unions having threatened, in December, to tie up all transportation, the Government, on the 27th, took over the roads, which under private management had done a magnificent war job. William Green, leader of the American Federation of Labor, criticized the seizure on the extraordinary ground that, though the men had voted to strike, they would not actually have done so. In other words, this leader bluntly said that, under his leadership, one of the finest bodies of skilled labor in America had merely tried to bluff the Government into paying higher wages by a threat of tying up, in mid-winter, all domestic transportation, thereby stopping transport for all war production and the export of matériel needed for 10,000,000 Americans in the armed forces, at home and abroad. Nothing more need be said. In spite of brave words about "holding the line" against inflation, establishing wages, prices and markets, the Government kept yielding to any labor leader who had brass enough to defy it and public opinion, regardless of the safety of the nation and of the future of organized labor itself, in the eyes of the nation, especially when the armed forces shall have come home.

The trouble was due to the fact that there was no clear-cut government labor policy. The Secretary of Labor faded out of the picture almost wholly. Other officials and Boards overlapped in their vague jurisdictions. The President took up each case as it came and often overrode his own appointees. Perhaps, as Vice-President Wallace told the Political Action Committee of the Congress of Industrial Organizations on January 15 of the following year, but referring to facts of 1943, "Many things which some of us have not been able to understand, have been explained by the fact that the President is keeping his mind on [winning the war and the peace] to the exclusion of anything else." No one man could possibly run the war, our foreign relations and all the domestic concerns of a people of 135,000,000 engaged in a war for survival. The extraordinarily complicated chart of various agencies, boards, etc., all heading up to the President, as compiled by the Office of War Information, explains much of the confusion which came to exist. As a result of this confusion and of the lack of clearly defined powers and responsibilities, the country itself became bewildered by a succession of resignations on the part of top-flight officials, and by quarrels between them, and even between Cabinet members, in public. As an example, we may cite the resignation of Chester C. Davis, whose appointment a few months earlier had been hailed by the country, and who, in resigning, expressed his opinion sharply as to the way things were being run. Among other examples was the open, and almost scandalously vituperative, quarrel between Jesse Jones and Vice-President Wallace, which ended in the President's removing them both from some of their official positions.

As far as can be judged from the acts of Congress, the polls taken of national opinion, and the election in November, the President was heartily supported by large majorities in his war and foreign policies but opposed for the increasing tangle into which domestic affairs had been brought. Also, showing the enormous advance, since the days of Woodrow Wilson, toward an international outlook, the Senate, a few days after election, voted 85 to 5 (and of the 5 opposers 2 were Democrats) to join in some form of international organization to maintain peace and security after the war, thus greatly strengthening the hands of the President in his negotiations with foreign nations. His own foreign missions, and especially that of Secretary of State Cordell Hull to Moscow (all of which will be mentioned in the section on the Fighting Front), were applauded and confirmed. In fact, I doubt if any other president since Washington has had such united and non-partisan support in his war and diplomatic policies as has Mr. Roosevelt.

However, even in war, the citizens, while supporting the Government abroad, reserve the right, and properly, to differ on domestic issues and policies. This was clearly

ALL'S NOT SO QUIET ON THE HOME FRONT
A cartoon by Draper in *The Richmond Times-Dispatch.*

revealed in the election of November 1943, although only
seven states and a few hundred municipalities voted for
candidates for important offices. The Republicans claimed
that the election should be fought on domestic issues,

63

whereas the White House made a personal issue of two of the leading candidates, W. C. Bullitt, former Ambassador to France and Russia, who ran for Mayor of Philadelphia and was defeated by over 64,000 votes; and Lieutenant General Haskell, who ran as a Democrat for Lieutenant Governor of New York State and was defeated by the Republican Joe R. Hanley by 450,000 votes. In New Jersey, Republican Walter E. Edge defeated the Democratic candidate, backed by "Boss" Hague, a supporter of the Administration, by 128,000 votes, and in the border Southern state of Kentucky, which had gone Democratic by 106,000 votes in 1939, the Republican candidate for Governor, S. E. Willis, won by a majority of a few thousand. The chief points to be noted are that the drift away from Roosevelt and the Democrats, so notable in the more important election of 1942, was continued; that the farmers were notably leaving the Democrats; that there was a split in the labor vote; and that the Negroes were in part going back to their former Republican allegiance. This was the comment of a backer of the Administration.

We may now turn to some other aspects of the Home Front. Rationing of certain foods and of other commodities began early in the year. The system was willingly accepted by our citizens and, on the whole, worked smoothly for a people who, above all others, were unaccustomed to red tape and to limitations on their own desires. It was a new and not a happy experience for Americans to be told what they could or could not buy even if they had the money. The tremendous job of registration and the handing out of ration books was handled by the teachers in the schools, who deserve much credit for this heavy extra duty. For the most part, at least, members of the local "ration boards," who had to do much, and often unpleasant, work among their neighbors, were unpaid volunteers. There was practically no grumbling on the part of the public, who willingly accepted the nuisances, and the cuts in living required, in a whole-hearted spirit of "win the war." As time went on, there were some "black markets," as there have been in every country, and some chiselling and hoarding, but not much, in view of the vast numbers who voluntarily submitted to the regulations.

In that respect, the Home Front made an admirable record. The chief complaints were with regard to the extreme shortage of gas for cars, mainly in the East, and the rationing, in December, of coal for heating homes, both of which, many felt, had been badly handled by the Administration. The life of all America, especially outside the big cities, had been built up in recent years around the car as an unfailing means of transport, and the sudden curtailment of this means, which was the only one in innumerable small towns and country districts, spelled real hardship, as well as abandonment of homes and disruption of accustomed social ways. The fact that the Government, through Fuel Administrator Ickes, had advised people to change their heating systems from oil to coal,

65

undoubtedly was the cause of much of the resentment felt, in the colder sections of the country as winter set in, when coal was rationed and even unobtainable. The resentment mounted also against John Lewis and his miners, who had won an extra $1.50 a day by the year-long strikes and bickerings, at the cost of danger to the nation at war and of the discomfort and even death of many citizens.

In spite of strikes on the part of some labor, both labor and industrial management did an astoundingly fine job during the year. The chief credit for this must go to business and the individual American. When, at a dinner during the Teheran Conference, Marshal Stalin raised his glass to toast the marvel of American production which had saved the war for the Allies, that head of a nominally Communistic country (although far from it now in fact, despite American Communists, who lag behind Moscow in their ideas) was really toasting private enterprise and individual initiative.

The vast American industrial machine for production had been built up on that basis, and the sudden conversion, in amazingly short time, from the huge output of peace-time goods for 135,000,000 people to an all-out production for war was due to the adaptability both of the executives and of the men in plants, large or small, all over the land. General H. H. Arnold, Commanding General of our Army Air Forces, in his Report to the Secretary of War, spoke of America as having had a "most valuable secret weapon" in "the self-reliant, resourceful American soldier." These qualities do not develop overnight. They are built up by a whole life and way of life, which calls them forth, day after day and year after year. As the General also said, elsewhere in his thirty-page Report (dated January 4, 1944), and which every American should read, "Only in America would a piano company believe that it could convert to building airplane wings in a few months, and do it. A tire manufacturer built fuselages and tail surfaces. A former pickle plant turned out airplane skis and floats, and a manufacturer of girdles and corsets began making parachutes."

In 1939, our total production of army and commercial planes had been 2400. In the fiscal year 1940 the Army Air Force received only 886 planes of all types. When, after the fall of France, May–June of that year, the President asked for 50,000 planes annually, the figure seemed fantastic. A year and a half later, on the very anniversary of Pearl Harbor, American manufacturers completed their one hundred thousandth plane! This was only one item in that marvel of American production which Stalin toasted with fervor.

By the middle of 1943 we had built the greatest naval fleet the world had ever known, building in June of that year alone as many naval units as had been built in the whole first eighteen months of the defense program. The increase in our merchant shipping was even more startling. Especially in the shipyards of that genius discovered by the war, Henry J. Kaiser, ships were being built, from keel-laying to final fitting out, in a few weeks each. In spite of a shortage of manpower, we raised 5 per cent more foodstuffs than in the previous record year. We made 50 per cent more munitions in 1943 than even in 1942. With some 10,000,000 persons in the armed forces, the nation did its best to maintain a working force of 65,000,000, including 3,000,000 women new to their jobs. As we have said, at various times during the year over 600,000 coal miners went on strike, 350,000 steel workers, and 1,450,-000 rail workers voted to strike, and there was a spate of smaller, but essentially important, strikes, in many other key lines. A great deal of the record is obviously not good but, in general, the average American, from the lowest employee to the highest and most harassed executive, showed up well. On the whole, they did a job, in business, industry and agriculture, which they can be proud of and which augurs well for the future.

With output directed primarily to supplying the needs of a total war, the production of civilian goods had to be greatly curtailed. This, combined with another factor, the enormously stepped-up national income, naturally raised the specter of inflation. The President had frequently pointed to the danger, and talked about "holding the line" but, under pressure from labor, he failed to do so and, before the end of the year, even the so-called "Little Steel Formula," designed to keep wages in relation to the cost of living, was scrapped.

It is unfortunate, with so much talk of a "planned economy," that no statistics are accurate, and that even those

GOING UP!

A cartoon on the rising cost of living in *The Cleveland Plain Dealer*.

of the various government bureaus and departments vary greatly among themselves. However, such as are as good as I can get, indicate that since World War II started, a little over four years ago, wages of factory workers have increased 82.4 per cent and, as living costs in the same period rose only 27 per cent, the increase in "real wages" was very substantial, estimated at 44.1 per cent between August 1939 and June 1943. Specific examples from among factory workers have been given by Congressional Representative A. J. Engel of Michigan, as a result of study in 47 war plants. This study reveals such wages as: for a machine-gun assembler, from $4700 to $8741 a year; for a filer of machine guns, from $4200 to $8000 a year; and so on. Representative Engel also noted that an advertisement of the United States Employment Service called for "Dishwashers, waiters and kitchen men. Wages $250 a month, board and lodging. Olympic Commissary."

There is, however, a great difference in the position of the workers in this war, as compared with those in World War I. This should be stressed, for it may prove an important factor after the peace. In both wars, wages rose to hitherto undreamed-of levels, but in this war they have, to an amazing extent, been *saved*. I am a trustee of one of the oldest and largest of the Mutual Savings Banks of the country, located in a war-plant district, and I have had opportunity to watch this saving process, at first hand. We have been getting, *every day,* from eighty to ninety thousand dollars of workers' savings. I have also watched the rise in life-insurance policies, more than 50 per cent of those I follow being taken out by persons who never before had had insurance. Again, in the concerns I know about, here, from 90 to 100 per cent of the employees have voluntarily accepted a 10 per cent deduction from their wages for war bonds. Mortgages are being paid off so fast as to make a serious problem. As far as we can make out, there are two forces at work. First, people really learned a lesson from the sudden and severe depression of the 1930's. Then, also, owing to rationing and the scarcity of civilian goods and pleasures, people have not been able to spend their money. This means that there is a tremendous dammed-up demand for goods—homes, furniture, cars, washing machines, etc.—which will be released when the men come home and we turn from war to civilian production. This is a very marked, and important, characteristic of this war. Another point to be mentioned is the great drop in instalment buying. Owing partly to government regulations and partly to lack of goods, "consumer credit" throughout the whole nation dropped approximately 50 per cent in the two years, 1941–43. The release from this burden of debt on goods bought, already enjoyed, and partly worn out—a debt which emphasized the depression of the 1930's—will be another factor in the release of buying power, demand for goods, and increase of employment, when this war is over.

Another marked difference between conditions in this and in the last World War is symbolized by the difference between "War Debts" and "Lend-Lease." In the last war, we sold war supplies of all sorts to the Allies and ran up bills as any merchant would do, creating the so-called "War Debts," only a fraction of which were ever paid and which were the cause, later, of much bitter international feeling. "Uncle Sam" was no "Uncle Shylock." It was just the way things were done then, as was emphasized in the famous remark of President Coolidge: "They hired the money, didn't they?" Perhaps the happiest augury for a better international order, when this war is won, is "Lend-Lease."

This time, the Allies have pooled their resources, genuinely pooled them. Accounts are kept, to some extent, although they are complicated, but no one is worrying very much about the final day of balancing and settlement. In fact, except for statistics, there may be no such day, and no one is worrying very much about that, either. The goods and services "lend-leased" embrace almost everything which we, or others of the United Nations, need to win the war. The United States, as the richest, both in cash and in available material resources, of the nations fighting for freedom, naturally heads the list on the ledger, but when, in March, Congress renewed the life of the Act, it raised no question about repayment. The vote was unanimous in the Senate, and 407 to 6 in the House. Under the able management of Edward R. Stettinius, Jr. (formerly Chairman of the Board of the U. S. Steel Corporation), who, at the end of 1943, was transferred from Lend-Lease to the post of Under-Secretary of State, Lend-Lease had not only proved one of the most successful of the Administration's experiments but had won the whole-hearted support of Congress and of the public because of the frank way in which Stettinius took both of these into his confidence and explained what he was doing.

Before we leave this topic, which in time may prove to be one of the most important in this chapter, we shall note one or two points. Lend-Lease was not a gesture of sentimental generosity on the part of Uncle Sam. This war began on the old sell-goods-and-send-bills basis of previous ones. Before Lend-Lease, Great Britain had already bought, in the United States, supplies to the amount of more than a billion and a half pounds sterling. As one nation after another was drawn into the struggle for survival against the Axis Powers it became evident that, in procuring from one another what we all needed to keep from having our throats cut, we could not treat each other as ordinary buyers and sellers. Some had money, some had shipping facilities, some had essential raw materials, some had production facilities. If we pooled all we all had, we might win. If we tried to make a merchandising business out of the war, we could not win. Problems of bargaining; problems of foreign exchanges; problems of bookkeeping and of man power; the all-important problem of *time*—all these came into the picture. So the miracle happened. Peoples as different as those of the United States, the British Empire, Russia, China, and of others of the United Nations, pooled what they had to give

73

for the common cause. Hitler, whose method was to divide his victims and kill them one by one, had wrought this miracle of unified and unselfish joint effort. Almost all the nations have contributed. "Lend-Lease" accounts for about 12 per cent of the total war cost for us and for about 10 per cent of the same total for the British, but it is impossible to calculate exactly. British, Russians, Chinese, and others are getting things from us, and we are getting things, of different sorts, from them. We have given (we might as well, all of us, look at it that way) our billions here in the U. S. A., but the United Kingdom had given, up to June 30, 1943, over £2,250,000,-000. Canada, with less than a tenth of our population, had, after paying cash for all she got from us, made a free gift to our Ally, the United Kingdom, of $2,000,000,000. It is impossible to keep accurate accounts. The items are too multitudinous and never before was there any world undertaking so decentralized. The British—to cite only one nation—are using our ships and railways, and we are using theirs. We, in some places, are sending food to them, and some of our boys in the forces are eating meals at the cost of the Australians. The American forces in England, according to our Government, get 90 per cent of their medical supplies and hospital service from the British. So it has been, all over, in a bewildering complex of friendly transactions. What has been needed has been supplied, whether *to* or *by* Americans, British, Russians, Chinese, and all the rest. The world has never before known anything like it. Americans may well feel proud that they inaugurated it. Let us hope that this extraordinary experiment may not be spoiled, at the end, by any resurgence of a huckstering spirit. Obviously Lend-Lease has not abolished nationalism and, after the war, we shall again compete for trade, but perhaps the example of what we have been doing, so potently and so successfully, will not be wholly forgotten.

We may mention here a few other planning schemes, on the Home Front, looking toward post-war conditions —plans of differing qualities and potentialities.

Other countries, notably Britain, which produced the Beveridge Plan for Social Security, and various other social services which have attracted much attention, were also looking ahead. In our country, the N.R.P.B. (National Resources Planning Board), to which the President in 1938 had appointed as Chairman his then seventy-five-year-old uncle, Frederic A. Delano, produced a Plan which aroused much criticism and perhaps contributed to the abolishment of the Board by Congress in March. The Plan called for a combination of governmental and private capital in industry, but also for "free enterprise," for a wide extension of social services, for continuing Federal controls of business for an indefinite number of years after the war should be over, and, incidentally, proposed a new "Bill of Rights," including such incompatibles as the "right" to security and the "right" to adventure, the "right" to the "amenities of life," meaning almost everything anyone could require, and at the same time "the right to live in a system of free enterprise, free from compulsory labor," etc. As Governor Dewey said of all the plans of all the planners, everyone seemed to believe that the post-war era could be made one "of full employment in which nobody has to work." Anyway, Congress cut off further payments to the N.R.P.B.

Another effort, this time at international planning, occurred in May. Our Government invited representatives of the United Nations, and of eight associated nations, to meet at Hot Springs, Virginia, to consider post-war food problems. Of this Conference, which might set the pattern for other important inter-Allied conferences, less is known historically than might be desired. For some reason, the Administration decided to exclude all members of the press. The American press, in contrast with the British press bureau, Reuter's, and the Russian press, kept scrupulously to the lines laid down by the Government, as it had already proved and was notoriously to prove later in the year, but the Standing Committee, representing 560 American and foreign journalists formally accredited to Congress, protested in vain against exclusion from any contact with the proceedings of the Conference as "the denial of legitimate news to the American public, and an abridgement of the freedom of the press." At the end of the meeting, June 3, a summary of its results was handed out, which indicated in a general way that food was important to man; that there would be shortages after the war; that some sort of organization should be set up to control production and prices; and that the governments should consider the matter further. The real results of the Conference may have been more important than the public could learn, with the army patrolling the grounds of the hotel where it was held.

Another international conference of representatives of the United Nations was held at Atlantic City, in November. It was organized under the name of the United Nations Relief and Rehabilitation Administration, and was added to the alphabetical jungle of administration organizations as U.N.R.R.A. This had as its province not only the problem of food but the general rehabilitation of devastated countries and, unhappily, a large part of the world has been devastated and will become more so. To indicate the magnitude of the problem, we may note that in Europe alone, over 20,000,000 persons, exclusive of war prisoners, had been torn from their accustomed homes and means of living. Forty-four of the United Nations were represented. A preliminary report, out of date by the time of the meeting, had been made in 1941, and Great Britain, Canada and the United States had all agreed to do their full share of the financing.

Although there were innumerable problems as to priorities, financing, the nature of population shifts, the obligations of each nation, organization, and so on, this meeting of delegates from forty-four nations proved more efficient, friendly and democratic than any other such international gathering in history. A permanent war and post-war organization was set up, with ex-Governor Herbert H. Lehman of New York State as its Director. U.N.R.R.A., the first international post-war "operating agency" of the United Nations, expects to be in full working form by the spring of 1944. Although the "Big Four" —the U. S. A., Great Britain, Russia and China—obviously have large powers, the smaller nations are protected by the provisions that every nation shall have equal voice in council and committee meetings, and representatives of the smaller nations were appointed to chairmanships of many important committees. A sort of "world community chest" of $2,500,000,000, to be made up by the uninvaded nations, was set up for the period of transitional reorganization, estimated as extending for perhaps two years after the ending of war. Each nation agreed to contribute on the basis of one per cent of its national income for the fiscal year ending June 30, 1943. The quota of the United States for the whole period was $1,356,000,-000. As I have often pointed out, governments, political traditions, and "constitutions," written or unwritten, evolve from the necessities and natures of people and not from the blueprints made by theorists. The fact that U.N.R.R.A., arising out of the basic needs of so many different nations—nations of different races, languages and backgrounds—was, in 1943, organized so easily and democratically in a three weeks' meeting which might, a generation ago, have ended in an explosion of nationalistic ambitions and jealousies, may be another of the year's good auguries for the future. It was not the "Parliament of Man" or "the Federation of the World," as envisaged by the Victorian poet Tennyson, but it was natural and instinctive, not theoretical or synthetic.

Before leaving the Home Front and turning to the overseas Fighting Front we may mention a few points on which we cannot here enlarge. There were further changes in the personnel of the Supreme Court, so that by 1943 a large majority of the Bench had been appointed by Roosevelt during his unprecedented number of years in office. There were some important legal decisions, of a radical nature, with regard to labor and property, but perhaps the most important situation evolved as a result of so many appointments by one President, with his own ideas as to the sources from which the Justices of our highest judicial tribunal should be drawn. This was, that owing to their previous positions and activities, an unusual number of them had to disqualify themselves from sitting as judges in cases with which they had already, in one way or another, been connected, so that even a legal quorum of judges could not always be secured. This extremely dangerous situation, for so it might prove to be in some highly emotional and important case, led to various suggestions, such as changing the number required to deliver valid judgments, or, by others, that appointments should, with such possibilities in view, be made with more care.

79

Aside from the strikes and serious labor disturbances which occurred during the year, there were, from time to time, riots in various cities such as Los Angeles, Detroit, New York, and elsewhere. Although Mexican Spanish were, to some extent, involved in California, Negroes in Harlem, New York, and so on, the riots do not appear to have been racial, and were due, rather, to hoodlumism and to the general unrest, particularly of the younger generation, incident to war unsettlement. Indeed, in spite of the melting-pot nature of the United States, and the fact that the homeland nations of many of our citizens were fighting against one another, it may be set down as one of the encouraging features of the war years to date that racial dislikes and bitterness have been less in evidence than in any previous war.

A week before Christmas, the President returned from his extended trip and from the conferences in Africa and the Near East, and on Christmas Eve addressed the nation and the world over the radio from his home at Hyde Park. As was probably natural (but it underlines what we have said about his foreign and domestic policies), his chief interest was in foreign policies and in winning the war. Winning the war is, obviously, our first and most important concern, but to win on the Fighting Front we must have a united and smoothly working Home Front. The President made no mention of the strikes, not even of the railroad strike looming a few days ahead, but he did say that he thought "the New Deal," as a political slogan, was outmoded and belonged to the past and that, as he put it, "it was too narrowly domestic to fit the Administration's concern with a global war."

We may now turn to the Fighting Front. It would be stirring to write about individual actions, and of American heroism as displayed in them, but such actions have been too multitudinous to be set down in a few words if any general picture is to be painted.

It is obvious, in a global war, where forty-four nations are allied on our side, that what has happened in those nations is of importance to us. Looking ahead of the year 1943, we may note that the Argentine, the one country in the two American continents which had not joined all the others in breaking with, or fighting, the Axis, finally came in, to make the opinion of all the nations of the New World, from the North Pole to the South, unanimous. Later events, however, were to disturb this.

Also, we have spoken of the "Big Four," which includes Russia, and as there is some misunderstanding of that country, due perhaps to the Communist Party in our own, we may cite a few points. The tremendous help given to the Allied cause by the massive effort and ability of Russia is well known, but some of her domestic changes are less so. Some know that the "Comintern" was scrapped; that family life and marriage were put on their former Christian basis; that the Church was re-established; and so on, but the economic implications of the "Stalin Constitution" appear still not to be understood.

Interpreting the new Constitution, Professor Trainin, one of the leading Soviet jurists, says that "only efficient work can secure the progress of society. . . . Everyone possesses an equal right to work. But does it follow from this that everyone has the right to equal compensation for his work? Certainly not. . . . That is why the Constitution establishes the principle of compensation *according to the quantity and quality of the work done.* He who gives most to society receives most for his work. . . . Innovators . . . by introducing new methods of work . . . raise the productivity of labor by as much as 1000 per cent. . . . The Stalin Constitution now safeguards the rights of citizens to personal property. . . . Citizens have the right to personal ownership of their incomes from work, to their savings . . . [etc.]. They have the right to inherit personal property." I need not quote more. Apparently Russia, in twenty-five years, has gone full circle from Communism back toward capitalism, and this has been one of the major factors in winning this war for liberty against the Huns and Hitler's "honorary Aryans," the Japanese. Clearly, in a world now so closely interwoven any important changes of viewpoint among the peoples of the Allied nations, fighting for their lives, are of importance to us. We cannot discuss them all, but the fact that a nation of such vast population, resources and vigor as the Russian Soviets is now steering in these new directions is of such significance for the future of our own and of all Western civilization that it must be mentioned.

Our necessarily too brief account of the Fighting Front must be broken into even briefer sections. First, we must mention the international conferences which laid the foundations for Allied strategy and understanding, and which were, perhaps, even more disastrous for Axis prospects than any single action in the military field. The latter, again, must be divided into the Oriental and Western sections.

There were six major conferences during the year, and several minor visits paid by President Roosevelt, such as his stopping off, on his way home from Casablanca, to visit the Presidents of Liberia and Brazil, and his visit to President Comacho in Mexico, in April. Comment on the major Allied conferences must perforce be limited. The fact that they were held, and in a spirit of cordiality, mutual confidence and good-will, was in itself a stunning blow to Hitler, whose only hope and chief policy was to split his self-made enemies. As for Japan, the British, on a number of occasions during the year, gave their most solemn pledges not to lay down their arms until the Empire and the United States together had completely defeated that nation.

The conferences were, of course, concerned with the war, and largely with matters of concerted global strategy in all its aspects. Obviously, information could not be given to the enemy, and the communiqués issued had, therefore, to be brief and uncommunicative. We know a little more about some of the conferences, but not very much.

The first was held in January, between Prime Minister Churchill and President Roosevelt, at Casablanca in

SHADE OF VON TIRPITZ—"I, TOO, COUNTED ON THEM"

A cartoon in *The New York Times* in June, 1943, as Allied shipping increased.

North Africa. There, with the Tunisian campaign still unfinished, was planned the future invasion of Sicily and Italy. In May, Churchill came to Washington, and there was a conference in the White House. In August, the two leaders met again, in Washington, at the President's estate

U. S. MARINES GO OVER THE TOP AT TARAWA

Leathernecks storm a Jap-held airport, in taking the two-mile-long atoll, a decisive step in the attempt to crack Japan's central Pacific defenses.

TWO GREAT CONFERENCES OF 1943

Top: The Cairo Conference. *Left to right:* Generalissimo Chiang Kai-shek, President Roosevelt, and Prime Minister Churchill. *Bottom:* The Teheran Conference. *Left to right:* Premier Stalin, President Roosevelt, and Prime Minister Churchill.

WAR ON THE HOME FRONT

Top: A Diesel engine being lowered into a submarine in a shipyard somewhere in the United States *Bottom:* Woman war worker applying sealing compound to the underside of a tank.

A CONFERENCE OF THE GENERAL STAFF

Left to right: (*seated*) Lt. General Henry H. Arnold, Air Force; General George C. Marshall, Chief of Staff; Lt. General Lesley McNair, Army Ground Forces; (*standing*) Maj. General Joseph McNarney, Deputy Chief of Staff; and Major General B. B. Somervell, Army Service Forces.

Madame Chiang Kai-shek, at a reception in Washington, during her visit to the United States to further "all out" aid to China.

CAPTAIN EDDIE RICKENBACKER, RESCUED IN THE PACIFIC AFTER SPENDING 21 DAYS
ON A RAFT, TALKS TO SECRETARY OF WAR HENRY L. STIMSON

TROOPSHIP OF THE SKY

A COLUMN OF SOLDIERS AND JEEPS OF THE U. S. ARMY BOARDS A NEW
GIANT CURTISS–COMMANDO (C–46) WHICH CAN SPEED TROOPS, MOBILE
EQUIPMENT AND FIELD ARTILLERY TO SCATTERED BATTLE ZONES

DEFENSE PLANT EMPLOYEES MAKING POSTERS STRESSING THE NEED
OF SAVING RUBBER

Harris-Ewing Photographic News Service

TROOPS OF U. S. ARMY TASK FORCE MARCH THROUGH HILLS OF THE FRENCH ISLAND OF NEW CALEDONIA

at Hyde Park, and in Quebec. In the latter city the decision was taken to invade Europe in 1944. In October, Secretary of State Hull and Foreign Secretary Eden went to Moscow for conferences with each other and with the Russian Foreign Commisar Molotoff, as well as with Stalin. These talks were enormously fruitful, and when Hull returned to Washington he was met at the airport by the President and, later, received a great ovation from Congress when he reported to both Houses.

In November and December came the climax of the series. Roosevelt and Churchill went to the Near East, with elaborate diplomatic and military staffs, meeting first at Cairo with the Chinese Generalissimo Chiang Kaishek and, later, at Teheran with Marshal Stalin of Russia. At these meetings plans were finally drawn for an all-out offensive in all quarters of the world. At the various conferences there were also formulated plans looking to the future. At Casablanca, the two leaders conferring there rejected peace feelers from the Nazis, and made the first of their demands for "unconditional surrender," a term which General Grant had made famous in our Civil War. It was after Quebec that demands were made for the punishment of the leading war criminals in the Axis countries, and at Cairo, in concert with China, it was decided to strip Japan of all territories she had forcibly annexed since 1895. At the end of the year many local problems, such as notably the troublesome Polish-Russian frontier line, were still left open for future adjustment

Incidentally, we may here note certain new international alignments that came into being during 1943.

January 16: Iraq declared war on the Axis.

January 20: Chile severed relations with the Axis.

April 26: Poland and Russia severed diplomatic relations.

July 25: Mussolini fell from power.

October 12: Portugal gave the United Nations use of the Azores.

October 13: Italy re-entered the war as a co-belligerent of the Allies.

Military operations of the year can be sketched in skeleton form only. We may mention the Pacific theaters first. The Japanese, who, after Pearl Harbor, had seized islands in the Aleutian group off Alaska, threatening attacks on our mainland, were finally completely driven off in 1943. In January, we took Amchitka, sixty-nine miles east of Kiska. By May 31 we had secured possession of Attu, and in August we landed unopposed on evacuated Kiska, thus completing the operations.

In the farther and southwestern Pacific, army, navy, marines and air forces cooperated in the hardest kind of jungle and other terrain fighting, on islands—the Solomons, New Guinea, and others—scattered over great distances. For those who played their gallant parts in these undertakings such brief references as can here be made must seem, as indeed they are, utterly inadequate. Of all the fighting, perhaps two affairs stand out most markedly.

The first was the Battle of the Bismarck Sea, March 1–4. A Japanese convoy had been spotted making for New Guinea. For three days 162 Allied planes struck almost continuously at the Jap ships, their land-based fighters, and at their planes on the ground at various near-by airfields. Our losses were 1 bomber and 3 pursuit planes, with a total casualty list of 13 men, whereas the enemy's known losses were 61 planes, 22 ships, and an entire division of 15,000 men and their officers.

On November 22 occurred the other best-known feat of the year, though it came near being a disaster. This was the battle of Tarawa, which Lt. Colonel Evans F. Carlson, in command of the Marines, described as the toughest job ever tackled by that branch of the service in its 168 years of fighting all over the world. This time, the amphibious expedition was against certain small islands of the Gilbert group, northeast of the Solomons. Through a series of mishaps, impossible to foresee, landing on the little atoll of Tarawa proved an extremely difficult and bloody affair, the Marines having to wade ashore for some 300 yards in the face of murderous mortar and machine-gun fire. Practically all of the 3000 to 4000 Japs on the island were finally killed, but our own losses were very heavy.

Under the leadership of General Claire L. Chennault, our planes are making themselves felt in China, but the main problem in that sector is that of supplies. Ever since the Japanese got Burma and cut the Burma Road, all supplies have had to be flown in. The difficulties of supply are almost incredible but are being met, as well as possible, largely by American fliers. First, supplies have to travel 10,000 miles by sea; then, with many intervening difficulties of transport, they have to be carried by plane, often flying by instrument and in atrocious weather, over mountain ranges 17,000 feet high, from Assam to the Chinese forces. If a mistake is made flying in one direction, there is a crash into 22,000-foot peaks, while a mishap, flying the other way, lands the flier in Japanese Burma.

In the European theater we may mention first the operations of our fliers based on Britain. The heavy bomber command of the R.A.F. was designed for night missions, while the American Flying Fortresses and Liberators were planned for daylight precision raids. As the year advanced, operations by both the Anglo-American forces became more and more effective and frequent until, by its end, they were of almost daily and nightly frequency, weather alone interfering. Not only had Berlin, the capital of Nazi misrule, met almost complete destruction, but vast havoc had been wrought on key points of German transportation and military production. As the production of the United States and its Allies grew by leaps, that of Germany declined, but it would appear, though there is a school of military thought which takes a contrary view, that air power—enormously effective as an auxiliary—cannot alone end a war. Throughout the year, Russia, which had been winning magnificent vic-

tories on the eastern front, at great cost both to herself
and to the enemy, had been calling for a second land
front on the west. By the latter part of 1943 the menace

COMING EVENTS CAST THEIR SHADOWS BEFORE
As Marcus in *The New York Times* pictured the Churchill-Roosevelt conference.

of the submarine had been so largely met and overcome
as to make comparatively safe the transport of vast numbers of men and huge quantities of supplies, and we may
now turn briefly to the progress of our overseas land

forces. Obviously, all the Allies are working for the same end, and if we speak chiefly of the Americans, it is not that we wish to ignore the great achievements of others but merely because of the nature of these annual additional chapters in what is primarily an American history.

In the preceding chapter, we spoke of the North African campaign, and of the long pursuit by the British of the German and Italian armies under Rommel, across the whole stretch of northern Africa. We spoke of the landing of the joint Anglo-American expeditionary forces for the Battle of Tunisia, as it is called. In the winter and spring of 1943 that battle took on a new form, and was finally decided.

Early in February, General Eisenhower was given supreme command of all forces in North Africa. Meanwhile, Rommel's German Afrika Corps, with its Italian auxiliaries, had steadily retreated to the Mareth Line in Tripolitania. On the arrival there also of the British Eighth Army under General Sir Harold Alexander, the British, too, came under the command of Eisenhower, and thereafter the British and Americans—in Africa, Sicily, and Italy—were to work in the closest harmony. It was reported, somewhat later, that an officer said to the American commander: "Well, the two teams work together pretty well." His immediate reply was: "Two teams? There is only one team here." The answer did not spring from any egoism on the part of Eisenhower. It simply stated a fact, and a happily remarkable one.

Those of us who served overseas in World War I and recall the heartburnings over efforts to keep the British, French and American units and armies separate, can better appreciate the extraordinary spirit of unity and comradeship in which British and Americans got together during the North African campaign and its sequels. If much credit is due to Eisenhower's personality and tact, much is due also to the officers of both nations in the army, navy and air services, who, in this post or that, from bottom to top, worked as though it were all just "one team." Credit goes also to the men of the rank and file, who came to know and appreciate each other's qualities as fighters and comrades. Allies have fought side by side in earlier wars, but never before has there been anything quite like this, or like the spirit of Lend-Lease of which we have already spoken.

The junction of the veteran Afrikan Corps with Von Arnim's command in Tunisia gave the enemy strength for offensive strokes, and in the third week of February the Germans broke through the Kasserine Pass and threatened the whole Allied position. In earlier wars, "battles"—Waterloo, Gettysburg, etc.—were often a matter of hours or, at most, of a day or two. In this war, they are of enormous scope and may, as their names, "the Battle of Britain" and the "Battle of Tunisia," indicate, last for months.

According to the official report of General Marshall, Chief of Staff of the U. S. Army, the last phase of the

Battle of Tunisia opened on March 20 when, under terrific attacks from the air and land forces, the enemy began retreat. Axis communications for supplies and reinforcements from Italy were largely cut off by attacking planes. Week after week, the enemy yielded one point after another, retreating finally into the Bon Peninsula. By May 10 the last resistance had been shattered. All Axis forces surrendered and the entire African continent was freed of the enemy, who had lost all their African colonies—German and Italian—and all their armies and supplies. 242,415 German and Italian troops, with all their equipment, were surrendered. A French army, which had newly been created, celebrated its first birthday by capturing nearly 50,000 of the enemy. The Mediterranean was again open to Allied shipping.

As we have stated, the decision to invade Sicily and thence the Italian mainland, when Africa should be cleared, had been made at the Casablanca Conference, in January. That invasion was, therefore, the next step. One interesting point had been revealed during the Tunisian campaign. Many of the German troops were picked and seasoned men from crack regiments, who had been told to fight to the last man. They did fight well and bitterly, as General Arnold, commanding all American Air Forces, stated in his Report for 1943, but, he added, "when it became clear to them that they would lose the battle, they gave up at once." The Italians, who had never had their heart in the war, and who hated the Germans, gave up readily. In Sicily, it was to be shown that they did so even gladly.

In the next move of the Italian campaign, the coordination of air, sea and land forces, which had stood the Allies in such good stead, was continued and, although the first land troops disembarked on the shore of Sicily on July 7, by August 17 the last Axis troops had surrendered, or fled across the Strait of Messina. By September 14, the Allies were ready to invade Italy itself and, on that date, landed on the beachhead at Salerno. The Battle of Tunisia had changed into the Battle of Rome, which is still in progress, and can better be considered in our next year's chapter. In the long-drawn-out battles which characterize World War II the daily moves cannot be detailed and they acquire little significance for the layman until the work of months can be seen in perspective and as a whole. Nor can we here recite the military actions in other sectors, such as the Near East. Such outlying sections by no means constitute "side-shows" but all of them help to form the pattern of global strategy which this war demands.

All the military action and industrial production, whose outlines we have been able merely to suggest rather than to describe in detail, called for a great extension of governmental functions and of expense. They would have done so, in any case, even if war were not notoriously costly and wasteful. Again, during this greatest of all wars, we have been indulging, for better or worse as individuals may regard it, in the added luxury of a social revolution.

We may note the cost and complexity, in two brief ways. It has been estimated that by the middle of the year now under review the cost of the war reached the astronomical figures of over $12,000,000 an hour, $289,000,000 a day or $7,000,000,000 a month. Once every few years, for the benefit of our readers and in order to enable them to understand the news in the papers, we have given a list of the more important Government agencies, with their alphabetical designations. Below is the current list, far from complete.

ABNPHSBM—Advisory Board on National Parks, Historic Sites, Buildings and Monuments
ANMB—Army-Navy Munitions Board
APB—Aircraft Production Board
ARA—Agricultural Research Administration
BAE—Bureau of Agricultural Economics
BLS—Bureau of Labor Statistics
BWC—Board of War Communications
CAA—Civil Aeronautics Administration
CAB—Civil Aeronautics Board
CCC—Commodity Credit Corporation
CCPA—Committee for Congested Production Areas
CFB—Combined Food Board
CMA—Coal Mines Administration
CPRB—Combined Production and Resources Board
CRMB—Combined Raw Materials Board
CSAB—Combined Shipping Adjustment Board
DLC—Disaster Loan Corporation
DPC—Defense Plant Corporation

DSC—Defense Supplies Corporation
FBI—Federal Bureau of Investigation
FCA—Farm Credit Administration
FCC—Federal Communications Commission
FDA—Food Distribution Administration, also Food and Drug Administration
FDIC—Federal Deposit Insurance Corporation
FEA—Foreign Economic Administration
FEPC—Committee on Fair Employment Practice
FHA—Federal Housing Administration
FPA—Food Production Administration
FPC—Federal Power Commission
FPHA—Federal Public Housing Administration
FSA—Farm Security Administration, also Federal Security Agency
FTC—Federal Trade Commission
FTZB—Foreign-Trade Zones Board
FWA—Federal Works Agency
HOLC—Home Owners' Loan Corporation
ICC—Interstate Commerce Commission
IWC—Inland Waterways Corporation
LOPM—Liaison Office for Personnel Management
MAB—Munitions Assignments Board
MRC—Metals Reserve Company
NHA—National Housing Authority
NIC—National Inventors' Council
NMCB—National Munitions Control Board
NLRB—National Labor Relations Board
NPPC—National Power Policy Committee
OCD—Office of Civilian Defense
OCIAA—Office of Coordinator of Inter-American Affairs
OCR—Office of Civilian Requirements

ODT—Office of Defense Transportation
OEM—Office for Emergency Management
OES—Office of Economic Stabilization
OFAR—Office of Foreign Agricultural Relations
OPA—Office of Price Administration
OPRD—Office of Production Research and Development
ORD—Office of the Rubber Director
OSRD—Office of Scientific Research and Development
OWI—Office of War Information
OWM—Office of War Mobilization
OWU—Office of War Utilities
PAW—Petroleum Administration for War
PRC—Petroleum Reserves Corporation
REA—Rural Electrification Administration
RFC—Reconstruction Finance Corporation
RRC—Rubber Reserve Company
SEC—Securities and Exchange Commission
SFA—Solid Fuels Administration
SWPC—Smaller War Plants Corporation
TFDRL—Trustees of the Franklin D. Roosevelt Library
TVA—Tennessee Valley Authority
UNRRA—United Nations Relief and Rehabilitation Administration
USCC—United States Commercial Company
WDC—War Damage Corporation
WFA—War Food Administration
WLB—War Labor Board
WMC—War Manpower Commission
WPB—War Production Board
WRA—War Relocation Authority
WRCB—War Relief Control Board
WSA—War Shipping Administration

CHAPTER III

THE RECORD OF 1944

I N the previous chapter I stated that the year 1943 was the most complex in our history for any recorder to recount, and that it might prove to be the turning point in favor of the United Nations and freedom. It did prove to be the latter but I am not sure that it was the former as I undertake, in a limited space, to tell the tale of 1944 during which the global war extended and intensified, and in which we had, here at home, an epochal Presidential election. We begin with domestic affairs.

During the second week of January, Mr. Roosevelt sent two Messages to Congress; one, of four thousand words, was the one called for in the Constitution, which states that the President shall "from time to time give to the Congress information on the state of the Union." Ever since the first term of George Washington this has been, each year, the first message transmitted from the Executive to the Legislature. The other, of eight thousand words, was in connection with the Budget for the ensuing year. The two, and one other, may be considered here together, because, even if somewhat vaguely, as might be natural in a year with a Presidential campaign at the end of it, they expressed in combination the ideas of the Administration as to the present and the future.

Considered as one, the Messages were interesting both

for what they said and did not say. For example, Mr. Roosevelt gave some startling figures as to the cost of war and normal government expenses. The war, he said, including the pre-Pearl Harbor defense program and post-Pearl Harbor operations, had cost $153,000,000,000 to the end of December 1944. This was six times the cost of World War I, $41,000,000,000 more than all the money spent by the Federal Government from 1791 to 1932 (when Roosevelt was elected), and represented nearly $1200 for every man, woman and child in the United States. Moreover, the President estimated that the actual war-cost would rise to over two hundred billions by June 30. In addition, Congress was asked to appropriate ten billions for the ordinary peace-time government agencies.

The war-cost, the President correctly said, mirrored "a gigantic effort," adding that in the output of munitions alone our production now almost equalled that of all the rest of the world combined. He expressed satisfaction with the progress of the war in its military aspects but added that our very victories were tending to slacken the war effort at home. He complained that Congress, with a national election in view in a few months, was loath to lay heavy enough taxes but he did not suggest that the Administration, obviously for the same reason, was equally loath to adopt a firm stand on labor, though he did mention some strikes, such as those in the coal and steel industries, and the threatened rail strike, which would have completely hamstrung the entire war effort and cut off the stream of supplies going to our forces overseas.

As we noted at the end of the chapter on the previous

year, Mr. Roosevelt, at a news conference, had discarded further use of the term "New Deal" as no longer adequate to cover the situation and his plans and interests. His several January Messages may therefore be taken to express his own new orientation. In general, they were vague, but some aspects stand out. They were not conciliatory to Congress; they were somewhat hostile to business; and they handled labor with delicacy.

To come to some of the details, he proposed a so-called "five-point plan."

1. The President asked for a law "which will tax all unreasonable profits, both individual and corporate," and added that the tax bill being considered by Congress "does not begin to meet this test." The bill then being considered called for a tax rate on "excess profits" of 95 per cent and was so worded that practically no one in the country could have a net income, after taxes, of more than $25,000, a measure advocated also by the Communist Party.

2. The President said that for "two long years I have pleaded with the Congress to take undue profits out of the war." There had been since 1942 a renegotiation law, administered by Presidential appointees, with no right of appeal.

3. He asked for a cost-of-food law which would place a floor under the prices farmers would receive and a ceiling on the prices consumers would pay, which virtually meant a subsidy to farmers of about $1,100,000,000 a year.

4. He asked for a re-enactment of the 1942 statute stabilizing farm prices, without which, he predicted, there would be "price chaos by summer."

5. He asked for a national service law which would "make available for war production or any other essential services every able-bodied adult in the nation." We might add that ours is the only leading nation in the war which has not passed some such service legislation.

The President also considered post-war problems. He spoke of the difficulties of reconversion from a war to a peacetime economy. He envisaged a vast government spending program, including the building of 34,000 miles of super-highways, and asked for a new eight-point Bill of Rights.

There have been a number of new Bills of Rights suggested either to supersede or overlay the original so-called Bill embodied in the first ten amendments to the Constitution, but this one received the official endorsement of the President in his Message on the Budget. It included the right to a job; to earn money for adequate food, clothing and recreation; of farmers to a decent living; of business men to be free of unfair competition; and the rights to a home, to protection in old age, during sickness and unemployment, and to a good education. It was not explained how all these desirable ends, described as "rights," were to be obtained or who was to pay for them. As was to be expected, public reaction to the several Messages was very mixed, depending on whether they were regarded from a merely political or from a serious economic standpoint.

Unfortunately the country, for the second time in its history—the first time being during Lincoln's second campaign—was confronted with a national election in the midst of the crisis of a war for survival. An important difference lay in the fact that, apart from whatever contrasts there may have been in the temperaments and ambitions of the two men, election had meant only the normal second term for Lincoln but it meant a fourth term for Franklin Roosevelt. In any history of the year, this situation deserves comment.

As long as the two-term tradition lasted, which was about a hundred and fifty years after Washington's inauguration, the President was independent, especially in his second term, nobody expecting any other. But now that a President has been elected for a third and a fourth term, this situation has changed. Just as a Representative in Congress, wholly dependent on pleasing the pressure groups which deliver the votes in his limited constituency, has to "go along" to a considerable extent, so now the incumbent of the Presidency, if the number of terms and perhaps the ambition to fill them are unlimited, is going to be forced to do so also. All of these factors, including the popular election of Senators, have been contributing to change our form of government from one made up of fairly independent thinkers to one of officials, of all grades, peculiarly sensitive to pressure and vote-getting.

Of course, there have always been group and sectional interests, such as the manufacturing tariff group, the farm bloc, the "Silver States," the Prohibition group, the veterans, and many others; but the more efficient political methods of pressure groups, combined with our gradually changing form of government, have been tending greatly to enhance the power of "pressure politics."

There is one more point which is a key to help unlock the history of 1944 and possibly of a good many years to come. If it is true that our entire government (Executive, Legislature and even Federal Judiciary) is going to be increasingly affected by pressure, it is important to know from whence that pressure may come, so as to get a sense of direction. Two trends have been notable in America in the past half-century or so—industrialization and urbanization. No American group, occupational or of about the same economic or social level, has ever voted unanimously alike. There have always been currents of individual and conflicting interests.

Where pressure comes in is in being able to deliver enough votes of voters who, from opinion or discipline, can swing the *balance* of an election in one important district or State. Capitalists may be high-tariff or free-trade, depending on what their capital is invested in. Industrial workers want high wages (which means high prices for manufactured goods), but low food costs. Farmers want low prices for manufactures but high prices for their food products; and so it goes. Business men are not united, but very vulnerable because of large fixed investments in plants. Farmers are scattered and notoriously independent. The big chance to build consolidated groups is among industrial workers and in the big cities, so that we have developed the powers of the trades-union leaders and of the city bosses and city machines, which are too well-known to name. All these factors are not new. Many have been operating for a long time but as they all combine, together with the popular election of Senators, an indefinite number of terms for the Executive, and a Judiciary largely the appointees of only one man and party, we are beginning to see more clearly the "shape of things to come." All have come about naturally. Even a fourth term *may* have been essential under the conditions. However, 1944 marked a more or less climacteric year, and now we touch on some of the high-spots more definitely.

Before going on to discuss the labor problem we may speak of a spectacular break between the Executive and the Congress in February. There was nothing especially novel about this. There has always been a tug-of-war between these two branches of government, dominance passing from one to the other depending upon the abilities and ambitions of each. But this conflict had new elements which have sprung from new conditions.

Briefly what happened was this. According to competent observers bad feeling between the President and Congress had been on the increase for some months. We are too near the events to appraise them with full historical knowledge, and can merely report them. After many months of delay Congress, in mid-February, passed a tax law. It was, indeed, inadequate, but that does not explain the extraordinary tone which the President adopted. He had originally asked for over $10,000,000,000 and the Bill, according to Congress, provided $2,300,000,000 or, by the Treasury computation, about $100,000,000 less. The President, denying the validity of both sets of figures, cut the result by another billion, and more. In his brief but almost unexampled Veto Message, he attacked the integrity of Congress and the ability of his own Secretary of the Treasury. He described the measure as "not a tax bill, but a tax relief bill providing relief not for the needy but for the greedy." Party leaders and the stanchest followers of Mr. Roosevelt were amazed and angered.

Without going into further details, we may say that he had attacked and impugned the motives of his strongest supporters, such as Morgenthau of the Treasury, Democratic Senate leader Barkley, Doughton the Democratic head of the Ways and Means Committee of the House, and others. No one could quite understand.

Some commentators suggested that the President, who was increasingly referring to himself less by that title than by that of "Commander in Chief," was deliberately seeking a break with Congress and the support of the soldier vote for a fourth term. Chairman Doughton said in the House that, knowing the President as he did, he could not believe he had written the Message. It had, he added, "none of his usual dignified, courteous, and helpful approach in matters of state. I see in this document the hands of a group of individuals not in any sense responsive to the will of the American people." In the Senate, Barkley, in an excoriating speech, resigned from his position of Majority Leader and said that the President's message was "a calculated and deliberate assault upon the legislative integrity of every member of the Congress." He said also a lot more! The Presidential veto was defeated in the Senate by a vote of 72–14 and in the House by 299–95. Mr. Roosevelt, evidently frightened by the terrific repercussion of his words, in all directions, begged Barkley to remain, and Barkley was upheld by the Senate, of which his party unanimously re-elected him as a real Majority Leader rather than as a rubber stamp for Administration policies. As a whole, the resounding episode probably did good and helped to restore proper balance between the Executive and leaders in Congress.

On the other hand, the amount raised in taxes by the Bill was, as we have said, inadequate. Both the President and the Secretary of the Treasury had properly asked for more but they had made no helpful suggestions, for political reasons which are part of the story of the trend of the times to which we have referred. They could not agree with each other, or with Congress, as to the sources from which additional revenue should be drawn. The President apparently thought only in terms of increasing the income taxes on individuals in the higher brackets and the profits tax on corporations, both of which had risen to points which endangered future economic progress. He would not consider a sales tax, which would spread small taxes over great numbers of people. Morgenthau had, on one occasion, rightly said that "we know where the bulk of the new money lies and where, therefore, lies the greatest danger of inflationary pressure. Today, four-fifths of all the income of the nation is going to people earning less than $5000 a year." That, of course, was true but, well, shall we put it in plain English and say the Administration wanted votes as well as money?—which brings us to another angle of the trend—its labor policy.

In regard to the Government's labor policy, good, bad or lacking altogether, as it sometimes has seemed in 1944, all three branches of the government—the Administration headed by the Chief Executive, the Congress, and the new Supreme Court as almost wholly reconstituted by the President during his twelve years of office and appointing power—have to bear their respective shares of responsibility. What does the record reveal?

First of all, our shift-over from peacetime production

of peace goods, in the most peace-loving perhaps of all the nations, to a wartime footing which has made the United States the greatest military power on the globe has amazed the world. Allowing what you will to government, there were other and very vital factors playing their parts. We are a democracy, with the highest standard of living of any people. That simple statement involves a good many subsidiary points. We can note some.

In a real and successful democracy, men and women learn to be self-reliant and to be *citizens,* not robot subjects. Our democracy has been steadily growing in maturity, and although in this war we have drafted over ten million citizens into the armed forces to face intense hardship, discomfort and death—or worse—there have been no "draft riots," as there were eighty-two years ago during the Civil War. The high standard of living for all has its implications also. There has, for many centuries past, always been "Big Business," but in the Old World, Big Business meant for the most part big fortunes for the few and high-priced goods for narrow markets. In the New World, owing to many favoring circumstances, "Big Business" came to mean "more goods for more people," lower-priced and higher quality, which, mostly in the preceding and present generation, have spelled our American form of large-scale mass production. From this and democracy came our "know-how" on the part of executives, our vast capacity to produce, and the sense of citizenship on the part of the people at large, and thus the "miracle of production," as Stalin called our achievement in this war. I do not like labels, but taking "labor" in its popular sense as applying to those who work in a factory or elsewhere for daily or weekly wages, I do not think there is any difference, on the whole, in sense of citizenship or patriotism, between "labor" and other elements in the community; and, what is more, I do not think there is a "Labor Vote." We all believe in democracy, self-government and America. (Leave out the fringes.) Now we come to our problem again as it is being revealed.

Early in the war, labor made a "no-strike" pledge for the duration. It has not been wholly adhered to by any means. In 1944, the year here under review, there were many ghastly examples to the contrary. But there have been such in other countries also as, notably, in England, which has been as a whole the most steadfast in its five years and more of war. Perhaps the answer to many things is Mark Twain's remark that "there is a lot of human nature in man." All in all, in America, labor has behaved well, but there *have* been inexcusable strikes endangering the lives of our forces overseas and threatening the success of the war effort. We need not list them all.

One of them, the one which caused the most resentment at home and perhaps among the armed forces, was that of 1800 foremen at the Wright Aeronautical Corporation in New Jersey in November, stopping work on the making of B–29 bombers. These foremen were highly paid and presumably especially intelligent. The Administration has persistently minimized the strikes by speaking only of "hours of man power" lost but it is obvious that it makes a great difference at what stage in the production of critical material the man-power hours *are* lost. The Foremen's Association of America, which is unaffiliated, was also included earlier in the year, in May, in a strike which made an estimated 60,000 idle in war work in Detroit.

Trying to stick to the facts and avoiding theory or personal prejudice, what do we find with regard to the increasing labor chaos as the war approaches its climax? First, let me repeat, what is only opinion and not capable of statistical proof, that I believe labor, in the accepted sense, to be as patriotic as any other group. It has, however, second, become split into conflicting parties, the A. F. of L., the C.I.O., and so on. We have not a long tradition of Trade Unionism or a strong Labor Party, as in England. Many of the strikes were "jurisdictional" rather than against employers or the public. "Labor Leaders," so-called, big or little, good or bad, have tended to play their lone hands much as the non-social-minded capitalists of, say, the 1870's did. Third, there has been the effect of government measures, including those of all three governmental branches.

The Wagner Act (1935) had given labor vast privileges denied to employers. The Smith-Connally Act, adopted by majority votes of both parties in both Houses of Congress in June 1943, has had fantastic results. Under this law, ostensibly designed to prevent strikes in wartime in essential industries, the government itself must count the ballots of the workers and, so, if the vote is for a strike, makes itself to a certain extent the official sponsor. On the other hand, there cannot be a strike against a government-operated plant, so that the strikers can force the government to take over operation if they choose, as happened in the case of the coal strike in the spring. The Smith-Connally Act was not a law against strikes but, practically, a law to enable the workers to decide whether or not they should force the government to take over. These facts are pertinent, because although they proved important in 1944 they may prove even more so in 1945.

We come now to the general attitude of the Government as a whole. We have mentioned Congress, which in spite of all criticism has refused to amend either the Wagner or the Smith-Connally Acts. The Supreme Court has trailed along, in spite of a continued succession of the formerly much criticised 4–5 and other split decisions. With regard to what is more particularly called "the Administration," we have mentioned the tendency to minimize news of all strikes. When John L. Lewis defied the President and Government, he "got away with it," and the President admitted he could do nothing. In the course of the year, the two disputes which attracted the most public attention were those with James Cæsar Petrillo, of the Musicians Union, and with Montgomery Ward & Co., both of which we must mention, as they held attention during most of the period covered by this chapter, and indicate trends following earlier legislation and policies.

We may note, by way of introduction, a victory scored by John L. Lewis and his mine workers. Originally, the Wage-Hour Act of Congress was supposed to stabilize wages, except for a few workers receiving sub-marginal pay. The "Little Steel Formula" was one of its accompaniments. However, late in March, just before the deadline of April 1, Lewis got an increase under the subterfuge of "portal to portal pay," although the Union had agreed in 1940 with the operators that such a method of computation would "result in complete chaos." The actual time of each miner was not figured but an "average" time for all was agreed upon, which simply meant a rise in the wages of all, and was approved by the Supreme Court with an eloquent plea by Justice Murphy, who had been appointed to the Court after his term as Governor of Michigan following the sit-down strikes in that State and a period in the Cabinet. In the previous year, 1943, when Lewis had refused to obey an order of the War Labor Board, the President had been asked what he would do, and he answered with the query whether he should write a nice little note on pink paper, saying, "Dear Mr. Lewis, I hope you will sign the contract."

The lesson had apparently not been ignored, and so, enter Cæsar Petrillo, head of a labor union, the American Federation of Musicians, so-called. The case goes back some years. Let us make it as short as we can without distorting the facts, and those are all we have to report. According to the War Labor Board, in its findings as of March, the "union" appears to be a very loose organization of followers of Petrillo, of which only one out of three depended on music for a livelihood. Petrillo had claimed that "canned music," *i.e.,* phonograph records, juke boxes, and so on, were depriving musicians of their living, and had demanded, as early as June 1942, that the companies concerned pay specified sums of money to the union for its "employment fund." Under Petrillo's ultimatum and orders, the making of records had stopped August 1, 1942. He allowed no member of the union to take part in such production, and apparently he had so built himself up, with the help of all departments of government, that he could prevent any musician not a member of his union from getting any job at all.

Since 1937 his musicians' wages had increased 50 per cent to 110 per cent, running as high as $18 an hour. Unions are not liable for accounting as are business enterprises but the N.W.L.B. estimated (1944) that the union (subject to Petrillo) was receiving $3,000,000 a year outside of wages. The size of the prize that Petrillo was after may be indicated by an estimated juke-box business of $200,000,000 a year and the fact that the three major phonograph companies had been making 130,-000,000 records a year.

What happened down the line? In 1942, Thurman Arnold, then Assistant Attorney General of the U. S., filed a suit in an Illinois District Court asking for an injunction to prevent Petrillo from carrying out his ultimatum. The old Norris-LaGuardia Act of Congress forbade injunctions in labor disputes. The Department of Justice lost its case. Later, through Elmer Davis, the War and Navy Departments *asked* Petrillo to *allow* the making of records because their absence was having a bad effect on the morale of service men at the front. Petrillo said No. The U. S. Senate investigated the situation and cross-examined Petrillo, only to get the same answer. In June, 1944, the War Labor Board issued an order to Petrillo to desist. Same answer. On October 4, the President of the United States telegraphed to Petrillo asking him please, even if he thought the decision wrong, "to accept the directive orders of the National War Labor Board. What you regard as your loss will certainly be your country's gain." The country gasped at this, but again Mr. Petrillo refused to rescind his ultimatum.

It is all a much longer story, including the opinion of a Circuit Court of Appeals that there had been conspiracy and coercion, and the decision of the Supreme Court that, in view of Congressional legislation, there was nothing to be done about it. Later, two of the leading recording companies capitulated and paid royalties to Mr. Petrillo or to his union. We had reached the point where one labor leader, motivated by the lust for money or power, could tell the entire American people what music they would hear and how, and defy the Government. Executive policy over a period of years, the Courts, Congress and the W.L.B., all have had a part in this.

The other leading case of the year, which shared the limelight, was quite different. Montgomery Ward & Co. is one of the largest businesses in the country, one of two leading old-established mail-order houses which reach into almost every village of the land. They got into trouble with the W.L.B. in November 1942, for having refused to sign a contract with the C.I.O. union as ordered by the Board. We have noted that when Lewis refused to sign and called an order of the Board "infamous" he was allowed to have his own way, and Mr. Petrillo has certainly had his.

A business, however, according to legislation and court rulings, is in a very different position from a labor union, both as to obeying laws and accounting for money handled. When the W.L.B. applied to the President to help them enforce their order against Montgomery Ward there was also a very different reaction than in the cases of Lewis, Petrillo and other labor leaders and unions. The President immediately sent a telegram which read, in part, "As Commander-in-Chief in time of war . . . I direct Montgomery Ward & Co. to comply without further delay." They complied. Although they had always, on principle, opposed the closed shop, they signed the contract demanded by the C.I.O. for the year, as ordered.

When the contract expired, the W.L.B. demanded that it be continued together with the "check-off" and other points which did not deal with wages. The company, whether wisely or not, refused until a poll of the employees had been taken. The issue became somewhat confused, although the main lines remained clear. The President again intervened, and Sewell L. Avery, Chairman of the Board of Montgomery Ward & Co., defied the order. The Post Office refused to deliver mail to the mail-order house, and the President ordered the army to take over the property. Avery, the sixty-nine-year-old Chairman, still defiant, was seized in his private office, carried out bodily and set in the street by soldiers of the army detailed for the unpleasant job. The W.L.B. had been unwise. Montgomery Ward may have been ill-advised, but the pictures in the newspapers of soldiers carrying an old, nationally known and respected business man out of his office to dump him on the street, as contrasted with the treatment accorded Lewis and Petrillo, raised a storm of protest and comment.

The whole thing was a mess but brought to light many complications in our present form of government and in our current Administration. We were supposed to have three departments of government, acting as checks on one another, the Executive, Judicial and Legislative. Owing to accidents of death and to the unexpectedly long term of office of the President, who would have been in office for sixteen years had he lived out his fourth term, the Supreme Court, which is the pinnacle of the Judicial system and the court of last resort, has been almost wholly made up of appointees of the Executive. During the past dozen years, Congress has abdicated many of its powers to the Executive by giving him almost unlimited powers and creating "Boards," or what you will, whose members are appointed by him. Many of these have assumed not only Executive and Legislative powers but also Judicial. Some of the most careful students of America and its institutions have pointed to this "government by commission" as perhaps the most dangerous element in current American public life.

In addition, we are at war, a deadly war in which all our national ways and institutions are at stake, a fact that too many Americans still appear to ignore. The war powers of a President are ill-defined but are supremely important and essential. They have in the past been variously interpreted by such war Presidents as Lincoln and Wilson, but no President before ever had such powers as had Mr. Roosevelt, either just taken by himself or conferred upon him by Congress.

However, the Montgomery Ward case brought all these points more or less into the clear. The confusion of government by commission became evident. For example, the War Labor Board held that this particular labor dispute was a war issue, yet the War Man Power Commission had refused to classify the company as an essential war industry. On the other hand, the War Production Board had decided that the company was sufficiently essential to the war effort to warrant granting it priorities for materials. The entire muddle placed before the public some of our difficulties, especially as regards the extent of the President's powers.

A new angle was brought out by Attorney General Biddle, who took the Montgomery Ward case to court and surprised the public by asserting in his argument that no court, in wartime, should seek "to substitute its judgment for that of the Executive." He held that there was an "aggregate" of constitutional powers in the hands of the President in wartime which would enable him to deal in his own judgment with any situation. He added that "no business or property is immune to a Presidential order"; "that the Government does not need a court order . . . to take possession." He went on that way, and the strongest Democratic newspaper supporter of the President said that people could not be blamed if they did not believe him when he said that they "were just seeing things under their beds."

Things were getting too bad. The President had been away on vacation. After his return, and on May 9, the army was taken out of Ward's and the property restored to its owners and management. In December, the President again ordered the seizure of Ward properties in seven cities, the crisis once more centering around problems of the closed shop and enforced union maintenance, not those of wages or production. On almost the last day of the year, Avery asked for a chance to appeal to the courts.

Meanwhile, the situation in organized labor had be-

come increasingly confused. In May, John L. Lewis had
finally refused, after long negotiations, to merge his
union with the A. F. of L. That feud remained with more
bitterness than ever. In an open letter, Lewis accused the
A. F. of L. through its President, William Green, of
"base hypocrisy, approximating moral turpitude." On
the other hand, the C.I.O. entered politics in a big way,
having organized its Political Action Committee (to become known in our alphabetical world as the P.A.C.), in
which Sidney Hillman, a Lithuanian who had come to
this country in 1907 at the age of twenty to become a
labor leader of the new school and an Administration
favorite, was a chief figure.

Lewis, in earlier years, as recounted in a previous chapter, had gone into politics with his half-million contribution to the Democratic campaign fund, only to quarrel
with the President later. Some of what might be called
the "elder statesmen" of the labor movement were deeply
opposed to political action. In September of the year under
discussion in this chapter, for example, Matthew Woll
repeated his oft-given advice that the sphere of labor action was on the industrial front and that "Labor cannot
and must not stake its whole future upon the success or
failure of any political campaign."

However, new days, new ways, and as early as the
middle of May, Hillman's P.A.C., claiming to act for an
"overwhelming majority of the C.I.O.'s five million members" called for a fourth term for Roosevelt, which brings
us along to the election, for this was most emphatically
an election year and, considering the fourth term, the
most crucial we have ever had.

We shall come to details in a few more lines but first there are a few general things to be said about this re-markable 1944 campaign. We have spoken of its being a war year. Undoubtedly the old saying about the danger of changing horses when crossing a stream influenced many voters. No one can say whether, except for the war, there would or would not have been a fourth term. Such discussion is guesswork not history, but there *was* strong opposition to it, as was clearly indicated by the resignation early in June, on the eve of the national conventions, of James A. Farley as Chairman of the New York State Democratic Committee. As Chairman of the National Committee, he had been largely responsible for Roosevelt's election in 1932, and had remained loyal as Postmaster General. He had opposed a third term and could not approve a fourth. As a wholly loyal member of the Democratic Party, he could only resign.

The action was symptomatic of the many crosscurrents in the campaign then starting. We have mentioned the increasing power of labor, especially Hillman's P.A.C. of the C.I.O. In his bolt, Farley found company in many Democratic leaders of the South, who, however, disliked the New Deal and the Vice-President, Henry Wallace, even more than the thought of a fourth term. Hillman and much of radical labor was insistent on having Wallace. If Roosevelt ran again, it was becoming evident that his running mate would have to satisfy both labor and the Solid South.

Another complication was the soldier vote. Nearly ten million men overseas, mostly of the younger generation, raised a tremendous question. For months, there was discussion in Congress and in State legislatures as to how proper and constitutional legislation could be framed so as to enable this overseas vote to be taken and counted. Ill-feeling was aroused and no wholly satisfactory adjustment reached which might serve as a future precedent for the nation as a whole. What was done might have caused great confusion had the vote been as close as in the Hayes-Tilden election of 1876 but, luckily, it was not, for such a contested election might have had terrifying consequences in the midst of our life-and-death struggle for national existence against enemies then far from beaten.

We need not detail the platforms of the two parties, but it is important to speak of certain aspects of them. Most important of all for the future of the United States and perhaps of the world, both parties agreed *in the main* on matters pertaining to the war and its conduct, and on the future assumption of responsibilities by this nation. That was something new. Party politics had stopped at last at the water's edge. Second, both parties vied with each other in offering baits to the public, such as extension of so-called security in the way of old-age pensions, medical relief and so on. Finally, labor, as a pressure group, loomed large.

The twenty-third National Republican Convention, with 1057 delegates, met at Chicago, June 26–28. Thomas E. Dewey, Governor of New York, was nominated for the Presidency by a vote of 1056 to 1, a fifty-four-year-old Wisconsin farmer, Grant A. Ritter, insisting on voting for General MacArthur, who had flatly stated he would not run. For Vice-President, the Convention nominated John W. Bricker, Governor of the often politically pivotal

State of Ohio. Dewey's nomination was pretty much of a foregone conclusion, and Bricker withdrew gracefully and took second place. Our nominating conventions are distinctly American, but they are more notable for noise, hullabaloo and a half hour of applause than they are for humor. Perhaps this one provided a characteristic example. When the Rev. George R. Cady, who was chairman of the Wisconsin delegation, tried to induce Ritter to make Dewey's nomination unanimous, Ritter shouted back, "I am a man, not a jellyfish," and the Reverend Cady shouted back, "Isn't he a damn fool? That is as far as a clergyman can go."

Willkie, the Republican candidate in the previous election, did not come out for Dewey and expressed some dissatisfaction with the platform. Moreover, the party was not well organized, nor wholly unified on important issues. Dewey, unquestionably, had been nominated for a tough fight.

The twenty-eighth National Democratic Convention also met in Chicago, July 19–21. There was no difficulty over the nomination of Roosevelt for the fourth time, and he received 1086 votes against 89 for Senator Byrd of Virginia and 1 for James Farley, who had declined to allow his name to be used. The real trouble came, as had been expected, over the nomination for Vice-President. Henry Wallace, who had been in that office for four years, was most anxious to run again, and was the candidate of the C.I.O.-P.A.C. He was, however, as I have noted, strongly opposed in the Solid South and by other elements in the party. Mr. Roosevelt, in a letter, made it clear that he did not back him. Finally, the choice fell on

Senator Harry S. Truman of Missouri. Writing to Chairman Hannegan, the President accepted the nomination for a fourth term, stating that he did not want it but that all the men in the armed forces had their Commander-in-Chief—who was himself—and that *he* had as commander above him the American people, and so, although he would "not run in the usual partisan, political sense," he *would* run. The campaign was on, and developed more or less according to the usual pattern and procedure.

A considerable change had occurred, however, during the time since the President had run at the beginning of his first term. In that fateful 1932, his support had been widely distributed among all sections of the people —farmers, many business men, labor, the disillusioned of all sorts among those out of work and discouraged, conservatives who agreed with Mr. Roosevelt's then campaign speeches as to the necessity for simplifying government and reducing its cost. By 1944, many of these followers had, for various reasons, fallen away, and those in reputed control of large blocks of votes, such as city bosses and labor organizations, had come to loom large.

At the end of August 1944, Sidney Hillman was called before a Congressional Committee of the House to explain about his two "political action" committees. His testimony was explicit and there is no reason to question its honesty but it raised important questions for American political life. Among other things, the investigation revealed that the Corrupt Practices Act excludes from its provisions both political conventions and primary elections, which latter are in many sections tantamount to election itself. The P.A.C. almost put over Wallace as

Vice-Presidential candidate in the Convention, against the wishes of a majority of the Democratic Party and of the President himself. The second loop-hole is the definition in the Smith-Connally Act of a labor organization. Hillman drew a subtle, and apparently legal, distinction between contributions for political purposes by a Trade Union and contributions by its *individual* members through *another* fund, though he was responsible for both.

Trade Unions are getting to be Big Business. No Union stands higher than the International Ladies' Garment Workers, of which David Dubinsky is the able leader. In June, he led the way for real accountings by unions, and advised others to follow. He showed that his international union, with its locals, had well over $16,000,000 of liquid assets. This indicates the financial power which unions *can* use in contested elections if the loopholes claimed by Hillman hold good.

On October 7, a few weeks before the election, Philip Murray, President of the C.I.O., and Hillman, chairman of the C.I.O.-P.A.C., issued a statement calling on all local union officers and shop stewards to get out the vote for Roosevelt. Compare this demand with any similar one which might have been issued, but could not, by the heads of any of our great business corporations. When asked, in connection with this unprecedented election order, how many of his claimed five million voters would vote for Roosevelt, Hillman merely said he did not know but that the number who would vote for Dewey was "so infinitesimally small that I don't care to estimate." The point is *not* that it was labor. It is whether *any* pressure group, farmers, labor, business corporations or other, should have such power to elect members of Congress, and the Executive, who in turn appoints the Judiciary, or whether that power should still reside in the people at large irrespective of their occupational groupings.

We can record the election briefly. Apparently the "soldier vote," as counted, did not differ greatly from what might have been expected had the men been at home. In any case, the total vote was not close enough to raise the dreaded problem of long delay. Within a few days after election, the figures showed a total vote cast of 45,568,024, of which Roosevelt polled 24,333,633 and Dewey 21,234,379. Any changes in the popular vote subsequently counted, owing to minor difficulties, did not alter the result substantially, and the sweeping plurality in the Electoral College of 432 for Roosevelt and 99 for Dewey remained unaltered after missing districts, belated soldier ballots and other readjustments were accounted for.

Mr. Roosevelt had won his victory but from the longer historical point of view there are a number of points to consider. There had been twelve years in which to build up patronage and political machinery. There was the war and there was the "swapping horses" argument. The vote of the Electoral College, in our antiquated system, was impressive—432–99. Yet it was the lowest Roosevelt had polled in his four elections. In 1932, it had been 472–59; in 1936, 523–8; in 1940, 440–82. Moreover, his party majorities in both Houses of Congress, except for a slight rise as regards Representatives, in 1944, have been steadily declining, bringing them to 241 but as contrasted with 313, 322, and 333 in his first three Congresses.

The popular vote also deserves mention. As the best

practical solution of a difficult problem in self-government, we have accepted the verdict of the majority until
it changes, but it is well to remember what our great
proponent of this rule, Thomas Jefferson, said of it in
his First Inaugural Address. He wrote that "though the
will of the Majority is in all cases to prevail, that will, to
be rightful, must be reasonable: that the Minority possess
their equal rights, which equal laws must protect, and
to violate would be oppression." In the election of 1944,
the "Minority" who voted against Roosevelt numbered
roughly 21,500,000 out of a total of 45,500,000. They
form a very important section of the total picture.

There was another significant feature about the popular vote. Not only had the winning party, playing for
sixteen years of office, gradually lost strength as a whole
but the sources of that strength had changed. Both geo-
graphical and statistical studies of the vote indicate that
there had been a big shift since 1932 and 1936. The
farmer of the Middle West, notoriously progressive, was
leaving the fold. The "Solid South" remained, for racial
reasons, but the party lines were dividing as never before
on narrow economic lines of cleavage. A huge mass of
votes came from the industrial cities and centers of the
North and West, garnered by city bosses and trade-union
political leaders. This is new and worth noting. It was
stated that the vote in seven big cities alone gave Mr.
Roosevelt 185 electoral votes, and the C.I.O.-P.A.C.
proved its importance. The two-term tradition was clearly
buried for good, and both the character of the electorate
and the nature of the Presidential office had altered.

Although Mr. Roosevelt's fourth term would not begin

until the following January, there had been many rumors of impending changes in the Cabinet after election. There was only one, though that was of supreme importance and had nothing whatever to do with politics or with the too frequent bickerings among high officials in the Administration. Solely on account of health, the Secretary of State, Cordell Hull, found it essential to resign on November 21, after an almost completed twelve years of service in that high office, a period of public duty unequalled by that of any other incumbent of the office in our history. He had struggled with frail health from the time when, against his own desires, he yielded to Mr. Roosevelt's insistence, in 1933, that he leave his seat in the Senate to head the Cabinet and assume duties which were to prove the heaviest that any Secretary of State has ever had to carry.

This, fortunately, is not an obituary but merely a reference to the most important resignation during the years of Roosevelt's Administration.

Cordell Hull was born of a financially humble family, in a log cabin—or shack, if you will—in a "cove" of the Tennessee mountains. He once told me, as I recall, that he had never seen a railroad train or a newspaper until he was twelve years old. He rose, through a succession of offices, to a leading position in the United States Senate. I was in London at the time of the Economic Conference, and well recall the ill-feeling aroused there when the conference was "torpedoed," as they called it, on orders from America. Mr. Hull was our chief representative, *in London*. I remember that several leading Englishmen expressed their feelings to me about what had happened, but they all said, "At least, you Americans can be proud of having sent us, as the head of your delegation, a *very great gentleman.*" The little barefooted boy of the mountains had made a reputation as a noble and distinguished statesman in many lands besides our own, and was perhaps the most beloved and respected member of the Administration at home, both by those who agreed with all his ideas and those who might not.

The President appointed as the new Secretary of State, Edward R. Stettinius, who had had a notable career in business and had given it up, at much cost to himself, to enter government service, and who had occupied many important posts, including that of Lend-Lease Administrator and, more recently, Under-Secretary of State. Joseph Grew, a career diplomat and former Ambassador to Japan, was made the new Under-Secretary, and five Assistant Secretaries were also appointed, and confirmed by the Senate. On the whole, this appeared to be a good team for the heavy international work facing America during the war and afterwards.

Stettinius had made a particularly good record as Administrator of Lend-Lease and a fine impression on Congress whenever called upon to discuss that important measure, which has done so much to bind the Allies together and to co-ordinate all their operations, both through our Lend-Lease to them and through their reverse Lend-Lease to us. Nothing like it had ever been done in the case of any previous military alliance, and the favor that it found with the people and with Congress was indicated when, on April 19, 1945, the House of Representatives extended it to July 1, 1948, by a vote of 334 to 21, the few dissenting votes being all Republican and 20 of them from the Middle West. A good deal of stress has been laid on the twenty billions or so that we have "Lent-Leased" to our Allies, but not enough on the reverse process.

We may note a few points regarding this from President Roosevelt's Message to Congress of November 24. By the end of June, he reported, the British Commonwealth had given *us* about $3,400,000,000. In the first six months of 1944, the British Isles had supplied our overseas troops with well on to the equivalent of 4,000,000 ship-tons of supplies. Our army in the European theater of war was supplied by the British with about 63 per cent of its Quartermasters' supplies and with 58 per cent of those for our engineers. In the Pacific, Australia and New Zealand gave us 1,850,000,000 pounds of food alone, and over 20,000 small ships and boats for our Philippines campaign. It has not been all one-sided, and the pooling of supplies has gone hand in hand with the extraordinary pooling of aims and of effort.

On the home front, things did not run so smoothly. We had been unprepared for war, but thanks largely to the individual initiative bred by democracy, to our extraordinary productive capacity, and to the "know-how" of our great corporations, we had done a marvellous job. In many ways, however, it is easier to transform a peacetime production to a wartime one than *vice versa*. With war, people are willing to sacrifice and to cut their standard of living; there is one big job, to win the war; one big customer for all goods, the Government; business and investors have not made money out of this war, but cost-sheets, like the machinery for many peacetime goods, are thrown out of plant windows; there is no choice as to type of goods; the Government decides those things.

But when peace comes, it is different. Producers will again have 138,000,000 potential customers with differing tastes, hungry to enjoy what they have been foregoing. Plants which have discarded their peacetime machinery are cluttered with machines and tools serving Government needs only. If, after the war, the Government is not to remain the sole customer, the sole buyer and distributor of goods, the problem becomes enormously complex. During the year, efforts were made to prepare for a transition to peace, and for the readjustment of individual lives, so that we might be better prepared for these than we were when the reverse transition to war and its shortages and rationings had had to be made.

The most important of these efforts was blueprinted in the Report made to the President and Congress in February by John M. Hancock and Bernard M. Baruch. It dealt not only with the whole problem of industrial conversion but laid special stress on the human elements involved in eventually transferring 20,000,000 service men and special war-workers back into their places in a peacetime economy. Its 131 pages cannot be summarized in a paragraph, but its importance as an example of industrial statesmanship of the highest order, as well as proof of the ability of its drafters, was generally proclaimed.

The size of the problem was indicated not only by the numbers of individuals affected but by the note that we were at that time producing war goods to the amount of $50,000,000,000 a year, a production which would almost wholly cease with the final end of the war. The Report came out solidly for private enterprise, and said, "There has been too much loose parroting of the slogan, that if individual enterprise fails to provide jobs for everyone it must be replaced by some of the other systems that are around. The war has been a crucible for all the economic systems of the world, for our own, for communism, fascism, nazism—all the others. And the American system has outproduced the world." However, the Report was switched on to a siding by both the Administration and Congress, and the year passed with no constructive work done, though in the campaign both the President and Wallace talked of the necessity of "sixty million jobs." With the end of the German war at least in sight, we are still as unprepared for peace as we were for war when Pearl Harbor was attacked.

We may now turn briefly to the Supreme Court which, as we have noted, had become almost the creation of one President. It affords an interesting example of the well-known fact that a man's job and environment have a great influence on his thinking and character. The newly constituted Court *is* new, and it will take time for the new Justices to work out their lines. Most of them, when appointed, had had little or no experience on the bench; of the nine Justices appointed by Roosevelt, only two had any previous experience as judges: Rutledge had been appointed as a Judge of the Court of Appeals for the District of Columbia in 1939, and Black had served eighteen months as a police judge, but independence, if not too great concern with the need for a continuing tradition, appeared early.

For example, on January 31, the Court divided 5-4 in

a decision denying the right of parents of the sect of Jehovah's Witnesses to send their nine-year-old children out into the streets to sell pamphlets in favor of the sect. In a rough estimate, the *U. S. News* called the box-score of the split decisions: in civil liberties cases, the individual won 9 and lost 6; in the regulation of business, the Government won 17 and lost 10; in tax cases, the Government won 6 and lost 5. Moreover, the Justices did not vote *en bloc*. Even Justices Murphy and Roberts have been found on the same side. Nevertheless, the confusion was dangerous for respect for law and the Constitution. In the 1942–43 session, 176 dissenting opinions had been written as against a majority opinion in 171 cases. It began to appear that the Court was not to interpret the law and the Constitution but to form a third House of the legislature.

Justice Roberts may be considered a conservative but certainly Justice Felix Frankfurter cannot, yet on February 2 they joined in a statement that the tendency, as displayed so far, was such as to leave the lower courts "on an uncharted sea of doubt and difficulty without any confidence that what was said yesterday [by the Supreme Court] will hold good tomorrow." Justice Roberts pointed out that the law must gradually change to meet changing conditions but that it must not become a mere game of chance with no precedents to go by.

The change in the Court was well illustrated in a decision, 8–1, handed down April 3, reversing a unanimous decision in 1935. The decision, which may prove to be a momentous one, invalidated the rule of the Democratic Party in Texas to the effect that Negroes should not be allowed to vote in primary elections. In the previous decision, the Court had held that party rules were not governmental acts; but the new decision (Justice Roberts alone dissenting) held that a State cannot cast "its electoral process in a form which permits a private organization to practice discrimination in the election."

Decisions during this session of the Court confused considerably the problems of taxation. One of the main reasons for forming the Constitution was to allow a free flow of commerce between the States and to abolish tariff barriers across State lines. With 3,000,000 square miles and 138,000,000 population, the United States was to become the greatest contiguous free-trade industrial area in the world, and to prosper accordingly. Little by little, by such subterfuges as use-taxes, regulation of interstate truck traffic, food-inspection laws, and in other ways, this free trade has been in steady process of being whittled down. Four decisions of the Supreme Court in 1944, regarding taxes (although the Court split differently in the different cases), helped to break down the original intent of the Constitution. Relief appeared to lie rather in legislation by the States or by Congress than in the Court, and the same was true of a most important decision in June declaring that insurance companies were engaged in interstate commerce, reversing a continuous course of highest judicial decisions for over seventy-five years, to which all insurance companies and their policyholders had adjusted themselves and their affairs, thus vindicating what had been said by Justice Roberts about a Court decision coming to be like a railroad ticket, good for only one train on only one particular day.

Before we turn to the inexpressibly complex international aspects of the year, including the war, we may note some of the Americans distinguished in various ways who died during 1944. The year took such a heavy toll that it is impossible to give to each the notice he deserves. Alphabetically arranged, there were: George Ade, humorist; Jules S. Bache, financier, art collector and benefactor of New York; Raymond Clapper, news correspondent, killed in a plane crash in the Pacific; Irvin Cobb, beloved humorist and lecturer; Norman H. Davis, public figure and head of the Red Cross; Charles Dana Gibson, artist; Dr. Walter A. Jessup, head of the Carnegie Foundation; Frank Knox, Secretary of the Navy; Judge Kenesaw M. Landis, czar of American baseball fairplay; Manuel Quezon, President of the Philippines; Brigadier General Theodore Roosevelt; Alfred E. Smith, ex-Governor of New York and Presidential candidate in 1928; Ida M. Tarbell, writer; William Allen White, editor; Wendell L. Willkie, leader and Presidential candidate in 1940. In a chapter already much too long, it is clearly impossible to pay proper tribute to those cited, all of whom were great Americans in their several ways.

We must now turn to the war and the international conferences of the year. We have heard much of our "forgotten wars," in this mondial one. They are far from being forgotten, but the acts of *this* vast drama *are* too numerous to be considered with any of the detail warranted by the heroism displayed by the individuals and forces in the various sectors.

Let us start with the Pacific. The war in that area has been perhaps the most difficult of all wars for a layman.

to understand, and it might be well for more of us to remember that, in military matters, we *are* laymen and not trained strategists. The water distances for transport, across the greatest of the world's oceans, are so enormous; the number of islands and mainland ports so great; the economic and military importance of them so different; the expansion of the Japanese was so rapid, after the destruction of our fleet at Pearl Harbor and the capture of the Philippines; that altogether it combines to make the most complex and little understandable picture of a combat zone that we have ever known.

Gradually, however, by late January, a pattern began to emerge. The apparently unrelated campaigns in the mountains and swamps of New Guinea and on the Solomon Islands began to make sense. We were headed for Rabaul and the open sea. Admiral Halsey and General MacArthur in different spheres were working together for a common end. We may mention two points. For one thing, although it was not announced until the end of August by Secretary of the Navy Forrestal, we had added to our navy since the beginning of the European war 65,000 vessels of more than 9,000,000 tons displacement, and our job, he said, was only half finished. That, and our airplane production, incredible to the Germans and to Hitler's "honorary Aryan" ally (combined, both here and all over the world, with the unexpected ability of Tom, Dick and Harry to leave peacetime jobs in a "decadent" democracy and become the toughest fighting force in the world), were to change the picture and save that world for freedom.

The second point was that the road to Tokio was not

by way train, *i.e.,* it was decided not to take island by island at great cost of life and time. The so-called "leap-frog" tactics were carried out. We jumped ahead to strategic points, over others. The result was amazing to the Japs, and even to our own public. By the end of 1943, we had captured the Gilbert Islands. By January 30, 1944, we started operations against the Marshall group. On February 8, we captured in that group the atoll of Kwajalein, the toll of dead being 286 Americans and 8122 Japs, a fine batting average. American guns destroyed practically every living thing on the island.

In the Marshall group was the island of Truk, which the Japs had fortified so heavily that they considered it a sort of impregnable Gibraltar and one of their most essential naval bases. An attack by carrier-based planes, followed by battleships, cruisers and destroyers, the force under command of (now) Admiral Spruance, captured the stronghold, February 17–18. News reports stated that the Japs lost 19 ships and 202 planes. With other islands also taken, the Marshalls were completely in our possession by the 20th. In the Bismarcks, a couple of days later, we heavily attacked Rabaul and sank a convoy of 9 ships. Rabaul itself was to fall to us, and our now successive victories had their repercussions in Japan with the dismissal of the heads of both the army and navy. In spite, however, of the immensely powerful and mobile air and naval force we had built up in the Pacific since Pearl Harbor, it was not realized at home what we had been doing. A leading journal, for example, stated that no nation before had ever undertaken to defeat at a distance of 10,000 miles from its own bases another nation of

80,000,000 people, and that we would be lucky if we got to the Philippines by the middle of 1945. We were to under-estimate the speed of the Pacific war and, at the year's end, to over-estimate that of the European one.

April 7, however, we struck again at Palau Harbor, less than 600 miles from Manila, sinking 28 enemy ships, damaging 18 others, and destroying over 200 planes. Early in August, the President paid a quick visit to Hawaii. By the middle of October, our forces were back in the Philippines. On the 25th, the President announced that in a sea-air battle we had routed the Japanese fleet, which had made a three-pronged attempt in the narrow waters between the islands to prevent our vessels, together with an Australian squadron, from entering. MacArthur, who had promised when he left in 1942 that he would "come back," *was* back, and reported the most "crushing defeat" the Japs had suffered. Apparently, the whole of the Japanese fleet had been engaged, and the victory was indeed overwhelming. Even before this fight, the score for the period since Pearl Harbor was 195 American naval vessels of all types lost on all the oceans as against 750 Japanese ones sunk or damaged. It was no wonder that Rear Admiral Clark said that "we're strong enough now out there to go wherever we want to go whenever we want to go." This statement was highlighted when on June 15 we began attacking the Japanese homeland with our new B–29's—the first air attacks since Doolittle's one raid on April 18, 1942.

In spite of that, it was to be a long job yet and a hard one, but the change from 1942 was amazing. America had become not only the greatest air power in the world but the mistress of the seas. The Japanese navy was on its way out, wholly; the German surface navy, at least, was practically wiped out by the end of the year; one-third of the Italian navy had been turned over to the Russians and the fate of the rest was in doubt; the French fleet was largely destroyed; as compared with the British, with an estimated · 2,200,000 tons of combat ships, we had 4,500,000 tons. With such power go heavy responsibilities.

Our return to the Philippines was hailed with genuine joy by the Filipinos, who had remained stanch and loyal throughout the Japanese occupation and who completely trusted us to carry out our pledges of eventual independence under American protection. They had given us much assistance in our landings, and the whole episode was a very promising one for the possible relations between a great power and a small one. The Japanese had treated the Filipinos with great brutality, and in January our Government had released the Report prepared by the Army and Navy Departments on the atrocities committed by the Japs on our own troops before we had been forced to evacuate the islands. The details of the "March of Death" at Bataan, and other incidents, had earlier been considered too horrifying for those at home, to be published. All of these factors contributed to our satisfaction in being able to regain our foothold and gradually extend our control again over the islands.

In the previous chapter, we spoke of the wiping out of the Germans in Africa, and the transfer of the struggle from Tunisia to Sicily and thence to the mainland of Italy. It might perhaps, at the time, have seemed to the layman that the campaign in that theater had been a disappointment. For a while, the public, at least, anticipated that the Germans would be driven out of Rome, northward, out of the peninsula altogether, thus opening a way through the back door into that portion of Germany in which Hitler and other leading Nazis recently talked of maintaining their last stand.

On January 22, landings were made at Anzio and Nettuno, on the coast below Rome, with the idea of getting behind the Germans and cutting off their lines. There was also heavy fighting at Cassino. The plans did not work out as expected but in spite of the bloody struggle on the Anzio beach-head we made our footing good; Cassino was eventually blown to pieces and Rome, mostly undamaged, fell to us on June 5. From then on, progress was slow. The Germans still controlled the industrial north of Italy and the passes over the Alps, in spite of our steady edging forward. The cost, however, may have been terrific, as the Allies, partly owing to mistaken German strategy, pinned down many divisions of the best German troops in Italy, who in 1945 were to be badly needed on the Rhine.

Italy also came over to the Allied side, entering the war as a "co-belligerent"; the King resigned, though he kept his title; the Crown Prince took over; Mussolini, who had been rescued from prison by agents of Hitler, pretended to organize a government; and unrest and uncertainty continued. Troops, American, British, French and of other smaller allied groups, had fought to the limit, but somewhere in the high commands, military or political, there were missteps, and Italy was disappointing. Again, let me say, that the campaign had a very great importance, and that the men who took part in its "blood and sweat and tears" have every reason to be proud of the part they played in the winning of the final victory.

Meanwhile, for nearly two and a half years, the most painstaking plans had been in the making for an invasion of the European continent from the north by way of England. We shall speak of these plans in a moment but may here mention two incidents in connection with them. We had been piling up, as we shall note, incredibly huge supplies of men and matériel in Northern Ireland (Ulster) and in Britain. On March 10, our State Department sent a note to Prime Minister de Valera of Ireland (Eire) explaining the situation, pointing out that the Japanese and German governmental representatives in that country had the opportunity of picking up and transmitting to their home offices information of the utmost importance, and asking whether Eire would not take steps looking to their recall. The answer from de Valera was a flat "No."

The second incident occurred in the middle of June. Robot bombs, later nicknamed "Doodlebugs" by our troops in England, began to fall on London and other parts of that country, and have continued to do so up to the present writing. Jet-propelled rockets, rising to the stratosphere and descending at terrific speed with no warning sound until they hit and exploded, directed at no specific target, military or other, were, nervously as well as physically, more devastating than had been the earlier Blitz from planes dropping bombs. The rocket bomb was distinctly a new weapon. At first, they were started from the Normandy coast, the send-offs later being moved farther east along the seacoast. But the time of retribution was drawing near, and we now come to perhaps the greatest military operation in history.

The preparations began at a morning meeting in London, on July 1, 1942, when about thirty top-ranking colonels and generals sat down to begin discussions. In April of that year, we had appointed as our representative Lt. General John C. H. Lee. I can touch on only some of the aspects here, but for further details refer the reader to an article by C. L. Walker in *Harper's Magazine* for March, 1945. His article was passed by the censors in the U. S. Army and Navy, and in the British Army, Navy and Air Forces, and so may be considered accurate history. I lean heavily on it in the following paragraphs, with full acknowledgment to *Harper's*.

In the approximately two years intervening between that July 1942 and the beginning of the actual physical invasion in June 1944, what were some of the things to be considered and done? The American Army had to put over a million men into the United Kingdom by D-day. Our own, and the British forces, had to supply these men with various amounts of *more than a million different items*. In over 1100 British towns, more than 100,000 buildings had to be erected. (This, and much else, came under Britain's contribution to Reverse Lend-Lease.)

For the air forces, landing strips had to be built equalling in total length the distance from Moscow to America. At least 18,000,000 ship-tons of cargo had to be transported from America and dumped all over the United Kingdom, but dumped in such a way that it could be known at a moment's notice what was in the tens of millions of crates and packing boxes, and where these were located. For the eventual Channel crossing, more than 660 *different kinds* of landing and escort craft had to be designed and built.

For the long preliminary air bombardment, which to many civilians may have appeared somewhat haphazard, thousands of hours had to be spent in study. Not only did German war plants have to be located and picked out according to their importance for the enemy war effort, but the thing got so fine that it was estimated not only how many planes had to be used for destruction at 5000, 15,000, 25,000 feet height, but even in some plants what *wing* of the building would have to be knocked out to destroy a particularly important part or instrument being made in it. Further, there was the question of what type of bomb would be best for each particular job, and there were numberless other details to be thought out and planned in advance. Nothing was haphazard.

Both ocean freight, which, with a recrudescence of U-boat attacks, seemed seriously menaced at one stage, and land transportation in the United Kingdom itself were headaches. We had to ship 3000 locomotives and 57,000 freight cars specially built in America for use on British rail lines. A month before D-day, there was not a single empty siding on any rail line in England, and the quip over there was that if American supplies kept piling up and the invasion did not start soon, the island would sink; that all that kept it above the water already were the barrage balloons! For example, we had shipped thousands of miles of four-inch pipes, the rot-proofing for 500,000,000 burlap sandbags, 2,500,000 miles of telephone wires. We had, over there, enough bridging to replace every possible destroyed bridge in France. We had 125,000,000 maps, so accurate as to show even the tides, so that the planners knew where a boat of given draught could touch a beach at any minute, any hour of any day. Blood plasma, drugs—such as sulfa, penicillin, morphine—special slings to carry the wounded—everything was ready, and emergency hospitals had been set up and time schedules so worked out that, when D-day *did* come, between eighty and ninety per cent of the wounded received expert medical attention within ten minutes. When that day came, the vast adventure started in darkness—no lights—and in radio silence. Every man knew the exact spot where he had to be at a definite *minute*. On the other side of the Channel, the plans were just as carefully drawn, so that as material was placed on the dumps on the beaches those who had to know knew that "At Dump 6, Aisle 2, Row 4, Tier 3, you will find your box of 300 spark plugs."

There has never been anything else like it, and it must be remembered also that two peoples, the British and the Americans, were working together as one, and that we had to transport all our men and matériel over three thousand miles of the Atlantic. There had been no full-scale invasion across the Channel since that of William the Conqueror in 1066. Philip of Spain had tried it, as had Napoleon and Hitler. Now the British and Americans were trying it, in "reverse Lend-Lease," against what the conquering Germans had declared to be their impregnable "Atlantic Wall." This time, success was complete, and marked the turning-point, in the European theater, of what has been the greatest war in all history.

The attack had been agreed upon by Roosevelt, Churchill and Stalin at the Teheran Conference, but the preparations had taken time. It had been time well spent. The exact date for its inception had been left to General Eisenhower, Supreme Commander. He had finally determined to set his vast and intricate machine in motion on June 5. The weather, however, was bad. The meteorologists told the General it would improve on the morrow. Whether to believe them or not? It was a terrible responsibility. Bad flying weather for the planes, a storm on the Channel, might ruin everything. He took the chance, and the scientists were right. The weather was not too good, but it had improved and continued to do so.

On June 6, 11,000 planes blasted a way, ahead, for the troops being transported on 4000 vessels, not counting the innumerable small landing craft. The biggest airborne force, up to then in history, was also carried over the beaches, and inland to behind enemy lines. The attack had been made before dawn, and that day, Churchill, paying high tribute to Eisenhower, could tell Parliament that all had gone "according to plan—and *what* a plan!"

Hitler's boasted "Atlantic Wall" was crashed. Caen was taken, after heavy fighting and considerable destruction of the historic city. The great port of Cherbourg was also taken, although the Germans, sensing the value of ports to the Allies, held grimly to Brest and others. The overrunning of the countryside was unexpectedly rapid. On August 23, the people of Paris rose, and both the Germans and the representatives of the Vichy regime were in flight or hiding. France, with troops advancing from the south as well as from the north, was rapidly becoming almost wholly free again. The Allies were advancing into Germany and approaching the Rhine. Parts of the "Low Countries" were freed, but it took time to get control of Antwerp, first its outlying defenses and then of the port itself, and we desperately *needed* ports for bringing in the matériel required by our own rapid advances and the increasing tempo of the fighting. It was these lacks which brought disappointment in the late autumn and early winter. We had, for the moment, after high hopes had been raised of a very early end to the war, reached the limit of our forward driving power. The Germans, under von Rundstedt, turned for a counter-attack. It was a perilous undertaking for them, and was in the end to prove fatal, but the deferment of our anticipations caused the year to end on a note of discouragement, not as to eventual victory but as to the amount of time required and the human cost.

During 1944, there were several important international meetings and conferences. For Americans, three stand out especially: those at Bretton Woods, Dumbarton Oaks and Quebec. The first two may be said to represent as yet "unfinished business" taking the form of suggestions and plans which have caused great discussion and still have to be passed upon, possibly at the coming international Conference in San Francisco in 1945.

The Bretton Woods Conference was participated in by representatives of forty-four nations, opening its sessions on July 1 and closing on the 22nd. Its fundamental concern was with post-war economics. The final plan dealt with two items: one, the creation of a Fund, to which all the nations should contribute, to help stabilize the wildly fluctuating currencies of the world; and, second, a Bank which would help as an investment institution "to bring about those economic conditions which are essential to sound currency stability and healthy trade." The Fund and the Bank were closely linked, but each of them has been subjected to exhaustive criticism by one school of economists or another and by one nation or another. Something will come out of it all, but the monetary, exchange and trade aspects of the whole matter are too complex to be discussed properly here, especially as it is all still in a state of flux.

The next Conference was held at Dumbarton Oaks, near Washington, and dealt with other aspects of postwar world organization. As contrasted with that at Bretton Woods, it was a four-power Conference—the United States, the British Empire, Russia and China were represented. It was to devise some sort of world organization, and, meeting on August 21, point was given to this aim by the news, on that day and the day or two following, that the Vichy government in France had disappeared and that Romania had abandoned Germany and joined the Allies. (In the following months, Hungary and Finland were also to desert the sinking ship.)

The tentative proposals made were that the above four powers, with France added, should have special responsibility and authority for maintaining peace, attacking aggressor nations, if necessary, before, and not after, these had started war themselves. Among the points suggested were the following:

1. A General Assembly of all peace-loving nations to

make recommendations looking to the maintenance of peace.

2. A Security Council of eleven members, including the above-mentioned five as permanent members and six others to be chosen by them for two-year terms. The Council would have full authority to use economic, military or other means to maintain peace.

3. An Economic and Social Council to deal with humanitarian problems.

4. An international Court to handle justiciable questions.

The decisions and plans of the Conference, like those arrived at at Bretton Woods, will have to be confirmed, probably at the international Conference in San Francisco.

From September 11 to 16, Roosevelt and Churchill, with very full advisory professional staffs, met at Quebec for the second Conference of the war held in that city. From the reports given out by each, apparently the chief topic discussed was the future conduct of the war in the Pacific, and Stalin did not attend, in part probably because Russia was still bound to Japan by a non-aggression pact. Both statesmen expressed themselves as highly delighted with the complete accord quickly reached, and there is no question but that Britain and the Empire will throw their full weight in with us against the Japs, once the European war is finished. Aside from what was agreed upon at this Conference, Churchill has now many times, in public speeches and before Parliament, made that pledge in the most solemn manner, and there is not the slightest reason to doubt his good faith or that of the people who, he has promised, will back it.

CHAPTER IV

THE RECORD OF 1945

O<small>N</small> January 1, 1946, Mr. Arthur Krock, the Washington correspondent of *The New York Times,* and by many considered the best informed, most accurate and sanest of Washington correspondents, headed his daily column in that journal, "The Mightiest Year in Our History." In his first paragraph he wrote:

The year now closing will be marked as the high point of achievement thus far in the nation's history and that of any people in the annals of the world. Perhaps there are contemporary historians with the skill and wisdom to subdue the rushing events of 1945 long enough to put them within the covers of a book. But if such there are the assignment would still be terrifying.

I agree. But the assignment to put them within the pages of a single chapter is infinitely more so. What *did* happen in those momentous twelve months? What are the events that I must touch upon for you, though I cannot begin to do them full justice?

The year witnessed the dying agonies of nations in the first total global war in the history of the human race. Utterly new weapons were employed on the sea, under

145

the sea, on land, in the air and even in the stratosphere. Military operations of hitherto undreamed-of intensity and complexity were under way. Our own nation rose to a height of industrial production which would have been inconceivable a few years earlier. There was the sudden death of Roosevelt, the first American President ever to be elected to a third and even to a fourth term. Then there was the collapse of the Axis Powers, Germany in Europe, and Japan in the Orient, that came about with an unexpected suddenness and completeness. Of the previous leaders, Roosevelt, as we have said, died suddenly. Mussolini ended in ignominy, his dead face stamped on by Italian heels in a muddy gutter. Hitler disappeared. The Churchill government in Britain was overthrown. The atomic bomb opened to all mankind a new era both of terror and peaceful power. One of the innermost and most dangerous secrets of the universe had been discovered. The great New World abandoned its traditional policy of isolation and set itself whole-heartedly, and almost unanimously, to the establishment of an organization for world peace in which we should play our part with vigor and responsibility. The world capital was obviously to be located in the United States. The end of the war, or rather of the several wars, did not bring peace and prosperity, and there were dark shadows, but the events had been staggering beyond the imagination of previous generations. Clearly, such a story cannot here be told in detail.

The first concern of all of us during the greater part of the year was the war itself, so let's begin with that. Before going into even moderate detail, we may repeat that it was the first total and global war in history. This meant, for our American men (and women), that they had to go to almost every quarter of the globe—Europe, Africa, the islands and lands of the Pacific—and that they had to learn to use every new weapon which science was devising against military enemies and civilian populations. It was not at all nice, but this was what the Axis had forced us to do.

The second general point to make here is this—that, before the war ended, the world had become divided into two camps: the Axis Powers, who wished to impose their will on all the rest; and the rest, who wished to go their own ways, although those ways might be very different from one another. There is, however, a tremendous difference in being governed by another in *his* way or running your affairs in your *own* way, be they Russian, British, North American or South American. We all wanted to be ourselves and not to have to do the Prussian "Goose-step." The variety and number of nations organized against the Axis called for the greatest coalition or alliance in all history. In the minor and more local wars of the past there have been many "alliances," and their histories have usually not been too happy. The alliances in this war were the most successful ever, and this was due, in the main, to the "Big Three"—the United States, headed by Franklin Roosevelt, the British Empire, by Winston Churchill, and the Soviet Union, by Stalin. We shall speak of their meetings later.

Now, for the details of the various wars, in so far as we can consider them. There are, first, the military details, in Europe and in Asia. We may begin with Italy.

In the preceding chapter, we noted the fall of Rome. These operations had entailed very heavy losses, which could not immediately be replaced. However, after some months, the pursuit of the enemy into the north of Italy continued. By April 29 the Allies had reached the great city of Milan and on May 2, after a general collapse of the Germans, their commander surrendered unconditionally. We may note that there were, at various times, fighting with the Fifteenth Army, troops who were Americans, British, Canadian, French, Japanese, New Zealanders, South Africans, Poles, Indians, Brazilians, Italians, Greeks, Moroccans, Algerians, Arabs, Goums, Sengalese and a brigade of Jews. Never before had peoples who wished to be free to lead their own lives worked together in this way. The surrender of the Germans ended the Italian war and wholly changed the situation in Yugoslavia. We need merely mention the end of the Fascist regime and of Mussolini.

This chapter of American history is no place in which to survey the career of "Musso," but, as he attempted for a while to stride the world, and killed his hundreds of thousands, his end is of interest. He was a small fat man,

THE MIRACLE OF PRODUCTION

Our shift from peacetime to wartime production, helping to make the United States the
greatest military power on the globe, amazed the world.

MacARTHUR *WAS* BACK

Accompanied by his aide and Chief of Staff, Lt. Gen. Richard K. Sutherland, General MacArthur fulfills his 1942 promise of return to the Philippines shortly after American troops landed on the last lap of the road back to Manila

From a photograph by Acme Newspictures

INVASION LANDING ON THE NORMANDY BEACH

While barrage balloons hold off German strafers, boats land an almost endless supply of matériel and troops which are carried inland by long lines of trucks.

Cordell Hull Opening the Security Parley Conference at Dumbarton Oaks, Washington, D. C.

Changing Guard at Dumbarton Oaks during the Conference.

Top, left: President Franklin D. Roosevelt. *Right:* General George Marshall. *Bottom, left:* Admiral Ernest J. King. *Right:* General Henry H. Arnold.

Photographs from Acme Newspictures, Inc. and Press Association, Inc.

Top, left: General Dwight D. Eisenhower. *Right:* General Douglas MacArthur. *Bottom, left:* General George S. Patton, Jr. *Right:* General Omar Bradley.

Top, left: General Carl Spaatz. *Right:* General George C. Kenney. *Bottom, left:* General James H. Doolittle. *Right:* Major General Curtis E. LeMay.

Photographs from Press Association, Inc., Kenyon and Eckhardt, Inc. and U. S. Navy.

Top, left: Admiral Raymond Amos Spruance. Right: Admiral Chester W. Nimitz. Bottom, left: General Alexander A. Vandergrift. Right: Admiral William F. Halsey.

and not at all the majestic figure he pretended to be in his hortatory press photographs. He had been captured by the Allies and had been mysteriously if not scandalously rescued from his prison by a German plane. He spent some months in a villa on Lake Como, and then, on April 28, on the eve of the German total collapse, was again captured by the Italians. He, his mistress, and sixteen Fascist aides were shot, thrown into a moving-van and brought to Milan. There they were tossed into the gutter at a street corner where Mussolini had had fifteen innocent Milanese hostages shot to avenge the murder of certain Germans. He lay in his Fascist uniform, with his head on the body of his mistress, while an angry crowd spat on them and stamped their heels into his bloody face. The next day, he and his mistress were hanged, heels up, and the career of the smallest and most miserable would-be dictator the world has seen was ended. It was horrible but was only a minor detail in the series of mass horrors to which men were to become accustomed in the year 1945. We thought we were living in a civilized era, but no other year has left on the spirit of man so deep an impression of the depths to which he could sink.

Now we move on to Germany. We had to end the chapter on 1944 with the counter-attack of the Germans under von Rundstedt in the battle of "the Bulge." This had been helped by the worst weather in many years for operations on a grand scale by our attackers. The slugging, up through the rugged mountain country of Italy,

149

had been costly and discouragingly slow. However, it had paid handsomely. Not only had we, for months, kept a large part of the German forces outside of Germany, but we had gained control of airfields from which we could take off to attack the vital German oil sources in the Rumanian fields at Ploesti and from which also we could begin shuttle attacks, with planes from England, in the all-important wearing-down process over the German home-land.

We were getting ready for the final "kill." Branches of all services shared in the task. We had at last gained control of the port of Antwerp, which was essential for pouring in supplies through the Low Countries. The air forces had done magnificent work—night and day—in softening German supply lines, defenses and morale. The Russians were getting ready for their drive on Berlin. During the last week in December, 1944, the weather turned in our favor. In general, the Allied plan—determined at the Yalta Conference—involved the greatest pincer movement in history. The Allies were to crush Germany by drives from the West and East. The invasion of Normandy and the defeat of the Germans at the battle of "the Bulge" had prepared the way for one; and the Russian advance for the other. Hitler, who had always said Germany could not stand a war on two fronts at once, but who, by his lies and conceit, had brought it on, was soon to suffer the consequences of his own perfidy and folly.

The Rhine was a barrier to attack from the West, but

on March 7 the 9th American armored division, probing the Rhine banks, found that the bridge at Remagen had not been blown up. The facts that the German officer in command was drunk and that a young American officer had led a detachment across, with only minutes to spare, were among the dramatic events in what was soon to become "the rat hunt" through Germany. We must, however, give credit to the brilliant staff work which took immediate advantage of the chance offered. The result was the establishment of an important bridgehead on the east bank of the symbolic river and, in time, of other bridges and bridgeheads. American, British and some French divisions began to wipe up the Germans, of whom, in the Ruhr alone, about 350,000 were captured or killed. Allied troops reached the Ilbe River, April 11, overran Bavaria and on the 20th captured the already largely destroyed Nazi shrine-city of Nürnberg, formerly one of the loveliest in Germany but now a heap of rubble.

Meanwhile, Russian armies had crossed the Oder River (March 24) on a wide front, and fought their way toward Berlin. We have mentioned the execution, or murder, of Mussolini on April 28. On May 1 the Hamburg radio reported that Hitler was dead and that Admiral Karl Doenitz had been made Fuehrer. Apparently, Hitler was not yet dead, and his fate will be mentioned later, but Germany *was* crumbling. On April 25, American troops from the West and Russians from the East had joined forces at Weismar and the "Holy Soil," as the Germans with characteristic insolence called their land, had been split in half. On May 2, Berlin fell to the Russians. Germany disintegrated, day by day. On May 5, the German commander surrendered unconditionally all his forces in northwest Germany, Holland and Denmark. As 500,000 Germans laid down their arms to the British General Montgomery, he remarked, "This is the moment." The next day, our forces captured Pilsen in Czechoslovakia. Other advances were made and, on the 6th, all German forces in Austria surrendered. The German dream of a retreat to impregnable positions in the mountains of Austria and Bohemia had vanished. At Reims, on May 7, with chaos everywhere, the emissaries of the Doenitz German Government unconditionally surrendered all land, sea and air forces of the Reich. The German war, which had lasted five years, eight months and six days, was over. Italy had collapsed, with the surrender of 1,000,000 Germans, and the Reich and its satellites were in ruins.

Throughout fanatical Germany city after city had been destroyed. Cologne, Nürnberg, the great port of Hamburg, and others, had become mere heaps of rubble. Berlin itself, which Hitler had proclaimed the capital of the new Reich for a thousand years, had gone down in a holocaust of fighting and flames. The greatest city ever to be conquered and ruined, it had had a population of nearly 4,500,000 spread over an area of more than 340 square miles. From its radio, as a final note, had gone forth, on May 1, a notice to Germans to stand by for important news. First, came the deep strains of Wagner's *Götter-dämmerung,* the "death of the Gods," which should have been dubbed "the end of the Devils," and then word that Hitler had died as a "hero" in defense of the city.

He did not die as a hero, although the details of his death are still obscure. The best documentary evidence we have indicates that, after a marriage to his mistress of many years—even her name does not deserve commem-oration—and a macabre wedding celebration, both took deadly poison and, with the aid of gasoline, were incin-erated in the underground apartments of the vast Chan-cellery which was to have lasted a thousand years. At any rate, there seems to be no doubt that they died as suicides and that their bodies were burned beyond recognition. At the same time, and in more or less the same manner, died the notorious Nazi leader Joseph Goebbels, the Ger-man propaganda chief.

In fact, the fall of Hitlerite Germany was unique. Other nations have been defeated in war but never has there been such a wave of suicides. On May 25—the date is unimportant—Heinrich Himmler, the former head of the noted Gestapo, committed suicide after being captured while in disguise by the British. He was stripped naked to see whether he had any poison hidden on his person, and killed himself by chewing a small glass tube contain-ing cyanide, which he had concealed in his mouth. One of the most hated men in the world, such was his end. There were others. Never before has a great nation and its leaders gone down in such a holocaust of destruction and infamy.

The end of the Reich was an amazing melodrama of unbelievable horrors and fantastic episodes. We need merely touch on some of them here, although in the global war in which the United States had been engaged it is hard to draw the line between what is American history and what belongs to the history of other countries. The insensate sadism of the prison and concentration camps has been recorded for all to read, and not by propagandists but by military authorities of unquestionable accuracy and veracity. Millions had perished of hunger, avoidable sickness and by fiendish torture, executed with all the efficiency of modern German science. The world had known barbarism but never before anything like this, and on the part of a people who called themselves not only civilized but the "Master Race." This was what we had fought against, and it is well to recall it, not in a spirit of vengeance but simply "lest we forget."

There were also fantastic incidents, such as the finding of hoards of loot, hidden away in caves, saltmines, and elsewhere, the plunderings of leading Nazis. There was, for example, one hoard of art treasures belonging to the bemedaled Field Marshal Goering valued as high as $500,000,000. Allowing for exaggerations in valuations the loot had still been colossal and made Napoleon look like a huckster. A trifling minor matter was the capture of Goering's private train of ten armored cars, one filled with the choicest of wines and liquors, one with his favorite music records, and others for lounging and sleeping, every room with its private bath. All this was state socialism and friends of the people with a vengeance! Well, they have gone, or are going—Mussolini, his face ground by Italian heels as his corpse sprawled in a muddy gutter; Hitler burned under the crumbling ruins of his vast Chancellery, from which he had hoped to rule the world; and the rest, dead or now being tried for their lives. The necks of a few cannot atone for the millions whose lives and happiness have been destroyed, but it is something, whether or not it may deter others in future from attempting to pursue the same mad course.

The war in Europe was over, but the best-informed opinion expected another year or two of bloody fighting in the Pacific, with possibly tremendous losses, against the fanatic and now desperate foe. On July 16, as day broke on the New Mexico desert, the innermost secret of the universe was shown to have been penetrated and solved. The dream of atomic fission became a reality. The first atomic bomb in history was successfully exploded in the lonely waste, and America found herself possessed of the most powerful weapon ever known to warfare.

We now shift to the vast ranges of the Pacific waters. The secret of the bomb was known to only a few in inner circles and even they did not know what the effects might be. The war had to go on.

The story of that war was one of infinite suffering and

155

of great losses. Minds were so concentrated on the European theater that many of the troops in the Pacific area perhaps felt that they were regarded as a sort of "sideshow." This, of course, was not true. Although the European war had to be won first, the Pacific war was, to us in America—facing two oceans—perhaps in the long run the more vital. At all events, that war had to go on, with the prospect of a long struggle and heavy losses.

We can only pass over it briefly, although it covered vast spaces and many land, sea and air engagements.

Both the Allied and Japanese operations in China and in the East near Burma had, according to General Marshall in his Report on Winning the War, been maintained at ends of the most precarious supply lines in history. General MacArthur's landings in the Philippines and the operations of our naval forces in the China Sea had cut the Japanese line to Burma. By the end of January, the Japs were in full retreat and by May the Burma campaign was practically ended, with 300,000 Japanese casualties, including nearly 100,000 dead, as stated by the British Admiral Lord Louis Mountbatten. In spite of the marvellous road built by General Stilwell (now abandoned after colossal cost), and the fact that in January 1945 we were transporting more than 46,000 tons of war material "over the Hump" to the Chinese forces, the enemy continued for some months to gain in the interior of China.

To touch on only a few points in what we may call the battle of the islands, we may note that on January 9 the

U. S. Sixth Army had hit the beaches of Lingayen Gulf in the Philippines, and that by nightfall the surprise attack had landed 68,000 troops in control of a beachhead 15 miles long and 6000 yards deep. MacArthur continued and, after recapturing Corregidor, Manila Bay was opened to us early in March. The General and his men had accomplished in less than two months what it had taken the Japanese more than six months to achieve after Pearl Harbor. MacArthur had made good his promise, when leaving the Philippines for Australia in the early dark days of defeat, that he *would return.*

Steadily we advanced, and the pincers closed on the homeland of Japan. The Philippines came gradually into our control. Other islands followed, notably, after a historic struggle, Iwo Jima, only 775 miles from the main Japanese island of Honshu and of vital importance to our air assault on Japan. The offensive against the Ryukyus began on March 26, when General Buckner and his forces made their first attack on Okinawa. The battle was long and bloody and did not end until three days after the killing of General Buckner on June 18, almost on the eve of victory. Meanwhile we had suffered 39,000 casualties, including 10,000 naval personnel, but almost 110,000 Japs had been killed and about 8000 taken prisoner. The long struggle had been notable for the particularly fierce suicide attacks by the Japanese, including rocket bombs, with a ton of explosive each, guided by live pilots, who inevitably died when they hit the target.

157

Steadily the Allies advanced here and there and closed in on the doomed Japanese Empire, now of the setting not of the rising sun. In June the Australians made an unopposed landing in northwest Borneo, establishing air bases which could be used in combination with those in the Philippines. Operations continued in the latter islands and the campaign in Luzon was practically completed by the end of June, by which time MacArthur's forces had killed 317,000 Japs and captured over 7000. As the encirclement continued, the whole Pacific Ocean from California to China was swarming with American sea-power—a marvellous change from the day of Pearl Harbor. Japanese shipping—naval and commercial—had been largely sunk or driven from the seas, and what was left was rapidly crumbling. In Malaya, the Dutch East Indies and China, troops were on the move.

On April 6, by order of the Joint Chiefs of Staff, MacArthur was appointed to the command of all United States Army forces in the Pacific, and he and Admiral Nimitz, commander of the Naval Forces, were ordered to prepare the final attack on Japan itself. Other appointments were made, including especially those affecting the Air Force, strategic command of which remained with General Arnold.

During July, thanks to our possession of the Marianas, Iwo Jima, Okinawa and other air bases, our superbombers, aided by the fleet and by British units, steadily shelled cities and industries on the Japanese home islands. There

158

were two plans for gradually bringing the war to an end, but operations according to either would have been long, and costly in Allied lives.

There was, however, another plan and weapon. The experiment in the Arizona desert had been successful. From the meeting of the "Big Three" in Potsdam, General Spaatz of the Air Force received orders to drop an atomic bomb on the industrial part of any one of four named cities. He could make his own choice and drop the bomb any day after August 3 when the weather permitted. On the 6th a bomb was dropped on the military base city of Hiroshima. The effect was as terrifying as it was devastating. Most of the city was wiped out. The loss in life has never been accurately stated but apparently about 160,000 persons met almost instant death. Nothing like it had ever been known before.

Two days later, on August 8, the Soviet Union declared war on Japan. Russian armies at once were on the march. The following day, the American Air Force dropped a second atomic bomb, this time on the great city of Nagasaki. It was even more destructive than the first, the smoke from the burning metropolis rising 50,000 feet into the air, visible throughout the surrounding country for 175 miles. On August 10, the Japanese Government sued for peace on the terms of the Potsdam Convention, which meant unconditional surrender.

I may mention for the information of readers, because I have had a number of inquiries from England and even here at home, that the term "unconditional surrender" is well over eighty years old; it was first used by General Grant in the capture of Fort Donelson in the Civil War, in 1862. As, owing to a mistake, Grant's name had been entered on the records at West Point as "Ulysses Simpson Grant," which characteristically he did not bother to correct, he became *U. S.* Grant, and the initials for the first two words of U. S. A. and also for "unconditional surrender" may have had some odd influences on his career. He became known, after his Mississippi River campaign, as "Unconditional Surrender Grant." Some Britishers seem to think it was a term invented by Franklin Roosevelt at Casablanca. Perhaps even some Americans do not know its origin.

The problems of the occupation of the various conquered countries may better be dealt with in the next chapter, but we may note here that, in the case of Japan, our military power was established in a somewhat different form from that set up in Italy or Germany. General MacArthur was made the Supreme Commander; the Emperor (who had traditionally been regarded by his people as a god) and the whole Japanese Government were placed under the absolute control of MacArthur, who in the remaining months did an excellent job.

The final ceremony of surrender took place on the deck of the battleship *Missouri*—mightiest warship afloat, then lying safely in Tokio harbor surrounded by other naval units and with planes circling overhead. Among other

American officers present were Admirals Halsey and Nimitz, and Generals MacArthur and Wainwright, the last thin and emaciated from his years in a Japanese prison camp after his heroic defense of Corregidor. It was a perfect ending to exactly six years of the most horrible war in history, a war brought on by the three powers which had aimed at the conquest and enslavement of all the rest of the world. The war had come within a hair's breadth of succeeding and we all owe it to Britain, who for some terrible months stood alone, that it did not succeed. The struggle had started on the plains of Poland on September 1, 1939, and, having involved the globe, ended on an American battleship lying within Tokio harbor, on September 1, 1945.

The losses had been greater than any dreamed of in previous wars. Without trying to estimate the millions upon millions of casualties suffered by Russia, the British Empire and our other Allies, we may mention only those sustained by the United States, as given in the final Report of General Marshall, Chief of Staff, and the losses of our enemies as estimated by him. The war in Europe cost the United States in round numbers about 773,000 casualties, with 160,000 dead; the Pacific war 170,000, with 41,000 dead. On the other hand, 1,600,000 Germans, Italians and Japanese were killed; 304,000 permanently disabled; and 8,150,000 taken prisoner and disarmed.

We have spoken of the new weapons, notably the atomic bomb. There were, in fact, several weapons which helped the Allies to win, although, for various reasons, the bomb has most stirred the popular imagination and apprehension. Throughout history there have been many new or secret weapons. But no other has struck mankind so aghast as has the atomic bomb.

I think it is not merely the number it can kill at once. Speaking realistically, was it not better to end a war, once and for all, with the instantaneous and therefore practically painless death of one or two hundred thousand people rather than by the agony of millions who, otherwise, might have died from painful wounds received in battle or after months of suffering in hospitals, concentration camps, and elsewhere? We had also been taught by our enemies that "total war" meant not only intense suffering for the men in the armed forces at the fronts but for the whole civilian populations in seemingly peaceful towns and cities far behind the lines. What struck us about the atomic bomb was not the numbers killed, but the fact that the bomb indicated that we had penetrated the secret of the most powerful force in the universe, and that no one could predict the future. That is what has worried us. The future control of atomic energy by the various nations is still in doubt. At present the "secret" is *supposed* to be mainly the possession of Great Britain, Canada and the United States. How long will it remain so? We, fortunately, stole a march on the other powers by developing this secret first, but they also have been carrying on scientific investigations which might—or may yet—lead to discoveries in this field of releasing incredible energies by the splitting of atoms.

Without going into minor matters such as the improvements made in the structure of tanks, planes, guns and so on, we may mention another technical discovery, less spectacular than the atomic bomb but considered by some equally effective in winning the war, and the value of which in peacetime may be more quickly proved than seems likely in the case of atomic fission. That is radar.

Radar may be briefly defined as "direction-finding and ranging by radio." What it can do is almost incredible. In the war its uses were, among others, to locate rockets, planes, ships and other enemy offensive weapons which were far beyond the limits of human vision even with the use of any aids up till then available. The location and direction of enemy weapons could be so accurately determined that they could be destroyed without being seen —for example, ships below the horizon or planes beyond the range of vision or behind clouds. Obviously, radar's peacetime uses are likely to be many and, for the present, far greater than are those of the energy released from the splitting of atoms. All great wars, especially of modern times, have brought about discoveries in medicine, mechanics, and in other branches of science, which have had their value in time of peace but, to date, as far as this war is concerned, radar seems to promise the most.[1] The race

[1] I speak as a layman but suggest for those who wish to investigate the problem farther the 52-page pamphlet *Radar* published by the Office of War Information.

between the Axis Powers and the Allies, in improving tanks, planes and so on, would carry us into analysis too technical for this short chapter, but we may note that the balance was finally won by American mass production and the "know-how" not only of those at the head of the great corporations but of the small business men and workmen all down the line. This does not mean that *we won the war.*" Had it not been for the amazing courage of the British in holding the front line in the "battle for Britain," and for the work of others at a time when we were as yet unprepared both in a psychological and in a military sense, we might well have had triumphant Germans controlling New York and Washington. What I mean is that we put into the scales at the critical moment just that extra weight which tipped them; and it was the plain American business man—big or little—who did it. The business man, of either category, has no *Congressional Record* in which to register his speeches, but *he* it was who did the job. That is now often forgotten, but it must not be.

We have spoken of weapons in the mechanical sense. In this greatest of all wars there were other weapons, of a spiritual and psychological sort, which the Allies possessed and the Axis did not. The first was the love of freedom. The plain fact is that neither the Germans nor their "honorary Aryan" allies the Japanese objected to being governed and regimented in their private lives. The Japanese, for example, may have regarded their Emperor as a god. Well, the British, with all their loyalty to the throne, and the Americans, with their loyalty to their form of constitutional government, have never regarded the head of the state in that way. We could say what we liked, and we have often said a lot not applicable to a god. The Allies simply could not conceive of being goose-stepped.

There was also the psychological viewpoint, which in this war may have had an unusually strong foundation in the spiritual. The wars of all history teem with alliances. But these alliances have been shifting and brittle. I need not run over them here. Any student of history knows them. Never before, so far as I know, has a Grand Alliance proved so close, strong and lasting as that of the Allies in the final and determining stages of what we call World War II but which, actually, was the concluding phase of a single war which had lasted, with an interlude, from 1914 to 1945—if it yet be over.

In the concluding and decisive years, the Alliance, chiefly of "the Big Three," held together as no previous one ever has done. You may give your own reasons, such as the spiritual one I mentioned above, the character and mental resources of the three heads of state—Franklin Roosevelt, Winston Churchill and Stalin—or whatnot. Anyway, they hung together in crisis after crisis as was the case with no other Alliance.

In respect of this team-work, there are two things to note. One is what we may call operative and the other political. As to the first, we want to call attention to the extraordinary and really amazing cooperation of American and British forces in the field. I do not know of any other two nations cooperating as closely and as intimately. In what was perhaps the most important, and certainly the most complicated operation of the entire war, the American General Eisenhower was placed in supreme command over both American and British Empire troops. At present writing, the high esteem in which he is held by both peoples would seem to indicate that he had been the major factor in bringing about this unusually close and harmonious cooperation between the two nations. Many other officers might be mentioned, but the chief fact is that there came to be such a complete harmony between the personnel—both officers and men—of the two nations as to make them practically one for the purpose of winning through to freedom and to the right to live their own lives as they wished.

There were also, however, the political aspects. In the absence, as yet, of the pertinent documents, these political aspects have been publicized chiefly through the meetings of "the Big Three." There were three meetings of special importance. In February—ending on the 12th—Stalin, Roosevelt and Churchill met at Yalta, in the Russian Crimea. Roosevelt had not been well, and, with his physical infirmities, the long journey and strain undoubtedly told heavily on him.

We do not yet know what agreements may have been

entered into at Yalta between the heads of the three states. At the time, it was announced merely that there had, in general, been agreement on the occupation of Germany when defeated, with reparations to be demanded from her, and that the Allies would remain united for peace as well as in order to win the war. From time to time since then, however, certain secret agreements have come to light, mostly in the form of territorial and other concessions made to Stalin, apparently as the price of continuing the absolutely essential participation of the vast and powerful Russian forces in the joint struggle. Stalin was in a position to strike bargains and, as an absolute dictator, the terms he made concerned only himself.

Roosevelt and Churchill were in more uncomfortable positions. They also represented great powers but powers which were democracies. These democracies had been exhibiting the enormous reservoirs of strength which derived from the initiative of free peoples, but their voters, either through Congress, Parliament, or public opinion, had the final say. We need mention here only that, as some of the secret clauses have had to be acknowledged, they have aroused a good deal of apprehension and resentment, not only because of the bargains themselves but quite as much from the uncertainty as to what may still remain hidden. The course of the war, with the successive defeats of Italy, Germany and Japan, would seem to indicate that the democracies of the world are, in the long run, stronger than the totalitarian dictatorships, but sitting around a table a dictator has certain, at least temporary, advantages. It may be added that, in a life-and-death fight for survival, every decision cannot be made a subject for public debate, as in the case of a tariff in peacetime. Nor can the public be even informed of every move. Hindsight is easy. Foresight, in a great crisis, is difficult. To me, this seems a valid excuse for whatever may have been agreed to at Yalta. The wars were, as yet, far from won; and civilization was at stake.

The next important conference of the Big Three, with a change in personnel, was held in Potsdam, ending August 1. In the meantime, two important events had occurred.

On the afternoon of April 12 the entire world was stunned by the sudden death of President Roosevelt. Not only was he one of the "Big Three," and the leader of America in the war and in its new international rôle but, owing to his unprecedentedly long series of terms in the White House, there were many young Americans who had never known or voted for any other President. There were many who believed this to be an unfortunate development in our system of democracy but, be that as it may, it made his sudden passing from the scene at the rising crisis of the war all the more of a shock.

A few weeks earlier, on January 20, he had been inaugurated for his fourth term, the first President to serve for more than two. It has been said that today no one can endure for more than eight years the terrific strain which the office entails. There were those who believed, as they heard rumors about the President's health and studied the newspaper pictures of his drawn face during the campaign, that he could not possibly last out the sixteen years for which he had asked.

His health grew worse and, as I have noted, the trip to Yalta was a heavy draft on his failing strength. One may say that in the circumstances, though they were such as to make the decision difficult for him, he should not have accepted a renomination; but not even his bitterest enemy can say that, having done so, he did not give of himself to the utmost for the cause he had at heart and, like a good soldier, fight to the very end.

By April 1 the final offensives, within Germany and on the Ryukyus in the Pacific, had begun, and the President had gone to Warm Springs to rest. He was still putting in heavy days and on the one on which he died he had signed a series of state documents at about 2 P.M. and was sitting for the painting of his portrait when, suddenly, he had a severe cerebral hemorrhage. By 4:35 he was dead. Two hours and a half later, in Washington, the Vice-President, Harry S. Truman, was sworn in as President, and the ship of state sailed on. Roosevelt had been one of the most powerful men in the world and head of what had become the most powerful of all the nations.

Nothing could illustrate better the essential difference between democratic and totalitarian government than the chaos which followed the deaths of Mussolini and Hitler, and which might follow that of any other dictator, and the orderly and wholly constitutional way in which nearly 140,000,000 people, at the pinnacle of their world influence, accepted the transfer of their highest office—no suicides, assassinations, mass murders or revolution, merely a quiet ceremony in the White House, at which, in the presence of the quickly assembled Cabinet members, a simple American, who forty years before had been a clerk in a haberdashery store, and who then had served in Congress, took on the mighty burden, unsought and undesired, of serving as the head of the United States in the greatest crisis of history.

We come now to another striking example of the democratic process at work as contrasted with that of the dictator-totalitarian type. The conference of the new Big Three—Truman, Churchill and Stalin—was scheduled to meet in Berlin—or, rather, near-by Potsdam—on July 16. Truman and Churchill were there, but Stalin, without explanation, failed for some days to appear. The meeting was held over. Eventually, there was a gathering but, meanwhile, there had been a general election in Britain, the first in over five years. Churchill, head of the Conservative Party, had been Prime Minister through all that period during which the British Empire had endured the greatest test of its courage and determination in its thousand-year-long history. Churchill had proved himself a magnificent leader in war, but a democracy has the right to choose, and wise democracies have learned that great leaders in war are not necessarily the best leaders in peace. In any case, over 20,000,000 English voters went to the polls, and the result was a surprisingly overwhelming victory for the Labor Party. Clement Attlee, almost unknown outside of Britain, became head of the government, instead of Churchill, who, like Roosevelt and Stalin, had towered in world affairs. As in America, where the change from Roosevelt to Truman was effected by the former's death and not by an electoral campaign, the shift was accepted without disturbance of any sort. A free people had spoken, and the "Big Three" of the Potsdam Conference became Truman, Attlee and Stalin instead of Stalin, Roosevelt and Churchill. At the Conference, it was agreed to decentralize Germany both politically and economically; to shift the boundaries of Poland; and to create a Council of Foreign Ministers, including those of France and of China.

At the Potsdam meeting, President Truman had courteously been made Chairman, but this was the last meeting, to date, of the heads of states. On December 6, Churchill stated in the House of Commons that he had heard with "great grief" that "the Big Three are never to meet again." However, the Big Three had formerly been more than merely the representatives of powerful governments. They had been men of wide experience in international affairs and of determined minds and wills. Attlee was no Churchill; Truman was no Roosevelt; and Stalin, whose health had not been good, seemed to be relaxing somewhat the reins of power. Neither Truman nor Attlee were as well known throughout the world as were their predecessors, nor did they have their world influence.

The final meeting of the year was held at Moscow, on December 15, but was attended only by Molotoff, the Russian Commissar for Foreign Affairs; James F. Byrnes, who had become American Secretary of State under the new administration; and Ernest Bevin, British Foreign Secretary under the new Labor Government. An earlier meeting of Foreign Ministers in London had ended in a more or less acrimonious stalemate. Although the Moscow meeting was thought by many to have cleared the air, the communiqués were vaguely worded and there was much difference of opinion as to the degree of success actually achieved. In general, an Allied Council was recommended to be set up to control Japan; it was also recommended that the General Assembly of the United Nations should deal with the new problem of atomic energy; that the United States and Russia should withdraw their troops from China and Manchuria; that Korea should be placed under a five-year trusteeship; and that peace treaties with Italy, Rumania, Bulgaria, Hungary and Finland be prepared; and, finally, that Rumania and Bulgaria should be recognized by Britain and the United States. No one can tell as yet just what loopholes there may be in these agreements; what other agreements may have been made, of which we do not know; or how well those agreements of which we do know may be kept.

Turning from these successive meetings of the Big Three, which had grown gradually from the military alliance of the three greatest of the Allies, we now go on to note other international events which involved the United States.

There was, first, the meeting of representatives from practically all the nations of the New World (except Canada) to consider hemispheric solidarity and mutual defense. The result of their deliberations was the document now known as the Act of Chapultepec, from the fact that the Conference was held in Mexico City. Briefly, the old unilateral Monroe Doctrine was superseded by a joint resolution of all New World nations south of the Canadian border to unite in the defense of these continents against the attack of any foreign aggressor, and to consult together as to when such an act had been attempted or contemplated. This Act was dated March 3.

On March 5, in pursuance of an agreement made at the Yalta Conference, at which the Big Three, together with France and China, had been authorized to issue an invitation to certain other nations to join with them at a meeting in San Francisco to form the organization of the United Nations, such invitations were sent out. France declined to sponsor the invitation but the other four powers did, and invitations were sent to thirty-nine nations. The meeting was a successor to that at Dumbarton Oaks, in which France had not joined. The feeling, and the

move of America toward internationalism instead of isolationism, was well expressed by Senator Vandenberg in
the concluding sentences of his letter of acceptance: "It
will be my prayer that the San Francisco Conference may
be successful in promoting dependable peace, with organized justice, in a free world of free men. Civilization cannot survive World War No. Three."

In the third week of April the Conference got under
way, after a delay due to the late arrival, via Washington,
of the Russian Molotoff. Representatives of fifty nations
assembled, and one of the minor difficulties, but one which
was of more significance than some advocates of a hasty
world federation will allow, was the necessity of gathering a fleet of taxicabs whose drivers should have a combined command of sixteen different languages! There
were many knotty problems, including the status of the
Argentine, the dispute with Russia over the Polish situation, and others which we have not here the space to
discuss. The main point at San Francisco—before we
move on again to Washington—is that a Charter for the
United Nations *was,* at length, successfully drawn up
and agreed upon.

Its objects may be best and most succinctly described
by quoting a sentence or two from the long address by
Secretary of State Stettinius before the Senate Foreign
Relations Committee. He said, in small part, that:

This Charter is not the work of any single nation. It is the work of fifty nations. . . . [It] is both a binding agreement to preserve peace and to advance human progress and a constitutional document creating the international machinery by which nations can cooperate to realize these purposes in fact. . . . Members of the organization are pledged to carry out in good faith the obligations of the Charter. They are pledged to settle their disputes peacefully . . . not to use force against the territorial integrity or political independence of any state . . . to give the organization every assistance in any action it takes under the Charter and to refrain from giving assistance to any state against which the United Nations is taking preventive or enforcement action.

The amount of work and thought and, it may be said, of "give and take," had been extraordinary, and the draft of the new association of nations emerged a far better one than observers at times could have dared to hope. If the fact was remarkable that, after the slow failure of the League of Nations, fifty nations had been willing to make a new effort to build a world structure of peace, and had, within a few weeks, at least agreed upon a Charter, perhaps even more remarkable was the change in attitude in Congress from that following World War I. The month of July probably marked the greatest shift in American foreign policy from isolationism toward international cooperation in our entire history. First, on the 13th, the Senate Foreign Relations Committee (Senators Hiram Johnson of California, Murray of Montana, and Shipstead of Minnesota not voting) approved the

United Nations Security Charter by a vote of 20–0. This was breathtaking. Then, on the 19th, the Senate passed the Bretton Woods Agreement by a vote of 61–16, the House having already passed it by 345–18. (It was ratified by twenty-eight nations and went into effect on December 27.) That was the result, after about a year of public discussion and congressional debate. Finally, on the 28th, the Senate ratified the UNO Charter by the astounding vote of 89–2, the only dissenters being Senators Shipstead of Minnesota and Langer of North Dakota. The United States was the first major power to adhere to the new world order, if such it is to prove.

Many men and events had contributed. The President, Truman, unlike Woodrow Wilson, was not at odds with the Senate but had been a former popular member of that body and knew how to get along with it. Leading Senators had been prominent at San Francisco and at the meetings that led up to and followed from it. The then Secretary of State, Stettinius, who had shown his skill in negotiating and smoothing over difficulties at the Conference, had always commanded the respect of Congress. But, aside from these and other personal equations, the world had changed and America had changed. The Senatorial debates were notably lacking in the rancor and bitterness of the days of Lodge and Wilson. In any case, America had set its course in a new direction, though it must remember that documents and words of humanitarian aspiration are not enough. We, as the most powerful nation in the world in 1945, took the lead. We cannot now, like the traditionary ground-hog, go back into our hole for another sleep.

In Great Britain, both Houses of Parliament voted for the Charter unanimously, so that the two great English-speaking Allies were standing together. Just at that moment, however, we took a step which was somewhat misunderstood in Britain and which caused not only alarm but much ill-feeling. The system of Lend-Lease had been one of the most brilliant and fruitful ideas of the late President Roosevelt, or at least of his Administration, whoever may have contributed to it. As Attlee said in Parliament, when Truman unexpectedly and suddenly terminated the arrangement:

The system of lend-lease in the United States and Mutual Aid from Canada and the accumulation of sterling by the sterling area countries have been an integral part of the war organization of the Allies. In this way it has been made possible for us in this island to mobilize our domestic manpower for war with intensity unsurpassed elsewhere and, at the same time, to undertake expenditure abroad for the support of military operations over a widely extended area without having to provide export to pay for our imports of food and raw materials or to provide the cash we were spending abroad.

Those who know what Britain achieved will recognize this as a very mild statement of the case. It had always been understood that the end of Lend-Lease would coincide, more or less, with the end of the wars; but no one, not only among the Allies but even in our own Congress, was prepared for the abrupt termination decreed without preparatory warning by Truman. It is true that the President, in making his twentieth quarterly report on Lend-Lease some days later, stated that in his opinion the United States should write off an "overwhelming portion" of the more than $42,000,000,000 which we had "lent-leased" to our Allies. However, Byrnes almost immediately made his own statement, which brought confusion and left those who had received Lend-Lease uncertain as to where they stood in their economic quandary, with shortages of food and all other imported materials.

In the President's practically final Report it was disclosed that of all Lend-Lease Britain had received, roughly, 42% or about $13,500,000,000; Russia 28% or about $9,130,000,000; and China only 2% or about $198,000,-000. As we have explained in earlier chapters, there had also been "Reverse Lend-Lease," and by April 1 we had received in goods and services over $5,600,000,000 from the various parts of the British Empire and elsewhere. Truman in his statement pointed out that in percentages of national income the United States had spent, including everything, no more than had Britain or Russia, but the whole affair of the termination of an arrangement which had done so much to promote harmony and military cooperation between the Allies was badly bungled at the end.

The President had also not been happy in his plans for

the domestic economy. In fairness, it must be said that he had inherited a colossal mess which had not been of his making and that he had not desired the office of Vice-President, which for the first time in our history appeared, in the circumstances, almost certain to lead to the Presidency. Washington, in more than twelve years, had become a vast and intricate network of politics and over-lapping alphabetical agencies forming the greatest bureaucracy in our whole national development. The new President understood politics in all its aspects, good and bad, and a President *has* to be a good politician to get anything done. But politics in the ordinary sense had, in the preceding few years, become inextricably mixed up with those of the warring labor factions, particularly those of the Left-Wing of the CIO and its political pressure offspring. This made for complications.

Also the planners and so-called experts, in the government bureaus, made some very bad mistakes in their estimates of post-war unemployment, the rate of reconversion of industry, and so on. We may note, for example, that on August 30, 1945, John W. Synder, then Director of Reconversion, estimated that there would probably be 6,000,000 unemployed by the end of the year, and possibly 8,000,000 by spring. The Chairman of the Social Security Board expected from 5,500,000 to 7,600,000 by December. The Secretary of Labor presaged 6,000,000 to 8,000,000 by spring; Henry Wallace concurred, while Sidney Hillman of the Political Action Committee of the

CIO said 10,000,000 within six to eight months (from August 13). These "experts" figured that there would be intense deflation and that government aid (which they would manage) and public works on a grand scale would be required. On March 23, 1946 (the date lies outside the scope of this chapter but the facts are pertinent), the United States Employment Service announced that the number of requests from employers for employees of all sorts was *ten times* the number of those applying for jobs. This indicates the difficulty of a planned economy in a highly complex industrial society of more than 135,000,-000 people. President Truman did not pretend to be an authority on labor relations. These expert bureaucrats did; so what?

The new President, thrown with hardly a moment's notice into the national driver's seat, had to find his way around. Furthermore, though there had been frequent strikes and labor troubles even during the war, the end of a major war is always the signal for an outbreak of violent demands. Peace seemed to presage not so much a lowering of wages as a reduction in overtime and the "take home," and living costs had advanced to some extent, although not in general as much as straight wages. Incidentally, labor had saved more and accumulated more reserves during this war than ever before, due partly to high wages and partly to the lack of consumers' goods to be bought. Finally, there were the specters of inflation or deflation—the government experts apparently could not make up their minds which—to be guarded against.

The situation and problems in the United States, and in the rest of the world, were of acute difficulty. To many it appeared that one thing was of primary importance: that production to the fullest capacity should get under way as rapidly as possible to prevent unemployment and *de*flation and also to provide the long-wanted goods which would absorb much of the swollen bank accounts of all classes, including labor, and thus help to prevent *in*flation. This was the view of business and, after VJ-day, factories were reconverted from war to civilian production with a speed which surprised all, including the government experts.

Unfortunately, labor, or at least some of the most influential labor leaders, did not share this view, and from April onward strike after strike occurred. First, among the major ones, came the usual April coal strike which, at that time, threatened not merely to retard reconversion but the winning of the wars themselves, at that time not yet won. We need not list all the strikes called by labor but may note only the beginning of the greatest of them all, which started in November in the automotive industry. If there was one industry which, above all others, had helped to win the war, it had been this one. If there was one industry which could produce civilian goods, such as cars, ice-boxes, motors for all sorts of things, from electric fans to Diesel motor engines, and so on, faster than any other, it was this one. Its employees numbered hundreds of thousands, and their pay was the highest in the world. But the strike came, and lasted for months, costing the people of America all that time in getting back to normal consumption and production, and General Motors alone, with its employees, about a billion dollars loss. The President's "fact-finding committees" and other nostrums of the government experts had proved a costly farce.

Meanwhile, there had been the usual shifting of offices in the top positions, though the rank and file, often highly important if less heard about, tended to cling to office. In the Cabinet, after Truman's accession to the Presidency, one by one—the dates are not important—old members were replaced by new, although Ickes was not to go until 1946. In December 1945 the new Cabinet was as below:

Secretary of State, James F. Byrnes of South Carolina, who replaced Stettinius, successor to Hull.

Secretary of the Treasury, Fred M. Vinson of Kentucky, who replaced Morgenthau.

Secretary of War, Robert P. Patterson of New York, who replaced Stimson.

Attorney General, Tom A. Clark of Texas, who replaced Biddle.

Postmaster General, Robert E. Hannegan of Missouri, who replaced Walker.

Secretary of the Navy, James V. Forrestal of New York, who had previously succeeded Knox.

Secretary of the Interior, Harold L. Ickes of Illinois, who did not resign until early in 1946.

Secretary of Agriculture, Clinton P. Anderson of New Mexico, who replaced Wickard.

Secretary of Commerce, Henry A. Wallace of Iowa, who had already succeeded Jesse H. Jones.

Secretary of Labor, Lewis B. Schwellenbach of the State of Washington, who succeeded Miss Perkins.

In the above list, the members of the Cabinet are arranged in the order in which they succeed to the Presidency in case of the removal, death, resignation or inability to serve of both the President and Vice-President. As Vice-President Truman became President within the first three months of Roosevelt's fourth term, this meant that there was then no Vice-President, so that this list of possible succession is therefore of importance. Truman himself soon made an effort to correct by legislation this defect in our Constitution, but there were objections to the specific suggestions offered and as yet nothing has been done.

On November 20, the trial of twenty-one top Nazis began at Nürnberg, and at present writing is still going on, so that there can as yet be no valid comment on this trial.

In spite of strikes, and what seemed the quite unnecessary delay in getting reconversion, and the release of a much-needed flood of goods for civilian use, under way, war regulations were gradually being relaxed in the latter part of the year: such as gasoline rationing, on August 15; the rationing of shoes, on November 1; of meat, on

November 23; and so on, leaving sugar the only rationed commodity by the end of the year.

Ordinarily, the necrology of the year would call for mention and some notice of the more important individuals who had died, but 1945 was so full of deaths, natural, or in battle, by assassination, suicide, judicial process or other, that it would be hopeless to try to record them here, at the end of this chapter on the world's worst year. The principal deaths were those of the three heads of states: Mussolini by murder, Hitler by self-administered poison, and Roosevelt of a cerebral hemorrhage. After these, we could name dozens of world figures. One whose name cannot be omitted and whose death, the result of injuries suffered in an accident, was internationally mourned, was General George S. Patton, affectionately called "Old Blood and Guts" by his men. This fighting soldier, who typified much that is the best in the youth of America, played an important part in the defeat of Germany and by his gallantry and superb leadership endeared himself not only to Americans but to all who had the Allied cause at heart. We may end, perhaps, by noting, at the close of this period of horror, the passing of one of our finest and most loved men, who had kept through all the miseries and terrors he had witnessed his sense of humanity and warm comradeship, the news correspondent, Ernie Pyle, who was killed at Okinawa, on April 18. *There* was a man, and a guiding hope for a better future—somehow, sometime.

CHAPTER V

THE RECORD OF 1946

THE year 1946 did not have the intense dramatic interest of 1945. It was a period of transition. That, in itself, does not mean too much, for individuals, nations, the world itself, are always in a state of transition from one period or phase to another, and, as the French say of life, "the more it changes, the more it is the same." What lends a sinister interest to what we are living through now is the certainty that if there is *not* a change there will be a complete and horrible end of Man. Civilization cannot survive a World War III of atomic bombs. So far, in spite of the hopes for the United Nations, in spite of the trials we have suffered and the lessons we should have learned, the signs of change do not seem to be bright on the skies over a whole globe which the inventions of science have made to shrink to about the size of a baseball. There are some encouraging points, but not many.

The social and economic patterns, or curves, after every great war—to go back only a century and a half, or so—have shown a remarkable similarity. This, by my own interpretation as I have tried to explain it in other writings, is due not to natural laws, such as those of chemistry or physics, but just to human nature.

During a war, at least on the part of those wholly in favor of it, every effort is bent to win, and every hardship willingly met. Then comes peace, and, especially if it is peace with victory, a huge load is lifted off the hearts of all. They go on a buying spree for all the things which have been denied to them. But they have not won Aladdin's Lamp. Merchants have stocked their shelves. Farmers have grown used to high prices. The economy gets out of gear—wages, prices for farm produce, manufactured goods, cost of living. A readjustment has to be made, and we get the usual *primary* post-war depression. Adjustments *are* made, things look good again, and we go on a big speculative spree. But war destroys capital, and its restoration calls for time and hard work. The big boom busts, and then we have the *real* post-war depression.

For example, let us take only the American Revolution and World War I. The "shooting war" of the Revolution may be said to have ended with the surrender of Cornwallis at Yorktown in 1781. Peace was signed in 1783. There was a spree until 1785, when the primary depression and first period of readjustment set in. This lasted till 1787, when our present Constitution was drawn up, largely as a result of the intense economic difficulties and social unrest. Next came the boom, till the crash of the early 1790's.

After World War I the "shooting war" ended in 1918; peace was signed in 1919. We were having the spree. Then came the first depression of 1920–21; then the big boom until the real post-war smash of 1929. In 1946, and perhaps 1947, we are at the customary stage of this apparently inevitable cycle.

We shall speak of the labor troubles a little later, but before we start on our more or less purely domestic concerns we may repeat what we alluded to in the last chapter, *viz.,* that the so-called history of America is becoming enormously more complex. It is not only that our own political, social and economic life is becoming more complicated but that formerly isolated America has spread over the globe.

I quote a few lines from an extremely important article, "Our Treaty Procedure vs. Our Foreign Policies," by J. Sloan Dickey, President of Dartmouth, in the April 1947 issue of *Foreign Affairs:*

During the first 150 years of our national history our major foreign policies were in the main unilateral in form, negative or merely declaratory in character and restricted in scope. Today they are dominantly cooperative, *i.e.,* contractual in form, and involve positive undertakings as to men and treasure. There is no place, there is no subject, not touched by our concern.

I recommend the entire article to the readers of this chapter, but what I have quoted indicates the difficulty

THE UNITED NATIONS: ITS

GENERAL ASSEMBLY

Up to five delegates from each of fifty-one member nations, but only one vote for each nation. Its duties are to discuss any questions within the scope of the Charter, and submit recommendations to the Security Council.

SECURITY COUNCIL

Eleven members — the Big Five permanent, the other six elected for two-year terms by the Assembly. Investigates international disputes; takes action against aggressors if necessary.

TRUSTEESHIP COUNCIL

Composed of any members administering trust territories; plus those of Big Five not administering such trusts; plus as many others as are needed to ensure equal representation of members who do and do not administer trusts.

SECRETARIAT

Headed by a Secretary General, it includes administrative and research staffs serving the entire United Nations.

ATOMIC ENERGY COMMISSION

Eleven members of the Security Council plus Canada. Will "consider problems arising from the discovery of atomic energy".

MILITARY STAFF COMMITTEE

Composed of Chiefs of Staff of U.S., Britain, U.S.S.R., China and France. Decides composition and directs forces against aggressors under the Security Council.

INTERNATIONAL ARMED FORCES

To be composed of a quota of forces readily available from all members for putting down threats to peace. (Not yet organized. To be decided by Military Staff Committee.)

Special text — revised for the Board of Education, City of New York

ORGANIZATION AND FUNCTIONS

ECONOMIC-SOCIAL COUNCIL

Eighteen members elected for three-year terms by the Assembly. Will coordinate the work of specialized agencies to eliminate economic and social roots of war.

INTERNATIONAL COURT

Fifteen members, chosen for 9-year terms, by Assembly and Council, from candidates nominated by national groups in Permanent Court of Arbitration. Will meet in permanent session to decide legal disputes between nations.

INTERNATIONAL BANK

Part of the Bretton Woods plan, ratified by thirty-five nations. Will provide funds for reconstruction and develop resources not fully employed.

INTERNATIONAL MONETARY FUND

Also part of the Bretton Woods plan. Will be employed by member nations to help stabilize currencies.

FOOD & AGRICULTURE ORGANIZATION

A research and study organization to help ensure freedom from want, increased food production, improved agricultural methods and higher food and nutrition standards throughout the world.

CIVIL AVIATION ORGANIZATION

Organized in 1944 to deal with complex economic and legal problems in commercial air transport operations, and inspect travelers and cargo to prevent spread of disease.

UNITED NATIONS EDUCATIONAL, SCIENTIFIC AND CULTURAL ORGANIZATION

Drafted at London 1945, to develop international cultural understanding and to help make the world's accumulated knowledge available to all.

CHART BY GRAPHICS INSTITUTE FOR THE NEW YORK TIMES

for any historian in telling the story of the U.S.A., even of one year. One can no longer stop at the water's edge. There are the plane routes through the stratosphere, and instead of the stormy Atlantic the North Pole has become the shortest route from the New World to the Old.

We obviously cannot write the history of the world in 1946 in one short chapter, or even cover all the contacts we have had with the rest of the globe; we can touch only a few high spots.

The year 1946 was, as we have said, a year of transition. The wars in the shooting sense had ended in 1945, but peace had not come. Some of the longest industrial strikes in our history were winding their slow way but were not to end until 1947. We were, in a sense, in slack, although very turbid, water.

On the international scene we noted in the last chapter the formation of the United Nations with fifty members. At midnight on April 18 of the year we are discussing, the League of Nations expired. It had not lived in vain, if its successor, the U.N., can build better on the basis of the knowledge we gained from the failures of the League.

Any organization formed by "nations" is bound to encounter its difficulties in the individual characteristics and ambitions of nations as such; but that is a chance which has to be taken. It is better than ironing the whole world flat into one pattern and mode of thought and action, like a gigantic ants' nest. The now-dead League failed for many reasons. The United States, which had been foremost in planning it, did not at last join it. Na-

BIG THREE

DISCORD

DANGEROUS INTRUDER
From a cartoon by Fitzpatrick in *The St. Louis Post-Dispatch*.

tions which had joined did not live up to their obligations. They permitted the Japanese invasion of Manchuria and the Italian invasion of Abyssinia, and other matters which led directly to the holocaust of World War II. What we can do now remains to be seen. By March, 1947, Russia, always with its satellite state or puppet government of Poland trailing along, had used its Veto Power ten times to defeat the purposes of the U.N. Security Council; it may continue to use that power to defeat the purposes of the new international organization to which it adhered.

It is too early to make a prediction, and the year 1946 in the U.N., as in so many other factors and phases of our post-war life, comes under the heading of "unfinished business." So much of the twelve months was apparently taken up with squabbles over forms, procedure, and even the site of a permanent location—Westchester, Connecticut, New York City, San Francisco and other points east and west—that the public may have lost interest, and to some extent may also have lost sight of what really had been accomplished. We have to reserve for the 1947 chapter the generous offer by the Rockefellers of $8,500,000 and the final decision to house the U.N. in a little city almost of its own within the city of New York.

A good deal of solid work in the way of handling international affairs and acute complications had been accomplished, and four new nations had been admitted to membership — Iceland, Sweden, Afghanistan, and Siam. The diversity of nations and peoples, and of the problems involved, was rather breath-taking. But we can only wait and see. "Unfinished business" again. Although the permanent home of the U.N. had not been decided in 1946, the year marked the first time that the Security Council held its meeting (the twenty-fourth) in Amer-

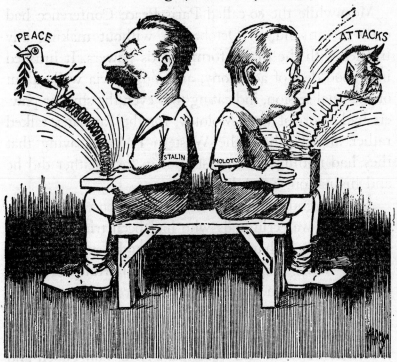

EACH TO HIS OWN
From a cartoon by Marcus. Reprinted by permission of *The New York Times.*

ica, at Hunter College, New York. On October 23 the meeting of the General Assembly was opened by President Truman at their temporary quarters in the New York City Building in Flushing Meadow Park. He

193

pleaded for peace and asked that the world should not be split into "irreconcilable parts." During the session, which ended in December, the problem of the veto so constantly used by Russia was discussed, but no final change was made.

Meanwhile the so-called Paris Peace Conference had come to an end on October 14 without making any treaties with the major former Axis powers. It finished in a good deal of acrimony, and Yugoslavia walked out of the final session, indicating that even the smaller powers had a sort of veto. Molotov, for the Russians, talked rather angrily about the Western Powers, saying that they had nothing to suggest; but in fact neither did he and his nation. So ended that.

Another end came on October 16, when eleven of the chief Nazi war criminals who had been tried at Nürnberg died, ten by hanging and Goering by suicide. Those hanged were Wilhelm Keitel, Ernst Kaltenbrunner, Fritz Sauckel, von Ribbentrop (the "von" denoting aristocratic origin was his own fancy decoration), Arthur Seyss-Inquart, Alfred Rosenberg, Julius Streicher, Alfred Jodl, Hans Frank, and Wilhelm Frick. Von Papen and Schacht were held for further trial by a German de-Nazification court, and were condemned by that court the following year. The multiple trial had necessarily been long-drawn-out, but it had been fair; and when ten top Nazis were hanged in seventy-five minutes, that at least was not "unfinished business" for the year. If we consider the ends of Hitler, Goebbels, Mussolini, Ciano and other leaders in the previous chapter, the world had never before seen Nemesis so thoroughly at work.

CAN'T HANG AN IDEA
From a cartoon by Poinier in *The Detroit Free Press.*

To extend the international scene, we can merely mention certain quarters without going into the details needed to understand the difficulties everywhere. Nobody can be a specialist on every country, however wisely columnists may appear to talk on all subjects; and apart from that, to offer information on the globe today calls for not a part of a chapter but a large book.

195

To indicate briefly some of the sore spots in which we had economic, military or diplomatic interest remaining in the year:

The Far East was in turmoil. We have always had a very friendly interest in China, and of all outside nations I think we have ever been China's best friend. Civil war between the parties of Chiang Kai-shek and the Communists was still going on when President Truman sent General Marshall, former Chief of Staff, to be his personal representative, with the rank of Ambassador. After many months Marshall, who had formerly been fully familiar with China, had to turn in a very pessimistic report, and we began to withdraw some of our armed forces. The problem, especially after the killing of four American Marines by Chinese Reds in August, was complex; but I would trust Marshall's judgment.

In Japan General MacArthur was carrying on the American occupation with considerable success, although the end is not yet. The Emperor Hirohito in his New Year's message to his people had set the stage for the house-cleaning of the Jingo element (which MacArthur later carried out) by announcing that he was not a God. The Emperor did not deny that he was descended from the Sun Goddess, but merely that he was not himself divine. This may seem absurd to us, but it was important news in Japan. However, the Emperor went further and made perhaps the more important pronouncements that the Japanese people were not superior to all other races, and were not destined, as centuries-long tradition had affirmed, to conquer all the world in war. The trials of the Japanese war criminals went on.

Also in the Far East, the Dutch colonies continued in revolt, and rebellion broke out in French Indo-China. The great sub-continent of India itself was seething; there were murderous mobs and every indication of wide civil war between Moslems and Hindus if the British withdrew and gave "India" its complete "independence," both indefinable terms under the circumstances.

In the Near East there were also vast upheavals following the global war. The British prepared to evacuate Egypt and the Sudan, with effects on the control of the Suez Canal and the "life-line" to India. There had been trouble brewing in Palestine between the Jews and Arabs, and Britain was primarily responsible for order in that country. The situation is an extremely intricate one and can be described only as an unholy mess. The sufferings of the Jews in Europe have been very real. We all know of them, but historically and racially the rights of Spanish, Polish, Russian, American or any other Jews to any large part of Palestine are certainly very vague and intangible. The Jews themselves are by no means agreed, and I myself have had letters from Rabbis asking me to speak up for Zionism, or, in other cases, to write against it.

Meanwhile the Arabs are determined that only a certain number of Jews be allowed to come in as immigrants each year. More insist on doing so, and hence the conflicts, the concentration camps, the terrorism, and the problem of what is to be done. The Labor Government in Britain is about through with carrying it alone. At various times, notably in October, Truman had suggested, on occasion tartly, that the British settle it. We sent a delegation to London to discuss the question, but the President rejected their findings. We have given advice but have declined all responsibility, and so far have succeeded only in keeping the kettle boiling.

Then there are Greece and Turkey, to say nothing of Persia—now Iran—and its oil. The Russians threaten a thrust that way, and if the Near East is important for the British Empire it has become increasingly so for us, because of trade routes, oil and other products, and because of the need of keeping alive countries which are threatened by the Communist glacier but would like to hold to their independence.

Moving nearer toward the old Europe, we find the Balkans largely under the sway of Russia, and Poland in the U.N., seems always to vote with the Soviets as just a "me-too." Practically all these countries are dead broke, for the physical destruction of war has been followed by the most fantastic of currency inflations.

For example, take Hungary, from which, oddly enough, I have recently received the first royalties from a Hungarian translation of one of my books. Before this last war a Hungarian *pengo* was worth twenty cents in American money, or five to a dollar. On June 12,

1946, paper pengos were one *trillion* (1,000,000,000,000) to the dollar, and three days later the same number were worth only thirty-five cents. The government were printing larger notes every week. What happens to the economy or the ideology of a people under such conditions?

We have had our troubles with Yugoslavia, another satellite of Russia, through the whole year—Yugoslavs carrying forbidden weapons in our zone of occupation, American fliers shot down, diplomatic notes shuttling back and forth, and constant recrimination on both sides. I cannot linger longer over the international complications—Germany, the strident Left-wing of the British Labor Party, Franco's Spain, or Peron's Argentine. I have said enough to indicate that 1946 was indeed a year of "unfinished business," and that it is going to take on our part a lot of money, courage, and above all knowledge and brains to finish it. With the world, as I said at the beginning of this chapter, shrunk to the size of a baseball we can never again take refuge by drawing into the shell of isolation. *There are no oceans any more.* We may not like it—I do not—but we have to face the fact of a new world and of new dangers, from within and without.

The shift from war to peace was being made, and in the process some things were being finished, or practically so, in the United States. We shall speak of politics later, but here we may say that in his first message to

Congress on January 22, President Truman, in one of the longest messages ever sent—25,000 words—discussed the coming transition from almost every angle. Later in the year he proved himself ready and willing to go a long way in cutting down the war-time agencies and his own war-time powers.

The O.P.A. came almost to a complete end. All price controls were to expire at midnight of June 30. The situation as to prices was chaotic for a time, but although some went up when the ceilings were off, others in time went down. There was, however, distinct anxiety as to what would happen. I need not go into all the details of bills passed, vetoed, repassed, replaced by other bills and so on, for some months through the summer. Suffice it to say that by the end of the year, the O.P.A. (Office of Price Administration), which had done much good work and some clumsy work, as is natural in war, had practically ceased, except for such items as sugar, rents, and a few others. There was also a strong movement to turn rent controls over to the individual States locally, and sugar control was expected to end in 1947.

In August another war agency came to an end: U.N.R.R.A., as it was called to alphabeticize—if I may coin a word—Roosevelt's rather long-winded name for the United Nations Relief and Rehabilitation Administration. The State Department announced that it would ask for no further funds. The organization had had two primary objects: (1) to supply the nations liberated by the Allies with foreign exchange with which to buy goods, and (2) to handle the problems of procurement and shipping. The U. S. A. had appropriated about $2,700,000,000 for these purposes. We had also agreed to contribute through the Export-Import Bank, through the International Monetary Fund, and in other ways, about $15,000,000,000 more. The other organizations had been established. The war had been over about one and a half years.

As always happens when a huge bureaucracy has been set going with billions, there was a clamor, but Under-secretary of State W. L. Clayton was unusually correct when he stated that there was no more need for U.N.R.R.A., and that "the United States is not a limit-less reservoir of wealth and goods. We have serious prob-lems of our own." He also remarked that "the gravy train is going around for the last time." The United States had contributed 70 per cent of the total cost for world rehabilitation, in some cases to bolster up regimes such as those in Yugoslavia and Poland which were not even friendly to us. Serious scandals, which had interna-tional repercussions had also crept into the Relief admin-istration. Both our State Department and Congress de-cided on sudden death for it.

Another war adventure which was being placed in the category of finished business was Lend-Lease. The idea of what came to be called by that term originated ap-parently with Franklin Roosevelt in 1941, and it developed into the most stupendous mutual-aid program in all history. We have spoken of it in previous chapters, and need merely say here that in effect it meant that the Allies would pool all their resources to attain victory —cash, food, munitions, everything. We were the richest nation in the world, and the burden naturally fell heaviest on us on a bookkeeping basis; but we must forever recall that we were not ready for war, and that for two years and more the enemy which nearly vanquished all of us was held at bay by "the blood and sweat and tears," in Churchill's phrase, of the British. It had been a gallant, daring, and perhaps an eventually decisive improvisation on the part of Roosevelt, and one for which all the world, including ourselves, in spite of the cost to us, must always be grateful.

In 1946, however, the time had come to wind up accounts. We ourselves had not been the only ones to "Lend-Lease." Other peoples had done the same for us in what was called "Reverse Lend-Lease." The balances were impossible to figure in dollars and cents, because money had been only part of the almost unthinkably huge and complicated set of transactions. There had been money—yes—but also materials, housing for troops, food, medicines, doctors and hospitalizations for our men as well as the Allies, transport, and everything which could be conceived in a nightmare of an expert accountant.

We opened negotiations with the thirty-four nations which had joined with us, and on December 27, President Truman informed Congress that as near as could be figured in the complications, the others had repaid in Reverse Lend-Lease, or in one way and another, about 70 per cent of the nearly $60,000,000,000 involved. Belgium was the only country which gave us more than we had given to her in her agony, but satisfactory settlements had been made with the United Kingdom, France, Turkey, Australia, New Zealand, and India. At the end of the year we were still awaiting results of negotiation with Russia, China, Greece, Holland, Norway, and the Union of South Africa. Russia was the largest remaining partner in the enterprise, having reecived over $11,000,-000,000 but so far has declined discussion, although it was claimed that she had passed on part of her share to her new satellite states. That was some of the unfinished business.

Meanwhile we had made the greatest single international loan in history. It was $3,750,000,000 to Great Britain, and it passed the House of Representatives by a vote of 219 to 155, with defeat of all suggested amendments which might somewhat have crippled it. The loan was made to enable Britain, which had become weakened in the war (which for a while she had carried on absolutely alone in the world against Germany and the other Axis powers), to regain her strength, and also to enable her to repeal certain regulations she had been forced to make to save the world, as well as herself, but which we felt might hurt us in times of peace.

Briefly we agreed that she could borrow all or such part as she needed, up to 1951. Up to then she would have to pay no interest, but after that she would pay 2 per cent on all she had borrowed, and the principal was to be repaid by 2001. If she suffered a severe depression in any year, interest would be waived for that year. On her own side, Britain made certain agreements in trade which were much to the advantage of the United States.

Although it was rather a year of winding up, one other new international commitment was entered into. This was UNESCO, which stood for the United Nations Educational, Scientific, and Cultural Organization. The 220 voting delegates meet at UNESCO House in Paris, formerly the Hotel Majestic. The plans are rather vague but far-reaching, including world-wide broadcasts, increased international freedom of the press, international exchange of students, and coordination of cultural surveys, among other things. What will come of it, aside from expense, no one yet knows, but forty-four nations joined, with the notable exception of Russia, which seemed to regard the organization as a vast propaganda machine for the capitalist powers.

During the year no final treaty of peace was made with a major power on the Axis side, although a treaty draft was drawn up with Italy, which had become a Republic in June after the abdication of the King and his flight to Egypt. The treaty, which still had to be ratified by the Big Four, stripped Italy of all her colonies, considerable territory adjacent to the home peninsula, her navy, most of her air force and army, and set aside $100,000,000 in reparations for Russia. The terms suited neither Italy nor Yugoslavia, and how it is to be enforced when the more general settlement of Europe ensues is problematic.

While still considering the unfinished business of the wars and before discussing our more purely domestic affairs, we must speak of that dread menace which has come to hang over all the world, the atomic bomb. For the most part it is all still "top secret," or supposedly so; but there are two matters concerning it which attained much and continuing publicity through the latter half of the year. One was the testing at Bikini, and the other our efforts to devise some sort of international control which might lift the thought of the horrors of World War III from the minds of all mankind. We have not yet succeeded in the second point and have been only partially informed as to the first.

Early in the year, or probably earlier still, it was decided to test the effects of the atomic bombs, which had been so devastating on Hiroshima and Nagasaki, on a fleet at sea. The question to be studied, especially important for the two great sea powers, Britain and the United States, was whether sea power could survive atomic energy. As Admiral W. V. Pratt, U.S.N., explained in an article in February on "Operations Crossroads," as it was called, the United States made the experiment because we had the secret of the bomb and a great store of all types of sea craft. A problem was where to conduct the Operation. The Mediterranean, Atlantic and other waters were ruled out for obvious reasons; in the Pacific winds, weather, harbors, populations and other matters had to be considered.

The choice narrowed down to Bikini, the most northern atoll of the Ralik chain of the Marshall Islands. The spot is unhealthy and produces scant sustenance. It had a population of only about 200, and has an enclosed lagoon ten miles wide and twenty-one miles long to harbor the vessels. The weather could be depended upon, and the winds were right to carry off the destructive radio-activity over wide empty spaces of ocean. The natives were moved to another and better island home, and every possible scientific preparation was made to record results, especially the power of the blast, the effect of intense heat, and of the radio-activity on material and animals.

On July 1 the bomb was dropped. It was the fourth. The first had been in the New Mexico desert, and the other two on the Japanese Empire, ending the war. On July 25 the fifth bomb was dropped, not on the surface but in a moderate depth of water. The effects were different.

When the first bomb was exploded above water, only one ship was within 1000 feet of the explosion, but twenty others were within a half mile. Of these twenty-one, six were sunk and the rest very badly damaged. Tests on the animals (goats, pigs, rabbits, mice and so on) showed that if the ships had been manned by human beings the initial flash of the lethal radiations would have killed almost all the personnel aboard vessels centered around the blast and many at greater distances.

When the second and sub-surface bomb exploded, a column of water about 2200 feet in diameter rose to a height of about 5500 feet, and for a few moments lifted the 26,000-ton battleship *Arkansas* into the air before it plunged to the bottom of the ocean. Waves of some several hundred feet high swirled around the column, which was estimated to have contained about 10,000,000 tons of water, which had become radio-active and fell back in spray on the other ships. The activity was the equivalent of that which would have been produced by many hundreds of tons of radium, and would have killed all human beings at once or within a short time. For some days ships continued to sink, and it was not considered safe to approach them on account of the lethal radium. We need not go into further details; those here have been taken from the official reports made to President Truman on August 2 by the civilian observers and the joint Army and Navy Chiefs of Staff. It has been suspected that the tests revealed even greater dangers to mankind from this demonic weapon than were disclosed.

At present the secret in its full manufacturing entirety

is *supposed* to be known only in the United States, but we do know that Germany had very nearly discovered it for herself, and it is now said that Russia is working on it with the help of scientists imported from Germany. While, as we have said, it is mostly all "top secret," yet we have learned enough to know that another war might be horrible beyond expression, and that something must be done. Atomic energy may indeed open vast vistas for peaceful industry; but though dynamite, gunpowder, and T.N.T. are useful in peace, no one bent on war has hesitated to use them for that purpose also.

Following our discovery, use, and experimenting with the bomb, we have been doing our best to control its use by all peoples. The Report by Bernard Barurch and others suggested one approach to the problem. We have taken it up with the United Nations, but so far no agreement has been reached. It is difficult to see what arrangement can be made to use atomic power in peace, to keep other nations from learning the secret in "one world" of science, or to trust anyone. In the past generation we have seen so many solemn treaties torn up as "scraps of paper," and been told so explicitly by international gangsters like Hitler and others that the bigger the lie the more useful it is, that at present one can only dread the future. It may be said that we should not have made the discovery of atomic fission or used it, but we have unfortunately to remember that Germany came within an ace of beating us to it—and if she had, then what? We finished

208

the gangsters of three Axis Powers—but is the world any safer today for democracy than it is for the atomic bomb? There are yet individuals and nations who care more for ambition and aggrandizement than for civilization.

We may now return to more purely domestic affairs, notably politics and economics. Both were heavily influenced by the labor situation; so we may discuss that first. The year was marked by prolonged and bitter strikes, some to run for a year or more and not to be settled until 1947. I have already noted that the primary periods of readjustment after great wars are always notable for difficulties with prices, wages, and social upheaval, partly purely economic and partly psychological. The year 1946 was bad, but on the whole, whatever may be ahead, I do not think it was as bad, from my memory, as around 1920, when I paid thirty cents a pound for sugar, bought the last barrel of flour obtainable on the East End of Long Island, paid $22 a ton for coal which was half slate, and national revolution was openly talked of. It is always well to have some perspective.

The main job of the year was to pass from a war-time program for industry to one of peace-time production. It was a colosssal undertaking. Business, big and little, with its executives and labor, had accomplished the greatest feat of production in world history, but it had entailed a wholesale turnover of goods and the machinery and tools necessary to make them. The end of the wars had come more suddenly than anyone had thought probable or even possible, and we were confronted with the immediate necessity for going into reverse. During the wars we had concentrated almost wholly on war material instead of peace demands—tanks, for example, instead of cars, bombs instead of refrigerators, and so on. We had built camps, hospitals, ships, and all sorts of things, but not dwelling houses. All of a sudden we had to supply the accumulated needs of peace, the needs of an increased population, of millions of returning veterans, need of replacements for wornout cars, of equipment of all sorts.

During the wars two things of prime economic importance had happened. On the one hand, all sorts of goods could not be obtained. On the other, labor had received immense sums in wages and there was a very limited chance to spend money as compared with World War I, when workmen wore silk shirts, their wives fur coats, and every luxury could be bought with the new high pay. In this war it was different. A mink coat, perhaps, but there was a limit to the number of mink coats any one person wanted, and most avenues of expenditure were closed because of lack of goods. So money piled up. I saw it in the savings bank of which I am a trustee in a big manufacturing city, and in the reports of other banks.

Peace came, but not world settlement, with an amazing lack of goods people had wanted—cars, houses, washing-machines, refrigerators, really good clothes, and all the rest—and with an unprecedented amount of cash savings and debts paid off. The one thing needful was *production,* not only to fill long-felt wants but to turn the superabundance of cash on hand into goods and to stave off inflation. A quick readjustment was essential. I think it must be admitted that business did a remarkable job in transforming plants and machinery in huge establishments, such as General Motors, and innumerable small ones, from war to peace; but the difficulty which may have caused us to "miss the bus" was labor with its strikes. I am a "friend of labor," as the phrase goes, and think that labor as a whole made a fine contribution to the war effort. Nor am I trying to compare what labor did at home, in safety and comfort and at high wages, as contrasted with what the ten million or more men and women of the armed forces, in discomfort, did at low pay and risking their lives. We will let that go. The fact remains that, with the plants and factories transformed, we had to *produce.* At that point labor fell down. If we have not got the houses for veterans and their wives and babies, or the goods, including cars and all the rest, that everybody wants and could pay for, the lack cannot be blamed on either capital or executive management. War profits were a myth. Let anyone look at the dividend records of the companies which did most to win the war.

We cannot go into all the details of the strikes which hampered the called-for production; we need mention only some of the long list which operated to raise prices and the cost of living. With a long-pent-up demand for things, with an unprecedented amount of savings with which to pay for them, with limited production, the answer would be obvious—*inflation*. And if the government clamped on "ceilings," then black markets would begin, as they did in some cases. With increased cost of living, increased wages would be asked, and the vicious spiral might be set in motion toward a *Pengo*.

The year opened ominously. The newspapers recorded actual or prospective strikes involving over 2,000,000 employees in leading industries, such as Western Union, Western Electric, the Bell Telephone System, steel, General Motors and others. At Stamford, Connecticut, the bitter strike at the Yale & Towne plant was threatening to become a general one, the first general strike in the history of the State. A strike in the meat-packing business was called for the 16th of January with demands for a 25-cent-an-hour increase in pay for 200,000 workers.

Meanwhile Truman, or his advisors, had lit on the idea of appointing "fact-finding" commissions to determine what increases of wages were called for and might be paid without increasing the cost of the finished products to the public, starting with steel. It cannot be said that the plan worked out. It smashed the government's so-called "wage-price policy," and with the first recommendation for an 18½-cent increase, set a pace for every labor leader, big or little, to aim at or surpass.

Naturally the factor of labor varies from industry to industry. In some, labor cost is as low as about 6 per cent

KEEPING HIM SPINNING
From a cartoon by Marcus. Reprinted by permission of *The New York Times*.

of the total cost of production. In others labor may represent 50 to 60 per cent of the total. There can be no straight line across all industries, but there is a tendency, natural in a way, for labor leaders, if one of them gets a certain rise, to try to get the same for their unions regardless. So when "fact-finding" pointed 18½ per cent in one case, that appeared to set the lowest figure for all to shoot at. Some of the broader aspects of the President-Labor situation will be mentioned when we come to the politics of the year, and we shall here continue with some of the strike news.

It was incessant, and marked by every arrogance on the part of so-called labor leaders, in disregard of the general public interest and even of our form of government. The Wagner Act and others which had been passed in the heyday of the New Deal, and which appeared to create one world of law, crimes and patriotism for capital and a much more comfortable one for labor, had been largely responsible, and Congress cannot escape its own share of blame.

To mention a few dates: We may note that the packing-house strike began January 16, causing a nation-wide shortage of meat for all. Five days later the steel strike began, resulting in dropping steel output, when it was so badly needed for cars, building, and everything people wanted, to the lowest point in fifty years. On April 1, John L. Lewis called out the soft-coal miners, and although the government under its still existent war-powers seized the mines from the owners on May 21, the strike continued. A nation-wide railroad strike precipitated by a few unions was forced to end by Truman on May 25. This strike, which would have paralyzed the whole effort of the nation to recover from the war, was one of the bad spots, because the railroads had been practically under government control for more than a generation as far as rates and other factors in operation were concerned, and the Railway Brotherhood had been almost the most conservative of unions among highly paid and highly skilled labor. A. F. Whitney, head of one of the rail unions, when thwarted in his purpose by the President and public opinion, threatened to raise a fund of millions to defeat Truman in 1948 should he run for President. We were used to the struttings of a John L. Lewis or a "Cæsar" Petrillo, but we had not expected that sort of thing from the Railway Brotherhood. On September 5, the maritime workers started a series of strikes which practically closed the ports of the nation to shipping, stopped commerce and our aid to the starving in other countries.

There were many other strikes of importance, or strikes threatened by unions which held a pistol at the head of the public, such as the Subway of New York, under Quill. The entire city of Pittsburgh, a most important producing city, was stalled for weeks with enormous loss of goods for the entire country and public and with intense discomfort to its own local inhabitants. Under the Wagner and other Acts already mentioned, labor leaders have come to consider themselves immune to the laws and penalties which control all the rest of us.

Who are the rest of us? Who is a laboring man? Who

is a capitalist? It is getting hard to say. Is a noted labor leader who is reputed to have a salary of $25,000 a year and a handsome house a laboring man, and is an old man who may be trying to get along on $2500 a year from a lifetime of accumulated savings a capitalist?

There are certain things which stand out in the strikes of this "year of transition." One is what I have just pointed to. Another is the recklessness of the leaders and their utter disregard for everybody else in the world. Two others are the needlessness of so many strikes and their enormous waste to both the workers and the public. This chapter is not an essay in economics but in history. The history of 1946, however, points a moral if it does not "adorn a tale."

We can touch on only two or three other labor conflicts, and must get on. The strike, marked by violence, which lasted more than a year at the Allis-Chalmers plant, was not over until 1947, but we can sample a few more.

There was the longest and costliest strike in the automotive industry, that against General Motors, which was ended in March. What happened? Of the C.I.O. Automobile Workers Union, 175,000 went without working and without pay for 113 days, in an endeavor to increase the company's offer of a 10 *per cent* raise to the figure set by Truman's committee of a 19½ *cent* raise. The strike was finally settled on a basis of 18½ cents, and some side benefits, but it was estimated that the workers would have to work steadily for five years to make up

in lost pay the difference between the company's voluntary offer and what the strikers got. At the Chrysler and
Ford plants the workers got 19½ cents and 18 cents
increase by negotiation without strikes and with no stoppage of production. The General Motors strike is estimated to have cost the workers $127,690,000 (the
figures of their union); it cost the company $600,000,000
in unfilled orders, the dealers $100,000,000 in lost com-
missions; and the public had to go without the cars and
other goods that they wanted and needed.

To note another case: the C.I.O. strike at the Granite
City Steel Company plant lasted 150 days, the longest in
the steel industry. The company had offered 20 cents-an-
hour increase, but the C.I.O. leaders demanded 26 cents.
The strike was settled after about five months at 21 cents.
The workers had lost an average of $1160 each, and it
would take them fifty-five years to make this up from
the one cent gained, which they had been fighting about.
The strike cost the public 150,000 tons of badly needed
flat-rolled steel. These are merely samples to show the
extreme waste in strikes for companies, men, and the
public—and most of us are "the public."

We cannot even mention the many other strikes
which, as we have already said, occurred all over the
country throughout the year. We will end with the second
coal strike.

Soft coal has, of course, been essential for industry of
all sorts, including to a great extent the railroads, although many are now changing over to oil on account

of the frequent and unpredictable strikes of the miners and consequent lack of fuel. We have already mentioned the strike which began on April 1 and ended only in May after the government had taken over the mines.

On October 21 Lewis, in a public statement, declared that Secretary of the Interior Krug had broken the government contract with the miners on two technical points. By the middle of November the issue was joined between Lewis and the government. The problem was whether to accept the dictation, even that of Green of the A. F. of L. who joined with Lewis, or to fight for the rescue of the economic and social stability of the nation. Even strong pro-labor Senators warned Truman that the time had come. The President decided to fight. Winter was approaching. The country had only thirty-seven days' supply of coal above ground, it was said. In two weeks steel mills would have to close; in twenty days railroads would stop running; in thirty days public utilities would have to discontinue service.

Lewis did not declare a strike. He simply said there was no longer a contract, and as miners would not work without one he knew what to expect. On November 20 the mining of soft coal in twenty-eight states came to a halt, and 10,000 anthracite miners also walked out. The production of over 2,000,000 tons of coal daily for American industry, for American health and comfort, stopped. Lewis kept silent.

However, on the 18th Justice Goldsborough of the

United States District Court of the District of Columbia, issued an order restraining Lewis from cancelling the contract with Krug, and if he did not obey it to appear November 25 to show why he should not be held in

STILL TO BE WEIGHED
From a cartoon by Herblock in *The Washington Post.*

contempt of court. Four hundred thousand miners were out and remained out. Two hundred and fifty thousand other workers had been forced into idleness; millions were expected to be out if the strike continued; 25,000,-000 tons of coal had not been mined; and 1,000,000 tons of steel had not been made, according to estimates.

On December 3, Lewis was declared guilty of contempt, and the following day he was fined $10,000 and his union $3,500,000. In pronouncing sentence Goldsborough is quoted as saying: "This is not the act of a low lawbreaker, but it is an evil, demoniac, monstrous thing that means hunger and cold and unemployment and destitution and disorganization of the social fabric; a threat to democratic government itself." Lewis's lawyer shouted "shame and double shame." Lewis joined himself to that and other remarks, but two hours later gave in. He ordered the miners back to work until *March 31, 1947.* The freight embargo was lifted; the 50 per cent of train service was resumed; Pittsburgh and other centers began to produce again; lights went on; hospitals, schools and homes were saved from the threat of freezing. Another strike was over for a time.

There is an old saying that figures do not lie but figurers do. I have no intention of suggesting that the Bureau of Labor Statistics under recent administrations have falsified figures, but it is often difficult to know just what they mean. Strikes are figured in lost hours of manwork, but it is a question how far the estimates are carried. Are they the lost hours in a "struck industry" or is the estimate carried through all the ramifications of a strike in coal, steel, railroads, makers of parts essential to some other industry, and so on? In any case, the government figures, not published until April, 1947, but relating to the year 1946, do give us some idea of what happened. The Bureau of Labor Statistics then reported that in the preceding year strikes had caused a loss of 116,000,000 man-days, more than a million each in the cities of Buffalo, Chicago, Cleveland, Detroit, Houston, Los Angeles, New York, Philadelphia, Pittsburgh and San Francisco. This indicated the nation-wide extent of the troubles, and the added fact that, even as the government figured, the lost hours were three times those due to strikes in 1945.

Without going into all the rest of the strike situation in 1946, we may now turn to the political scene of the year.

Truman, who had not particularly wanted the Vice-Presidency, had been hurtled into the Presidential office in an hour or so after Roosevelt's sudden death in 1945. Such changes in position have often been extremely sudden, as for example after the assassinations of Lincoln and McKinley; but it is one of the shortcomings of our form of government that the man who thus finds himself, with hardly any warning, the most powerful individual in the United States and perhaps the world, had not been an understudy, or sufficiently familiar with all the problems he is unexpectedly called upon to handle or solve. After World War I, a President did try to have the Vice-President sit in at Cabinet meetings, but the plan proved somewhat impracticable. The Vice-President, under the Constitution, is the presiding officer of the Senate, and it is impossible to combine that job with that of an active member of the Cabinet. It has not been tried again; so the man who at any moment may be called upon to assume the office of President perforce remains more or less outside the constant inner councils of the administration.

When Truman, on the afternoon of Roosevelt's sudden death, had to take the oath of office and become the leader of the nation, he was extremely modest and even humble in the face of the task ahead of him. We Americans are a kindly folk, I often think—from living and observing in many lands—the most kindly in the world. We sympathized with Truman, wished him well, and waited.

He had, I think, about the hardest job which ever awaited a Vice-President when called almost at a moment's notice to be President. Some other Vice-Presidents, with somewhat limited experience and background, had done well, such as Chester Arthur after Garfield; but when they had to take the helm the ship of state was on a fairly steady course and the weather was not stormy. Truman came in at one of the greatest crises in American and all world history. Moreover, his predecessor, Roosevelt, for the first time in the history of the Presidency, had been elected for a third and a fourth term. His power had been great. He had been immensely popular with at least more than a majority of the electorate. A large percentage of the younger voters, men and women, had never known any other President. He had been a leading figure in the years of depression and war. He had appointed eight of the nine justices of the Supreme Court, a contingency never anticipated. He had built up his continuing power on an odd combination of pressure groups and city bosses, including labor, having taken $500,000 from the miners' union in one election and having built up John L. Lewis for a while. He had had immense "war powers," and those which were granted in the continuing "crises" which he had declared. He was the center of the stage.

Truman, although a Senator, was not a world figure or even a national figure, and had not been in a position, except on the sidelines, to see how the New Deal "clicked." But at first he seemed to feel—which was perhaps natural—that he must carry on the Roosevelt policies, where he could find them, and make the Deal click with something of the former tick-tock. The public began to feel that he was bewildered, and that he was trying to be just a "me-too" in the cast of a play in which he had not rehearsed. His stock went down rather sharply.

Gradually, however, he appeared to be learning to stand on his own. Little by little the Gallup polls and other indications pointed to a rising popularity. Also he was becoming more used to the responsibilities of his office. Between the two, his confidence in himself and his enjoyment of power and responsibility increased. He began to become more President in his own right instead of just someone pledged to carry out the known policies —or unknown, like Yalta—of his predecessor.

Two things were possibly effect and cause of the change in his own attitude and that of the public. One was that during the year the remnants of the New Deal Cabinet were wiped out, and the other was Truman's position as to labor. Truman is, of course, friendly to labor, as most Americans are, but under the New Deal labor had, thanks to the administration and Congress, gradually been relieved of many of the legal restrictions placed on all other citizens. Congress sensed that public feeling was beginning to shift, and although Truman vetoed the Case Bill and some other strongly anti-labor acts, he ended the year with a knock-down-and-drag-out fight with John Lewis, some years back the pet of Roosevelt. The end is not yet, but Truman and the administration won the final round of 1946. It began to be evident that Truman was no longer the trustee, so to say, of the Roosevelt political estate, but President of the United States from Missouri, and popular polls indicated that the public acclaimed the change.

As to the Cabinet: On page 182 I noted the changes in the Truman administration to the end of 1945. There were two familiar figures remaining, Harold L. Ickes, Secretary of the Interior, and Henry A. Wallace, Secretary of Commerce. There were a number of "blow-outs," so to say, in both the Cabinet and the Supreme Court during the year.

The first was especially pungent, as Mr. Ickes always was. Ickes had been Secretary of the Interior for thirteen years, and had been an able and faithful public servant, although there were many, including myself, who were far from agreeing with all that he did. He was a self-styled "old curmudgeon," and it was a tribute to his underlying honesty of intention that many who did not like some of his acts or much of his language nevertheless accepted the title with a certain degree of genuine affection.

Truman had nominated Edwin W. Pauley, a man with large private interests in oil, to be Under-Secretary of the Navy, and a feud broke out between Ickes, who opposed the nomination, and the President. The public did not like the nomination too well either, for Teapot Dome still smelled. Without reflecting in the slightest on the personal integrity or capacity of Mr. Pauley, I may say that the suggested appointment seems to have been unwise; but the President stuck to it. Ickes insisted that there was a question raised between his own veracity and that of Truman, wrote an extremely caustic letter, and handed in his resignation, which was accepted. The change did not strengthen the administration, but it did mark another step away from its being the administrator of the Roosevelt household and four terms of office. The new Secretary was Julius A. Krug of Wisconsin, who still holds the position.

In June there was another shake-up. Truman made the nominations, later confirmed by the Senate, of Secretary of the Treasury Fred M. Vinson to become Chief

Justice of the Supreme Court succeeding the late Harlan F. Stone, which placed eight Democrats on the highest Court. He also nominated John W. Snyder to take Vinson's place as Secretary of the Treasury, and John J. Sullivan to the contested post of Under Secretary of the Navy.

Before going on to the last change in the former Roosevelt Cabinet, we may speak of another occurrence in June, perhaps the most unseemly row which the Supreme Court has ever offered to a public which has always had the highest respect for it. Justices Robert H. Jackson and Hugo L. Black attacked each other violently in the press. Such terms were bandied between them as "war," "weapons of the open warrior" and "stealthy assassin." I recall in history nothing like it. Both men were Roosevelt appointees. That President had had apparently little understanding of the function and high position of the Court, for in spite of some of the magnificent services he had rendered, he had suggested at times that the Justices consult him before handing down their decisions; he had tried to pack the whole Court so that it would interpret the Constitution as he wished, and had appointed men who had rendered party service rather than men who had had experience in the judiciary. So much was this true that in a number of cases Justices could not take part in decisions because in one way and another they had already been involved in the litigation before it reached the highest tribunal of the land. Justices are appointed practically for life, in spite of the talk of the "nine old men" when Roosevelt was trying to pack the Court, and that is one of the serious dangers to the people in the break from the two-term tradition established by Washington and maintained until 1940. We are supposed to have three branches of government—the Executive, Legislative, and Judicial, each acting as a possible check on the other. But if the Executive is elected for three, four (as Roosevelt) or more terms, the Judicial branch may be wholly appointed by one Executive, as it practically is now. It is interesting, however, to observe that men remain men, and that although Roosevelt appointed men who, he thought, would decide as he wanted, there have been more 4–5 decisions than before.

In September came the final important blow-up in the Cabinet. Henry Wallace had lived in the public eye and at public expense from 1933, when he had been made Secretary of Agriculture by Roosevelt. He has long been a center of controversy, and there was considerable opposition when in 1940 Roosevelt insisted on the Convention's naming him as his running-mate as Vice-President. He served in that office until 1945, but Roosevelt had consented to drop him and had run with Harry Truman. He was then made a member of the Cabinet as Secretary of Commerce; but there had been a row with Jesse Jones, and although the Commerce Department had presumably absorbed the R.F.C., of which Jones had been head, the Senate split the two when con-

227

firming Wallace. In 1946 there was the trouble with Ickes, Wallace, and Bowles. Then in September came the speech by Wallace at Madison Square Garden in favor of Russia and against Byrnes; it was what some journals called "the Wallace nightmare." The President fumbled the ball at first, but he had to stand by Byrnes. The public that had been treated to the squabble between two Justices of the Supreme Court, now witnessed that of two Cabinet members: the Secretary of Commerce attacking the Secretary of State. Wallace had to resign and his resignation was accepted. He is now editor of the left-wing *New Republic*. With his departure the Roosevelt Cabinet came to a complete end. Averell Harriman, previously ambassador to Great Britain, became the new Secretary of Commerce. It cannot be said that the New Deal was ended, but there was a new head of state, and new faces around his council board.

Meanwhile Congress had adjourned in the first week of August. In its seventy-ninth session the legislative body had made history and had also disappointed some hopes. The honeymoon of the accidental President and of Congress had somewhat come to an end the preceding September. During the session the President had submitted in all thirty-two major programs. Of these Congress went with him on ten, refused to follow on fifteen, and compromised with the White House on seven. The two important points were that it was no longer a rubber-stamp Congress that would take orders, and also that it had reversed a legislative trend of years in international affairs. The charter for the United Nations had been accepted, as well as our participation in that organization. The huge loan to Britain had been favorably acted on, and other international agreements made. If the old isolationism was not completely dead, it was evident that the people, through their representatives, had changed their course and embarked on the new responsibilities with which our tremendous influence in the War had saddled us. This time we did not scuttle; we tried to carry. Elections proved the changed temper, and that in the fall recorded a marked reversal from the previous sixteen years.

The election was an "off-year" one, but the total number of votes cast was 35,874,568 out of a possible total of voters over twenty-one of 91,634,472. It was not only an "off-year," but there was an enormous dislocation of votes due to changes in residence during the war and the forces which were still overseas. However, in comparison with the preceding "off-year," 1942, the 1946 vote showed an increase of nearly 6,500,000 ballots cast, which indicated interest. The Republicans outvoted the Democrats in thirty states with electoral votes of 362. The eighteen states in which the Democrats won have an electoral-college vote of only 169. The Republicans gained control of both Houses of Congress for the first time in fourteen years. This did not settle 1948, but it did indicate that the trend notable for several elections was continuing.

Truman accepted the defeat of his party, in what was a political landslide, with good grace. He indicated that for the good of the country he was anxious to work in harmony with a Congress controlled by his political opponents. All of these things—the winding up of the old New Deal Cabinet; the defeat, at least temporary, of the John L. Lewis who had first climbed to power by contributing $500,000 for the election of Roosevelt; Truman's increasing grasp of foreign affairs, his ready acceptance of his party's defeat in November—all contributed perhaps to the marked rise in his popularity from the low point to which he had fallen in popular esteem at the beginning of the year.

Although this account of 1946, in which the United States was playing a part in almost every quarter of the world, is necessarily inadequate, we can mention only a few more points with which to conclude it. This is, after all, only a chapter and not a book.

We may speak first of a matter not usually touched on in history—the weather, which Mark Twain once said every one talked about, no one did anything about. The winter of 1946–47 will long be remembered as the worst in two or three generations, particularly in Britain and on the continent of Europe. Blizzards blocked roads and railroads by snow; intense cold and floods and gales killed crops and vast numbers of domestic cattle, caused intense suffering, prevented distribution of food and fuel, especially coal for manufacturing, and in every way helped further to disrupt an already disrupted civilization. In a word, the weather increased our obligations to other suffering peoples, and added to the economic and political unrest everywhere. It seemed almost as though Heaven were punishing man for the horrors which he himself had let loose in the world since 1939.

At home our national debt had risen to fantastic figures, and, in spite of efforts to cut the cost of government, that too kept rising in the number of federal employees and their pay. There were, however, marked contrasts. The salary of the Chief Justice of the Supreme Court was raised from $20,500 to $25,000; the salaries of Congressmen from $12,500 to $15,000, and so on. But although office boys in government employ were raised from $1440 to $1690, there was no increase for the President of the United States from $75,000, for the Vice-President from $15,000, or for a member of the Cabinet from the same figure. The great democracy may figure that $75,000 is a large income, as it regards salaries of some of the executive heads of large corporations with great responsibilities, but it forgets the taxes and the necessary expenses attached to the job. Later in the year it was figured that after income taxes and such expenses as he *had* to pay for the White House (although the government pays some) the President of the United States had a "take home pay," as labor calls it, of $4500 a year. It is interesting to compare that with the huge fortunes in palaces, works of art and property of all sorts accumulated by a Hitler or by any other prominent man in a totalitarian state, including possibly Communist states.

Among the notable deaths of the year were Harry Hopkins, who had been Roosevelt's most confidential adviser; Senator Carter Glass of Virginia, who had been for a generation or more a leader in finance in the Senate; the retired Justice McReynolds of the Supreme Court; General Stilwell, who had won fame in the war in the Pacific and had built the Stilwell road to China; and "Jimmie" Walker, ex-Mayor of New York City.

On the whole the year ended in a gradual emergence from war to peace but with serious labor trouble behind us and more to come in 1947. Two things stood out. Democracy had proved its worth in the war, and we had made not only enormous but sudden and unexpected transitions from an old order to a new. We took the elections in our stride. We did not collapse when Roosevelt died. The ship of state sailed on, even though the waters were rough and stormy. Moreover, we seemed at last to have grown up and to be willing to assume our role as the most powerful country, or one of the two most powerful countries, in the world. The gradual collapsing of the old British Empire presaged a new world in which we should have to play a leading role. We had cause for pride as well as for anxiety.

CHAPTER VI

THE RECORD OF 1947

THE field to be covered by each of these Supplementary Chapters, as also the task of writing them, has increased enormously since in 1933 I undertook the first one in order to keep the original four volumes up to date. After World War I, and, specifically, with our refusal to participate in the League of Nations, we had turned our backs on the rest of the globe. Our thoughts were almost entirely concentrated upon ourselves within the forty-eight states, with an occasional uneasy glance at Alaska and our outlying island possessions.

In those earlier additional chapters, there were to be chronicled the great depression of the '30s; the glittering promises of the "New Deal"; and surprising developments in politics and constitutional government. The story of those years was not simple but, from our present viewpoint, extraordinarily local. Then 1939 brought the beginning of World War II and our history veered in an entirely new direction. The history of what happened I have tried to tell, year by year, as far as mere current reporting may be considered history.

With the Spanish War of 1898, we had become a great power, to be reckoned with by other nations, but we still went pretty much our own way. With World War I, we became a "world power," but afterward shied away from what that entailed. We emerged from World War II as the most powerful of all nations except as regards military man-power, in which Russia exceeded us. In wealth, in production of goods for peace or for war, in "know how" in techniques, in inventive ability and other elements of strength no one could any longer compete with us. There was another and tremendously fateful factor, fateful for ourselves and for the whole of world civilization. After World War II we did not "shy away." We are still a bit dizzy and overwhelmed by the responsibilities and obligations which we have found thrust upon us, but, with the exception of a comparatively small number of die-hard isolationists, both the people at large and their leaders have this time accepted our new position. Popular polls and congressional votes clearly indicate this.

The steady shrinking of the British Empire to which, in spite of its faults, the whole world, including ourselves, had looked in large part for international stability and security, political and financial, in the four quarters of the globe and on the Seven Seas, left vast vacuums which must be filled by some other nation capable of taking over with the same strength and the same ideas of human freedom, individualism and personal liberty. I do not mean that we have to step in and govern those peoples whom the Empire has freed from its own control, but we are called upon to stabilize in freedom the rapidly developing new world of independent and free nations, so that they shall not fall into a worse condition than before, thus endangering their own liberty and ours.

In our recent post-war history, perhaps the most important item is the fact that we have accepted the challenge of that job. The outstanding fact in the history of 1947, made clear by a multitude of continuing incidents, may well be this—that the U.S.A. and the U.S.S.R. have become the two giant nations contending with each other for determination of the future course of world history. On that we shall have more to say later on and may merely mention here that, though *we* have no desire to expand *our* limits, Russia, already the largest territorial unit on earth, most evidently proposes to expand *hers*.

A CARTOON COMMENT ON RUSSIA'S FOREIGN POLICIES
From a cartoon by Manning in *The Arizona Republic*.

Again, the difference is ideological—to use an ugly and clumsy current word. America has been made what she is by the traditions and the immigrants brought to this land from Britain and western Europe, and especially by their hopes of becoming free and independent with a chance to say and think what they wish and to make the most of themselves as men and women untrammelled, as far as that is possible, by government or by the chains of the past. Russia is a totalitarian police state. The events of 1947 have made that clear. The new world-alignment of powers has set new problems. That is why I quoted, in the chapter covering the preceding year, a sentence from an article by the President of Dartmouth: "There is no place, there is no subject, not touched by our concern." And so we begin this chapter with our world concerns rather than with our domestic ones.

In dealing with the former, it might be simpler to discuss them country by country or topic by topic, but a chronological treatment of the year's foreign affairs will, I think, give a better understanding of the complex and constantly shifting problems to which we have had to accustom ourselves. Two points may be mentioned first, as background.

Toward the beginning of the year, January 7, President Truman announced the resignation of the Secretary of State, James F. Byrnes, and the appointment of General George C. Marshall to succeed him. Although this would ordinarily call for comment in the section devoted to our domestic and political news, the center of gravity for America had so shifted toward international affairs that the unexpected change of the head of our State Department was news of the first importance not only to ourselves but to all the world. Although unexpected, the transfer of office was not, as some papers said, "sudden." Byrnes had long been an ill man and had wished for many months to be relieved of the strain of office. He had remained only at the repeated insistence of the President. Marshall while still in China had known of his own appointment but the secret had been well kept by all three men. The retirement of Byrnes was generally regretted, but the name of his successor was widely acclaimed both at home and abroad.

The Senate acted with unprecedented speed in confirming the nomination by unanimous acclamation. That a Republican-controlled Senate should so act on the nominee of a Democratic President was notice to the world that the country was, this time, wholly united in a bipartisan foreign policy. Politics appeared at long last to have "stopped at the water's edge." This was the more welcome inasmuch as at a time when we needed continuity and unity in our relations with the rest of the world Marshall was the fourth man within the space of twenty-five months to be in charge of them.

The second factor which we may mention as background was the United Nations. It might be thought, in view of the high hopes raised by its organization, that we could more or less follow international affairs through its proceedings as recorded during the year by press and radio. In fact, however, although it has started some important projects it has been too largely preoccupied with matters of procedure, organization, and, unfortunately, violent recriminations (mostly on the part of Russia and her satellite states) to serve the purpose of a guiding thread to our story. And now we shall start on our journey. It will take us to many far parts—parts to which, a generation or more ago, "American history" did not have to travel, except in the wake of business.

For the thirteen months before he flew home to become Secretary of State, General Marshall had been in China vainly trying to bring peace between the warring factions there. His Report to the President was not encouraging. In brief it stated that the Kuomintang party contained too many dyed-in-the-wool reactionaries and the Communist party too many dyed-in-the-wool Marxists, the latter determined to make all China Communist eventually. Each party completely distrusted the other although each contained very considerable liberal minorities. These minorities, however, were without cohesion, political experience, arms or other resources. Without American aid they could do little. The Americans have always been friends of China and were formerly popular there, but the propaganda of the Communists, in Marshall's official words, "has given plain evidence of a determined purpose to mislead the Chinese people and the world and to arouse a bitter hatred of Americans. . . . Sincere efforts to achieve settlement have been frustrated time and time again by extremist elements of both sides." This is part of what, in the preceding chapter, I called "unfinished business."

We shall mention later, under domestic affairs, the President's various messages to Congress, but may mention here his Proclamation of the last day of 1946, published in the news of January 1, 1947, which did in some ways mark a piece of finished business. Although its chief effect was on home legislation, even the straddle of dates is suggestive of the increasing straddle between what was becoming domestic and what foreign in our growing complexity. The Proclamation was brief, and declared, after a few words of introduction, that "although a state of war still exists, it is at this time possible to declare, and I find it to be in the public interest to declare, that hostilities have terminated."

The President emphasized that the "states of emergency" declared by Franklin Roosevelt in 1939 and 1941, and the state of war itself, had not been terminated. The last would presumably not be terminated until Congress had authorized peace treaties with the many belligerents. The declaration of a termination of hostilities, however, had the effect of terminating immediately eighteen statutes based on the use of that phrase and, within six months or at a later definite date, thirty-three others. Some were important and some had then ceased to be so, although in one case the declaration had involved the termination of $1,500,000,000 in taxes. The Proclamation seemed, nevertheless, to indicate that Truman was then willing to relinquish *some* of the swollen power which the Roosevelt administration had accumulated. It appeared also to suggest, in spite of certain technicalities of phrasing, that the time had come for peace-making and starting the world on the way toward reorganization and recovery.

A year has gone by since then and there has been no general peace conference like that of Vienna in 1815 or that of Paris in 1918–1919. However, a start was made with the completion, after fifteen months' work, of treaties between the Allies and (separately) five of the satellite states of Hitler—*viz.* Italy, Hungary, Rumania, Bulgaria and Finland. With the exception of Finland, with which the United States had not been at war, each treaty was negotiated between the individual enemy state and, on the side of the Allies, Russia, Great Britain and Northern Ireland, the United States, China, France, Australia, Belgium, the Byelorussian Soviet Socialist Republic, Brazil, Canada, Czechoslovakia, Ethiopia, Greece, India, Holland, New Zealand, Poland, the Ukrainian Soviet Socialist Republic, the Union of South Africa, and "the People's Republic of Yugoslavia." The list is interesting as indicating, even with the exclusion of Germany, Austria,

Japan and other nations which had participated in the struggle, not only the mondial character of the conflict but also the new geography of nations and peoples to which we have had to get accustomed.

The drafting was finally completed by the Foreign Ministers Council of the Big Four (the U.S.A., the U.S.S.R., Great Britain and France) in New York on December 12, 1946, but the texts of the five treaties were not made public until January 17, 1947. It was hoped that when signed in Paris they would make possible the early evacuation by the conquerors of some parts of Europe and ease the important task of drawing up peace treaties with Austria and Germany when the Big Four should meet in Moscow in March.

It is impossible to go into the details of the terms imposed in each case. (The texts of the treaties were published in full in *The New York Times* of January 18, and fill eleven newspaper pages of small print.) In general, they dealt with boundaries, reparations, and demilitarization. Italy gave up all claim to her African colonies, the future disposition of which was left to the Big Four; ceded territory to France, Greece and Yugoslavia; agreed to pay a total of $360,000,000 in reparations to Yugoslavia, Russia, Greece, Ethiopia, and Albania; her armed forces were cut to a nominal figure and the bulk of her navy was turned over to the Allies. The other treaties, with varying details, followed much the same pattern but provided that Allied troops should be withdrawn from Italy and Bulgaria within ninety days after the signing.

It is evident from a reading of the treaties that Russia

was building up herself and the former Hitler satellite states—now satellites of Russia—which she intended to

HOPING IT WILL HATCH
From a cartoon by Seibel in *The Richmond Times-Dispatch*.

absorb into her own system. It had been hoped, as we have said, that the work of the Big Four might ease the situation for the Moscow Conference, but there are some interesting points to be noted. Except for the radio "Voice of America" the one to two hundred millions of ordinary Russians are allowed to learn little or nothing of other countries and how conditions in them compare with those existing in the Soviet republics. "The iron curtain" is very real, and radios are so scarce that broadcasts reach only a small fraction of the people. Few foreigners are allowed to visit and move freely within Russia. For example, at the end of September Russia refused visas for passport entry to the American Assistant Secretary of State Peuifoy and ten Senators for the limited purpose of "Inspecting the American Embassy in Moscow," a purpose similar to that for which the group had already visited many countries. As was said at the time, it was "a distinct shock to State Department officials as well as to Congress." Russians are not permitted to travel, and therefore get their ideas from the officially allowed and controlled newspapers, notably *Iszvestia* and *Pravda.*

A fortnight or so before the opening of the Moscow Conference, *Pravda* had an editorial in which it stated that Russia, due to Soviet socialism and the genius of Stalin, had won the war "in single-handed combat unprecedented in history." It added that the Allies had delayed as long as possible so as to weaken Russia and had opened a second front only when Russia had already won against Germany and Japan. This would seem calculated to justify to the Russians their disproportionate demands when peace terms were being fixed. Also, just before the Moscow Conference an incident occurred in the United Nations which was another movement to justify Russia's huge annexations and demands for reparations.

With the Peace Treaty of Versailles in 1919 the system of "mandated territories" had been inaugurated. The mandated sections remained under the control of the League of Nations and were in no sense transferred as possessions to the nations receiving them but were held in trust, so to speak, under strict rules. Japan had received the mandate for many small islands in the western Pacific, which she had treated as her own and which proved to be important points in her secret and felonious attack on America. The United States asked the United Nations, as successor to the League of Nations, to award the mandate to us and to grant us exclusive air, naval and military rights over these strategic points for attack upon us. There were some objections voiced and, in view of the long-sustained verbal duel between Russia and the United States throughout the whole history of the U.N., it came as a surprise when Russia readily acquiesced. Apparently, however, the Kremlin wanted to make it appear that we were a partner with her in loot. The mandated islands had altogether a territory of only 846 square miles and a total population of 48,000. The islands belong to no nation but to the United Nations and, as Japan as mandator had broken all her pledges to the League, we asked to be allowed to take her place merely for our own safety and for the good of the inhabitants. We had just fulfilled our own pledge to give the Philippines, with 115,000 square miles and 16,000,000 people, complete independence, although obviously "independence" did not mean military strength, and we should still have the responsibility of standing behind them, should they be attacked. On the other hand, Russia, after the war, had taken

—as apparently accurately stated—more than 250,000 square miles belonging to other nations, with a non-Russian population of almost 25,000,000. By unanimous vote of the United Nations Security Council at Lake Success the Japanese mandated islands were placed under the trusteeship of the United States on April 2. The episode of Russian agreement with America, unexpected and unique, had its humorous aspects. With such incidents, and many others round the globe, the Moscow Conference opened.

The Conference started on March 10, its main object being to draw up peace treaties for Germany and Austria, although Molotov tried to make a démarche at the beginning with consideration of the Chinese Civil War. The Foreign Ministers of the Big Four who participated in the conference were Marshall (U.S.A.), Bevin (Great Britain), Molotov (U.S.S.R.), and Bidault (France).

We shall speak of the failure of the Conference but may mention first, in chronological order, two items tending toward stability. On March 4, a fifty-year treaty of alliance was signed between Great Britain and France within the framework of the U.N. charter "to prevent the recurrence of the German menace" and in no way forming a bloc against the Soviet. On the same day, President Truman, who had flown on the 2nd to Mexico City on a good-will visit to President Aleman, won all Mexican hearts and a tremendous ovation by placing a wreath at the national shrine to the band of youths who fell in the final attempt to defend their country during the battle of Chapultepec, in the war between Mexico and the United States, in 1848. This was said to have been suggested by the American Ambassador. However that may be, it was a gracious act of the sort which the proud and emotional Mexicans would and did appreciate to the full. In spite of the Marxists and other followers of that belief, history is not wholly determined by economics, and this simple act of chivalric friendliness had resounding effects which may last a long time, after a century of distrust on the part of our important southern neighbor. Aleman that evening hailed Truman as "the new champion of solidarity and understanding among the American republics."

And now back to the Conference at Moscow, which, although a failure in a sense, may have marked a turning-point in the history of our civilization. It dragged its way until the patience of all but the Russians, who were doing the dragging, was exhausted. Every question, even when it could finally be brought up for consideration, was deadlocked. For example, on one fundamental point the Coördinating Committee reports that "The United Kingdom and United States delegations do not agree to reparations from current production. . . . The acceptance of reparations from current production is an absolute condition of the Soviet delegation's acceptance of the principle of the economic unity of Germany." It is reported that Bidault said: "Where are we? God knows," and that Bevin answered: "Yes, and He isn't a member of the Council of Foreign Ministers."

So it went, with a number of amusing incidents, however, such as the Russians' giving a gala performance of the ballet on the night of the Greek Ambassador's dinner, in order to keep the members of the delegations away

245

from the latter, after the announcement had been made of Truman's plan for Greek aid. On April 23, Marshall assailed the Soviet Union for having blocked any possible peace treaty with Austria, as well as a four-power pact to keep Germany disarmed. Molotov denied the charges, and the Conference ended the next day.

On his return to Washington, after his Report to the President, Marshall spoke to the American people on the air (April 28) and said in part, "Agreement was made impossible at Moscow because . . . the Soviet Union insisted on proposals which would have established in Germany a centralized government, adapted to the seizure of absolute control." There had been very plain speaking and a full report. Moscow was no Yalta or Potsdam, and we now knew where we stood. No more evasions or secret compromises. "Bed rock," as the *Herald Tribune* called it, instead of the "quicksands" of the past. A new era in the relations between Russia and the West was opening, in which spades would become spades.

Even during the Conference, there came the first announcement of "The Truman Doctrine," which hustled the Russians into their invitation to the gala ballet mentioned above. On March 13, Truman presented before a Joint Session of the Houses of Congress a new foreign policy of vast possible import. He demanded that the Federal Government should have the right and the power to intervene in the affairs of other nations when their national integrity was threatened by Communism or other totalitarian ideologies. Specifically at the moment he asked for $400,000,000 to give economic and other aid to Greece and Turkey. Russia was not named as the menace but was clearly indicated.

The President pointed out that already we were seeing totalitarian regimes forced on such countries as Poland, Rumania, Bulgaria, while others were struggling to maintain their freedom of choice. "Greece," he added, "is today threatened by the terrorist activities of several thousand armed men, led by Communists," along its northern boundaries. The independence of Turkey was also being threatened, and, he went on, "Should we fail to aid Greece and Turkey in this fateful hour, the effect will be far-reaching to the West as well as to the East."

He made it plain that our move was not a threat to Russia but only to the unlimited expansion of the Soviet system and the forcing of its way of life on unwilling peoples. For more than a century, whether under the Czars or under the Communists, Russia had been trying to control the Dardanelles and to overrun the Balkans, Greece, Turkey and the Near East. She had been held off her neighbors time and again, notably in the Crimean War, largely by the British Empire and its occasional allies. As I have already noted, the Empire was no longer able to perform the duty of world policeman in maintaining a reasonable balance between the great powers.

The part of the world in question was of the utmost strategic importance for any single nation bent on domination of the world. The huge bulk of Russia was rolling on across all northern Asia to the Pacific, and across country after country in Europe which had never been in its possession. Its strength is in its inexhaustible reserves of docile man-power, whereas that of the United States is on the sea, in the air and in its inventiveness and high production. Nobody can roll back the masses of Soviet infantry. The one point from which we can exert pressure which will be recognized by the Kremlin is the eastern end of the Mediterranean. We did not go there, however, to attack Russia, but to protect free peoples in their right to live their lives independently and in their own way. The announcement of the so-called "Truman Doctrine" was in general well received by the American people and press, although it marked the most decisive swing from traditional isolationism since the Monroe Doctrine of 1823. In Congress the support was notably bi-partisan, the most bitter opposition coming not so much from the Republicans as from a small minority in the President's own party. The bill which implemented it by appropriating the $400,000,000 was passed toward the end of May and the "Doctrine" may be said to have been then accepted as an integral part of our foreign policy and a fateful step in the willingness of the United States to assume its grim task of defending the freedom of the human spirit wherever it might desire to be free. The future is on the lap of the gods.

There had been, as I have said, opponents to the plan, but we may concentrate on one, not only for the furor which he created in 1947 but for his probable prominence, if not importance, in 1948—Henry Wallace.

Wallace had been in the Cabinet of Franklin Roosevelt for about five years when Roosevelt forced his nomination as Vice-President, and he rode into office with his chief, who dropped him in 1944 in favor of Truman. Had Roosevelt's sudden death come earlier, Wallace might have been President now instead of Truman. The disappointment must have been bitter. He was made Secretary of Commerce, but the office was shorn of much of its power when he was confirmed by the Senate. Later, after an unseemly Cabinet row, his resignation was accepted and he became a free lance. He became also a bitter opponent of the Administration and its policies. In addition, he steadily and rapidly, judging by his speeches and writings, became a defender and friend of Communist Russia. He had often been used by the Communist official papers in Moscow to indicate that American "Liberals" (words no longer have any definite meaning) favor the Soviet regime. On one occasion, during the Moscow Conference, he advocated that America make a large "non-political" loan or gift to the Soviets to help restore their devastated regions.

In *The New York Times* of March 18 there was a full-page address by Wallace, apparently paid for by his backers, the "Progressive Citizens of America," in which he violently attacked the Truman plan for Greece and Turkey and said that Truman "proposed, in effect, that America police Russia's every border. There is no regime too reactionary for us, provided it stands in Russia's expansionist path."

On April 7, he took a plane for England for a European speaking tour. According to *Newsweek,* he was handed, as he left, a beautiful embossed scroll signed by such Americans as Senator Pepper, Louis Adamic, Guy Tugwell and Elliot Roosevelt—a "Henry Wallace Scroll of Greeting" to the liberals of Britain. Arrived, he at once launched into a fierce attack on America. He accused us of wanting to stretch an American empire round the globe. He even called America's course "a wild and mad nightmare of ruthless imperialism." He said that "no

powerful idea—and Communism is a powerful idea—
can be countered by a gun." The comment in America
was hot. In the Senate, both Democrats and Republicans denounced him. For example, Senator Vandenberg
(Rep.), head of the Foreign Relations Committee, said,
"it is a shocking thing when an American goes abroad
to organize the world against his own government"; and
Senator McClellan (Dem.) of Arkansas said, "I wonder
if he [Wallace] is not trying to establish himself as a
favored Communist Quisling." Having been, by the grace
of Roosevelt, Vice-President for four years and a Cabinet
member for many, his name carried more weight in
Europe—never too well posted on American domestic
politics—than it did at home. There was talk of a cancelling his passport or of proceeding against him under the
Logan Act, but a longer length of rope was decided on.

In the spring, came the further shrinking of the British
Empire by a complete withdrawal from Burma and India. India at once split into three parts—the present state
of "India," Pakistan and the Princely states—with ensuing bloodshed and terror.

Throughout the year we continued to try to enforce
the treaty with Russia regarding Korea. That little but
very important nation on the Pacific had been promised
independence, with the right freely to choose its own
form of government, but meanwhile it had been split
into northern and southern parts, the first occupied by
the Russians and the latter by the Americans. There was
constant friction between the Communists in the one part
and the Americans in the other, and Russia consistently
blocked all efforts to carry out the promises made to the

Korean people, even to the extent of refusing to allow a delegation of the United Nations to inspect the Russian zone. The deadlock continued into 1948 and we need not go into the details here. We may note, however, that for Russia the importance of little Korea was largely in relation to Soviet plans for controlling the great Chinese province of Manchuria, a territory approximately as large as France and Germany taken together. Manchuria is the most highly industrialized part of China and also extremely rich in such raw materials as coal, iron ore and oil. There are possibilities there of eventually far greater production than in our own Pennsylvania-Great Lakes section.

From time to time Russia was accused of not living up to her agreements in other nations, and on June 5 Truman denounced as "an outrage" and a breach of the Yalta agreement her actions in Hungary, where the government was overthrown with Soviet connivance. The State Department was more guarded in expression, but a strong note of protest was forwarded.

On the same day that the President denounced Russia, Americans got their first view of what has come to be known as "the Marshall Plan," a project of enormous importance. At Harvard, where he had gone to receive an honorary degree of Doctor of Laws, the Secretary of State made a historic speech.

After endorsing the statement made by Truman at Washington earlier in the day to the effect that our aid to Europe was necessary, Marshall added that Europe "must have substantial additional help or face economic, social and political deterioration of a very grave character." He went on to say that help should no longer be on a "piecemeal basis," but that the initiative must come from the countries of the Old World in drafting their needs and in evincing among themselves a spirit of union and cooperation, and that then we would help as far as we could. He denied that the United States would foist a plan on any country that was unwilling to accept it or that the plan was directed against "any country or doctrine," but he added significantly that we would give no aid to "any government which manœuvres to block the recovery of other countries," and that any which sought to benefit politically by perpetuating human misery would meet "the opposition of the United States." In a brief but extremely lucid speech he pointed out the completeness of the breakdown of the European economy in such matters as currencies, investments, banks, insurance companies, exchange between the industrial and the food-raising sections, and called attention to a vast complexity of factors which were retarding recovery and confidence and were even more important than was the obvious physical destruction of machinery, buildings, railroads and the loss of manpower.

Meetings were held in Europe and the plan gradually took shape. In his Harvard speech, Marshall had said that the extraordinary complexity of the interlocking problems and the mass of facts presented to the public would confuse its judgment, but as discussion continued in Congress, in the press and everywhere else, the unanimity in favor of some such form of help was not only remarkable but another indication that Americans were growing up to a comprehension and acceptance of what the Secretary called "the vast responsibility which history has clearly placed upon our country." The amount suggested as necessary gradually grew to $18,000,000,000 to be distributed over a five-year period, with the deadline for beginning set as April 1, 1948. The final action of Congress with regard to this project will be recorded in next year's chapter.

June 5 was a day of historic importance. On that day, in addition to the items already mentioned, the Senate confirmed treaties with four countries—Italy, Hungary, Bulgaria and Rumania. The first was passed by a roll-call vote of almost 8–1, and the others without a call but by an almost unanimous shout. As proof of the bi-partisan character of our present foreign policy, which I have noted as indicating a most amazing change in our political climate, there is the fact that the treaty with Italy, presented by a Democratic President, was voted for by 42 Republicans and 32 Democrats. We had come a long way from the days of Wilson and 1919.

For centuries the problem of the Jews has been an extraordinary one, affecting both themselves and the peoples among whom they have lived. It is impossible to discuss it here in all its controversial aspects. All that we can do in the space at our disposal is to comment on the question of Palestine, one of the most difficult among the political and racial puzzles of our time. The Zionist movement, which claimed that the Holy Land was the "Homeland" of the Jews, has been active in various forms for a long period, but it may be noted that even now not all Jews are united in favoring it. There are able Jewish leaders and Rabbis who are opposed to it. I know of no other problem which involves such a complex play of forces of all kinds—racial, economic, political, passionately emotional, and others—as that of Palestine. It was coming to a head in 1947 and we have no idea to what it may lead. It is beyond our scope here to go into the bloody events already occurring in 1948. In the case of so complicated and controversial a subject, we must, however, outline the background of the past few years.

During the latter part of World War I Britain signed the ambiguous Balfour Declaration to the effect that she would "facilitate . . . establishment in Palestine of a national home for the Jewish people . . . it being understood that nothing shall be done which may prejudice the . . . rights of existing non-Jewish communities in Palestine." (Lord Balfour was an interesting philosopher but by no means adept at drawing up intelligible State Papers.) When, after the Peace and the formation of the League of Nations, the system of Mandates came into effect, Britain received, though not too willingly, the Mandate for Palestine, and the full-of-trouble pledge of Balfour was written into the Mandate. Although any account of this problem is "charged with dynamite" and likely to suit nobody, it would appear that, as compared, for example, with the complete disregard by Japan of her pledges for the Pacific islands mandated to her, the British had done their best to carry out the difficult and fuzzy-worded Mandate given to her. (In the post-war world after World War I, the United States, although asked to do so, had refused to assume responsibility for any Mandate.)

When, early in 1946, the League of Nations voted itself out of existence it passed a Resolution that League members holding Mandates should "continue to administer until other arrangements have been agreed upon between the United Nations and the respective mandatory powers." Britain was anxious to be relieved of the responsibility and obligation to solve an almost insoluble problem and, after consultations with the United States and other nations, which led to no solution, Britain, in May 1947, laid the matter before the United Nations, with a request to report in September.

Meanwhile, as far back as 1939, when war was again threatening in Europe, Britain had restricted Jewish immigration into Palestine to 75,000 over a five-year period, although after the war she raised it to 1500 a month. At the time of the hearing before the U.N. it was estimated that there were 1,300,000 Jews on the European continent who had survived the Nazi terror. The Jews and Arabs were represented, the former by Rabbi Silver and the latter by Henry Cattan, a lawyer from Jerusalem. Silver spoke of the "desperate urgency" of the human problem of increasing the immigration quota, whereas Cattan said that linking the refugee problem with that of Palestine would make "both problems infinitely more difficult." Meanwhile Jews embarking from ports, usually not named in the newspapers, were trying to enter Palestine against regulations, and were often intercepted by the British and taken to camps in Cyprus. The situation became increasingly tense.

A little more background is called for. One estimate of the time placed the number of Arabs at 1,200,000 and the number of Jews who had been there, or who had recently entered, at 600,000. Viewed historically or otherwise, who, after two thousand years or more, can be said to hold title to all or even part of the Holy Land? Also, it was later said that the Soviet was sending Jews and, with them, Communist agents. We have spoken of the "vacuums" left by the withdrawal of the British Empire from various strategic parts of the world. To mention *oil* is to suggest machinations on the part of that pet bugaboo of the demagogue, "Big Business." But the fact remains that at the eastern end of the Mediterranean, in the Near East, are the greatest reserves of oil outside those in Russia and the dwindling ones in the United States. Oil is not just "big business," as a large part of America, with its oil-burners, its motor age and its planes, has discovered during the last few years, and if our supply, as some alarmists predict, will be used up in twenty-four years, what becomes of our whole life? Also, if Russia moves into the Near East and adds its oil reserves to her own, how could we defend ourselves in war? Again, the Arabs are not just "Arabs." They could set the whole Moslem world against Western civilization. The leader of the Arab Higher Committee, organized in 1936, was the Grand Mufti of Jerusalem, who fled from Palestine to Berlin during the war because of his Nazi sympathies and is now directing policy from Cairo, though Mr. Cattan spoke for him at the U.N. When I mention oil it is not because I believe in the economic interpretation of history. The Arabs threatened a "holy war," and that is something different and equally important.

One or two more points. There are about 40,000,000 Arab sympathizers in Arab League countries. If it came to a complete instead of a sniping and guerrilla war, it is quite obvious who would be wiped out. It would not be the 40,000,000 Arabs, unless the United States and other nations became engaged in war against them on the grand scale. It would be the Jews. The Arabs and Americans have always been friendly. The Arabs have regarded us as helping them toward democratic ways and a higher standard of education and living. Yet they are now turning against us in bitterness because, under Truman, the United States took the lead most energetically in inducing the Assembly of the U.N. to vote for the partition of Palestine.

Here oil comes in again. It is the greatest, and an enormous, asset of the Arabs. They *have* to sell it to get the money to import modern machinery. They had planned to make a two-way trade with the United States, and on November 7 Truman, in his Report on Foreign Aid, counted on getting from the Near East 15 per cent of the oil called for by the Marshall Plan. If we go to war with the Arab League, Russia will step in and get the oil, in exchange for Communism, although, as I have said before, we are committed to hundreds of millions of dollars of expenditure in Greece and Turkey to protect the Near East *from* being overrun. The Palestine problem is extremely complex, as complex as human nature itself. We Americans like simple answers, but there are some world problems to which there are none.

To conclude the record as regards Palestine during the year 1947, we mention the meeting of the General Assembly of the U.N. on November 29 at which it was voted, 33 to 13, with ten abstentions and with Siam absent, to partition Palestine into two states, one Jewish and one Arab. The Arab delegates walked out of the meeting. For once, Russia voted with the United States in favor of the plan but with some uncertainty as to just what they meant to do in the future. The intricate problem of the boundary lines between the two states was postponed. There are 4,770,000 Jews in the United States, of whom 2,035,000 are in New York City, and New York State has the largest vote of any in the Presidential Electoral College. The whole problem has an almost infinite number of angles, and we must now leave it until we come to the record for the year 1948.

During 1947, the Palestine question was perhaps the most discussed of all international problems which might bring on war. Otherwise, what was important was precisely what was *not* done and—to make an Irish "bull"— *how* it was done. For the most part, it was a year of almost complete frustration for the U.N. I recall no other case in history of international meetings where the leading figures of great and small nations poured out such a torrential volume of scurrilous, insulting and mendacious adjectives and nouns without war resulting. Perhaps that in itself was something. Perhaps time will bring an improvement in manners. The Russians won the prize with the almost unbelievable remarks of such men as Gromyko, Vishinsky, Molotov and others, but even they were outdone by the Yugo-Slav, Dr. Bebler, who threw into the delicate negotiations over Greece, and over what the Balkan states were doing, such mollifying terms as "assassination," "quislings and traitors," "a slanderous and infamous document," and added that those who had reported on the situation were "without shame." As the Belgian Prime Minister Paul-Henri Spaak observed, "If the force of an orator can be measured by the number of his insults, Dr. Bebler has reached the summit of eloquence."

Fortunately, in spite of provocation during the two sessions held—one regular and the other a special one called to consider Palestine—representatives of other member powers kept their discussions of affairs on a higher level. Russia, nevertheless, and her satellite states, managed to block almost all progress toward world settlement. Only once has there been practical unanimity. Vishinsky had been vitriolically denouncing as war-mongers the United States, Great Britain, and many of their leading statesmen, as well as other countries such as Greece. He had presented a resolution denouncing in especial "war-mongering in the United States, Greece and Turkey," but feeling ran high and, for once, there was a unanimous vote of 56–0 on a compromise denouncing "war-mongering" by any country.

The veto power, however, was the strong weapon of the Soviet. When the U.N. was formed, the four great nations insisted on a power of veto and it is likely that we ourselves would not have joined with an indefinite number, possibly before long more than seventy, of small and many of them powerless nations, if we had had to be completely controlled by their collective decisions, with no right on *any* occasion to say "No." The veto power, however, was expected to be used very sparingly by anyone, and only *in extremis*. In 1946, the United States and Britain used it twice, but they have not used it since then.

France has used it only once. Russia, during the two years, has used it *twenty-two* times. This has very definitely clogged the machinery of what was intended to be an instrument for the adjustment of world problems and for the maintenance of peace, but which has largely become an amazing world sounding-board for speeches made by representatives of the Soviet and its satellite nations.

In September, Secretary Marshall had proposed that there be a limitation of the veto power and that a "Little Assembly" of the U.N. be set up to remain in session and to prod the Council into action. Vishinsky replied in a violent speech of more than an hour and a half, denouncing the United States as preparing for a Third World War "to satisfy the limitless desires of its influential circles . . . which is the crazy idea of world domination." Nevertheless, after a tempestuous session, on November 6 the American plan for the "Little Assembly" was voted 43–6, with six abstentions. Russia and her satellites said they would boycott it and they have done so ever since.

Without entering upon the details of other and minor matters we must note that throughout the year it was the constant opposition by Russia to plans proposed by the other great powers which has thus far prevented any settlement of the problem of control of the atomic bomb in war. Incidentally, in an unexpected move which surprised all the Allied capitals, Russia suddenly signed peace treaties with five former satellites of Germany— Italy, Rumania, Hungary, Bulgaria and Finland—with all of which (except for Finland, with which, as I have noted above, none of the Allies other than Russia had been at war) treaties had already been signed by the others of the Big Four, in Paris, February 10.

We may now mention, much more briefly, certain other world matters which were a part of our history in 1947.

On June 30, after four years of service, the United Nations Relief and Rehabilitation Administration, commonly known as U.N.R.R.A., came to its legal end. It had spent nearly $3,000,000,000, of which the United States had contributed 72 per cent. The seventeen countries receiving food, clothing and other supplies had been Albania, Austria, China, Czechoslovakia, Hungary, Finland, Korea, Yugoslavia, Greece, Italy, Poland, White Russia, the Ukraine, San Marino, the Philippine Republic, the Dodecanese Islands and Formosa.

On August 14, we crossed off from Italy's account with us approximately $1,000,000,000 of war debt and also lightened her burden in other ways, such as freeing $60,000,000 worth of blocked property and returning to her 28 of her captured freight ships. In October, the first comprehensive report of our foreign relief was made by a Joint Congressional Committee. It disclosed that *since* the war the United States had contributed between $19,000,000,000 and $20,000,000,000 to other peoples, and the Marshall Plan still lay ahead for possibly as much again. In spite of Russian gibes and opposition, representatives of sixteen Western European nations met at Paris, July 12, to develop a plan for cooperating in their own relief and in working out the necessary machinery for carrying out the plan. Russia objected as far as she was able, but this time she had no veto power. Molotov claimed that the plan was aimed at destroying the independence of sovereign nations and wished the money to be given to each or any nation, individually, for such purposes as it might choose, including political ones. The Paris Conference of the Big Four, to which we shall refer later, had just ended disastrously and the split between East and West was plainer than ever, but while speaking of American aid in its various forms and amounts we shall conclude by recording the meeting of the sixteen nations who welcomed the Marshall Plan.

With reference to Russia's claim that the plan would destroy independence of action among the nations which accepted it, it is illuminating to note that she quite brazenly denied independence of action to her satellites. For example, although Russia was twice asked to attend the Conference but refused, all her vassal states were also invited. The Moscow radio announced that Finland, Rumania and Poland had rejected the invitation, yet all three nations denied this. Almost immediately, however, they *did* decline. Hungary accepted and, later, sent "regrets." Czechoslovakia accepted officially on a Monday. On Wednesday its Communist Premier and its Foreign Minister, Jan Masaryk, flew to Moscow, were talked to by Stalin in the Kremlin and, the next day, a Czech official communiqué declined the already accepted invitation with the comment that participation in the Conference by Czechoslovakia "could be interpreted as an act directed against its friendship with the Soviet Union and our other allies." In view of the evident desire of at least five of the satellite nations to participate in the discussions and share in the benefits of the American plan, it may be asked who was interfering with their sovereignty and freedom of action?

We have still to consider three other international con-

THE "RED" HERRING
From a cartoon by Marcus in *The New York Times*.

ferences which carry American history of 1947 to France, Brazil and Britain.

The Paris Conference was called during the first week of July, with invitations to practically every European country, except Franco's Spain, to consider some form of coördinated self-help as a preliminary to the Marshall

Plan. The United States was purposely not represented because its turn would come if Europe decided favorably. After five short sessions that conference ended in complete failure. The Foreign Ministers of Britain, France and Italy laid down principles which would lead the Old World out of its post-war morass and re-establish an economic basis for recovery and for a continuance of the peaceful development of European life and culture. The Eastern European nations, now under control of Russia, would normally exchange their goods with the West, but the iron curtain fell, and on July 13, in one hour, against the eloquent pleas of Bevin, Bidault and Sforza, Molotov divided the world into two parts. Including, to look ahead to February 1948, the coup d'état of that month in Czechoslovakia, the Soviet Dictators, who called themselves the "People's Government," had added to the Soviet control 650,000 square miles of land and roughly 110,000,000 people formerly outside Russia. The countries overrun and annexed were Czechoslovakia, Esthonia, Latvia, Lithuania, Yugoslavia, Albania, Poland, Bulgaria, Rumania and Hungary. The split was complete but for the sixteen nations, which met in Paris in July and, on September 22, signed an agreement in the free desire to use the Marshall Plan. With the help of the United States, which I have just detailed, they showed that European civilization and hopes were not all dead.

While the sixteen Western European nations were holding their fateful meetings in Paris, another conference was being held in the New World with the same aim of protecting life, as we have known and enjoyed it, from destruction by primeval forces.

This meeting had been provided for in the Act of Chapultepec (see previous chapter). Its official title was "the Inter-American Conference on the Maintenance of Peace and Security," but it is generally referred to as "the Rio Conference," because it was held at Petropolis, a small town near Rio de Janeiro, Brazil, and the beautiful city of Rio is much better known than its small suburban neighbor, Petropolis. The official title of the Conference would conceivably have accommodated almost any topic which a constructive or obstructive delegate might have wished to have placed on the agenda, but the main object had happily always been understood and was firmly adhered to. That object was to draw up a formal treaty or agreement for union in American hemispheric defense. Truman, as already noted, had on his Mexican trip made a most happy impression on our proud South American neighbors, and when on September 1 he arrived at Rio by plane from Washington to take part in the closing sessions of the most friendly and important Conference ever held among the American nations, he was given a great ovation by a crowd of Brazilians estimated at 1,000,000. The following day, September 2, a pact was signed by representatives of nineteen American nations, including, of course, the United States, to protect one another mutually in case any one of them were attacked.

On December 8, the United States Senate ratified the Treaty by a vote of 72–1, the sole dissenter being Senator Millikin (Rep.) of Colorado. The treaty took into consideration the Charter of the United Nations, and the contracting parties agreed, in accordance with the terms of the Charter, not to resort to the threat or use of force among themselves and also to consider an armed attack against one American state as an attack against all, and then immediately to employ the best means of repelling such an attack, though no state was to be forced to use arms without its consent.

Meanwhile, in our quest for American history during 1947, we have to make one more trip to the Old World before settling down to record domestic politics and other home affairs.

On November 25, there was a meeting of the Foreign Ministers of the Big Four in London. Throughout the preceding months, relations between Communist Russia, Western Europe and the Americas had been steadily worsening, not only because of the almost obscene attacks, especially on the United States, by Russians or representatives of her puppet states in the U.N., but also on account of increasingly outrageous statements from the Kremlin and by so-called Russian statesmen. The main objects, supposedly, of the Conference were to resolve the problems which were preventing the long overdue peace treaties, especially those with Germany and Austria, and thus the restoration of peace and of some sort of political and economic order to Europe.

The long-drawn-out overture, so to say, had not been promising. It had been becoming more and more obvious that Russia, for its own purposes, did not wish peace or prosperity in the world at large. That is not the environment in which world revolution flourishes. The crescendo of vilification had been rising steadily until it finally called forth from our long-suffering Secretary of State,

George Marshall, such remarks, in his now famous speech at Chicago on November 18 (less than a week before his leaving for London), as: "The clarity of the record and of our intentions, however, has not prevented Soviet officials and Communist groups elsewhere from waging with increasing venom a calculated campaign of vilification and distortion of American motives in foreign affairs. These opponents of recovery charge the United States with imperialist design, aggressive purposes, and finally with a desire to provoke a third world war. I wish to state emphatically that there is no truth whatsoever in these charges, and I add that those who make them are fully aware of this fact."

The same thing went on in London. By the middle of December, it was obvious that the Conference would get nowhere. In demanding enormous reparations from Germany, Russia, without admitting the vast additions to her own population, resources and territory, acquired by stealing from others, made fantastic statements about the huge sums which the other powers had made out of the war. Marshall made an angry reply, not only denying Molotov's statements but stating that Molotov himself knew that they were not true. Bevin, Foreign Minister of the British Labor Government, and Bidault, Foreign Minister of France, were equally furious.

Three weeks after it had begun, the Conference "adjourned indefinitely." It was more than the temporary winding up of a meeting. It was the break-up of the brittle war alliance, the splitting of East and West, evidence that the three Western nations can confer, compromise and agree but that Russia does not suggest but only demands and makes those demands in lying and insulting terms. There was no use going on. Several small items remained to be swept into the dust-pan. Vishinsky had declared that Russia was so strong militarily that no other power could stand against her. Russia cut the nominal value of her war bonds (to which she had forced her citizens to subscribe) by two thirds, and the value of the ruble (the standard coin) by 90 per cent. The Government paper, *Iszvestia,* speaking of the belief in certain countries that Czechoslovakia could be a "bridge between East and West," commented that "they forget that in a vital struggle there can be no middle position." In less than two months we were to learn what had so obviously been meant by that. And now we may return from our journeyings, to see what 1947 has been like within the United States itself.

If, in 1947, international affairs loomed larger in proportion to our domestic ones, it was because never before in our history had we been so involved with the entire world and, also, because, for reasons we shall at once relate, in home politics it was a year of "slack water." It was not a Presidential election year nor even an "off" election year. The year 1944 had been a resounding Presidential one politically, with a President, for the first time in our history, nominated and elected for a fourth term. We must go back to that for a moment, to understand the Truman term.

The long tradition handed down to us from the days of Washington and of Jefferson, both of whom inveighed against even a third term, was, it is now fairly evident, broken in the case of Franklin Roosevelt because the party leaders and the electorate believed he was the only man who, from his knowledge as Commander-in-Chief and his personal international ties with other world leaders throughout the greatest struggle in which we had ever been engaged, could carry on to a successful conclusion. The war and the possible peace appeared to be all that mattered. It was not a fourth term for the New Deal, as the dumping of Wallace for the Vice-Presidency, and the by-election of 1946 clearly showed. It was the war, and the experience and connections of the man who had thus far seen it through, which made possible this complete break with American tradition and even with our theory of constitutional government. It had never been envisioned, for example, that any Chief Executive, by serving for sixteen or more years, would be the appointer of practically the entire judiciary branch of the government, including the whole of the Supreme Court.

It came about, nevertheless, but when, in April 1945, the President suddenly died and the war with Japan, Germany and the other Axis Powers ended a few months later, Roosevelt's successor, Truman, was left dangling. The war, to conduct which the nation had elected Roosevelt, was over. The peace was indeed still to be made but, after one attempt at Potsdam, Truman gave up the Roosevelt rôle with respect to that. His experience as Vice-President, merely a presiding officer of the Senate and not a member of the Cabinet, had left him unprepared for it. He had not been elected to carry on the policies of the New Deal. Like the man in the old story of "Japhet in Search of a Father," where was he to turn? The public had been sympathetic toward him in his sudden elevation to an extraordinarily difficult position. He himself appeared willing to try to work with a Congress controlled by the opposite party. The year seemed to promise as well as could be expected.

That promise, however, was none too good. Truman's personal popularity and prestige were nothing like what Roosevelt's had been. Let us look at the beginning of 1947. The Presidential election was due in 1948. It was unfortunate, but in our American political system that fact is bound to have its deflecting influences. A national election, after sixteen years of one-party, almost one-man, rule acted for many like a bar of iron held near a magnetic compass. When Roosevelt had been elected for his fourth term, Congress had been safely Democratic:

The Senate		The House	
Democrats	56	Democrats	241
Republicans	39	Republicans	192

The set-up of the 80th Congress was quite different:

The Senate		The House	
Democrats	45	Democrats	187
Republicans	51	Republicans	245

The war in Europe was twenty months behind us; that in the Pacific, sixteen. The Presidential election was only twenty-two ahead. There was, due to the accident of death, a Democratic President in the White House; a Supreme Court of whom eight of the nine had been appointed by one Democrat by reason of the accident of unprecedented tenure of office; a Congress, after sixteen years in the wilderness, overwhelmingly of the opposite party. The entire situation was explosive and, to say the least, difficult for all. That it worked out even as well as it did is a high tribute to the American way of life.

The new Congress was quickly organized and, in general, with a minimum of disharmony. In the Senate, Senator Vandenberg of Michigan was elected President *pro tempore,* and became also chairman of the immensely important Committee on Foreign Relations. In the House, Representative Martin of Massachusetts was named Speaker. In these cases, as in most others, there was full harmony, and in those in which there was some bitterness it could be ascribed to the already advancing shadows of the presidential election of the coming year. Before beginning to recount political events in their chronological order, we may skip for a moment to the summer. At that time, an event occurred which materially changed the possible positions of Vandenberg and Martin in political history.

As had happened a number of times before, the death of a President and the succession of the Vice-President had left the Senate without its presiding officer and the office of President without an elected successor. Since 1886 it had been legally provided that, if both the President and the Vice-President should die, or be otherwise unable to serve, the line should run down the list of members of the Cabinet in the chronological order in which their departments had originally been established —that is, from State, Treasury, and so on, down. There had been many flaws in this arrangement. For example, a Secretary of State, who might have held office for a day only, might become President in place of some other Secretary who had been a Cabinet member for many years. Moreover, Cabinet members are appointees of the President and are not elected by the people. Truman had brought up the question a number of times and the bill he suggested was passed by the Senate on June 27, 1947. It provided that, regardless of party, the first in order of succession to a deceased President and Vice-President should be the Speaker of the House of Representatives, next the elected President-pro-tem of the Senate, and then on down the list of Cabinet officers.

This plan had many advantages. It would not only make the first successor to the two Presidents, in case both should die, a man who had been elected by the people but, as Representatives are elected every two years and Senators only every six, the succession of the Speaker of the House would bring the possible President, at the time of his accession, still nearer to the people.

It must be credited to Truman that he stuck to his idea in spite of the fact that the election had brought it about that both of his possible successors were Republicans. That, however, under certain circumstances, might well be a great advantage, and Truman in this case was working on a high constitutional and not on a merely political plane. He and his predecessor had both been able to do this on occasion, and with far better results than those achieved by the narrow partisanship of Wilson. Before the war, the appointment by Roosevelt of Stimson and Knox, both Republicans, as Secretaries respectively of War and the Navy, had undoubtedly greatly helped the war effort when it came. So also, under Truman, the constant use of the Republican and Democratic Senators, Connally and Vandenberg, undoubtedly helped to form a consistent and dependable bi-partisan foreign policy. On July 10, the House passed the Succession Bill by a vote of 365 to 11. Passed by the Senate, and with the signature of the President assured, an important step had been taken in our constitutional development and stability. The remainder of our domestic political chronicle was, for the most part, of a more ordinary sort.

At the opening of the 80th Congress the personnel and political complexion of that body had largely altered and there were many new faces in other parts of Washington, due to actual or immediately impending resignations, such as that of Bernard Baruch and his able aides, who had been dealing with the atomic bomb situation; Eugene Meyer and Harold Smith as President and Vice-President of the International Bank; former Ambassador Winant as American member of the U.N. Economic and Social Council; Dean Acheson as Under Secretary of State; Admiral Leahy as Chief-of-Staff to the President; and others.

Moreover, due partly to the political set-up and partly to recent legislation, the nature of the President's Message to Congress at the opening of the year had also changed. In fact, for the first time, there now had to be three Messages. The first was the one which had always been known as "the President's Message," and which has been sent or, rarely, read in person, to Congress by the President ever since the days of George Washington. The Constitution provides that the President "from time to time shall give to the Congress information of the State of the Union, and recommend . . . such measures as he shall judge necessary and expedient." Purely as a matter of

273

custom, every President, annually, immediately after Congress convenes, has sent an elaborate message and this is considered "the state of the Union" message, although during the course of a year there may be many more special messages. Now, however, two more are specifically required—the Annual Economic Report called for by the Employment Act of 1946, and a Message on the Budget also required by special Act.

Truman had already declared that hostilities in the Second World War had ceased and, with them, many of his own special powers. A few days later, on January 6, he appeared personally before Congress to deliver the first of his required three Messages.

Certain facts and figures would be contained in the other messages that were to follow. For a Democratic Executive speaking, for the first time in sixteen years, to a Republican-controlled legislature the tone and attitude were more important than precise recommendations as to what he might "judge necessary and expedient." Although somewhat vague regarding practical details, the Message seemed more evenly balanced in its reference to the need for capital and labor to work together to make the free-enterprise system function than had been some of the later New Deal pronouncements. Truman asked that industry reduce prices wherever possible; that labor refrain from unjustified wage boosts; that everything be done to bring about a high production of peacetime goods; that some reforms be made in labor practices; and he was conciliatory in his attitude, as a Democratic Executive, to his Republican Legislature. A honeymoon seemed a possibility.

On January 8 came the second of the Messages, the first of the Reports required by the Act of 1946—the Report on Economic Conditions. Under that Act, a permanent Council of Economic Advisers had been created to assist the President, and a Joint Committee of the two Houses of Congress to consider it. The theory had been that not only would the President have a continuing body of experts but that Congress would have a guide for the growing number of committees created for the steadily expanding functions of big government. To what extent the multifarious forms of private enterprise in a nation of some 145,000,000 people, spread over 3,000,000 square miles at home, and in more or less responsible contact with almost every corner of the globe, can be wisely guided by a small group of so-called experts, and by Congressional committees, remains to be seen. So far, all that we can say is that the reports, forecasts, and actions of these have been somewhat confused. Some experts have been afraid of inflation, some of deflation, some predicted a near boom and some a bust, some even foresaw that, some months hence, 8,000,000 would be unemployed when, actually, we came to have 60,000,000 gainfully employed, the record number on the country's pay-roll. In any case, the Report was made.

The next of the three Presidential Messages now required, by statute or by custom, at the beginning of a Session was that on the Budget. This, although the President insisted it was "realistic," was also somewhat confusing. He estimated the expense of government for the ensuing fiscal year at $37,500,000,000, with receipts of $37,700,000,000, which would permit a "surplus" of

$200,000,000. With figures so vast and unpredictable on either side of the ledger, the small "surplus" hardly appeared "realistic." We say "unpredictable" because, only a year before, the President, in consultation with his advisers, had said that the expenditures of the Government during the second year after the war would run to only $35.1 billions and now, in the third year, he asked for between $2 and $2.5 billions more. Moreover, in October 1946 he had stated that the budget would, according to his figures, be balanced by June 30, 1947, whereas there promises to be a deficit of well over 2.3 billions and, if the Government figures had not underestimated income by $8.7 billions, the deficit would have been over $11 billions! Yet to get a "surplus" now of only $200,-000,000 he estimated that business during 1947–48 would be much better, despite many estimates to the contrary. He also asked for "a prompt expansion of the Social Security system" and a much larger contribution by the Federal Government to the State Governments, for education.

Apart from the specific increases asked for, he had stated that the cost of government could not be reduced, although in the third year after World War II they were still at about 38 per cent of their wartime peak, whereas in the third year after World War I they had been reduced to 19 per cent. Of course, the comparison is not quite fair, for the world came back to normal—or seemed to do so for a while—more rapidly after the first than after the second war. This does not explain it all, however. When, in February, the Report of the Joint Committee on Reduction of Non-essential Federal Expendi-

THE SECURITY COUNCIL MEETS AT HUNTER COLLEGE

A tense situation developed in one of the meetings of the Security Council at Hunter College, New York City, when Andrei Gromyko, the Russian delegate, stalked from the chamber because the Council refused to postpone discussion of the Iranian dispute.

OPENING SESSION OF UNESCO

The Foreign Minister of France, Georges Bidault, addressing the opening session of UNESCO in the amphitheater of the Sorbonne University in Paris.

Photograph by Navy Department

HELEN OF BIKINI IN ACTION

The Baker Day explosion of the fifth atomic bomb, at Bikini July 24, 1946, as recorded by an automatically operated camera on a nearby island. This picture shows the column of water as it began to fall.

A NEW CHIEF JUSTICE FOR THE SUPREME COURT

Fred M. Vinson being sworn in as thirteenth Chief Justice of the United States by D. Lawrence Groner, Chief Justice of the United States Court of Appeals for the District of Columbia.

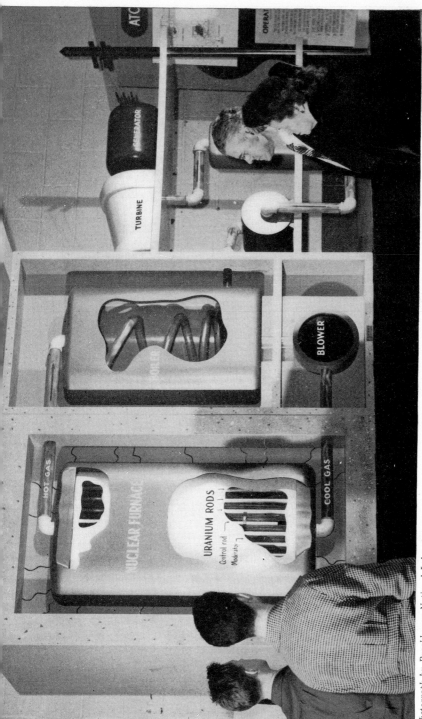

Photograph by Brookhaven National Laboratory

A MODEL ATOMIC FURNACE

This atomic furnace is similar to the one being built at Oak Ridge. When the uranium atoms in the furnace split, intense heat is given off. Rods of uranium become red hot and heat gas that is pumped over the rods. The gas flows from the furnace around coils through which ordinary water is flowing and boils the water to make steam. The steam flows to a turbine, which turns over a generator that produces electricity.

TRUMAN PLACING A WREATH ON MONUMENT IN MEXICO CITY

President Harry S. Truman, accompanied by U. S. Ambassador Walter Thurston, walks up the steps of the Monument of Mexican Independence towards the huge wreath which he placed at the foot of the monument during his good-will visit to Mexico City.

TIMES SQUARE AFTER THE CHRISTMAS SNOW STORM

A lone pedestrian braves the drifts in Times Square, New York, on the morning of December 27th following the blizzard of the day before.

THE AUTOMATIC DOUGLAS C-54 SKYMASTER WHICH CROSSED THE ATLANTIC WITHOUT A PILOT

The automatic flight was made by self-controlled pre-set mechanisms. The plane carried the emergency crew shown at right, though no human hand touched the controls on the entire flight.

tures, of which the Democratic Senator Byrd of Virginia was Chairman, was made public it showed that, outside of the Office of Emergency Management, which dealt with war problems, the departments and agencies of government were much more numerous at the beginning of 1947 than they had been even at the peak of war activity in 1944. The Senator stated that the investigation showed clearly that there had been "little reduction in the tremendous war-expansion of the Government" and that, on the contrary, with the exception of the Army and Navy and the war agencies, the growth of government "was constantly increasing." In thinking of bureaucracies one is reminded of the rise and fall of huge animals, such as dinosaurs and others, during geologic periods. Their bodies increase enormously in bulk and food needs until they are out of all proportion to the size of their skulls and brains, and then . . .

Of the proposed budget, well over $11 billions, or about one-third, was allotted to the armed forces and, including that, about 75 per cent to items connected with war or arising from past wars. We may speak here, therefore, of the greatest change ever made in the military organization of the United States. Congress, which had got off to a somewhat slow start, partly by reason of its political realignment, did pass a number of important laws before recessing at the end of July. There had always been, as in all countries, much jealousy between the Army and the Navy, each of which had a Secretary of Cabinet rank. War has changed in its character, and it had become evident that power in the air was as important as power on land and sea. Everywhere this added new complications as regards organization and prestige.

Finally, while Congress was anxious to adjourn and the President to fly to his dying mother, who was ninety-four years of age, a bill was passed and the President held up his flight to sign that bill in his plane, an incident symbolic of the new age which had so complicated both war and peace.

The bill provided for the unification of all our armed forces under a single military establishment with a single head, the Secretary of Defense, who was to be a member of the Cabinet. Under him there were three departments—the Army, the Navy and the Air Force, each headed by a Secretary with sub-Cabinet rank. The Secretary of Defense appointed was James V. Forrestal, former Secretary of the Navy, a very able man, popular with all the services and who, it had been said, gave up during the war a salary of $180,000 in private business to serve as an adviser to the President at $10,000. It is interesting to note, in passing, that the Government had grown steadily in strength and activities since the days of George Washington and that this was the first time that the number of members in the President's Cabinet had been reduced rather than increased.

Besides the reforming of our military organization, we may mention briefly some of the other more important legislation passed during the First Session of the 80th Congress.

The Taft-Hartley Labor Act, amending in many important respects the National Labor Relations (Wagner) Act, was passed by both Houses in June, vetoed by the President and passed again over his veto the same month by a vote of 68–25 in the Senate and 331–83 in the House. Long and complicated as it is, it helped to redress the balance of management and public interest against the excess powers given to unions and autocratic labor leaders in earlier measures, but it by no means deserved the name which the latter at once gave it, terming it the "Slave Labor Law." It is impossible to discuss clause by clause so controversial a measure, but we may note one clause which is important and has already been invoked by Truman. This clause provides that, in case of an industry-wide strike or lock-out which imperils the national health or safety, the President may appoint a Board of Enquiry and direct the Attorney General to petition for an injunction to last for 60–75 days, during which time a secret vote shall be taken of all the employees of the employers involved in the stoppage.

In May, a Portal-to-Portal Act was passed and approved modifying the liabilities and punishments under certain obscure prior Acts which had involved, by a Court decision, both the Government and private employers in potential damages of some five billions of dollars. The earlier Acts had threatened, for a while, to play havoc with the whole economic structure.

Two bills for reduction of taxes were passed by large majorities in both Houses, but both were vetoed by the President and could not muster the two-thirds vote necessary to over-ride the vetoes, although the second one did so, in the House of Representatives, by a vote of 299–108.

The honeymoon was over. Truman had given the impression that he would work with Congress, in spite of the difference in parties, but the 80th Congress was hampered by the constant threat or use of the veto, even when both Congress and public opinion seemed over-whelmingly in favor of a measure. In the case of the Labor Bill, both the President and organized labor—or its leaders—had used every means to influence both Congress and the public, but without effect. The President, nevertheless, vetoed in scathing terms not only that bill but both tax relief bills. In the case of the Taft-Hartley Bill, the tremendous vote in the Senate over-riding the veto could be compared with the stinging rebuke suffered by Franklin Roosevelt in connection with his Court-packing plan.

Historically, the development of the veto power of the President has been interesting. Before the Revolution, Acts passed by the colonial popular Assemblies were in many cases subject to a double veto by outside powers —the Royally appointed Governor of the Colony and the Privy Council in London. The statesmen who drew up our Constitution and administered it for the first generation or so feared an over-strong Executive as against the popular will. The power of the veto was put in the Constitution but it was understood to be for limited purposes only. Throughout the one or two terms of each of all the first sixteen Presidents none of the first six used the veto at all and by all the remaining ten it was used, inclusively, fifty-seven times. The Government had three distinct branches—the Executive, almost exclusively occupied with the enforcement of laws; the Legislature, to make the laws and to appropriate money; and the Judiciary, to pass on constitutional and other legal questions.

Andrew Jackson, who vetoed twelve bills, may be said

to have been the first President to set up his own judgment as regards the wisdom or advisability of a measure passed by the elected representatives of the people. It is not uncommon to find, in any country, that putting in the seat of power a man who claims to stand for the common man has had similar results. As compared with the first sixteen Presidents, who vetoed in all only fifty-seven Acts of Congress, the sixteen who followed Lincoln have vetoed over 1785! The tripartite nature of our government, with its presumed "checks and balances," was threatened most by Franklin Roosevelt, who tried to become a sort of Legislature in himself by vetoing more than 630 Acts of Congress and by his effort to make the Supreme Court an adjunct of the Executive. He *did,* in fact, name eight of the nine Justices, and if he had lived out the balance of the sixteen years for which he had been elected he would almost certainly have named them all. Both Congress and the nation—at least in considerable part—had become uneasy, and the latter, having voiced their wishes in the change of Congress in 1946, the increasing number and tone of Truman's vetoes, even of finance bills, began a split between him and a considerable number of even his own Democratic followers.

About a month after Congress had recessed, the President made his mid-year review of the Budget. It showed that there had again been rather amazing miscalculations by the fiscal authorities and advisers. Not only had the Budget for the fiscal year shown a surplus for the first time in seventeen years but the amount of this surplus and the miscalculations in advance were startling. Owing to misjudgment, the expenditures as estimated in January had decreased by $700,000,000 and the income had increased above the January estimate by $4 billions, leaving a surplus for the whole fiscal year of $4.7 billions. The President, having vetoed the two tax bills passed by the Legislature, which by old English and American tradition is supposed to hold the purse strings, somewhat blandly stated in his Message that the unexpected [and miscalculated] windfall of well on to five billions, including "the present cash balance, will be devoted to retirement of the public debt."

There were other troubles. Administration advice and practice had fluctuated, as I have said, between the fear of inflation and the fear of depression, "boom or bust." Prices were to be kept down, yet wage rises had been encouraged. The shortages in goods for peacetime domestic consumption and the increasing need of exports for European aid placed an added strain on the economy and turned up the thermostat on price rises. On October 1, the Council of Economic Advisers is said to have made a secret report to the President predicting a depression on account of rapidly rising prices and falling purchasing power, though we have noted the huge unexpected surplus and the two vetoes of tax relief. Money for Europe was also fast running out. For these, and for other reasons, there had been many demands that the President call a special session of Congress immediately but he had refused, for many weeks, while in Brazil and after his return. Finally, on October 23, there was an unusually long Cabinet meeting lasting more than two and a half hours, then other meetings and, later in the day, Truman called a special session of Congress for November 17, seven weeks ahead of the scheduled return to Washington of the 80th Congress. The reasons given were "the alarming and continuing increase in prices . . . and the need for emergency foreign aid."

After Congress convened, they received first the Marshall Plan. Secretary Marshall was three whole days on the witness stand explaining it. Then, five different volumes were boiled down to a little over 1150 pages, for members of Congress to study. In brief, there was to be without delay stop-gap aid to certain nations amounting to $597,000,000. The long-range program, which was to cover four years and extend to the sixteen nations already mentioned as signing the agreement in Paris, plus Western Germany, would get somewhere between $16 and $20 billions. That posted Congress as to European aid. The President, in his 4500-word address, talked of prices at home, which he said had risen 23 per cent since mid-1946 and were still rising. He asked for restoration to him of almost all the economic controls of the past war years, which Congress, under his leadership, had been abandoning since V-J Day two years before.

On December 19, the President again addressed the Congress, stating that to keep Europe from going Communist we must adopt the Marshall plan, or, as it has come to be known, the European Recovery Plan—E.R.P. He asked for $17,000,000,000 to cover four years, of which $6,800,000,000 would be needed during the first fifteen months. The continuation of the story will fall in the following months of 1948.

In the field of labor, the year following 1946, which

had topped all records for strikes and for lost work and production, was again a very disturbed one. Without detailing all examples, we may point to a few unusually interesting cases. As noted in the section on labor in the previous chapter, Lewis and his union, the United Mine Workers, had been fined respectively $10,000 and $3,500,-000 in December 1946. In fact, some of his leading labor leader colleagues had blamed Lewis for bringing about the Taft-Hartley Act and a changed attitude in Congress by his coal strikes and other actions during the war. On March 6, 1947, the Supreme Court, 7–2, upheld the decision of the lower Court, and a majority confirmed the $10,000 fine against Lewis personally but reduced the fine against the Union to $700,000, provided that it would rescind its notice to the Government (then in control of the mines) of cancellation of contract. Lewis yielded at last and signed the order. Later in the year, however, there were more mine strikes, and in one of these Lewis appeared to have gained a victory in the matter of wages and other benefits.

Nevertheless, the feuds went on among the big Unions and big leaders. Lewis, after getting out of the C.I.O., had rejoined the A.F.L. and been made a Vice-President—one of thirteen. Among other clauses in the Taft-Hartley Bill, was one which refused to labor unions the right to bring their cases before the N.L.R.B. unless their officers signed an affidavit that they were not members of the Communist Party and did not believe in the overthrow of the Government by force. If the general officers of the A.F.L. did not sign, the effect would be to bar all their sub-unions from access to the N.L.R.B. All the officers signed except Lewis, who claimed that the demand was insulting. He was dropped from office but remained head of the U.M.W., after expressing his opinion of the A.F.L.

There were many strikes and, especially from the end of April on, the "pattern" was set for a second general rise in wages and consequently in costs. The strikes in coal, steel, motors and other industries followed the usual form, and the details need not concern us year after year.

A strike of school teachers, on the scale of that in the city of Buffalo in February, was something new, as were the several strikes, with picketings and the usual trimmings, of "white collar" employees in banks and stock exchanges both in New York and elsewhere. There was a big strike among that highly paid and usually public-spirited and intelligent group, the telephone operators. There were even strikes in hospitals. On the whole, it may be said for 1947 that, although there was far less violence or bloodshed than in some of the great strikes of the past, such as the Pullman or Homestead, there was a disturbing factor in that there seemed to be developing a more cold-blooded disregard of the rights, necessities, health and even lives of large sections of the public of all ages who had nothing whatever to do with the causes or settlement of the strikes. It is not to be wondered at, if labor in vital trades is "getting that way," that the public, caught helpless, is becoming increasingly insistent that government take a hand, and that Congress is reacting to the public sentiment. It is unfortunate but natural. The pendulum always swings too far, either way.

Among the provisions of the Taft-Hartley Act is one

which requires labor unions to make accounting of their finances and internal affairs in detail to the Labor Department and, if fully complied with, this may yield interesting information on the salaries of the leaders. In August, when Daniel Tobin, the old president of the International Brotherhood of Teamsters (A.F.L.), startled his followers by refusing an increase in pay, a few figures were published in some of the daily newspapers. Tobin had been president for forty-one years, was well off, his children grown up and in good jobs, and his own salary was $30,000 a year. Harrison, of the clerks' union, was said to have a still larger salary, and Caesar Petrillo received $45,000 a year from his union. The salaries of certain others would make interesting reading. Justices of the Supreme Court now get $25,000 a year; members of the Cabinet $15,000 each; the President of the United States $75,000, and the Vice-President $15,000.

Of the unusual events of the year we need mention only a few. First the weather, of which Charles Dudley Warner once said that "everybody talks about it but nobody does anything about it." The winter of 1946 had been a record one for severity all over Europe, but in 1947 they had a mild winter in the Old World and the record passed to the United States, where rains, floods, hurricanes, tornadoes and snow wreaked their havoc on us. In the East of the country, the winter of 1947–48 was the worst in more than a generation. New York City had the most expensive succession of snow storms in its history; the storm that began on the day after Christmas cost $6,000,-000 to clear up the streets. In November, one of the most disastrous fires in the history of the eastern section of the country swept the forests of Maine and was pronounced a national emergency. It caused also the almost complete wiping out of the old and fashionable resort of Bar Harbor, with the destruction of perhaps $25,000,000 worth of houses and invaluable treasures within them.

There were also a notable number of airplane catastrophes, with a long list of casualties, but in September a remarkable feat was performed which may have a great effect on the use of planes both in peace and in war. An American Douglas C–54 Skymaster crossed the Atlantic from America to England, and made a perfect landing at an indicated field, without a pilot. There were fourteen persons on board, but as observers only. Not a human being during the entire trip touched any of the controls. The machine was equipped with what is called a "mechanical brain," which responded to the least impulse sent to it by radio from shore. It was evident that the contrivance would almost insure safe landings, even under conditions of "zero visibility." It was also evident that if, without human aid on board, we could send a plane across the ocean carrying fourteen people, we could also send such a plane, without people, but loaded with an atom bomb.

This extremely difficult and nerve-wracking year had included this new air development, talk of a "germ war," steadily rising tension with Russia, and the labor and political complications of a pre-Presidential-election year. Perhaps partly due to the increased strain, the year took also an unusual toll of the lives of prominent Americans, two of them unhappily by suicide—Herbert L. Satterlee, aged eighty-three, a distinguished New Yorker, son-in-law of the late J. P. Morgan; and John G. Winant, fifty-eight, former Ambassador to Great Britain. Both tragedies pointed to the strain under which men were living.

Among the other deaths, we may mention that of former Mayor Fiorello La Guardia, three times mayor of New York City and one of the ablest and most notable Americans in public life. We have already spoken of the death of Mrs. Truman, the President's mother, and have also to record that of Mrs. T. J. Preston, widow of former President Grover Cleveland, and one of the best-loved First Ladies the nation has had. There were too many deaths of outstanding individuals to permit us to go into biographical details and we merely cite some of them as indicating the passing of an era: the widow of Thomas A. Edison; Henry Ford, who did so much to transform American industrial life; Nicholas Murray Butler, President of Columbia University and a national and international figure for three generations; Senator Bilbo from Mississippi, long a stormy petrel in our political life and whose re-election was being contested at the beginning of the 80th Congress; Willa Cather, a distinguished novelist; Mrs. Carrie Chapman Catt, in her eighty-ninth year, long a leader in the Woman's Movement; Andrew Volstead, father of the Prohibition Act; and many others, noted in business life, politics, and in the arts and sciences, who if young could ill be lost to our culture and whose passing, in old age, seemed to set the seal on the transition from one type of life and thought to another.

The next chapter promises to be an exciting one, with turmoil at home and abroad—far-reaching decisions and vast responsibilities.

CHAPTER VII

THE RECORD OF 1948

THE year 1948 was one of unusual interest and of marked change in trends, both national and international. Internationally, the chief factor was the continued refusal of Russia to join with the West in re-establishing a real peace, and in consequence the continuance of the "cold war" between the greatest two powers in the world, the Soviet Union and the United States. We have spoken, in earlier post-war chapters, of the political vacuums left by the disappearance of Germany as the strongest state in the middle of Europe and by the partial liquidation of the British Empire. Although, during 1948, there were crises in China, Korea, and elsewhere, which concerned us in our new and not wholly welcome position as the strongest of all nations, we were in the main to concern ourselves with the rebuilding of Europe as offering, in our opinion, the best prospect of establishing once more a world of peace, civilization and progress.

Nationally, it was a presidential year, with all that that means in the various phases of our life. Moreover, the election, as Arthur Krock wrote—and he is, in my opinion, the ablest and most historically minded of all newspaper correspondents in Washington—was unique. For these reasons we shall reverse the order of the previous chapter and, after discussing world matters, concentrate at greater length on domestic affairs. Owing to our vast power and prestige, we are now obliged to discuss global affairs; but to talk over, later, that typical American event, a presidential election, will give us a sense of getting home again.

Turning, therefore, to international matters first, we shall speak of the United Nations. Much important work was accomplished at Lake Success during the earlier part of the year, but when the third regular session was opened in Paris, on September 21, it was faced by what our Secretary of State Marshall called "an unusually critical world situation." As early as March 28, the Pope, in his Easter address to a vast throng in St. Peter's Square, had warned that the world was facing a year of great danger, in which events which might prove "definitive or irreparable" for religion and society would occur. The all-important election in Italy was, at that time, only three weeks off. President Truman had just asked Congress for both an economic and a military program to check Russian "internal and external aggression." War clouds hung over all the earth.

Russia had persistently used the United Nations as a sounding-board for its propaganda which, shamelessly, bore little relation to facts. The debates were among the most remarkable in any public assembly, as when the Russian, Vishinsky, asserted that the report of the Special Committee on the Balkans was merely a "pile of garbage." Throughout the year, the United States and Britain were constantly accused by the Kremlin, its controlled newspapers and representatives, of almost every crime. But we shall have to treat of the East-West conflict as a matter by itself, and are here concerned only with the U.N.

Its Paris session opened under sinister circumstances. A few days before the members met, Count Bernadotte and his aide had been assassinated in Jerusalem, apparently by members of the notorious Stern gang, which boasted of the murder. The Palestine situation became more complex than ever. Russia had just tried a clever trick in Korea, but, as we cannot in one short chapter write the history of the United Nations as well as that of the United States, for even one year, it will make for clarity if we discuss, one by one, the various international problems of the U.N. as they concerned us. We must, however, summarize U.N. accomplishments.

In the first place, in spite of Russia's obstructionism, the U.N. survived as a world force. That, in itself, was a great step forward. Even Russia, with often insulting language, felt obliged, for some reason, to be represented there, if only to block progress and cast votes. (On October 25, Vishinsky, in a Council vote of 9–2 in a clear-cut decision between East and West, cast the 28th veto of the Soviet Union, joined as usual only by the Ukraine.) During the life of the U.N., while more and more nations, large and small, had been clamoring to join it, Russia and her satellites had steadily been losing in influence. The almost inevitable veto might block and delay, but the lying propaganda and the vituperations were losing their effect, much as a drug for pain which is overused. The Korean resolution, carried against Russia and her five satellites by a vote of 48–6, was an example.

During the Paris session of the representatives of 58 nations, 600 meetings were held and 17,000,000 words spoken, in various languages. The East-West issue emerged clearly, and two very important measures were passed. One was the Declaration of Human Rights for all human beings everywhere, and the other was the Genocide Convention. On reading the Declaration, you may say "just more words," yet words have often been winged. As the *Herald-Tribune* said, in an editorial, think of Magna Carta, the English and American Bills of Rights and other documents which have changed our histories and our lives. When the U.N. Bill of Rights is put into a treaty between the genuinely democratic nations, which is the next step, the fundamental difference between them and present or future dictatorships terming themselves democracies will be increasingly difficult to cover up by bad language or vetoes. The Genocide Convention also promises to be of marked influence in international law and in warning future

Hitlers, and other dictators, what may lie in store for them. The U.N. has not been operating in the expected time of normal peace; even so, it has not done badly.

Before passing from the U.N. to our relations with certain individual nations and with certain sore spots in the world, we must note what has been referred to as the most generous action ever taken by any people in history. In the preceding chapter we spoke of a speech made at Harvard, on June 5, 1947, by Secretary of State Marshall, outlining his ideas for helping to put Europe on its feet again according to what came to be popularly known as the "Marshall Plan" and, later, more officially, as the European Recovery Program (E.R.P.). After much discussion, here and abroad, the matter came to a head in Congress, in January 1948.

Appearing before the Senate Committee, Mr. Marshall took personal lead in getting the measure through Congress. The opposition came mainly from a few remaining isolationists, who dubbed the plan "operation rat hole," and from the supporters of Henry Wallace, who feared it would lead to war with Russia. It did not, though Russia opposed it from the start, apparently on the ground that it would help to bring peace and prosperity to Europe and thus interfere with her plans for world revolution and Communism. Marshall himself had said at Harvard that "our policy is not directed against any country or doctrine but against hunger, poverty, desperation and chaos." He had added that we must not interfere with the sovereignty of any country; that we must count on enough of them helping us to help them to help themselves.

Great Britain and France immediately sent out invitations to all European nations, including the Soviets, to join in a meeting to discuss the proposal. Sixteen joined in the Paris Conference, although Moscow and eight of its controlled countries declined, two of them apparently under orders and against their own desires. The nations attending the Conference through the year up until September were Britain, France, Austria, Belgium, Denmark, Greece, Eire (Ireland), Iceland, Italy, Luxembourg, Norway, Holland, Portugal, Sweden, Switzerland and Turkey. Meanwhile, the United States had set its shoulder to the wheel and, on January 2, signed bilateral agreements with France, Italy and Austria, granting them "interim emergency aid" to the extent of $522,000,000. Before Congress, Marshall had asked for an "all or nothing" adoption of his plan; as late as April 1, Senator Taft and some others thought nothing could be done until July 1. However, by April 3, the Bill had passed Congress and had been signed by the President, although the entire four years' needs were not voted at once. Congress, to start the ball rolling, did vote over $6,000,000,000. Later, in September, the Paris Conference, at its final session, asked for a total of $21,-780,000,000 of loans and credits from 1948 to 1952. I know of no country emerging from a great and costly war that has ever voted nearly $22,000,000,000 and perhaps much more, most of which its citizens never expected to get back again. The act, however, was not one of thoughtless generosity but, we hope, of enlightened statesmanship. We have at last learned that we cannot, under modern conditions, live and prosper to ourselves alone.

Congress was slow in appropriating the money, then moved quickly when Russia, in one of its customary coups, took over Czechoslovakia. Meanwhile, two points had been gained. The work of handling the help to Europe had been put under one head, Paul G. Hoffman, a Republican, and former president of the Studebaker Company. The appointee was to hold Cabinet rank but under control of the State Department. At last reports, at the beginning of 1949, it was going well for such a vast and unprecedentedly complex undertaking. Besides what was requested, under the Marshall Plan, from our government (which means of course all of us individually), the 16 nations attending the Paris Conference asked for additional credits of over $3,000,000,000 from the International Bank for Reconstruction and Development, and from private investors. The reason for such huge amounts was also clearly stated. The official report went on to say that "The scale of destruction and disruption of European economic life was far greater than that which Europe had experienced in the First World War. Industrial production in Belgium, France and the

Netherlands was reduced to 30 to 40 per cent of pre-war and in Italy to only 20 per cent; production of bread grains fell to only two-thirds of pre-war; 300,000 freight cars had been destroyed but a total of 2,800,000 were damaged." The participating nations also pledged themselves to a "wide range of actual and potential mutual help," though adding that the task was so great it would take at least four years. They needed not only rehabilitation but a period of security in which to work out their difficult, long-term problems. The later discussions of some sort of a United States of Europe, and of an Atlantic union for mutual defense, appear to have sprung from the Paris discussions.

As we have noted, Russia and her satellites would have nothing to do with these plans; and those of the Kremlin, as far as an outside observer can determine, seem to be directed toward a further demoralization of the old European system and civilization. As we have also noted, the whole year was taken up with vituperative threats and rumblings of war in an atomic age. The "cold war," and ideas of revolution and further conquest, instead of peace and rehabilitation, had followed apparent victory. Some of the abortive efforts to get together in meetings, at various diplomatic levels, may be mentioned, although we cannot enter into all the details of the "garbage," to paraphrase Vishinsky, of the twelve months. We shall touch first on a few of the high spots with regard to Russia.

In December of the previous year, 1947, the meeting, in London, of the Ministers of the Big Four had broken down, and, on the 31st, Molotov declared in Moscow that the United States had been mainly responsible for the failure because it had blocked discussions of the peace terms for Germany. This was as fantastic as many other statements made by the Russians throughout the meetings of the U.N. and at conferences, but may, in the opinion of the Communists, have served their purposes of propaganda, domestic and foreign. At the Conference, Marshall had already referred to Molotov's accusations as "insults and abuse," and the meeting broke up when the Russians demanded a $10,000,000,000 indemnity from Germany and Four-Power control of the rich Ruhr.

What came next was the publication by the American State Department of a volume of 362 pages containing the cream of about 2,000,000 documents, from the German Foreign Office, captured, in April 1945, by our Ninth Division in lonely châteaux in the Harz Mountains. Fortunately, the keeper of the archives had disobeyed orders to destroy them, and they have been studied ever since by American, French and British scholars. Extracts from the correspondence and agreements were printed in *Newsweek,* issue of February 2, 1948. Stalin, Molotov, Hitler, von Ribbentrop and other leaders all had a hand in the witches' broth. Among other things, they show that it was the Soviets, not the Nazis, who asked for the non-aggression Pact which led Germany to invade Poland, and that Moscow had asked for a secret division of Europe into Nazi and Russian spheres, as well as much else. We had had the documents but Marshall had kept them secret to facilitate negotiation in London, and when all hope of success came to an end, with the consent of France and Britain, he ordered immediate publication. Moscow registered rage, and from then on has included all three leading Western nations in her vituperative slander.

As there seemed no hope of making a real peace treaty to fill the vacuum left by the disappearance of Germany, the three started, under great difficulties, to build up some form of government in western Germany. This again infuriated the Russian Bear. It is impossible to write definitive history, if there ever is such a thing, based on the contemporaneously recorded events of the moment. Especially in the past, it has usually taken many decades, or even centuries, for original documents to be released or come to light. I recall, when working on research in the Manuscript Division of the Library of Congress, looking with envy at two piles of cases, one of Theodore Roosevelt papers and the other of Taft papers, neither to be open to the public for, thirty-five years, I think it was. How could a historian write of that celebrated feud until he had read those papers? Time, like distance, however, seems to be shortening; not only generals' and statesmen's memoirs but official documents appear with hitherto unheard-of promptness.

Judging by the Russian-German papers published as above, and by the actions of the Russians since, it would appear that Russia had had an eye on Germany, whose disruption would serve the purpose of enabling her to absorb such parts of it as she needed, using the same methods she had used in Poland and in the Balkan countries she had coveted. She had fought the Marshall Plan for bringing peace and prosperity, and did not want a settled government in western Germany. The "cold war," as the East-West situation had come to be called, had been intensified, and one of its most spectacular episodes was initiated on April 1, when the blockade of Berlin began. On that day, the Russian general in that city announced many restrictions on rail and road traffic with the western zones, controlled, under the Potsdam agreement, by Britain, France and the United States respectively. A few of these unlawful restrictions were accepted, though not all. The Russians were evidently willing to sacrifice the Berlin civilian population. Our General Clay replied that he could supply the 10,000 Americans in the city by air, and the British joined us by putting thirty-two planes in all into the service of carrying food. The celebrated "airlift," or "Operation Vittles," began. It expanded amazingly and, by November 1, the United States alone had 600 crews in the work, with planes arriving at three Berlin airfields, one every three minutes. The Germans, as well as the Americans and others, received the needed food and fuel at the rate of 3000 tons each twenty-four hours. The Berlin agreement of June 5, 1945, had been signed by the four Allies, stipulating that Berlin should be occupied and administered by all four jointly, through their military representatives. Russia, who had obviously broken the agreement, claimed that her Allies had done so, but they held firm. There were many war scares. Among other incidents, on April 5, a Russian pilot in a fighting plane dived on a British passenger plane, killing not only himself but 14 on the passenger plane including, besides British, two Americans. The matter dragged along its diplomatic course, and there were other incidents, in the air and on the ground. There were Communist demonstrations against the German-elected municipal government, the squabble over the currency of the four sectors of the city, and other moves that seemed headed for trouble.

On September 17, after meetings with Stalin and Molotov in Moscow—wholly fruitless—our State Department published a White Paper entitled, "The Berlin Crisis: a Report on the Moscow Discussions, 1948." At one meeting it had been agreed that the four military governors in Berlin should proceed, according to a Moscow "directive," to lift the blockade and to do certain other things of a hopeful character. The Russian General Sokolovsky ignored the directive and the fat was in the fire again. In October, the Berlin crisis was placed by a vote of 9-2 on the agenda of the Security Council of the United Nations, the dissenters being, as usual, Russia and the Ukraine. Without going into further details, by the end of 1948 the Berlin imbroglio was as unsettled as ever, although "Operation Vittles" was astounding both the Berliners and Russia. In the middle of November, however, Russia refused to lift the blockade and the Western powers declined another conference until she should do so. Another stalemate!

In the meantime, the American-Soviet drama had taken, in New York, a dramatic turn, which reminded one of Hollywood and klieg lights. The propaganda war of reckless lying had been waged by Russia since V–J–Day in 1945, but in August 1948 it met with a mad disaster. The lie machine had claimed that a Russian widow of fifty-two, by name Kasenkina, a schoolteacher who had taught chemistry to the children of Russians here on official missions, and another Russian teacher, Ivanovitch Samarin, had been "kidnapped" by Americans. Moscow broadcast it wildly and made official protests to Washington. It proved the worst boomerang in the history of the "cold war." As the facts gradually emerged from the shadows of mystery they proved to be that Mrs. Kasenkina, in terror at being forced back to Russia, had taken refuge on the farm of Miss Alexandra Tolstoy, the sixty-four-year-old American-naturalized daughter of the celebrated Russian novelist. From there, Kasenkina was snatched away by Jacob Lomakin, Soviet Consul in New York City, and the Vice-Consul Chepurnykh. She was kept incommunicado in the Consulate on 61st Street and the Consul answered all inquiries to the effect that she was well and not a prisoner. A writ was served on Lomakin, who later denied having accepted the paper. In Washington, Secretary Marshall said that, while he would not invade Soviet rights, any individual who complied with our laws would be assured of freedom and government protection. The Soviet Ambassador held a press conference to denounce the American Government as abetting abduction and a criminal conspiracy. In Moscow, Foreign Secretary Molotov called in the American Ambassador at midnight to accuse our government of conniving with a "gangster organization." The Ambassador replied that if the Samarins "wished to return to the Soviet Union, their travel would be facilitated." Meanwhile, Samarin had said that he would be returning to his death and, with his wife, had escaped to a hide-away in New Jersey—a man hunted on free American soil by a foreign nation. Mrs. Kasenkina preferred death in America to life in her own Russia, and, at 4:30 P.M., on August 12, she jumped out of a window in the room of the Soviet Consulate, falling several floors to the concrete-paved court. She would have suffered instant death had not some telephone wires broken her fall. She was, however, very seriously injured. In spite of her protests, employees of the Consulate tried to drag her into the building. New York police were happily quick in scaling the high iron fence of the yard and sent her in an ambulance to Roosevelt Hospital, out of reach of Soviet power. Both she and the Samarins came under the protection of the United States, which demanded the recall of Lomakin. He went.

Gradually, during the summer, which was taking on a distinctly Hollywood-ish atmosphere that made staid Americans incredulous, other things developed. The Congressional Committee on Un-American Activities, which did some very useful work, though in an unfortunate manner, uncovered evidence that a Communist spy-ring had been busy for years and had abstracted and microfilmed highly important papers from the "top-secret" files of the State Department. The Chambers-Hiss case carried over the end of the year, another bizarre touch being added to the news by the discovery of some of the films of these top-secret papers in an otherwise empty pumpkin on the farm of Chambers. During his campaign Truman spoke of the Committee findings as a "red herring." Both the State Department and many citizens appear now to have adopted a different view.

We shall come to Russia again, but may I add here that what I consider the ablest report on international affairs, a report published in London and New York, has for long been pointing out that, in spite of all that Russia is scheming for in Western Europe, the real menace is in her designs on the vast populations and resources of the Orient, in China, in Indonesia, in the subcontinent of India; also the continent of Africa. Pausing a moment at the front door, we must mention Korea, for Russia and ourselves face each other there. A glance at a map will show the great strategic importance of this Asiatic peninsula with a coast line 6000 miles long, dividing the Yellow Sea of China from the Japanese Sea. During its 900 years of history, it has been the scene of many contests and conquests, and was the chief cause of the Russo-Japanese War of 1904–05. The Japanese called it the "dagger aimed at their hearts" by Russia and, as a result of the war, obtained control of it. After Japan's defeat in World War II, Korean independence was restored but with a temporary provisional government (1946) of ten members, five from the United States and five from the Soviet Union. Elections were to be held, local popular governments were to be formed and the foreigners were to withdraw. On May 1, 1948, a puppet government was set up in Northern Korea, which claimed jurisdiction over both North and South, and some 700,000 local troops, it is said, were trained. Southern Korea, however, refused to be drawn under this Communist cloak and, a week later, elections were held there and a government formed under observation on the spot by a special committee of the United Nations. Russia would not accept this and demanded that the United States withdraw her troops if Russia did. The trouble was that if we did so the Northern puppet government, with its trained army, could overrun the South, and we should have abandoned our trust. We have gone rather into detail regarding this apparently minor matter taking place so far away, because it shows in some degree what our new world position has entailed and the essential difficulty of dealing with the Kremlin. Korea is not only rich in minerals; but in its relation to Manchuria and facing China and Japan, as it does, it cannot be neglected.

One of the most unselfish and steadily pursued of the foreign policies of our government has been that with regard to China, one phase of which was initiated by John Hay and known as the "Open Door" (1899–1900). By the end of 1948, however, it looked as though the Chinese Nationalist government, headed by Chiang Kai-shek, would have to yield to the Communists and, owing to their propaganda, Americans had come to be hated by large numbers instead of being considered, as of old, China's best friends. Some of our last grant of $400,-000,000 remained at China's disposal but we had refused the billion which Madame Chiang had come to Washington to procure. China, with its huge resources and a population of some 462,000,000, remained for us, at the year's end, an unsolved problem. So did Indonesia, with regard to which we had sent a rather sharp note to the Netherlands, also an old friend. South Africa was seething with native unrest, and the government headed by the great statesman, Jan Smuts, had been defeated. Something was happening all over the world.

At Bogota, Colombia, an important Conference began

on March 30 (adjourning May 2), with delegates from 21 republics in North and South America. It adopted an Organization of American States, superseding the old Pan-American Union of 1890, although the earlier organization was retained as a central organ and secretariat. Among much other business accomplished, perhaps the two most important items were approval of a treaty of hemispheric economic co-operation and a resolution, sponsored by the United States, for united resistance to the threat of international Communism. This brings us to an interesting point.

Moscow had apparently decided to break up the Conference. Our C.I.A. (Central Intelligence Agency) had known of this and reports had been made out to be sent to Washington but some minor State Department official in Bogota had, with the approval of our Ambassador there, suppressed the dispatches so as not to "alarm the delegates unduly." In any case, an important assassination occurred April 9, followed by a revolution lasting five days. (*Newsweek,* April 26, p. 23.) Bogota was hardly a place for quiet negotiation, but Secretary Marshall, lacking some of the suppressed documents regarding what was being planned, had insisted on going on, and then had insisted on staying. The Conference began and ended in Bogota, and probably fortunately, as showing that the United States was not to be intimidated by such "Commie" tactics.

The later European compact, already mentioned, the

North Atlantic Pact, which was in the making at the close of the year, the Italian election, the failure of the general strike in France, and many other straws in the wind all pointed to a gradual decrease, during the year, in the power of the Russian *Politburo,* although it is still too early to take out our pipe and put on our slippers. Czechoslovakia had been swallowed, but Italy and France seemed to be getting safe, and Yugoslavia had, under Marshall Tito, openly rebelled, not against Communism, however, but against Russian domination.

Meanwhile, in Havana, in March, there had been another meeting, with representatives from fifty-three nations, from all over the world. It was a corollary of the Geneva Trade Conference of April 1947 and designed to continue the rehabilitation of world trade, which the two World Wars, and subsequent economic restrictions, had so severely disrupted. Besides signing a "Charter of the International Trade Organization," known as the I.T.O., 123 trade agreements between individual states were signed, to simplify and otherwise facilitate trade.

There were, however, always reminders, great or small, of the flux in which the downfall of the old system, paralleling the downfall of the Roman Empire, had left the world. On our side of the Atlantic, an ocean which has ceased to be a sundering sea to become merely a highway, two such reminders occurred that deserve mention. At the very beginning of the year, an international quarrel developed over, of all places, Antarctica.

Nobody knows to whom its barren wastes belong, yet it may prove valuable—because of its hidden resources, strategic importance in war or peace, or, with the world and its transport changing so fast, in almost any way. Claims to at least sections of it, based on all sorts of alleged factors, have been made by Britain, Australia, New Zealand, Norway, France, South Africa, Argentina, Chile and, of course, the United States. Suddenly, Chile and Argentina decided to make their claims very vocal indeed. Chile dispatched a warship and sent along its President to unfurl a flag and make speeches. Britain sent a warship to what she had always claimed were *her* Falkland Islands. At the end of the year, these almost *opera bouffe,* but nevertheless dangerous, performances were still unfinished business. In December we had another headache. We had just signed with the South American nations the International Treaty of Reciprocal Assistance, of which Article 3 reads: "The High Contracting Parties agree that an armed attack against an American state shall be considered as an attack against all the American states, and, consequently, each one of the said Contracting Parties undertakes to assist in meeting the attack." Costa Rica suddenly claimed that she had been invaded by armed troops from Nicaragua. Hurried meetings were called by the Council of American States but on New Year's Day this too was still unfinished business.

We shall touch on only one more of the sore spots which involved the United States abroad, leaving Greece and certain others in much the same condition as we found them in the preceding chapter. In that chapter, we spoke at length of the complex Palestine question. It was too complex to be solved, at least in 1948. With regard to no other country or race has our foreign policy been more shifting or less understandable to the general public, unless it be with regard to China. Truman had insisted on the partition scheme and urged it on the U.N., then suddenly discarded it. The U.N. sent Count Bernadotte of the royal family of Sweden to the Holy Land to effect some sort of compromise; we have already mentioned his assassination by a band of Hebrew terrorists. His assistant took over; but neither individual nations, the United Nations, the mediators or anyone else proved able to bring about a solution. Conferences went on, war went on, between Hebrews, Arabs and Egyptians. Boundaries, religion, history, previous possession, and many other factors, precluded a peaceful settlement. The United States was not alone in its undecided and vacillating policy. Great Britain's Foreign Minister, Bevin, was as uncertain as was Truman. Britain, however, had had far more experience in dealing with problems of the Near and Far East, though perhaps the Laborites had not. At the end of the year nothing had been settled except that before, or soon after, the New Year, many of the leading nations, including the United States, Britain, and others, had given either diplomatic recognition, or promise of such recognition, to the somewhat ill-defined new nation of Israel. The prospects of some final settlement seemed brighter early in 1949. What may happen in that year is still hidden and belongs in the next chapter. We may now stop our globe-trotting and return to the domestic scene with its more familiar landscape of economic and political affairs.

Although they are closely intertwined, we shall start with the former. Economically, the year 1948 was a very prosperous one, in spite of Truman's warning to Congress, on January 14, that a severe recession might be coming, and his recommendation that grants in aid be given to the States to help support perhaps 4,000,000 unemployed. This message belongs later in the political section of the year and we shall note here only that, instead of 4,000,000 unemployed, employment had, by summer, risen to an all-time high of about 61,500,000. There *was* inflation during the year, but, instead of there developing any need for a return to rationing and other wartime restrictions, business made a rather amazing approach to peacetime quantity of production. Rising prices came from other causes, such as the amount of money in circulation, high wages and other high costs, including unprecedented taxes due to war and to governmental extravagance.

Strikes continued, but with a marked difference. In 1946, they had resulted in a loss of 116,000,000 man-power days; in 1947, of 34,600,000 of them; and in 1948, of, apparently, still less, although the final accurate figures are not yet computed. These, of course, retarded the production of goods long desired during the war and brought about a consequent rise in prices due to the discrepancy between the amount of goods and the amount of money in circulation. The high cost of living affected most seriously those living on fixed incomes and the white-collar workers on salaries which always move upward more slowly than do wages.

The position of the wage-earner was a matter of dispute, and it was the much-debated relation of wage income to the cost of living which was to deflect the strike movement and tactics throughout the year and probably for some years to come. We shall mention a few strikes or threats of strike which illustrate the point.

In January, Walter Reuther, one of the ablest labor leaders, and more broad-minded than many, led his United Automobile Workers in their third round of wage demands from General Motors. They made their demand on the claim, based on very questionable statistics, that living costs had gone up much faster than had wages. This was not borne out by the figures prepared by the U. S. Government through the National Conference Board and based on data collected by the Bureau of Labor Statistics. Who were more likely to be correct—Reuther and his union or the highly paid government bureaus of supposed experts? This had been, more or less, the standard pattern for strikes since the war. Later in the year, General Motors headed off another threatened strike by giving a small increase but tied up with a clause relating future wages to the Cost-of-Living index as reported by the Bureau of Labor Statistics. The cost of living for all had shown a marked tendency to level off and even to decline. As regards this new form of bargaining it will be interesting to see what labor unions will do when the cost of living goes down.

Meanwhile, however, there had been another coal strike, which gives us one more lead for the future. John L. Lewis claimed he had not ordered a strike but that 360,000 men had decided, at the same moment, to take a vacation. On March 23, President Truman was obliged to invoke the Taft-Hartley Act, something the Administration had to do, several times, during the spring, but for us here the interesting point about the strike is the fact that 360,000 out of 400,000 soft-coal miners had taken a walk, reducing the nation's vital coal production for industry and transport by 80 per cent, not for an increase in wages but for pensions of $100 a month for all miners who had reached sixty-two and were otherwise eligible under the pension plan. This was one of those "fringe" demands which were coming to be more frequent as the old gag about wages *vs.* cost of living was losing the argument and, consequently, its effect.

The President, as has been said, had to invoke the Taft-Hartley Act, which, during his campaign, he continued to damn, and, in order to avert the breakdown of transportation through the threatened action of three recalcitrant Railway operating unions, he had to turn to an old law passed for the war emergency, and seize the railroads. These points should be borne in mind, as they will play a part in the story of 1949. There were many other strikes, such as those in the industrial plants of Ford and Chrysler, strikes of dock workers, maritime workers and others, which need not be described in detail. The main two points, I think, are the shift in emphasis from the wage increase to those matters included in the "fringe" (and no one can tell where the latter may go and what they may add to costs, but Lewis has led the way and the other labor leaders must follow), and the happy fact that the Communist influence in Labor groups, especially in the C.I.O., has markedly waned.

We now turn to what we may call the more purely political events of the year and, toward the close, to what was perhaps the most extraordinary presidential election in our history. In the previous chapter, we noted that under new laws the President, beginning with 1947, had to deliver three messages to the Congress, when it convened, instead of one. The second Session of the 80th Congress, which was to loom large in the campaign of this election year, convened with brief ceremony on January 6. The next day, it received the first of the President's three messages, that on the State of the Union. In it the President, who had been steadily opposed to any reduction in taxes, advocated a $40 cost-of-living credit, and an additional $40 for each dependent of a taxpayer. He also advocated that the $3,200,000,000 loss in revenue which would ensue should be made up by increased taxes on corporations. "Corporation" is a wealthy word which sounds as if it could be soaked without hurting anything human, but any one who knows anything about the American economy knows that a great corporation—and it is the great ones which pay the great taxes—is a cross-section of American human life, owned by tens or hundreds of thousands of stockholders, often women with small holdings and means, such as is the case with the huge American Telephone and Telegraph Company; and affording employment in like numbers of thousands.

Both Congress and the people knew this and Truman's rather naïve system of taxation or non-taxation did not get across. He also pleaded for the passage of his equally unacceptable anti-inflation measure but at the same time urged an increase in minimum wages from 40 to 75 cents an hour. The "honeymoon" had long been over, and the start of the new Session was not auspicious.

On January 12, the President presented his second required Message, that on the Budget. He indicated that the necessary outlay for the coming fiscal year would have to be about $39,700,000,000, the largest peacetime Budget in our history, and this with the war three years past. He added that about 79 per cent of what he asked for represented the cost of the last war, its aftermath and prevention of another war. He did admit that some tax relief should be given to those suffering hardships—but who was not? He also thought that the national income would leave a surplus of about $7,500,000,000, which should be used to pay off a small part of the government debt. Nothing was said about reduction in government expenses as a contributing factor to that very desirable end. The required Message on the Budget had been made obligatory, with the thought that it would give both Congress and the people a view of what was in prospect and what would be needed, but the very wide difference, as noted in the preceding chapter, between the figures presented in former estimates and the realities, made this new Budget Message fall somewhat flat.

Finally, on the 14th came the President's Economic Report, as required to be rendered to Congress. He continued to urge the $40 credit to taxpayers, an amount which meant nothing to those above the small wage-earner brackets, and a 75 per cent corporation excess-profits tax, whatever that might be. He also urged again his whole anti-inflation program lest otherwise we might have a recession and could not be sure that it might not be "severe, and recovery slow and painful." It was an election year and the President was not beginning well. His "honeymoon" with Congress had long been over and his public popularity seemed to be declining. His three Messages already mentioned had contained practically nothing new or interesting, and were unmistakably political. When Truman delivered his Message on the

315

State of the Union, the Republican Whip of the House is said to have commented later that it suddenly occurred to him that for the first time he "was participating in a Democratic Convention." To quote a few words from *Newsweek*: "Some Congressmen scowled. Some twiddled their thumbs. Others squirmed in their seats, suppressed yawns, or fell fast asleep. What the 80th Congress thought [of the Annual Address on the State of the Union] was all too obvious. Its mood, on both sides of the aisle, ranged from frowning annoyance to soporific boredom." What the President thought of the 80th Congress was also to become "all too obvious" later in the campaign! At the moment, as the correspondent of the Baltimore *Sun* was reported to have remarked, "To get Harry out of here they'll have to chop a hole in the ice."

We emphasize the first few days of Truman's new year partly in order to bring out in strong relief the most amazing story of his triumph now to come, which was to set him apart in history as the darkest of dark horses who ever won a presidential race, though he himself, almost alone of the whole nation, refused to consider that he was such. But before we continue with the various campaign incidents, we shall go on with the business of Congress.

The work of Congressmen, Senators and Representatives alike, has become, like that of a President, almost too heavy to be borne. For example, during the approximate six months of the second Session of the 80th

Congress alone, 3871 measures were introduced for consideration, most of them complicated and calling for careful study. Of these, 505 were enacted into law. Of the 17 regarded as of major importance by the President, who had submitted them, 7 were passed and 10 thrown out. Of those which Congress had favored but not the President, he had vetoed 6 and, in the case of 5, his veto had been over-ridden by the necessary increased vote.

Taking its two Sessions together, the 80th Congress had passed notable legislation. It had, for example, resisted isolationism; maintained a bi-partisan foreign policy; passed the European Recovery Program; and if it did not reduce taxes as much as had been hoped from it, that was largely because the Democrats fought against any reduction in government expense. The overriding of 5 presidential vetoes by a two-thirds majority would, in a Parliamentary form of government, have been considered as a vote of "lack of confidence," automatically turning out the administration in power, and Truman did not like it. It appeared to be a repudiation of his leadership. That may be what led him, in his campaign speeches (almost everything he said in 1948 may be so termed), to call this Congress "the worst in history." He softened this later but, even after he had had time to think, he dubbed it "the second worst." A superlative is a very hard thing to prove and a series of them still more difficult. However, Truman was not yet through with the 80th Congress, as we shall soon see.

317

Truman's campaign had already begun in the first week of the year. At that time, the most conspicuous candidates were Truman, Henry A. Wallace and Senator Taft, with the shadow of General Eisenhower looming over both parties. Except for his "inherited" position as President, Truman would probably not have been considered. His record in solving or understanding government finance or other problems connected with the change from war to peace had not been impressive. A simple, genial soul, who liked people, he had none of the abilities or qualities which led such vast numbers of voters almost to worship, or else to hate, Franklin Roosevelt. Few, if any, hated Truman. They just did not think much of him, one way or the other, and were waiting for another President, be he Republican or Democrat, as the election might go. The war was over, and there was now no question, as there had been with the ill Roosevelt, of swapping horses while crossing a stream. The world, however, had not settled down to peace, everything was in turmoil, and there *was* a question as to whether Truman was strong enough to steer the ship. He had tried to play Roosevelt in world affairs, going to Potsdam to meet Stalin, but he soon gave up that role. He was indeed in the White House, though that, as history has shown, does not count for much. Of the six Vice-Presidents who, in the past, had succeeded to the Presidency because of a President's death, only two had been later elected to the office, or even been nominated by their party, and both had been Republicans: Theodore Roosevelt and Calvin Coolidge.

The Democratic Party leaders did not like Truman's candidacy at all. They did not think he had the slightest chance of leading the party to victory, yet it would be difficult, when he had been President for almost four years as successor to, and choice of, Franklin D., to push him out without seeming to stultify their own record as Democrats in office for sixteen years. Everyone knows, but we shall record later, what so amazingly happened.

There was another odd point. Roosevelt had not only made himself President for four successive terms, he had virtually chosen two Vice-Presidents and another President, besides a Supreme Court, practically all of whose members were his own appointees. Of Wallace we shall have more to say in a moment. When, after he had been Vice-President for four years, Roosevelt dropped him, and insisted on Truman instead, the public felt that Roosevelt had appointed his own successor. The Presidency, even under the best of circumstances, and for the usual eight years, is killing work. Roosevelt not only had the physical handicap which he had so heroically overcome, but had served twelve years during the greatest war in history, and the colossal strain was beginning to show. Pictures of him, from the one taken at Yalta to the one taken in a Pullman car in California during his last campaign, indicated to many of us that he could not complete another term and that Truman would become

President by inheritance, as he did very soon. Whether this was obvious to the two men perhaps no outsider will ever know but it must have been so to the discarded Wallace who, if he had not been discarded, would have been President, instead of Truman, for at least the nearly four years of Roosevelt's unfinished term. We now turn to the candidacy of Wallace.

As far as I can judge from contemporary comment and personal observation, Wallace had been even less generally popular with party leaders than had Truman. I recall, for example, listening in on the radio to the Democratic Convention when Roosevelt, with Wallace as his running mate, was nominated for the third time. Others who also listened in confirm my very clear recollection of the boos and hisses which greeted the nomination of the Vice-Presidential candidate. He had, during the previous twenty-five years, been a Harding-Coolidge Republican and an Al Smith Democrat, and had jumped like a sand-flea from one issue to another, finally becoming a New Dealer. Thanks to Roosevelt, he was nominated and elected, with the rest of the Democratic ticket.

Why Roosevelt did not want him a second time, I do not know. It may have been because of an inkling that whoever got the Vice-Presidential nomination in 1944 would be President before 1948. He did appoint him Secretary of Commerce, however, a post from which he was removed by Truman, as explained in an earlier chapter. Wallace had always claimed to remain true to

Roosevelt. Apparently, it had rankled that Truman, through no fault of his own, not only spent four years in the White House, with all the immense power and prestige of office which Wallace thought should have been inherited by himself, but had also fired him out of the Cabinet and from his job as Secretary of Commerce. All that may, or may not, explain a great deal, as an old mountain woman once said when told that her name was the same as that of the English royal family.

In December of 1947, a group of Leftists, who, with a good deal of conceit, call themselves the Progressive Citizens of America, had urged Wallace to start a new political party, and, on the Monday night before the New Year, he broadcast from Chicago, on a nation-wide hook-up, saying, "I shall run as an independent candidate for President of the United States, in 1948." He damned both the old parties, especially with regard to their policy as it related to Russia. As yet, he had no organized party, no platform or running mate. Comment was lively, running from the huge headlines and shrieks of joy of the Communist paper, *The Daily Worker,* which spoke of Wallace's candidacy as "historic," to that of the New York State Democratic Chairman who merely remarked that "Henry has read himself into oblivion."

During this century, somebody has tried to start a third party about once every twelve years and in only one case has it vitally affected a national election—I refer, of course, to Theodore Roosevelt and his Progressive Party. Despite his great prestige and enormous popularity, he could not succeed in getting himself reelected but only in defeating Republican Taft and electing Democratic Wilson. Wallace had no chance of being elected in 1948. His following was made up of the ragtag and bobtail of extreme Left-wing radicals with emphasis on the Communists. He was partly motivated perhaps by his peeve against the Party which had honored him for thirteen years as Cabinet Member and Vice-President. It has been suggested that he knew he could not be elected but was looking forward to 1952. This seems to have been the case as regards the Communists, both here and in the Kremlin, who supported him. Their idea was, it has been suggested, that the best way to defeat the Marshall Plan, Universal Military Training and the Democratic Party in general would be to run Wallace, and, if the Republicans put up an isolationist or an ultra-Conservative, this would hasten their downfall also, so that in 1952 the field would be fairly clear for a "New Messiah" campaign by Wallace, who had clearly shown he would follow the Party line.

For just a little while, it looked as though this long-term scheme, if there had been any such, might bear some fruit. However, all went askew.

Governor Dewey of New York had not yet "thrown in his hat" but, though not popular with a considerable number of the G.O.P. leaders, he was generally thought of as the most likely nominee of his Party. Senator Taft, son of former President Taft, and head of the Party in the Senate, had been angling for the nomination openly and for some time. By many it was thought that Wallace's Third Party might destroy the nominal chance that Truman might have and make the election of any Republican certain. Following the argument further, Republican leaders could say: "If the bird is already in the hand, why bother about hunting with Dewey, who has already been defeated once? Why not nominate Taft? He is not too popular nationally but he is safe, conservative, a member of the 'Old Guard' and dependable."

Fortunately, it did not work out as the Kremlin, badly informed and with its usual ignorance of other countries, had planned, though, amazing as it may seem to us, the Kremlin seemed to remain certain to the end that Wallace would be elected and become its man here even without waiting for 1952. We shall have to skim events for the next six months, politically, until the race really starts. Many things happened, however, to alter the list of chief characters and their chances.

Toward the middle of January, General Eisenhower, in an extremely dignified and statesmanlike letter, which an editorial in the *Herald-Tribune* said would remain "a classic statement of the duties and obligations which fall upon military leaders in a free country," and which was an appreciation of the division between military and civilian service, which, the same editorial said, "only the rarest of soldiers could possess," refused the Republican nomination. It was meant to be final, and was so taken by most, although the refusal had later to be twice repeated. Senator Vandenberg also again declined to be considered. On the 16th of January, in Albany, a few days before the meeting of the Republican National Committee, Dewey announced that he was available. On February 23, young Senator Glen H. Taylor of Idaho, who had campaigned as the "singing cowboy," left the Democratic Party to become the Vice-Presidential running mate for Wallace, thereby adding another bizarre touch to Wallace's caravan of fellow travellers and others. From the standpoint of the presidential campaign, until the Conventions of all three parties in the summer, we need dwell on only a few points.

After Wallace had announced his intention to run, there was much discussion within the two old parties regarding from which party Wallace might capture the more votes. It was not thought he would make much of a showing with the farmers, and labor was very widely split over him. His movement had been openly called a "Red Front," by the A. F. of L. Still, one never could tell. How far Left the people had gone would be an interesting question to have the answer to, in November. At this point, we are speaking of February, when he gave the Democrats a jolt.

There was a Congressional election to be held in the Bronx on the 17th, and Wallace backed for this office one

Leo Isacson, the extremely Left-wing, if not Communistic, candidate of the American Labor Party. The victory was overwhelming. As one local Democratic leader, quoting General Stilwell's famous remark, said: "We got the Hell beat out of us." That settled the fact that Wallace would from then on stick in the campaign. The Democrats were despondent, the Republicans jubilant. The vote cast had been light, but the shrewdest politicians of both parties realized that the result could not all be blamed on the small vote. On the Pacific coast, former Governor Stassen (another Republican aspirant) said that his party would have to "present a progressive, humanitarian program in keeping with the early traditions of the party under Abraham Lincoln." On the other side, Bowles advised Truman to "get back to the principles of the New Deal and outline a second new deal." This local election was a turning-point and, in the light of a greater election a few months off, very interesting.

From that time on, Wallace turned steadily to Russia and Communism, although he has said he himself is not and never was a Communist. He even started a correspondence with Stalin over Palestine and seemed, in his foreign policy, uniformly pro-Russian and anti-American. We need not go into the details of one primary or another, of one State campaign or another, which eliminated, or greatly reduced, the chances of certain temporary candidates, such as General MacArthur. They were probably of some influence in shaping the course of events at the Conventions but it would take too much space to discuss them at length. The campaign may be said to have gotten its real start with Truman's 8500-mile trip over the country, beginning in June.

The trip was remarkable in many ways. Truman started it with a beaming face just when his political fortunes and future appeared, to almost all the politicians, to be at their extreme nadir. Many things, some of which we have mentioned, had steadily been reducing his popularity, while, owing to his insistence on his civil-rights program, the South had broken out into open revolt the middle of May. On the 10th, under powerful Southern leadership, 1000 "Dixiecrats," as they called themselves, representing ten States of the old Confederacy, held a mass meeting to secede formally from the President and to hold their own Rump Convention, should the Democratic one nominate Truman. In other words, in 1948 a large body of Southerners were willing to bolt Truman and their party just as in 1860 their ancestors had bolted Stephen Douglas. There was indeed much of the 1860's in the air.

Franklin Roosevelt's party, that of the New Deal, had always been a good deal of a hodge-podge, although not quite so much so as that which Wallace was trying to weld into form. Roosevelt, however, had had a personality and a popularity far transcending those of either Wallace or Truman, *and* he had counted on the "Solid South" as a back-log.

Nevertheless, Truman, to the amazement, and often to the despair, of the old-timers in the political game, remained supremely confident. On June 3, with the Congress he had so damned still in session and the international situation in a crisis, the President started his trip, in a sixteen-car Presidential Special, Truman himself settling down in the "Ferdinand Magellan," the private car with armored sides which the Association of American Railroads had built especially for Franklin Roosevelt. Truman had tried to maintain that his long swing around the circle was wholly non-political in character, but, after a day or so of speaking, that faded pretense had to be discarded, unless perhaps in the disbursing office of the Treasury. He had, however, changed his tactics, and gave up his long speeches read from prepared manuscript, which, like Coolidge's, were very dull, and, except for large meetings in cities such as Los Angeles, he gave offhand folksy chats. Even so, the audiences did not seem enthusiastic and those who were sure Truman could not possibly be elected did not change their minds. Meanwhile, and right up to the November election, the vast majority of the best political writers in leading newspapers and magazines, as well as all the poll reports, were equally certain that Truman could not win. I have never known such almost complete unanimity of expert opinion against any candidate. We must now get on to the three nominating Conventions.

The Convention of the Republican Party came first

and was held in Philadelphia from June 21 to 25. On the first day, there were seven serious contenders, with the usual fringe of "favorite sons" in the wings. It looked like Dewey, however, and the next day the supporters of Senator Taft and Governor Stassen tried to start a last ditch "stop Dewey" drive, but neither of the two just mentioned would step aside in favor of the other. On the fourth day, on the third ballot, Dewey was nominated unanimously. It was the first time in its ninety-two years of history that the Party had renominated a candidate who had previously been defeated. (Dewey lost to Roosevelt in 1944.) Governor Warren of California was nominated for Vice-President.

The Democratic Convention was held in Philadelphia, in the same hall, from July 12 to 15. Truman remained confident as ever, but the Party was alarmed lest he get the nomination, which, in their view, would mean certain defeat in the election. Some still hoped to draft Supreme Court Justice Douglas or General Eisenhower. The latter had already expressed himself positively, not only in the letter already mentioned but in another letter to the publisher of the Manchester (N. H.) *Evening Leader,* in which he wrote: "I am not available for and could not accept nomination to high political office. . . . My decision to remove myself completely from the political scene is definite and positive. . . . I could not accept the [G.O.P. presidential] nomination even under the remote circumstances that it were tendered me."

In his January letter, to which he referred in the one just quoted, he had said, *inter alia,* "It is my conviction that the necessary and wise subordination of the military to civil power will be best sustained, and our people will have greater confidence that it is so sustained, when life-long professional soldiers in the absence of some obvious and overriding reason abstain from seeking high political office."

In spite of these letters and other public pronouncements, some jittery Democrats, who apparently could not believe the straightforward statements of an honest man, still wanted to preserve the Party from defeat as they foresaw it by forcing Eisenhower to run, among them James and Elliott Roosevelt and Senator Pepper of Florida. Pepper telegraphed Eisenhower to draft him and received a wire in return again declining the nomination and calling attention to his earlier letters and statements. The heat was then turned on Justice Douglas. In reply, he said, on July 9, "I am not a candidate, have never been a candidate, and don't plan to be a candidate." The refusals of Eisenhower and Douglas left James Roosevelt and others of the "stop-Truman" group out on a limb and some of them, including the politically minded son of the late President, swung down like monkeys from that limb to the band-wagon of Harry Truman.

For three days, however, the Democratic Party had been threatened with destruction and not merely with defeat in one election. There were incipient booms for a dozen or so minor Senators and others, such as Pepper of Florida, while, on the other hand, the Dixiecrats had threatened to bolt if Truman were nominated with a Civil Rights plank in the platform.

Nevertheless, Truman rode the pandemonium of the three days and was finally nominated on the first ballot, after an inspiring speech by Senator Barkley of Kentucky. Before this, however, the adoption of a strong Civil Rights plank by a vote of 651½ to 582½ led not only to the walking out of the Convention of the entire Mississippi delegation of 22 but, likewise, of 13 of the Alabamians, and to the unexpected nomination by the remaining Dixiecrats of former Governor J. Strom Thurmond of South Carolina against Truman. The latter was an easy winner, with 947½ votes (he had needed only 618) against Thurmond's 263. Senator Barkley, whose keynote speech had restored some hope to the shattered nerves of the Party, was nominated for the Vice-Presidency, unanimously, by acclamation.

A week later, the so-called Progressive Party of Wallace held its first national Convention. It was not important in itself but interesting in indicating, with other minor Party conventions, some of the trends of thought in the electorate. It adopted the name that Theodore Roosevelt gave to his third party in his Bull Moose campaign. There were 3240 delegates, who nominated Wallace for President and the "Singing Cowboy," Glen H. Taylor, for Vice-President. Both refused to repudiate

Communist support. Rexford Guy Tugwell headed the platform committee, and Vito Marcantonio and Leo Isacson, both of the American Labor Party in New York, were mainly influential in drafting the Party's program. The campaign slogan chosen was the somewhat misleading one, "Wallace or War."

The platform called, among other things, for negotiations to find areas of agreement with Russia, destruction of all atom bombs, repeal of the draft law, scrapping of the Truman Doctrine and of the Marshall European Recovery Plan, restoration to Communists of all their constitutional rights, abolishing the Committee on Un-American Activities and the loyalty requirements as of the present, together with such other matters as repeal of the Taft-Hartley Act, a minimum wage of $1 an hour, government control and lowering the cost of food, clothing and housing.

At the Convention of the Communist Party, held in New York from August 2 to 6, the ticket of the Progressive Party was adopted and virtually the same platform, including an offer of friendship with Soviet Russia. Wallace, in his acceptance speech, had gone the same way, claiming that the tension between the United States and Russia was due to American policy and that we should get out of Berlin.

Of the other minor Party conventions it is not necessary to do more than mention their names: The Socialist Labor Party, The Socialist Party, The Prohibition Party.

331

There was one more—the seceding Dixiecrats, who held their Convention in Birmingham, Alabama, on July 17, after their defeat in Philadelphia. Their hope was not that they could, on their separate ticket, elect a President but that they might take enough electoral votes to prevent either Truman or Dewey from receiving the required number, in which case the election would be thrown into the House of Representatives, where the South held the balance of power. Among the signs in the hall were such strongly worded ones as "To Hell with Truman." Even if the Dixiecrats were uncertain about being able to send the election to the House, they did feel, as they laid their plans, that they could at least defeat Truman.

Then came the weeks before election. The President made another campaigning trip, a shorter one, and Dewey did so also. The hullabaloo of Conventions and speech-making was coming to an end. From a political standpoint, it had been an interesting and, in many ways, a dramatic summer. On the other hand, as "the shouting and the tumult" died, there was, or seemed to be, no drama, nor excitement left. Never, since the first election, that of Washington, had the people, regardless of their own personal preferences, been so absolutely certain who would be the next President. All the small parties, including Wallace's, could be dismissed without a thought. Of the candidates of the two great parties, Truman did not stand a chance. Many of his own party had not wanted him. The panic and dismay had been all too evident. The "bosses" of the big cities, Hague in Jersey City, those in Chicago and elsewhere, had shown themselves cold to Truman; the Solid South, backlog of the Democratic Party, had not only been alienated by his Civil Rights program but had put up a candidate of its own. During the week before election, it was taken completely for granted that it would be Dewey—so completely, in fact, that, in spite of my professional interest, I, like innumerable others, did not even take the trouble to sit up as usual so as to get the late returns over the radio, and did not learn, until I took up my morning paper the next day, that Truman and Barkley were elected. I shall not repeat what I said at the time but only what Barkley was reported to have said when the news was brought to him: "Well, I'll be doggoned!" I have long been an observer of, and commentator on, the American scene and have never before known such absolute consternation over a political event. I have known such an event to produce anger, fright or what-not. This was plain consternation, mixed with a lot of jocosity because so many of us, and particularly the specialists in politics and public opinion, had been so wholly wrong.

We shall give the figures below, but may pause to ask why we had all been so positive and just how it all came about. There have been many post-mortem, as it were, explanations, and many of them do not, perhaps, belong in this brief review. Yet certain aspects of them *are* important historically. Of course, there were the usual ways

333

of approaching Truman's candidacy. I have already mentioned some of these, such as the fact that of the six Vice-Presidents who had become President by the death of the President only two had, later, been elected, which made Truman's chance only one in three. This was, of course, by no means decisive. Then there were all the other adverse factors I have already mentioned. The party which Franklin Roosevelt had held together had been made up of a most heterogeneous lot of elements. He was not only personally popular, he had always kept the Solid South and the city bosses of the big Northern cities. These were opposed to Truman, who, besides, was certainly not of the caliber of a Roosevelt. In addition to these and other points already mentioned, there is one that should give us pause.

We Americans like short-cuts and are given to getting our supposed knowledge from headlines and polls. During this campaign, almost every daily and weekly pumped into us the notion that Dewey was so far in the lead there was practically no election coming—that Dewey, from the moment of his nomination, was already in. To be sure, Truman's unprecedented "non-political" trip of 8500 miles of speech-making was far more vigorous and effective than such speeches as Dewey delivered. Nevertheless it had seemed obvious that every card was stacked against Truman; all the polls, headed by the trusted Gallup, had been for many months so unanimously certain Dewey had an unbreakable lead that the campaign seemed as dull as a horse-race with only one horse. The next morning, a stunned America, somnolent the day before, woke up.

As finally corrected, the count showed that 49,363,798 ballots had been cast and that 683,382 failed to indicate any choice for the Presidency. Of the total votes which did so indicate, Truman received 24,104,386; Dewey 21,969,312; Thurmond (States Rights) 1,169,312; Wallace, 1,157,100; and the rest were scattered in small numbers among the minor Parties. Truman got 49.5 per cent of the total and Dewey 45.1 per cent.

Although Truman's popular vote, large as it unexpectedly turned out to be, was less than any vote cast for Franklin Roosevelt, the election indicated certain interesting things. Truman, on his long trip, had not only travelled in Roosevelt's former private car, but had tried, at the suggestion of his advisers, to live himself into a new "New Deal." He had promised, if somewhat obliquely, all sorts of things to all sorts of groups, which pledges might turn up later to plague him. Roosevelt's influence still carried weight, and the beliefs he had tried to inculcate in people as to what they should expect from government. In the two years since the previous Congressional election, there had been another swing to the Left but not toward Communism or Socialism. The complete flop made by Wallace must have been a great blow to the Kremlin. The election also showed the vagaries of our electoral system. The popular votes have been given above; in the Electoral College, the votes were: Truman, 304; Dewey, 189; and Thurman 36; no other candidate any. Truman's luck was to win some States by very slim margins yet enough to give him the entire vote of such States in the Electoral College.

The election was, of course, the chief event in our domestic history for 1948. We may mention a few minor ones which are still of some interest. On December 26, 1947, a snowstorm began in the East which, between dawn and midnight, buried New York City and vicinity under a fall of 25.8 inches, almost 5 inches more than fell in the great blizzard of March 1888. Continued falls, with no thaw, played havoc all through New York and New England and made the winter a memorable one.

Population showed notable gains and California became the third in population of the forty-eight States. The political center of gravity was shifting. Another change of a different sort took place in Kansas when that center of Prohibition voted wet during the summer. Also, in August, the American Indians were finally given the full privileges of American citizenship. To end on the unfortunately usual funereal note, the following leading Americans died during the year: Thomas W. Lamont, banker, diplomat and philanthropist; Lewis B. Schwellenbach, Secretary of Labor; General of the Armies John J. Pershing; Wilbur L. Cross, educator and for several terms Governor of Connecticut; and Mrs. Theodore Roosevelt, the widow of the President.

INDEX

INDEX — Volume VI

FOR INDEX TO VOLUMES I–V, SEE VOLUME V

337

INDEX

Argentine, 31, 81, 174

Arizona, battleship sunk at Pearl Harbor, 2

Arkansas, battleship used in atomic bomb test, 207

Armed Forces, 24, 25, 34, 37, 60, 61, 86, 138, 150; *also see* World War II

Army Appropriation, passed, 57

Army Nurses, at Bataan, 8

Arnold, General H. H., 66, 67; in command of all American Air Forces, 92

Assam, Americans fly supplies to China from 88

Atlantic Charter, accepted by United Nations, 6, 7

Atlantic City, New Jersey, International Conference at, 77

"Atlantic Wall," Hitler's boasted wall crashed, 140, 141

Atomic Bomb, opened new era, 146; first bomb in history successfully exploded by United States, 155; dropped on Japanese cities, 159; a new weapon, 161, 162, 163, 185; tested at Bikini, 205, 206, 207, 208; problem of control, 260

Attlee, Clement, 171, 177

Attu, in Aleutian group, 86

Australia, 134, 158, 308; feared invasion by Japanese, 9; attacked by Japanese, 17; American forces in, 74; Reverse Lend Lease, 203

Austria, 294

Automobiles, new cars disappear from American life, 10; retail sales prohibited, 10

Automobile Workers Union, C.I.O. strike lasted 113 days, 216

Avery, Sewell L., Chairman of Montgomery Ward & Co., 112, 113, 114, 115

Axis Powers, 7, 37; surrender in Africa, 92; collapse of, 146, 147, 164, 194, 209; *also see* World War II

Bache, Jules S., financier, death of, 131

Balkans, vote wtih Soviet in United Nations, 198; report on Balkans attacked by Vishinsky, 291; Russian tactics in, 299

Bar Harbor, resort in Maine almost destroyed by fire, 287

Barkley, Alben, resigns as Majority Leader, 104; nominated for Vice President, 330; elected, 333

Baruch, Bernard, Report on reconversion, 127, 128; Report on atomic control, 208, 273

Baruch-Conant Report, 43

Bataan, Americans forced to retreat, 8; "foxholes" of, 9; epic will live, 32; "March of Death," 135

Battle of Bismarck Sea, 87, 133

Battle of the Bulge, 142, 149, 150

Battle of Coral Sea, 30

Battle of Indian Ocean, 18

Battle of Java Sea, 17

Battle of Midway, 30

Battle of Solomons, 32; *also see* World War II

Battle of Tarawa, 87

Battle of Tunisia, 91, 92, 93

Bavaria, overrun by Allies, 151

Belgium, 7, 294, 295, 296; Reverse Lend Lease, 203

Bell Telephone System, strike, 212

Berlin, almost destroyed, 88; falls to Russians, 150, 151, 152; end of Hitler, 153; *also see* Germany

Berlin Agreement, The, 300

Berlin Blockade, British join Americans in carrying food by air, 299; Russians refuse to lift blockade, 300, 301

"Berlin Crisis," The, White Paper published by State Department, 300, 301

Bernadotte, Count, assassinated in Jerusalem, 291

Bevin, Ernest, British Foreign Secretary, 172; at Moscow, 244, 245; London Conference, 267; Palestine question, 309

Bidault, Georges, Foreign Minister of France, 244, 245, 267

Biddle, Anthony D., U. S. Attorney General: Montgomery Ward Case, 115

"Big Business," 106

"Big Four," 78, 81, 204, 205, 240, 241; at Moscow, 244; at Paris, 261; at Potsdam, 269; at London, 266, 267, 297

"Big Three," Alliances, 147, 148, 173; Grand Alliance, 165; at Yalta, 166, 167; at Potsdam, 168, 170; Truman and Attlee in place of Roosevelt and Churchill, 171; *also see* Conferences

Bikini, atomic bomb tested at, 205, 206

Bilateral Agreements, "interim emergency aid," 294

Bilbo, Senator, stormy petrel from Mississippi, death of, 288

"Bill of Rights," new one proposed, 75, 100

Black, Justice Hugo L., row with Justice Jackson, 226

Black Markets, 65

Bogotá Conference, 305, 306

Bon Peninsula, enemy retreats to, 92

Borneo, 16; Australians in Northwest, 158

Brazil, 15, 83; accepts Atlantic Charter, 7; declared war against Axis, 31

Brest, 141

338

INDEX

Bretton Woods Conference, 142, 143, 144; Agreement passed by Senate, 176; ratified, 176

Bricker, Senator John W., 44; Dewey's running mate in 1944, 118, 119

British Government, 30, 76, 78, 83, 88, 205, 289; accepts Atlantic Charter, 6; loss of Singapore, 16; loss of capital ships, 17; other naval losses, 18, 19, 21; seizes Madagascar, 26, 27; relinquishes rights in China, 32; war in North Africa, 34, 48; Lend Lease to, 74, 75; ship tonnage, 135; robot bombs, 137; pledge to stay in war, 144; Churchill government voted out, 146; "battle" for Britain, 164; Labor Party wins, 170, 172; not prepared for termination of Lend Lease, 177, 178; crisis in India, 197; in Near East, 198; receives greatest single International loan in history from U. S., 203, 204; shrinking of Empire, 232, 234; signs fifty-year alliance with France, 244; withdraws from Burma and India, 250; problem in Palestine, 255, 256; accused by Kremlin, 291; joins Americans in flying food to Berlin, 299; Russian pilot dives on passenger plane, 300; policy for Palestine, 309

Buckner, General, killed at Okinawa, 157

Budget, 9, 52, 97, 274, 275, 276, 281, 282; 1948 largest in peacetime, 314, 315

Bulgaria, declares war on United States, 29; annexed by Soviet, 264

Bullitt, W. C., 64

Bureau of Labor Statistics, 220, 221, 311, 312

Burma, occupied by Japanese, 17; Burma Road cut off, 17, 87, 88; end of campaign in, 156; Briitsh withdraw from, 250

Butler, Nicholas Murray, President of Columbia University, death of, 288

Byrnes, James F., appointed secretary of State, 172, 178; the Wallace "incident," 228; resigns from Cabinet, 236

Cabinet, Secretary Hull resigns from, 124, 125; Edward Stettinius, Jr., new Secretary of State, 125; James F. Byrnes, Secretary of State, 172; new Cabinet, 182, 183; Secretary Ickes resigns, 224, 225; new appointments to, 226; Secretary Wallace forced out of, 228; Secretary Byrnes, resigns, 236; General George Marshall appointed to succeed Byrnes, 236

Cady, Rev. George R., 119

Caen, captured by Allies, 141

Cairo Conference, see Conferences

California, third in population of States, 336

Cameroons, Free French in, 26

Canada, 14, 15, 53, 77, 173; accepts Atlantic Charter, 7; Lend Lease of, 74

Cape of Good Hope, 21

Carlson, Lieutenant Colonel Evans F., Marine commander at Tarawa, 87

Casablanca, 52, 53, 83, 160; occupied by Allies, 34; Conferences at, 84, 85, 92

Case Bill, vetoed, 224

Cassino, 136

Casualties, at Pearl Harbor, 2; at Tarawa, 87; at Kwajalein, 133; in Burma, 156, 157; at Iwo Jima, Okinawa and Luzon, 158; in European and Pacific wars, 161

Cather, Willa, novelist, death of, 288

Celebes, 16

Central Intelligence Agency, 306

Chambers-Hiss Case, 303

Charter of International Trade Organization, signed at Havana, 307

Chennault, General Claire L., in China, 87

Cherbourg, French port captured by Allies, 141

Chiang Kai-shek, Generalissimo, 33, 196, 305

Chiang Kai-shek, Madame, comes to Washington, 305

Chile, 31, 32, 308; severs relations with Axis, 86

China, 7, 32, 33, 78, 171, 172, 203, 303, 305, 309; at Dumbarton Oaks Conference, 143; Americans fly supplies to, 87, 88, 156; Lend Lease aid to, 178; Civil war in, 196; General Marshall Ambassador to, 196, 237; Kuomintang and Communist parties in, 237, 238; crisis in, 289

Chrysler Motor Plant, 217, 313

Churchill, Winston, British Prime Minister, 16, 30, 31, 36, 165, 202; at Washington, 5, 6; visits Stalin, 33; at Quebec and Cairo, 85; at Yalta, 166; voted out of power, 146, 170, 171

Circuit Court of Appeals, Petrillo incident, 112

Civil Rights, plank of Democratic Party in 1948, 330

Civilian Defense, 12, 13

Civilian Goods, curtailed, 68, 71; retarded by strikes, 181, 182, 183, 210, 211

Clapper, Raymond, news correspondent, death of, 131

Clark, Tom A., U. S. Attorney General, 182

Clay, General Lucius, problems of Berlin blockade, 299

Clayton, W. L., Under Secretary of State, 201

Coal Mines, strikes, 59, 60, 181; strike of soft coal miners, 214; mines seized by

INDEX

INDEX

Forrestal, James, Secretary of Navy, 132, 182; Secretary of Defense, 278

Forty Hour Week, 25, 40

Four Power Conference, 143, 297; *also see* Conferences

France, 197, 203, 295, 296; Free French, 25; Laval confers with Axis, 26; Vichy Government surrendered Indo-China, 27; Government in Africa, 35; French ships in American ports seized by U. S., 35; French Fleet, scuttled by its officers, 36, 135; Paris liberated, 141; Vichy Government in flight, 141; declines to sponsor invitations to join United Nations, 173; Dumbarton Oaks Conference not joined in by, 143, 173; signs fifty-year alliance with Britain, 244; signs bilateral agreement with United States, 294; general strike fails in, 307, 308

Frankfurter, Felix, Supreme Court Justice, 129

Freight Embargo, in 1946, 220

French Indo-China, rebellion in, 197

Fuel Administration, 65, 66

Gallup Poll, in 1948 Presidential election, 334

General Assembly of United Nations, *see* United Nations

General Motors, 10, 182, 211, 216; costly strike, 217, 311

Genocide Convention, 292

Germany, 29, 31, 289; Nazis in Paris, 26; German saboteurs captured in United States, 38, 39; key points bombed by Allies, 88; surrender of Forces in Africa, 90, 91, 92; unconditional surrender at Milan, 136, 148; von Rundstedt's counterattack, 149; war on two fronts, 150; Rhine crossed by Allies, 151; Admiral Doenitz becomes Fuehrer, 151; "Holy Soil" split in two, 151, 152; Berlin falls to Russians, 152; unconditional surrender of, 152; suicide of Nazi leaders, 153; Hitler believed dead, 153; Goering's hoard of loot found, 154; ten top Nazis hanged at Nürnberg, 194; almost had atomic bomb, 208; Russia demands large indemnity from, 297; Russia demands Four-Power control of Ruhr, 297; secret documents captured by Americans, 297; difficulties of Western Powers in, 298; Russian blockade of Berlin, 299; Americans and British supply food by air to, 299; Berlin crisis, 300; Russians refuse to lift blockade, 301

Gibson, Charles Dana, artist, death of, 131

Gilbert Islands, 87, 133

Giraud, General, French commander aided Allies in Africa, 35

Glass, Senator Carter, death of, 232

Global War, 29, 49, 81, 83, 97, 145, 147, 154; *also see* World War II

Goebbels, Joseph, notorious Nazi, 153

Goering, Hermann, 154; a suicide, 194

Goldsborough, Justice T. Allan, issued order restraining Lewis, 218, 219, 220

Government, *see* United States

Granite City Steel Company, C.I.O. strike lasted 150 days, 217

Great Britain, *see* British Government

Greece, 198, 203, 245, 246, 247, 257, 294; accepts Atlantic Charter, 7

Green, William L., A. F. of L. leader, 60; feud with John L. Lewis, 116

Grew, Joseph, Under Secretary of State, 125

Guadalcanal, epic will live, 32, 33; *also see* World War II

Guam, unprepared for attack, 7

Guatemala, accepts Atlantic Charter, 7

Haiti, accepts Atlantic Charter, 7

Halsey, Admiral William F., commander of Fleet in Pacific, 33, 132

Hamburg, German city destroyed, 152

Hancock-Baruch Report, 127

Hancock, John M., 127

Hannegan, Robert E., 120; Postmaster General, 182

Harper's, 138

Harriman, Averell, new Secretary of Commerce, 228

Haskell, Lieutenant General William, 64

Havana, meeting of nations at, 307

Hawaii, attack on Pearl Harbor, 1; Secretary Knox flies to, 2; Short and Kimmel, Army and Navy commanders at, 3; Knox and Roberts reports on disaster at, 2, 3, 4; U. S. forces distributed in, 7 (*also see* Pearl Harbor); sugar supply lost to United States, 12; President Roosevelt visits, 134

Hebrews, war with Arabs in Palestine, 309

Henri-Hay, M. Gaston, Vichy Government representative, 35

Herald-Tribune, 246, 292

Heydrich, Richard, "The Hangman," notorious Nazi, 26

High Cost of Living, 69, 70, 212, 283, 310, 311

Hillman, Sidney, chief figure in P.A.C., 116, 117; called before Congressional Committee, 120, 121

Himmler, Heinrich, chief of Nazi Gestapo, a suicide, 153

342

INDEX

Stern Gang, in Palestine, 291

Stettinius, Jr., Edward R., 72, 73; Secretary of State, 125, 174, 175, 176

Stillwell, General Joseph, won fame in Pacific war, death of, 232

Stock Market, 22

Strait of Messina, 93

Strikes, 40, 41, 107, 108, 190, 209, 313; in essential industries, 59, 60; of steel workers, 68; of coal miners, 68; in automotive industry, 181, 182; steel, 212; of meat packers, 212; Subway of New York threatened by, 215; in city of Pittsburgh, 215; at Allis-Chalmers Co., 216; of soft coal miners, 217, 218; Lewis and his Union fined, 220, 221; 1946 topped all records for, 284; of school teachers in Buffalo, N. Y., 285; rise in prices due to, 310, 311; "fringe" demands, 312

Succession Bill, 182, 183, 221, 222, 272; passed, 273

Sugar, supply to United States cut off, 12

Sullivan, John J., appointed Under-Secretary of Navy, 226

Sumatra, 17, 21

Supplies, cut off by Pacific war, 20, 21, 87, 88; for Normandy Invasion, 138, 139

Supreme Court, convenes for trial of German saboteurs, 38; dissenting verdicts of, 45; changes in personnel of, 79; approves "portal to portal" pay, 109, 110; Petrillo incident, 112, 113; new appointees to, 128; split decisions of, 128, 129, 130; Fred M. Vinson new Chief Justice, 225; Justices Jackson and Black feud, 226

Sweden, joins United Nations, 192; attends Paris Conference, 294

Switzerland, 294

Taft, Senator Robert, 294, 323, 328

Taft-Hartley Labor Act, passed over President's veto, 278; provisions of, 279, 284, 285, 286; President Truman obliged to invoke, 312

Tarawa, Marines "toughest job" at, 87

Tarbell, Ida M., writer, death of, 131

Taxes, 22, 40, 103, 104, 105, 279, 313, 314

Taylor, Senator Glen H., Progressive Party candidate for Vice President, 324; refused to repudiate Communists' support, 331

Teheran, 66, 85, 141; also see Conferences

Timor, occupied by Japs, 17

Tito, Marshal, rebelled against Russian domination, 307; also see Yugoslavia

Tobin, Daniel, Union leader, 286

Tobruk, 31

Tokio, bombed by American fliers, 19, 132

Tolstoy, Alexandra, gave refuge to Mrs. Kasenkina, 301

Toulon, French Fleet stationed at, 35

Trade Agreements, signed at Havana Conference, 307

Trade Unions, 121

Treaties, 239, 240, 241, 244; four confirmed by U. S. Senate, 253; Russia signs with former satellites of Germany, 260; signed in Paris, 261; signed at Rio de Janeiro, 265; at Bogotá Conference, 306; International Treaty of Reciprocal Assistance signed, 308

Tri-partite Pact, The, of Axis, 6

Truk, Jap stronghold captured, 133

Truman, Harry S., nominated for Vice President, 120; becomes President on death of Roosevelt, 169, 170; at Potsdam, 171, 172; terminates Lend Lease, 177, 178; plans for domestic economy, 179, 180; 1946 Message to Congress, 199, 200, 203; forces end of railroad strike, 214, 215; was humble in face of task ahead, 222; rising popularity, 223; friendly to labor, 224; opposes Lewis, 224; vetoed Case Bill, 224; the Pauley incident, 225; "take home pay," of President, 231; Proclamation of, 238, 239; visit to Mexico, 244, 245; "The Truman Doctrine," 246, 248; at Rio de Janeiro, 265; difficult position of, 270; Message to Congress, 274, 275; vetoes Taft-Hartley Labor Act, 278; "honeymoon" with Congress over, 279, 280; calls special session of Congress, 282, 283; asks Congress for Economic and Military program, 290; had urged partition in Palestine, 309; recommends grants to States, 310; forced to invoke the Taft-Hartley Act, 312, 313; Message to Congress, 314; Budget for 1948 largest in peacetime, 314, 315, 316; rift with Congress, 317; begins campaign for election, 318, 319, 320, 325, 326, 327; nominated on first ballot, 330; was elected, 333; "Solid South" alienated by Civil Rights program of, 333; post-mortem of election of, 333, 334

Truman Doctrine, 246, 247, 248

Truman, Mrs. Martha, mother of President, death of, 288

Tugwell, Guy, 249; supported Wallace for President, 331

Tulagi, 32

Tunisian Campaign, 36, 84, 90, 91, 92, 93

Unemployment, post-war estimates, 179, 180

INDEX

Unification of Armed Forces, bill passed by Congress, 277; Secretary of Defense to be single head, 278

United Automobile Workers, 311

United Kingdom, *see* British Government

United Mine Workers Union, fined, 284; *also see* John L. Lewis

United Nations, Declaration signed by, 6; accept Atlantic Charter, 7; resources pooled by, 72, 73; at Hot Springs, Va., 76; organize UNRRA, 77, 78; Portugal grants use of Azores to, 86; Foreign Ministers at Moscow, 172; at Mexico City, 173; at San Francisco, 174; agree on Charter, 174, 175; Bretton Woods Agreement ratified, 176; Security Charter ratified by U. S. Senate, 175, 176; Organization and Functions of, 188, 189, 190; Russia uses veto, 192; Rockefeller offer of site in New York City, 192; Security Council holds first meeting in U. S. at Hunter College, 193; General Assembly of, 193; UNRRA ended, 200, 201; UNESCO in Paris, 204; problem of atomic power control taken up with, 208; grants trusteeship of mandated islands to United States, 244; Alliance between Britain and France, 244, 245; problem in Palestine, 258; veto power of, 259, 260, 261; countries aided by UNRRA, 261; progress at Lake Success, 244, 290; Count Bernadotte assassinated in Jerusalem, 291; survives as World Force, 291; Korean resolution passed by, 292; the Declaration of Human Rights passed by, 292; in Paris, 294; Berlin crisis placed before, 300

United Nations Educational, Scientific, Cultural Organization, U.N.E.S.C.O., 204

United Nations Relief and Rehabilitation Administration, UNRRA, organized, 77; Herbert Lehman Director, 78; terminated, 200, 201; countries aided by, 261

United Nations Security Charter, 175, 176; *also see* United Nations

United Nations Security Council, 192, 193, 244; *also see* United Nations

United States, Japanese attack Pearl Harbor, 1, 2; the Roberts, Knox reports on disaster, 2, 3, 4; Churchill comes to Washington, 5; A.E.F. landed in North Ireland, 6; Atlantic Charter accepted by, 6, 7; Guam and Wake unprepared for attack, 7, 8; General MacArthur escapes from Bataan, 9; 1942 Budget of, 9; National documents moved to hiding place, 10; rationing begins, 10; Civilian Defense, 12,

13, 14; great highway to Alaska completed by, 14; sends mission to India, 18; American fliers bomb Tokio, 19; possession of New Caledonia taken by, 20; *Normandie* burned at pier in, 21; industries convert to war, 22; increase in savings in, 23; Armed Forces goal of, 24, 25; debt limit raised, 25; Navy Supply Bill passed, 25; difficulties with Vichy government, 26, 27; Women's Organized Services of, 27, 28; naval victories in Coral Sea and Midway, 30, 31; epic of Guadalcanal, 32, 33; extra-territorial rights in China relinquished by, 32; Naval victory in Solomons, 32, 33; American troops land in North Africa, 34, 35, 36, 37; Fifth Column at home, 37, 38; German saboteurs captured in, 38, 39; strikes in, 41; New Deal "red tape," 42; President's Message to Congress, 49, 50, 51; nation united in war effort, 51; the national debt, 52, 54; Executive Salary Order killed by Congress, 54, 55, 56; Debt Bill, 54, 55, 56; Army Appropriation passed, 57; Smith-Connally Bill passed, 57; Congress deprives President of power to devaluate dollar, 57; mines taken over by Government, 59; railroads taken over by Government, 59, 60; American production toasted by Stalin, 66, 67; "Lend-Lease" by, 74; NRPB abolished by Congress, 75; Conference at Hot Springs, Va., 76; UNRRA organized in Atlantic City, N. J., 77, 78; global war, 81; six major conferences attended by President, 83, 84, 85; Secretary Hull confers in Moscow, 85; epic battles in Pacific, 86, 87; difficulty of flying supplies to China, 87, 88; Italian surrender in Sicily, 93; list of war agencies, 94, 95, 96; President's Message to Congress, 97, 98, 99, 100; greatest military power in 1944, 106; Tax Bill passed, 103, 104, 105; Democracy proves its worth, 106, 107; strikes in 1944, 107, 108, 109; Lewis and Petrillo incidents, 109, 110, 111; Montgomery Ward & Co., case, 112, 113, 114, 115; President Roosevelt candidate for fourth term, 116, 117, 118, 119, 120; decision on Soldier vote, 117, 118, 122; changes in Cabinet, 124, 125; Lend Lease Act renewed, 72, 73, 125, 126; President's Message in 1944, 126; Hancock-Baruch report, 127, 128; Supreme Court's "split decisions," 128, 129, 130; victories in Marshall Islands, 133, 134; greatest air power in 1944, 134; American Forces re-

INDEX

turn to Philippines, 135; mistress of seas, 135; Tunisian Campaign of, 135, 136, 137; State Department send note to Eire, 137; Normandy Invasion, 138, 139, 140, 141; Conferences at Dumbarton Oaks and Bretton Woods, 142, 143, 144; atomic bomb opened new era, 146; Battle of the "Bulge," 150; unconditional surrender of German Forces, 151, 152, 153; first atomic bomb in history exploded by, 155; General Marshall reports on progress of war, 155, 156; epic of Iwo Jima and Okinawa, 157, 158, 159; atomic bombs dropped on Japanese cities, 159; final ceremony of Japanese surrender, 160, 161; General Marshall's final report on war, 161; problem of atomic power control, 162; Radar another great discovery, 163; American business man's aid in winning war, 164; Conferences at Yalta and Potsdam, 166, 167, 171; sudden death of President Roosevelt, 169, 170; Truman becomes President, 169, 170; Moscow meeting, 172; Conferences at San Francisco and Mexico City, 173, 174; U. N. Security Charter ratified by Senate, 176; Lend Lease terminated, 177, 178; reconversion, 179, 180; new Cabinet, 182, 183; New World role for, 187, 190; difficulties with Yugoslavia, 199; O.P.A. almost ended, 200; UNRRA ended, 201, 202; greatest single loan in international history made to Britain by, 203; atomic bomb tests at Bikini, 205; a "top secret," 208; many strikes in 1946, 209, 210, 211, 213, 214, 215, 216, 217, 218, 219, 220; Lewis and his Union fined, 220, 284; salary increases for some Government officials, 231; "take home" pay of President of, 231; rise in national debt, 231; President's Proclamation, 238, 239; trusteeship of mandated islands given to, 243, 244; Secretary Marshall reports on Moscow meeting, 246; the "Truman Doctrine," 246, 247; Wallace attacks policy of, 249, 250; President advocates Marshall Plan, 251, 283; Korean crisis, 250, 251; Senate confirms treaties with four countries, 253; the Palestine problem, 255, 256, 257, 258; "Little Assembly" of U. N. boycotted by Russia, 260; Italy's war debt cut by, 261; contributions to other peoples by, 261, 264; Treaty of Rio Conference ratified by Senate, 265; Secretary Marshall's rebuke to Soviet, 266, 267; Succession Bill passed, 271, 272; President's Message to Congress, 274, 275; Unification Bill passed, 277, 278; Taft-Hartley Labor Act passed, 278, 279; Portal to Portal Act passed, 279, 280; President calls special session of Congress, 282; President's Message to Congress, 283, 290; "cold war," 289, 291; the Marshall Plan, 251, 283, 293, 294, 295, 296; Bilateral Agreements signed by, 294; Americans and British join to supply food to Berlin by air, 299, 300; Russians refuse to lift blockade of Berlin, 300, 301; Kasenkina and Samarin incidents, 302; Communist spy ring uncovered in, 303; the Chambers-Hiss case, 303; the Korean incident, 304; at Bogotá Conference, 305, 306; Trade Agreements signed at Havana, 307; International Treaty of Reciprocal Assistance signed by, 308; problems in Near and Far East, 309; employment gains in, 310; production retarded by strikes, 311; Taxes, 313, 314, 315; President's Message to Congress in 1948, 314, 315, 316, 317; Presidential election in 1948, 321, 322, 323, 324, 325, 326, 327, 328, 329, 330, 331, 332, 333, 334; Truman elected, 335

United States Employment Service, 180

Utah, sunk at Pearl Harbor, 2

Vandenberg, Senator Arthur H., refers to San Francisco Conference, 174; Wallace incident, 250; President *pro tempore*, 271; declined to be candidate for President, 324

Versailles Treaty, gave Japs mandate for Marshall Islands, 18

Veto Message, of President Roosevelt, 103

Veto Power, of President, 280, 281; in United Nations, 259, 291, 292

Vichy Government, 25, 26, surrenders Indo-China to Japs, 27; in Africa, 34, 35, 37; in flight, 141

Vinson, Fred M., Secretary of Treasury, 182; new Chief Justice of Supreme Court, 225, 226

Vishinsky, Andrei, Russian Foreign Minister, 258, 259, 268, 296; denounces United States, 260; casts 28th Russian veto in U. N. Council, 291

V-J Day, 159, 181

"Voice of America," Radio broadcasts to Russia, 242

Volstead, Andrew, father of Prohibition Act, death of, 288

von Ribbentrop, Joachim, Nazi leader hanged, 194

351

INDEX

AMERICA's place as a world leader today is due mainly to two circumstances, one planned by man, the other not. By great good fortune America is blessed with rich natural resources, and because of the foresight of her founding fathers, her government is such that these resources may be utilized for the benefit of all. For America encourages, and sometimes insists, that her citizens use their various abilities to increase or at least conserve these resources and ingeniously to implement them whenever possible. For it is only thus that America's rich natural heritage can be increasingly enjoyed by all.

The final pages of each volume of this edition of James Truslow Adams' *History of the United States* are devoted to picturing the theme of the volume. And on the following pages are depicted many typical scenes, showing why this country is great and rich and enjoys the highest standard of living any country has ever known.

This photograph would seem to be an almost perfect illustration of the first stanza of the song "America the Beautiful." Truly the spacious skies, majestic Mt. Nebo (11,871 ft.) and neighboring peaks in Santaquin National Forest form a beautiful backdrop for the modern harvest scene here depicted. A combined harvester-thresher is shown operating in a field of barley, located in the fertile Elberta Valley of Utah, some 70 miles south of Salt Lake City.

CONTOUR STRIP CROPPING

Courtesy of Soil Conservation Service—U. S. Department of Agriculture

This photograph shows both contour and strip cropping as practiced on a Wisconsin farm.

It has long been known that hillsides may safely be farmed by fitting the crop pattern to the slope of the land, for by running his cultivator across the slope on the contour, the farmer creates a whole series of dams lying across the path of the escaping rain water. Strip cropping, which is the practice of alternating bands of cultivated and non-cultivated crops on the contour, further increases water conservation and decreases soil erosion. Here we see alternating crops of corn, grain and alfalfa. In addition strips of close-growing, erosion-resisting crops, such as hay, may be planted above and below cultivated strips further to check the flow of water over long slopes. This method of farming also offers a convenient means of crop rotation.

A MECHANICAL COTTON PICKER

Courtesy of The International Harvester Company

Pictured here is one type of machine recently developed which bids fair to revolutionize the economy of the South. Although not in general use at present, the mechanical cotton picker is certain to attain widespread popularity among cotton farmers, for it equals the work of from 40 to 50 average field hands in the harvesting process.

CALIFORNIA CITRUS GROVE

By courtesy of the California Fruit Growers Exchange

Spanish adventurers brought the lemon to America and supposedly it was introduced into California at the same time as the orange—though its commercial development was much slower. Approximately 95 per cent of all lemons grown in America are produced in California. Although oranges are grown as far north in California as the latitude of New York City, lemons require a somewhat warmer climate and the majority of the plantings are in southern California. Because of the protection from cold northern winds afforded the interior valleys by the high mountain ranges, because of other favorable climatic factors, and because both orange and lemon trees are evergreen, California can ship fresh citrus fruits to market every day of the year.

FRUIT PRESERVATION

Photograph by Moulin Studios, courtesy of National Canners Association

America is probably the best fed and healthiest nation in the world. One of the main reasons for this happy condition is the fact that our canning and preserving industries have reached such a high state of efficiency. The great volume of total American production of canned and preserved foods comes from canneries located in the rural areas. The proximity of the cannery to the source of raw produce is one of the principal attributes of this industry, for fresh produce is canned while still in its freshest state, thus preserving the most nutritious elements of the produce. In 1947 the average person in the United States consumed 19.5 pounds of canned fruit alone. This photograph shows one stage in the processing of peaches; in this instance the container is a glass jar. It is interesting to note the sanitary precautions taken here such as the use of hair nets, rubber gloves and aprons and clean uniforms.

REFORESTATION OPERATIONS

By courtesy of the United States Forest Service

America has only recently awakened to the fact that our timber reserves have dwindled dangerously, not only because of indiscriminate lumbering operations and carelessly started forest fires but also because there has not been a comprehensive reforestation program to replace losses.

The United States Forest Service is now working tirelessly to remedy this situation. This photograph shows a planting crew climbing the trail up Lookout Mountain located in the Columbia National Forest in Washington. Each member of the crew carries a planting mattock and bag of tree seedlings. The snags and fallen logs are all that remain of a once beautiful stand of virgin timber which was burned over in the Yacolt fire of 1902.

"PAUL BUNYAN" TOOTHPICKS

From a photograph copyright by Asabel Curtis

These massive timbers were hewn from Douglass fir trees. In addition to its other uses Douglass fir is the principal wood from which plywood is fabricated. Leading lumber companies are now cooperating with the United States Forest Service in a program of conservation in order that such sources of timber shall not be irretrievably lost. As an example of how seriously our government is thinking about the problem, the Supreme Court in a recent decision ruled that lumbermen who cut down forests are bound to replant them.

GLASS BLOWER AT WORK

Courtesy of Du Pont Company. Lofman-Pix Photograph

An example of an art abetting a science. Glass blowers supply chemists with all types of special laboratory apparatus essential to exploring the chemical world. This complicated piece of equipment is a part for a high-vacuum still to be used in chemical research at the experimental station of E. I. du Pont de Nemours and Company.

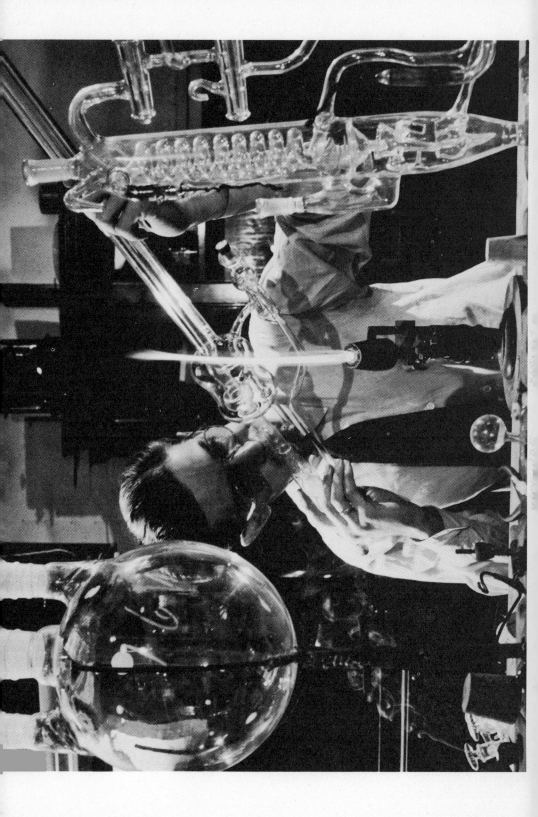

SUBMERGED LAND WELLS, ELWOOD FIELD, CALIFORNIA

From a photograph copyright by Spence Air Photos, Los Angeles

The continental shelf covers an underwater area of roughly 10 million square miles, about one tenth of which is contiguous to the coastlines of the United States and Alaska. Because of the geological character of the shelf it is believed that beneath it may be the greatest petroleum resources yet to be found anywhere. In 1945 President Truman decided to proclaim federal ownership of those lands off our own coast, and several states, primarily Louisiana, Texas and California, are fighting for State rather than Federal ownership. Although costs of drilling offshore wells are roughly three times those of comparable land operations, still the tremendous reserves (estimated roughly at 500 times the world's current consumption as of 1947) will make them increasingly valuable as our land reserves are depleted. In this picture the wells are directly offshore but in Louisiana some platforms are as far as 27 miles offshore in water up to 55 feet deep.

WORLD'S LARGEST OIL REFINERY

Courtesy of the Standard Oil Company (New Jersey). Photograph by Corsini

The Humble Oil and Refining Company's refinery at Baytown, Texas was commissioned in 1920 and now has a capacity to produce over 250,000 barrels of oil a day. It also has facilities for storing more than 21,000,000 barrels of crude oil and products and is operated 24 hours a day by some 6,000 workers.

NATURAL GAS PIPELINE

A section of the 30-inch Texas-New York pipe line under construction in Mississippi. It will stretch some 1,840 miles and will bring natural gas from the fields of Texas and Louisiana to New York City. There it will be reformed and mixed with manufactured gas and will replace considerable quantities of oil now used for enriching the present type of manufactured gas. Four hundred and seventy thousand tons of welded steel plate will be required to fabricate the pipe used. The project was begun in May, 1949, and construction is expected to be completed so that natural gas can be delivered to New York City in the winter of 1950-51.

LONG-DISTANCE DIAL TELEPHONE EQUIPMENT

Courtesy of The American Telephone & Telegraph Company

Automatic switching equipment in telephone toll offices permits operators to put through calls to distant telephones directly without the aid of other operators en route. This method of Operator toll dialing will increase immeasurably the speed and efficiency of long-distance phone calls. This system is being planned to give service to all parts of the United States and Canada.

NEW COLOR–CONVERTIBLE PRESS

Courtesy of The Christian Science Monitor, Boston, Massachusetts

This is a view of the new Hoe presses which are being installed for *The Christian Science Monitor*. They will make it possible to print 40-page papers at the rate of 120,000 an hour. To the right of the massive substructure may be seen the small railway tracks along which the 1,500-pound rolls of newsprint are brought to be fed to the giant presses.

FORD'S ROUGE PLANT

The Ford Motor Company's Rouge plant is the world's largest industrial city. Grouped into a single unit covering 1,196 acres are blast furnaces, coke ovens, docks, assembly lines, machine and repair shops. Here are railroad and bus systems, the world's largest production foundry, a paper mill and a glass plant, power house and laboratories. In the immediate foreground is the Rotunda building, exhibit building for Ford products, and facing it is the Administration Building.

SIGHT-SEEING TRAIN

The new Burlington Vista Dome Zephyr recently put into operation along the upper Mississippi. The eight-car diesel-engined train has five glass-domed sections for sight-seeing purposes. These trains do not ordinarily exceed 100 miles per hour, although speeds up to 122 miles per hour have been recorded. This stainless steel train averages from 75 to 90 miles per hour and makes the trip between Chicago and St. Paul, a distance of 427 miles, in 6 hours and 15 minutes including stops.

FLYING BOX-CAR

Courtesy of Fairchild Aircraft, Hagerstown, Maryland

This is a photograph of the model C-119 plane now being produced for the armed forces which will be the standard troop carrier transport plane of the Air Force. Access to the interior for bulky equipment is gained through clam-shell doors which open the entire rear of the square-cornered cargo hold. The plane is powered by two 2,650 hp. Pratt & Whitney radial air-cooled engines and has a cargo capacity of 2,700 cubic feet.

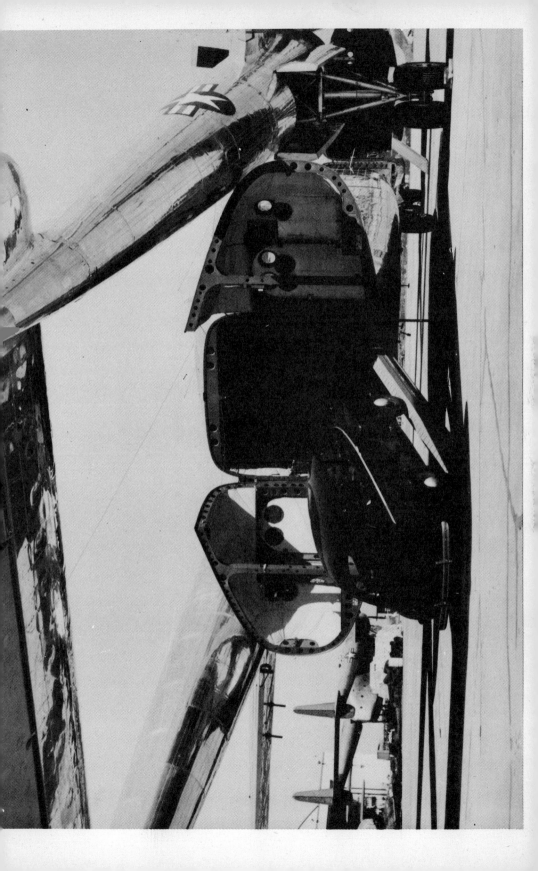

HISTORY OF
THE UNITED STATES

VOLUME VII

From an Acme Photo by Charles Corte.

HARRY S. TRUMAN

THIRTY—THIRD PRESIDENT OF THE UNITED STATES

THE MARCH OF
DEMOCRACY

A

HISTORY OF THE UNITED STATES

By

James Truslow Adams

Volume VII

THIRD PART OF ANNUAL CHRONICLE

By

ALLAN NEVINS

Professor of History
Columbia University

NEW YORK

CHARLES SCRIBNER'S SONS

CONTENTS

CONTENTS

ILLUSTRATIONS

ix

ILLUSTRATIONS

ILLUSTRATIONS

xi

xi

VOLUME VII

THIRD PART OF ANNUAL CHRONICLE

CHAPTER I

THE RECORD OF 1949

O N THE whole, 1949 may be placed among the happier days in American annals. Material well-being was maintained at a fairly high level, for a brief and minor recession was followed by a return to steady industrial production and rising income. To be sure, the cold war with Russia continued, a mighty tactical and psychological contest between the two greatest Powers of the globe. A deep tremor passed through all democratic peoples when President Harry Truman announced in September: "We have evidence that . . . an atomic explosion has occurred in the U.S.S.R." But though it was a frightening fact that the Russian Politburo, able to act secretly and without accountability to their own nation or world sentiment, now shared possession of the most horrifyingly devastating weapon ever made, the cold war gave no sign of generating great heat. Even as mutual hatreds and suspicions rose, the West showed a growing unity which made an Eastern attack seem less likely than before. Meanwhile, measures were taken in America to diffuse welfare more widely. Art, letters and science made gratifying progress.

I

Not only Americans themselves, but the people of other democratic nations, were interested above all else in the economic stability of the United States. Any business crisis, any really threatening depression, would have had disastrous effects in Western Europe, Australasia, and Latin America. Such was the situation of the non-Communist world, tossing in the trough left by the Second Global War, that everything depended upon the vigor, optimism, productive power, and statesmanlike altruism of the great republic. Fortunately, neither its energy nor its morale flagged.

The recession which appeared early in the year never really became alarming. A sharp setback in grain and livestock prices was accompanied by what experts called an "inventory recession"; for business, apprehensive of the future, cut down on reorders of goods. In response both commodity and stock-market prices dropped, and the number of unemployed rose. From November, 1948, to July, 1949, production as measured by the Federal Reserve Board index fell by 17 per cent. But these unfavorable factors were checked by the high purchasing power and hopeful outlook of the masses. In the first half of the year the public reduced its spending by only 5 per cent—and the industrial slackening soon ended.

As, in midsummer, the production of steel, cotton textiles and a great variety of consumer goods began rising steadily, unemployment became less troublesome. At one time estimated at nearly five million, it dropped to perhaps three million. Steel output, which in August had been but 82.2 per cent of capacity, recovered in December to 94.5 per cent. For 1949 as a whole, Secretary of Commerce Sawyer was able to report that gross national production (that is, the market value of goods and services combined) amounted to $259,000,000,000, and that total personal income was $212,000,000,000. These figures were only about 2 per cent below those of the rich year 1948. Employment for the year maintained an average of 58,500,000, which again was only 2 per cent below 1948. Construction had reached the highest level in the nation's history. Individual savings were unprecedentedly large, and were rising.

Although the American farmer was made uneasy by dropping prices, he continued to enjoy good times. Net farm income for the year was roughly fourteen billions, as compared with eighteen billions in 1947, and sixteen billions in 1948, the two record years of American history. Yet average income for the year was still about three times as high as in pre-war times. Crops were large. For the fifth consecutive season wheat production exceeded a billion bushels (1,126,000,000); for the fifth time in recent years corn production exceeded three billions (3,358,-000,000). From every part of the country came stories of the practical elimination of farm debt, the steady improvement of buildings, and the widened use of implements. In certain wheat and stockgrowing areas millionaire farmers were now too numerous to excite comment.

3

Nevertheless, the economic skies were by no means without their clouds. The net income of the farming population was expected to drop again in 1950. About two thirds of American exports to Western Europe were being financed by the Marshall Plan; and that program was to be gradually curtailed, and if possible brought to an end by the close of 1952. Businessmen were worried by what they thought the exorbitant demand of labor leaders for a "fourth round" of wage increases, or their equivalent in pensions and welfare benefits. They grumbled about a labor policy of "superimposing wartime gains on a peace economy." Above all, government expenditures remained almost appallingly high. So liberally did Congress vote money that the 1949 appropriations or commitments, $43,000,000,000, were a peacetime record.

Ordinarily in a post-war period of great prosperity, the country would have expected a systematic reduction in its debt-load. But as spending thus outstripped tax receipts, the national debt actually increased, reaching the $257,000,000,000 mark in December. A budget deficit of about $5,500,000,000 was in sight for the fiscal year ending June 30, 1950. Some observers were worried also by the size of consumer credits, which, thanks to the relaxing of controls on installment selling, were creeping near the end of the year to the eighteen-billion mark. The country as a whole took the combination of heavy debt, heavy spending, and fairly heavy taxation some-

4

what insouciantly. Much of business, however, though in a cheerful mood as the year ended, was following the motto: "Proceed with caution."

The sequence of recession and renewed prosperity had its effect on the Administration's financial policies. When the year began President Truman was pressing urgently for higher taxes to furnish a four-billion increase in reve-

PREVAILING HEADWINDS
From a cartoon by Long in *The Minneapolis Tribune*

nues. In July, however, he withdrew this demand, declaring that "in a declining national economy" there could be "no greater folly" than to try to balance the budget. Then, toward the end of the year, when the rise in production and income made inflation rather than deflation a danger, and rendered pump-priming of the economy unnecessary, he changed his attitude. Mr. Truman declared in October that deficit financing must end. "We have got to find money to run the government, period," he told the press.

All the principal economic groups of the nation kept

an anxious eye upon the future. In order to stabilize exports as the Marshall Plan supports declined, the government and various industrial groups prepared to push a great import drive. Paul Hoffman of the Economic Cooperation Administration declared that for the health of the democratic nations a rise of two billions a year in American imports was necessary. This would of course stimulate a balancing flow of exports. In other words, the United States had a plain economic as well as political stake in the ability of Europe to pay its own way after 1952. Labor seemed inclined to moderate its demands in the interests of national stability. Meanwhile, agricultural leaders showed a realization that large crop-surpluses, the cost of government support, and high food prices aroused discontent among the urban population.

I

The most spectacular events of the year were a series of trials involving Communist activities in the United States. At one time, three cases were attracting attention simultaneously. They were the trial in New York City of eleven Communist Party leaders, indicted on the charge of violating the Smith Act of 1940 by conspiring to "advocate and teach" the violent overthrow of the government; the trial of Alger Hiss, formerly a figure of some importance in the State Department, for perjury —behind which lurked the implied charge that he had transmitted copies of important government documents

to Russian hands; and the trial of Judith Coplon, a minor
Justice Department employee, on the charge of stealing
documents from government files and giving them to
a Russian agent. These trials were accompanied by a
somewhat feverish public feeling, so that many observers
feared the development of an anti-Red hysteria. Much
antagonism was aroused in the spring by a so-called conference on international peace held at the Waldorf-As-
toria hotel in New York under strongly pro-Soviet auspices. Some unofficial delegates of Communist allegiance
were denied entry by the American authorities; other
foreign delegates were forbidden to make a tour of inspection through the country. Entry was also refused to
the Rev. Hewlett Johnson, the "Red Dean" of Canter-
bury, who wished to make a lecture tour for the National Council of Soviet-American Friendship.

The most important of the trials, that of the "Politburo" of eleven Communist Party leaders, dragged into
the autumn amid a blaze of headlines. The main questions at issue were three: Was the Communist Party a
conspiracy?—Did the Party advocate the overthrow of
the government by force?—and, Did the American Party
take its orders from Moscow? Judge Harold Medina presided with dignity and impartiality as the defense maintained an exasperating barrage of quarrelsome arguments, challenges, and demonstrations. On October 14
the judge delivered a 16,000-word charge to the jury, telling them to assume the constitutionality of the Smith

Act. Next day, all eleven defendants were found guilty. They appealed, and the case was expected eventually to reach the Supreme Court, which might rule on the validity of the Smith Act.

In the Hiss case the prominence of the defendant (he was president of the Carnegie Endowment for International Peace) and its obvious elements of mystery raised interest to a still greater height. Hiss was accused of lying under oath when he denied to a grand jury that he had ever given State Department papers to Whittaker Chambers, a confessed Communist agent, or that he had seen Chambers after January 1, 1937. A six-weeks trial ended inconclusively in midsummer as the jury disagreed, eight voting for conviction, four for acquittal. On November 18 a second trial began under a new judge, with a wider array of evidence admitted. It was destined to close early in the new year in Hiss's conviction and his sentence to five years in prison. Meanwhile, Miss Coplon had been quickly convicted on the charge of removing papers from government files, and sentenced to forty months to ten years in jail. She was then remanded to a new trial, along with her alleged confederate, V. A. Gubitchev, on the much more serious charge of conspiracy to commit espionage.

Partly because of the disclosures in these trials, but more largely because of the threatening attitude of Russia, feeling against the Communists rose to a high pitch. This was in spite of the fact that the Communist Party

8

has negligible strength in the United States. Although it claims a membership of 70,000, actually the total is much smaller. Born in 1919, the Party reached its greatest vigor in the United States early in the depression of the 1930s, when it had perhaps 100,000 well-disciplined members, with a much larger number of sympathizing "fellow-travelers." But the Party never fully recovered from the Hitler-Stalin Pact, while recent events have kept it weak and discredited.

The Department of Justice took steps in 1949 to deport a considerable number of aliens charged with Communist affiliations. Harry Bridges, the noted Australian-born president of the CIO International Longshoremen's and Warehousemen's Union, was brought to trial in San Francisco on a charge of perjury and conspiracy. He had sworn in 1945 that he had never been a member of the Communist Party, while the government contended that he had been. Several legislatures, led by Maryland, passed bills to outlaw the Communist Party or place severe restrictions upon it. The noted German Communist Gerhard Eisler, facing punishment for refusing to supply evidence demanded by a House Committee, escaped to Europe while his appeal was pending in the Supreme Court. A number of educational institutions, including the University of Washington, dismissed faculty members for Party activity. Many States considered, and some passed, bills requiring stringent loyalty oaths from teachers in tax-supported schools or universities. In New York the sweeping Feinberg Act, which required the State Board of Regents to list subversive organizations, thus laying a foundation for the dismissal of teachers belonging to them, aroused a vociferous wave of protest. Finally it was annulled.

To many Americans the whole fierce movement against Communism seemed a token of healthy vigilance —for if war came, a Communist fifth column might do terrible harm. To many other citizens the outburst of feeling seemed exaggerated and dangerous. Led by the American Civil Liberties Union, numerous organizations took steps to curb the excesses of officials and to protect innocent individuals. The general belief of well-informed men and women was that "guilt by association" was unjust and untenable; that it was impossible to make fair lists of "subversive organizations"; and that "purges" of government offices, colleges, and other places would miss most guilty persons (who would lie), and crush many harmless people. The House Un-American Activities Committee proceeded with more fairness in its inquiries after Representative John S. Wood of Georgia replaced Parnell Thomas of New Jersey as chairman, and after John Rankin of Mississippi was excluded by a rule requiring that all the members be lawyers.

II

In governmental affairs the Truman Administration essayed, with much success, to press its "fair deal." But observers noted that while public support for welfare measures remained great, regulatory measures met increasing opposition.

It was "a streamlined Congress," with special research aids and an improved committee system, which met in January. But though the first session of this 81st Congress proved in the end to be fairly fruitful, the tempo of its action was dismayingly slow. For months, obstruction and indolence had free rein. An illustration of the languid temper of Congressmen was provided by the Reciprocal Trade Agreements Bill, renewing the authority of the executive to negotiate treaties for lower tariff rates. The bill passed the House February 9; it did not get through the Senate until August 15. This new measure, promptly signed by the President, restored the trade-agreement policy to the basis established by Secretary Hull in 1934, shearing away the unfortunate amendments which the 80th Congress had attached.

The most important domestic measures passed by Congress related to housing, minimum wages, and farm price supports. They were measures, that is, to furnish or preserve a certain degree of welfare to great masses of people. The Housing Act was especially noteworthy. It authorized Federal funds to assist local housing authorities in constructing no fewer than 810,000 homes over a six-year period, at the rate of 135,000 a year. Under this legislation, the national government would be obligated to pay local housing authorities about $233,000,000 annually over a period of approximately thirty-three years. This sum would make up the difference between the amount that low-income families could afford to pay in rent, and the amount needed to amortize the cost of the housing.

The Housing Act also provided for slum clearance, authorizing the government to make loans aggregating not more than a billion dollars and free grants amounting to not more than a half-billion more to help city housing agencies get rid of these social plague-spots. In addition, low-income farmers were to be assisted in erecting better houses by loans up to a quarter of a billion dollars, and by outright grants of not more than five millions annually for five years. This was the most generous housing measure that the country had yet known, and its authors hoped that in half a dozen years it would give far better living conditions to the poorest stratum of the population. In principle it did not differ from the pre-war housing program.

Another important enactment raised minimum wages of labor in various categories of workers from 40 cents an hour to 75 cents. This was by amendments to the Fair Labor Standards Act of 1938, which was simultaneously changed to restrict somewhat the number of workers thus protected. Most persons in covered employments already received at least 75 cents, but it was estimated that about 1,500,000 wage-earners would get increases ranging from five to fifteen cents hourly. The child labor provisions of the law were strengthened. It is eloquent of the changing standard of values in the country (and also of the rising standard of living) that the hourly wage-rate of 75 cents in 1950 had been about the daily average wage-rate of unskilled labor in 1850.

The six million farm families of the country were too important to the general economy, and their votes were too vital to politicians, to be neglected. A continued program of support for farm products was taken for granted, but its nature aroused violent controversy. Secretary of Agriculture Charles F. Brannan brought forward a new plan. He proposed that farm production should be more rigidly controlled by the government; that payments for it should be made direct from the Treasury; and that farm commodities should be allowed to drop to their natural price-level in the market. Thus consumers would no longer be taxed to keep their food prices high. Farmers naturally regarded this scheme with suspicion. Tightened government controls were repugnant to them. They realized also that direct payments from the Treasury could be more easily attacked than indirect payments. Of the four major farm organizations, only the National Farmers' Union lent the Brannan Plan support; the Grange, the Council of Farmer Cooperatives, and the powerful Farm Bureau Federation all vigorously opposed it.

The farm legislation passed in 1949 followed the familiar lines. Senator Clinton P. Anderson, former Secre-

tary of Agriculture, took it in charge. By its provisions
the existing 90 per cent of parity support for five basic
crops would be carried through 1950. Then in 1951 these
crops would be supported at from 80 to 90 per cent, and
after the beginning of 1952 at from 75 to 90 per cent
of parity. Everyone knew, however, that the legislation
would be revised again for 1951 and 1952, and revised
under the same pressure to buy votes by extending benefits. The farm-support program had its merits, for nobody wished to see the farmers slip back to the desperate
position they had occupied in the years 1920–1933—the
years of poverty, foreclosures, and the McNary-Haugen
agitation. But it also had its glaring defects.

The outcry of consumers and taxpayers against the
program steadily increased in volume. By the end of the
year the government had about $650,000,000 tied up in
carrying the cotton-surplus; a surplus of some fifty million bushels of potatoes had become so burdensome that
Secretary Brannan unavailingly offered to sell them for
export at a cent a bushel; and the cost of other surpluses
was grievous. The Commodity Credit Corporation estimated that it could not get through the crop year 1950
unless its authority to lend money on crops was increased
to a total of $6,750,000,000. Some observers believed that
as farmers took note of the rising complaints, and as the
fall in farm prices and income continued, rural organizations would swing to the support of Mr. Brannan's plan
for guaranteeing stable farm income by direct payments.

Certainly his proposals would give consumers the benefit of a free market and lower prices.

Among the minor measures which Congress passed and President Truman signed were a bill extending Federal rent-control until the summer of 1950; an authorization of loans for the expansion of rural electrification service; and an assent to American participation in the international wheat agreement, which controlled over a period of years the price of wheat exported from the United States to certain nations.

III

No measures before Congress aroused keener national interest than those which dealt with Federal aid to education. A widespread conviction had grown up that the government must assist the poorer States, and especially those in the South, to improve their schools. At the same time, many educators and many members of Congress were apprehensive that national aid would lead to strict national controls. Such leaders as Senator Taft of Ohio were deeply concerned to safeguard State jurisdiction in the field of education. Moreover, the question whether Federal money should go to parochial as well as public schools aroused much feeling. Many if not most Protestants and Jews held that Federal funds should be restricted to the benefit of tax-supported public schools. Many if not most Catholics believed that Federal funds should be paid for "auxiliary services" (transport, text-books, health aids) to parochial school pupils even in States where the constitution or laws forbade that the State assist any private institutions.

At the present time, some thirty States forbid the payment of public funds to non-public schools; in eighteen States publicly supported bus service may be given to pupils in private schools; and in five States non-religious textbooks may be bought for such schools out of public moneys. Senator Thomas of Utah reported in the upper chamber a $300,000,000-a-year Federal aid bill which would have left the disbursement of the funds to the States. The measure provided for a graduation of the aid in inverse proportion to State provision, so that the poorer States would get more per capita than the richer. In some Southern States upward of $25 per pupil each year would be paid, while some Northern States would get only the minimum of $5 per pupil, or a little more.

It was in the House, however, that controversy raged most hotly. The Committee on Education and Labor under Chairman John Lesinski of Michigan assigned the subject to a subcommittee under Graham A. Barden of North Carolina. The result was the introduction of the Barden Bill, which like the Senate measure would have granted $300,000,000 annually to the States, with a minimum of $5 per pupil. It proposed to confine this Federal aid to "tax-supported grade schools and high schools which are under public supervision and control." This was distasteful to Catholic groups. A rival measure, the Kennedy bill, introduced August 1, required that out of the $300,000,000 a sum of $30,000,000 must be used for pupil-transportation, State-approved non-religious textbooks, and health services, and empowered the government to pay funds for these auxiliary services direct to parochial schools wherever the State authorities could or would not do so. Naturally this was distasteful to most Protestant and Jewish groups, and to many believers in the principle of the separation of church and state.

The temper of the debate was not improved when Cardinal Spellman made a heated attack on the much-beloved Mrs. Franklin D. Roosevelt for what he thought her intolerant views; an attack in which he made statements which he later qualified. In the end, four main groups appeared in Congress: those who opposed all Federal aid to education; those who rallied behind the Barden bill; those who supported the generally similar Thomas bill in the Senate; and those who insisted that some of the Federal money should benefit church schools. The session ended without any action.

It similarly ended without action on a number of measures which fitted into the pattern of Mr. Truman's "Fair Deal," but which were in conflict with a rising dislike of Federal controls and interventions. This dislike had been strongly expressed by the 80th Congress, which Mr. Truman so sternly denounced; it was manifest in milder form in the first session of the 81st. The President had expressed himself in favor of a national health insurance plan, sending Congress a special message on the subject April 22. Three days later a bill embodying his main views was introduced in both houses. Setting up an elaborate organization under a National Health Insurance Board, it would have created a system of prepaid personal medical, dental, hospital, and home nursing service on the general pattern of the existing social insurance plans; the expenditures to be financed largely by taxes on wages and other earnings. A vigorous debate ensued, with the American Medical Association leading the attack on the measure. Senators Taft, Smith, and O'Donnell offered a much milder and more cautious National Health Bill. Most physicians favored a national health program with an enlargement of voluntary health insurance organizations, and with State aid to the "medically indigent." Much was said both for and against the British scheme of health insurance. In the end, Congress decided to wait upon further study of the subject and further scrutiny of the ambitious British experiment.

The White House failed to gain any ground for its proposals with respect to the application of the TVA principle to other river basins: the Columbia, Missouri, and Ohio in particular. Majority sentiment in Congress seemed willing to approve of separate schemes for flood control, power development, and irrigation; but it was apparently quite unwilling to create grandiose new organizations for integrated river-valley development. The

President's proposals for a Fair Employment Practices Commission met strong Southern opposition, and came to nothing. Nor did the Administration bill for extending social-security coverage pass Congress. The House voted it by a narrow margin, but the Senate held it over until the session of 1950. Mr. Truman had promised a repeal of the Taft-Hartley Act regulating labor relations, but this was denied him. Among the general measures on which Congress failed to act was the Celler Bill for increasing the number of displaced persons specially admitted to the country from 205,000 to 337,000, and for liberalizing the terms of their admission.

Altogether, Congress ended with a record of fairly efficient action on urgent national problems (we shall now consider those met in the foreign field), of great liberality in appropriations, and of caution as regards legislation that would have augmented Federal and especially executive power.

IV

The foreign situation changed unmistakably for the worse during the year. The main elements in this deterioration were the triumph of the Communists in China over the Kuomintang Nationalists; the development by Russia of an atomic bomb; the substantial failure of the Big Four Ministers' conference in Paris in May and June; and the slow progress of the European Recovery Program. Throughout the year the democratic world felt the pressure of unremitting Russian hostility, backed by the enormous power of Russian military might. The Soviet Union conjecturally kept at least 1,800,000 men under arms, and controlled in addition the growing forces of its satellite states. It was credited with 15,000 first-line airplanes, and with 10,000 in reserve. A large program of submarine construction was known to be making rapid progress.

The twenty-year civil war in China came substantially to an end in 1949 with a startlingly rapid Communist sweep under Mao Tze-tung. At the beginning of the year Chiang Kai-shek's forces had still controlled about half the mainland area and population in China. But the Communists soon began a relentless advance. On April 24 they captured Nanking, capital of the Nationalist government. Then they steadily pressed forward to drive Chiang's forces out of Canton, Chungking, Shanghai, and other cities. By December the remnants of the Nationalist troops, hopelessly defeated, were fleeing to the island of Formosa. The victorious Mao Tze-tung had meanwhile convoked a Political Consultative Conference in Peiping which was nominally a constitutional convention but which actually merely rubber-stamped a framework of government already drafted by Communist leaders. Mao used the occasion to announce the formation of "The People's Republic of China." The end of the year found him arriving in Moscow for a conference with the Soviet leaders, and for the drafting of a political and economic agreement.

That these events constituted a major defeat for American policy, and posed a direct challenge to the West, was all too plain. The United States had to write China off as temporarily lost. With it were lost nearly three billion dollars' worth of aid which had gone to the Nationalists since the defeat of Japan. The State Department issued a White Paper which used 1100 pages of print to excuse and explain the American failure. Great forces of revolt and renovation had been at work in China; the Communists had capably employed them, while Chiang's corrupt and inept regime had steadily disintegrated. "The unfortunate but inescapable fact," declared the White Paper, "is that the ominous result of the civil war in China was beyond the control of the Government of the United States. Nothing that this country did or could have done within the reasonable limits of its capabilities could have changed that result. . . . It was the product of internal Chinese forces; forces which this country tried to influence but could not."

For the future, the United States could only warn the Communists that it would oppose them if they did not show genuine independence, and became mere puppets of Russia. The State Department declared that Washington would encourage by every possible means the development of China as a free and stable nation. But it would resist any effort by the Chinese Nationalists to attack the countries of Southeastern Asia. In every way, declared Secretary of State Acheson, America would support the measures of the United Nations "to maintain peace and security in the Far East." The attitude of Mao Tze-tung's government toward the United States was one of defiance. Although just after Christmas the government of India recognized the Communist regime in China, the United States held aloof; and Peiping made it plain that it disdained American recognition.

Meanwhile, the meeting of the Council of Foreign Ministers (Messrs. Acheson, Bevin, Schuman, and Vishinsky, for America, Britain, France, and Russia respectively) in Paris had resulted inconclusively. They began their work on May 23 under apparently favorable auspices. The Russian land-blockade of Berlin, so effectively countered by the Anglo-American air-lift, had just been ended by an agreement made in New York. Hopes ran high in some quarters that the Soviet Union would now show itself more reasonable. The three great aims in view were (1) to overcome some of the more absurd implications of the division of Germany between East and West; (2) to remove some of the obstacles to a treaty of peace with Austria; and (3) to reduce the tensions between the Soviet Union and the Western Powers.

Not one of these objects was really attained. In talks which lasted almost a month, which ranged over the whole field of Western-Soviet relations, and which found Vishinsky much more on the defensive than he had theretofore been, some agreements were reached—but they amounted to little. The lifting of the Russian blockade of Berlin was confirmed; but in various ways the Russian authorities continued to harass and impede land traffic. A consultation on trade and transport between Western and Eastern Germany by the occupation authorities of the four powers was provided for; but the Russians were so plainly determined to get the best end of any internal trade bargain that the Western conferees drew back. It was agreed that in return for certain Austrian concessions to Russia on reparations, oil-properties, and Danubian shipments, Russia should assist in the preparation of a draft treaty with Austria by September 1; but the Russians ditched the work on this treaty. All in all, the limited agreements reached by the Big Four ministers became increasingly meaningless.

When, in September, the American and British governments announced that an atomic explosion had been detected in the Soviet Union, most Western observers were taken aback. It had been supposed by such well-informed men as former Ambassador Averell Harriman that the Russians could not make an atomic bomb before 1952. Lieutenant-General Leslie R. Groves, who had been in charge of our atomic work during the war, declared that he would lose no sleep over the announcement. "The question is not if they have built a bomb, but how good that one is, and how many they have, and how soon they can catch up with us," he remarked. But

others took the matter more seriously. It seemed more
urgent than ever for the United Nations to bring Russia

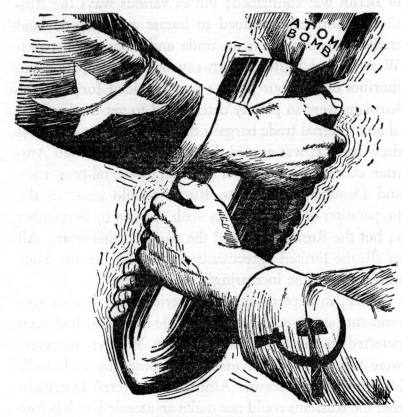

HANDLE WITH CARE!
From a cartoon by Marcus in *The New York Times*

to an agreement for the regulation of this horrifying
weapon. The event, said President Truman, "emphasizes
once again, if indeed such emphasis were needed, the
necessity for that truly effective and enforceable interna-

tional control of atomic energy which this government and the large majority of the members of the United Nations support."

But what could be done? Russia had offered her own plan. It called for the destruction of all bombs (that is, of the American stockpile); for the assignment of the development of atomic energy to individual nations, instead of an international body; and for an intermittent inspection by an international agency whose operations should be subject to the veto of any one of the Big Five powers. This was wholly unsatisfactory to the Western nations, which felt that continuous control and inspection were indispensable.

Long before Mao Tze-tung brought the 450,000,000 people of China under Communist sway, long before Russia succeeded in her first atomic explosion, the Western powers had taken momentous steps toward unification. Months of negotiation brought the governments of the United States, of Canada, and of ten European countries to a readiness to sign a treaty of mutual assistance. On April 4 the foreign ministers of the twelve nations, gathering in Washington, set their names to the North Atlantic Pact. "The parties agree," ran the treaty, "that an armed attack against one . . . shall be considered an armed attack against all." They further agreed that if such an attack eventuated the twelve nations would take effective action "to restore and maintain the security of the North Atlantic area."

25

This treaty was the Western reply to the threat of Russian aggression. It united more than 330,000,000 people, dwelling in a highly industrialized area of some seven and a half million square miles, in a compact to meet force with force. When placed before the Senate, reservations were quickly defeated, and it was ratified by a vote of 82 to 13. The size of this majority vote is the more impressive when we consider that the treaty marked a dramatic break with past traditions. For the first time in its history, the United States was committed to the principle that its frontier lay in the heart of Europe, along the line which divides Communist and non-Communist nations. There could be no question that an overwhelming public sentiment in the country regarded the treaty as vital to our safety.

Even as it was being ratified, the Truman Administration made it plain that another step was imperative. It at once proposed to Congress a Military Assistance Program, under which the United States would furnish its treaty partners with weapons to make their resistance more effective. This program already had a considerable history. In the autumn of 1948 American officers had begun to "observe" (that is, assist) the military planning which Western Europe had placed under the direction of Marshal Montgomery, the victor of El Alamein. Then, early in 1949, a board of three men, one for the army, one for the State Department, and one for the European Recovery Program, had been established in Washington to consider the defense needs of the Western nations. This body had explored the stocks of weapons on hand, the requirements of the various European forces, and the cost of sending American surpluses overseas.

CONVOY
From a cartoon by Seaman in *Justice*, ILGWU

The final Military Assistance Bill placed before Congress by the Truman Administration called for authority to spend $1,450,000,000 within a year in supplying arms to the eleven co-signers of the North Atlantic Treaty, and to five other nations: Greece, Turkey, Iran, Korea, and the Philippines. The omission of Nationalist China was significant. To some critics the sum demanded seemed too large, especially in view of the fact that Sec-

retary of Defense Louis Johnson declared that the arms-
aid program would have to be maintained for four or
five years. Senator Taft and others thought that the
grant of aid should be postponed until the Defense Council of twelve nations which the North Atlantic Treaty
had envisaged had been established, and had formed a
careful set of plans. But as September ended, the bill,
with its authorizations slightly reduced, passed Congress
and was signed by the President.

V

Meanwhile, the economic problems of Western Europe continued to trouble the United States even more
than its military weakness. During 1949 it became plain
that the Marshall Plan was in one light a brilliant success, and in another a partial failure. American assistance
under that plan had brought the production of Western
Europe decidedly above the pre-war levels. Great Britain
in particular had made a magnificent record in increasing
its industrial output. Yet the shortage of dollars in parts
of Europe, and the unbalanced condition of international
trade connected with this shortage, stubbornly persisted.
The British "dollar-gap" was particularly serious, for
Britain more than other countries needed imports from
the United States which could be bought only with dollars. By midsummer, it seemed imperatively necessary
for Great Britain to effect a dollar saving of about £100,-
000,000 a year.

It was evident that Britain might easily earn more dollars, especially in the Canadian market, if British goods were made more competitive in price and in rapid delivery in the hard-currency countries. A financial conference of the British Commonwealth nations in midsummer resulted in some minor measures for dollar-saving. This was followed early in September by an important gathering of American, British, and Canadian leaders, including Sir Stafford Cripps, Chancellor of the Exchequer, in Washington. Immediately afterwards, Sir Stafford announced (September 18) the devaluation of the British pound from $4.03 to $2.80. This cut was at once imitated by more than a score of other countries. Before the end of the year it was plain that devaluation was proving genuinely effective in reducing the dollar shortage.

The economic position of Western Europe remained painful, however, and American pressure was steadily exerted for a better unification of resources and markets. Paul G. Hoffman, head of the Economic Cooperation Administration, spoke to the officials engaged in the Marshall Plan, on October 31 in Paris. Europe, he said, desperately needed "economic integration" into "a single large market" in which eventually all tariff barriers would disappear. Some hopeful steps were being taken toward such an integration. In midsummer, a Council chosen by the Western European nations had met in Strasbourg to discuss means of achieving greater political, economic, and cultural unity. It was evident, however, that years of labor would be required to reach the goal that Administrator Hoffman had in mind.

Legislation for extending the Marshall Plan through the fiscal year 1949-50 brought on an exhausting wrangle in Congress, with an exhibition of more isolationist feeling than most Americans would have thought possible. One Arkansas Senator had the effrontery to propose that of the sum granted, $1,500,000,000 be earmarked for the purchase of surplus American farm produce! Another Senator sapiently declared that the Marshall Plan ought to be stopped because it was "a gigantic interference in the internal affairs of the countries of Western Europe." But on August 8, with bipartisan support and in particular with the valiant assistance of Senator John Foster Dulles of New York, the European Recovery bill passed the Senate, 63 to 7. Full second-year funds in the four-year program were thus provided.

American sentiment has now clearly been converted to the principle that the safety of the republic is indissolubly connected with the safety and economic stability of Western Europe and of the British Commonwealth countries. And American opinion in 1949 unmistakably held to the view that only heavy and efficient armaments could meet the Russian menace. Government expenditures in 1949-50 for defense, now more or less satisfactorily unified under Secretary Louis Johnson, would fall between fifteen and sixteen billions of dollars. Our huge military establishment, combined with the Marshall Plan and the Atlantic Defense Pact, was the answer to the continuous threat of Soviet aggression.

VI

The autumn elections came on with the American people in a reasonably contented and hopeful frame of mind. It is true they were worried—at least casually—by the heavy expenditures of the government. They were impressed by the exposure of waste and inefficiency made in the reports of the Commission on Organization of the Executive Branch of the Government, a body headed by ex-President Herbert Hoover, which during the spring issued a telling series of analyses of the multitudinous departments, bureaus, and agencies of the executive establishment. Mr. Hoover and the experts he had recruited made a number of highly important recommendations for improving the work of all the principal Washington offices, and cutting down their costs. But the country, as the recession disappeared, was generally prosperous. The farm population was pleased with the immense gains it had made during and since the war. Labor felt that it was on the high road to success in establishing the rule that capital must accept responsibility for the health and welfare of the workers, and must provide for this by pensions and social insurance. A short strike in the steel industry, beginning October 1, virtually ended just before election when the employers' front cracked, and the steel

31

companies began signing contracts under which they bore all the costs of a pension system.

The election was generally hailed as confirming the strength of the Democratic Administration. In New York a spectacular contest for a seat in the Senate was waged between Herbert H. Lehman, campaigning for "the welfare state," and John Foster Dulles, who opposed it. The Democrats ran up a vote of 2,585,074 for Lehman as against the Republican vote of 2,395,189 for Dulles. At the same time the Democratic candidate for mayor in New York City, William O'Dwyer, was swept back into office by a plurality of more than 300,000. To offset these results the Republicans could point to nothing better than the re-election of Governor Alfred E. Driscoll in New Jersey. The "Fair Deal" seemed to possess genuine popularity, and it was obviously necessary for the opposition to find some issue that would give them voting strength in the 1950 Congressional elections.

New Year's Eve was popularly greeted throughout the nation as ending the first half of the twentieth century, and ushering in the second half. It was universally agreed that the half century just closed had brought the country a series of heavy calamities and severe tests. It had involved the nation in two fearful World Wars, and had sunk it for a time in the deepest depression of history. But it was also universally agreed that the American people had gained in maturity, in resourcefulness, and in a sense of responsibility not only to one another but to the whole world.

ALL GREAT wars are followed by a prolonged period of international tension as the new forces they have called into existence find a balance and as the rough new solutions they impose are gradually adjusted to circumstance. Radical critics pointed out after the First World War—"the war to end war"—that the flames of conflict crackled in China, India, Egypt, Syria, the Balkans, and Ireland, that Russia invaded Poland and Italy attacked Greece, and that Latin America seethed with revolt. The Second World War had a still unhappier aftermath. Though actual bloodshed was limited to China, Southeastern Asia, and other remote areas, the cold war between Russia and the West (actually a Soviet attack waged by every weapon of threat, propaganda, espionage, infiltration, and economic pressure) posed the appalling danger of a great new conflict fought with atomic bombs, germs, and other implements lethal to whole nations. Five years after Versailles, the world had achieved a fair degree of peace. Five years after Potsdam, peace and equilibrium seemed remoter than ever.

In American history the year 1950 will stand out as

that in which the incalescent war suddenly became in-
candescent, devouring lives and treasure. The West,
after defeating Germany and Japan, had disarmed too
rapidly; in facing Russia it had depended too heavily
on the atomic bomb, whose secret Russia stole with unexpected swiftness and ease. (We did not learn until
1950 how rapidly and completely that secret *had* been
obtained, through Klaus Fuchs and others.) Aware of
Western weakness, the Soviet leaders had undertaken a
series of aggressive movements. The first, an attempt to
undermine the independence of Iran, Turkey, and
Greece, had been blocked by American and United Nations support of these threatened nations. The second,
an effort to cut off Berlin by blockade and make it the
capital of an East German satellite, had been frustrated
by the spectacular Anglo-American air-lift. In 1950 we
met the third, a bold movement to destroy South Korea
as a prelude to Communist subjugation of French Indo-
china, Burma, the Malay States, and even India.

The Korean War, which broke out on June 25, when
Communist troops of North Korea, largely armed and
trained by the Russians, and beyond question strategically
directed by Russian staff officers, crossed the South
Korean border in overwhelming force, was the central
event of the year in American history. It was at once
evident that Moscow had presented a grave new challenge to the Western Powers and to the United States.
For hours, the world waited breathlessly to learn what
action the Truman Administration would take. Its response was swift and decisive. From that moment the

Korean conflict dominated American interest and radically affected every department of American life: political, economic, military, social, and even cultural. The change paralleled the drastic redirection and concentration of American energies which had followed the fall of France in the spring of 1940.

BACKGROUND OF THE KOREAN EXPLOSION

From the beginning of 1950 American watchers had been aware that Asia was in a state of sullen upheaval. Much of the vast population of this continent, estimated at approximately one and a quarter billions of people, was in revolt against such vestiges of colonialism as yet remained, against many Occidental ideas, and in a vague, undirected fashion, against its own poverty, backwardness, and social misery.

Dutch Indonesia had just been given equal status with the Netherlands as a free nation under the Dutch crown; but fighting continued in Java, a revolt broke out in Macassar in April, and spring found the eastern islands, including Celebes, rising in a demand for an independent state. These difficulties were rapidly composed—American advisers lending a hand. In October, the Republic of Indonesia was admitted to the United Nations. Meanwhile, in British Malaysia bitter guerrilla fighting gradually diminished. French Indochina, now autonomous in its domestic and economic affairs, was also the scene of stubborn warfare, the Viet Nam forces and French troops battling against the Communists of the Viet Minh, who appeared to be receiving aid from the Chinese Communists across the border. By the end of 1950 the French forces, about 150,000 men, were being strengthened. In all these areas Russian-trained agents were active.

As for China, the Communist regime of Mao Tze-tung was now solidly in power, though large forces of Nationalist guerrillas, estimated as high as 500,000, kept up a spasmodic resistance. Early in the year Mao, visiting Russia, concluded a treaty with the Soviet Union (February 14) by which the two governments confirmed their alliance, Russia agreeing to aid China if she were attacked by Japan or by any Power associated with Japan (that is, the United States). The attitude of Mao toward the United States, as toward other Western lands, became increasingly hostile as the year advanced, and after the Russian treaty China gave still greater scope to Soviet technicians, economic advisers, and political agents.

The question whether the United States should recognize Mao's Communist regime, or continue to support Chiang Kai-shek's Nationalist Government in Formosa, was a subject of warm American debate during the early months of 1950. Great Britain on January 6 gave *de jure* recognition to the Mao Government, as the Asiatic members of the (British) Commonwealth of Nations had previously done. Many Americans believed that Washington should take the same step; that by recognizing the Peiping regime the United States could preserve something of China's oldtime friendship, and gradually drive a wedge between China and Russia, which in the past had been traditionally jealous and antagonistic. When Britain, India, and Pakistan supported a proposal for admitting Communist China to the United Nations, many Americans thought Washington should do the same. It was evident that had Secretary Acheson been a free agent, he would have favored a recognition of the Mao Government; but he and President Truman had to keep in view the violent opposition of a majority of Congress and a probable majority of plain citizens to this decision. The United States had no such sensitiveness to general Asiatic opinion as Great Britain had.

Many Republicans, indeed, demanded from the beginning of the year that the United States use naval and air power to protect Chiang's Formosa Government against attack. On January 5 President Truman flatly negatived such a policy. The Joint Chiefs of Staff had informed him that Formosa, though important, was not vital to American defense. Moreover, such an American intervention, without overt cause, would probably drive Mao deeper into the arms of Russia, which was just the result we wished to avoid. Unfortunately, Mao did much to offend American opinion. He seized American consular and other property. He took an unfriendly attitude toward all Western religious, educational, and medical establishments, which were largely American.

Meanwhile, the Kremlin lost no opportunity to enhance its influence over Peiping. In a gesture, that was to have fateful consequences, Russia on January 13 began a boycott of the United Nations, Jacob Malik dramatically walking out of the Security Council when it refused to approve his resolution for the expulsion of the Chinese Nationalist delegate and the seating of a Chinese Com-

37

munist representative. He remained absent until August, the Soviet Union and its satellites meanwhile withdrawing from about thirty organizations connected with the United Nations. The boycott was deplored in the United States as in other Western nations, but it had unexpectedly happy results when the crisis came in June.

Expert American observers knew throughout the spring that Russia, the Mao Government in China, the Viet Minh in Indochina, and Communist agencies elsewhere in Asia, were acting in concert. But they did not know what later became clear, that they were making preparations for a powerful surge to expel all Western influences, establish their domination over the whole teeming continent, and use it to help prepare the way for world revolution. We do not know the inner history of this conspiracy. The Communist skill in suppressing, distorting, and forging historical evidence is such that we may never know it. But it evidently comprehended an effort to drive France and Britain out of Southeast Asia, a plan for the seizure of Formosa and the elimination of Chiang's forces in that island, a thrust for the subjugation of South Korea, and the ultimate staging of a grave threat to Japan and the Philippines. Junks and other vessels were massed in the spring at Foochow, and other ports, for the invasion of Formosa. Nearly half a million North Korean troops were put in readiness to surge across the 38th parallel and inundate South Korea. The foreign ministers of the United States, Britain, and France met in London in May in happy ignorance of this plot.

When on June 25, in pouring rain, the North Korean
columns, led by Russian-made T–38 tanks, rolled toward
Seoul, their onslaught seemed irresistible. The ill-armed

STARTING SOMETHING?

From a cartoon by Marcus in *The New York Times*

South Koreans were quickly routed. It was doubtless the
Soviet expectation that the United States would not intervene, and that the United Nations would prove helpless. The Kremlin knew that Korea was seven thousand
miles from American shores; that the United States had

only a few divisions ready for combat; that with massive Chinese forces at hand and Western Europe under threat of invasion, any American government would hesitate to commit the major part of its land strength in so perilous an area. The result, however, dramatically belied Soviet calculations.

The very day the news of invasion reached New York, the Security Council of the United Nations hurriedly met at Lake Success, and appealed for a cessation of the fighting and a withdrawal of the North Korean forces to the 38th parallel. Hurried conferences were being held in Washington. If the leaders of the Administration hesitated, it was but momentarily. On June 27, President Truman announced that he was sending American air and naval forces, but not as yet troops, to the aid of the rapidly retreating South Koreans, and that he had also ordered the Seventh Fleet to protect Formosa from attack. A few hours later that day the Security Council called upon members of the United Nations to help repel the Red assault on South Korea. The President thereupon (June 30) ordered American troops to the battle-front. It will be seen that the Truman Administration lent armed assistance to the South Koreans even before the United Nations requested it to do so, and that this help was extended to the use of troops within sixty hours after the United Nations' request. There was neither time for gaining the assent of Congress as a whole (though leaders were consulted) nor necessity for doing so. The prompt action of the government had the wholehearted support of the vast majority of Americans. It halted a wave of panic that had begun to sweep over Western Europe. As the free world rallied behind American leadership, it gave the United Nations a prestige and power that the League of Nations had never achieved.

By the end of the first week of July, Great Britain, Australia, New Zealand, and the Netherlands had taken measures to send armed forces to South Korea, while Canada was certain to do so. Turkey, France, Thailand, the Philippines, Brazil, and India (a hospital unit) eventually furnished aid. The Security Council on July 7 called upon the United States to establish a Unified Command for United Nations forces, and Washington at once designated General Douglas MacArthur as chief commander. On July 7, too, the Administration announced a draft to fill up the ranks of the Army. The United Nations flag soon waved above the combat lines.

It was a happy fact that the absence of Russia from the Security Council had permitted this rapid action, for her veto would have been a grave obstacle. It was another happy fact that the presence of veteran American troops in neighboring Japan, and of large naval forces in Eastern waters, permitted a quick reinforcement of the South Koreans. But for these circumstances the North Korean army would quickly have conquered the peninsula, and the Stalin-Mao alliance, the United Nations defied, the United States humbled, and the rest of the world intimidated, would have stood ready to establish its domination over all Asia. As it was, the United Nations was vindicated, America was strengthened, and Russia was frustrated.

TIDES OF BATTLE

During 1950 the Korean conflict passed through three phases: retreat, counterattack, and Chinese intervention. During the first six weeks the United Nations troops fell back, step by step. The North Koreans, many of them veterans of Chinese, Russian, or Japanese forces, proved formidable fighters; their night attacks and infiltration tactics, learned from the Japanese, were highly effective, and their tank equipment was initially superior to that of the Americans. When superior American airpower, and in coastal areas the American naval guns, came into play, the North Koreans showed themselves able to stand terrible losses without flinching. The combat was often desperately confused in character. "I'll be damned if I know who's got who surrounded!" exclaimed an American officer at one point. Over rough mountains, down tangled valleys, across ill-smelling rice-swamps, the United Nations forces were pushed back by superior manpower, once losing sixteen miles in two days. By September 10 they were pent up in a narrow rectangular pocket in the southeastern corner of Korea, with a battle-front perimeter of about 120 miles. They had lost the auxiliary port of Pohung with its valuable airfield; the northern arc of the front at times seemed in danger of collapse. A preliminary and very incomplete count of American casualties to September 1 totalled nearly 7000. The Western nations steeled themselves for an evacuation, a new Dunkirk, through the tip port at Pusan.

Then, as reinforcements arrived, came a sudden shift

to the offensive. It had been well advertised in advance. President Syngman Rhee of South Korea had declared, "We are about to go"; Lieutenant-General Walton H. Walker of the Eighth Army had announced a thrust "in a short time." Every newspaperman knew that a huge invasion armada (it finally counted 261 vessels) had been gathered in Japanese ports. American, British, and Australian airplanes softened the North Korean resistance by hundreds of daily sorties in which they dropped vast quantities of explosives, fire-bombs, and napalm or jellied petroleum, and used deadly rocket-fire. American and British warships blanketed Red ports with heavy gunfire. Then, on September 15, with the advantage of high tides, the blow fell on Inchon Harbor, the port of Seoul.

The preliminary bombardment of the well-fortified Wolmi Island in Inchon Harbor was so tremendous that one marine officer said, "That island quivered until I thought it would roll over and sink," and an official dispatch spoke of "rearranging the Wolmi land mass." At dawn the First Marine Division took the island by assault, and that afternoon they scaled the Inchon sea-wall and swarmed into the heart of the smashed city of 300,-000. Then, with the Seventh Infantry Division, the marines moved rapidly upon Seoul. As they did so, the troops in the southeastern beachhead surrounding Pusan threw all their strength against the over-extended Communist lines. Here the First Cavalry Division, the Second, Twenty-fourth, and Twenty-fifth Infantry Divisions, and the Twenty-seventh British Brigade steadily rolled back the North Koreans. Simultaneously, strong

43

forces of South Korean troops, landing at Pohang and Yongdok on the eastern coast of the peninsula, struck inland. Great fleets of B–24 bombers and smaller planes smashed roads, bridges, and installations back of the North Korean lines, and the battleship *Missouri,* which had come 11,000 miles from Norfolk, bombarded enemy positions on the east coast with its biggest guns. The Communist resistance, at first stubborn, soon collapsed. On the Seoul front, MacArthur, seeing six Russian-built tanks destroyed within five minutes while Americans started lines of prisoners to the rear, observed: "That's a good sight for my old eyes."

On the afternoon of September 26, General Mac-Arthur, announcing that Seoul was in United Nations hands, declared: "Liberation of the city was conducted in such a manner as to cause the least possible damage to civil installations." The fact was that when at 3:05 next day the American flag rose above the Korean Capitol building, the city of Seoul was a shambles, three-fifths of it wrecked or badly damaged. It was a much-debated question whether the city should not have been surrounded rather than invaded, and left to wither away into United Nations hands while the armies pushed on north. But the important fact was that President Syngman Rhee's government could return home. Meanwhile, the North Korean remnant forces were still fleeing. On October 1, the South Korean Third Division crossed the 38th parallel in pursuit of them. Fifteen minutes later General MacArthur, in a broadcast in the Korean tongue, demanded that the Communist army, in whatever part of Korea it stood, should "forthwith lay down your arms and cease hostilities under such military supervision as I may direct."

CROSSING THE 38TH PARALLEL

A momentous decision now had to be made: Should the United Nations forces halt active operations at the old boundary, the 38th parallel, or should they pursue the aggressor beyond this imaginary line and bring all Korea, a once homogeneous country, under the authority of Seoul? It was a difficult question. As the Red Koreans fell back in rout, both Mao and the Chinese Prime Minister, Chou En-lai, asserted that if the 38th parallel were "violated" Chinese troops would be sent to aid their fellow Koreans. An American army standing on the Yalu River would seem both to China and Russia a distinct threat to those nations. Yet if the North Koreans were not pursued to the Yalu, they could reform and rearm in the mountainous northern terrain, obtain more troops from China and more munitions from Russia, and renew the attack on South Korea as soon as conditions seemed favorable. Moreover, Korea ought to be unified. The line which had severed the populous agricultural south from the partly industrialized north had been a vicious temporary expedient which would have been ended long before but for Russian obstruction of the United Nations plan for free national elections.

The issue was quickly resolved. Late in the afternoon of October 7 a unit of the First Cavalry Division sent a tank-and-jeep patrol across the 38th parallel just above the town of Kaesong; and at dawn two days later a heavy drive toward the North Korean capital of Pyongyang was opened by the Eighth Cavalry Regiment. Already large South Korean forces were beyond the boundary line, and American, British, and Australian infantry soon followed. It appears that as early as the middle of September the State Department had assented to a thrust beyond the parallel. On October 7, just after the first American troops had moved, the General Assembly of the United Nations passed a British-drafted resolution authorizing the step, 47 to 5. Simultaneously, the British Foreign Minister, Ernest Bevin, asked that "all Korea" be given a democratic government.

Much evidence exists, however, that MacArthur's ideas of the extent and nature of the counter-offensive northward differed radically from those of the Truman Administration, the British Ministry, and many United Nations leaders. In Washington, at Lake Success, and in London it was expected that MacArthur would capture Pyongyang and establish a well-fortified line across the narrow waist of Korea, roughly from Sinanju to Hamhung. This seems to have been the concept of the State Department. There, and at Lake Success, men spoke of the coming "MacArthur Line" at this waist. Prime Minister Attlee and Winston Churchill later sharply criticized MacArthur for not stopping at this easily defensible zone. But MacArthur was convinced that neither China nor Russia would intervene, that by pursuing the North Koreans to the Yalu River he could win a decisive victory by Thanksgiving, and that he could restore the Eighth Army to Japan by Christmas. He therefore pushed steadily forward. On October 20 he captured Pyongyang.

In the closing days of October several United Nations columns, hotly pursuing the 65,000 men left in the shattered North Korean army, moved rapidly toward the Yalu and Tumen Rivers separating Korea from Manchuria and Siberia. The battleship *Missouri,* with three airship carriers, bombarded the port of Chingjin, only fifty miles from Siberian soil. Victory, final and complete, seemed within the American grasp.

CHINESE INTERVENTION

Then came a blow that made the Western world gasp and that took the whole United States aback. On October 30, American troops captured sixteen Chinese armed with grenades and mortar ammunition. Next day, Major-General Edward M. Almond reported that a Chinese regiment, thrown across the Yalu a fortnight earlier, had come into action in front of two power plants near the Manchurian border. On November 1, half a dozen jet planes, evidently Russian-built, fought American planes on the northern front. The following day, a heavy force of Chinese troops overwhelmed two battalions of the First Cavalry. The Indian delegate to the United Nations, who had steadily warned his associates that China would strike if her boundary were approached, could say "I told you so." Many Americans and Britons could, and did, say: "MacArthur went too far."

47

It was reported, no one knew how accurately, that Molotov during an August visit to Peiping had asked for Chinese intervention in Korea. It was also reported that on October 24 the Peiping Central People's Committee had voted by formal resolution to place troops in the war. What was certain was that China was taking a course pregnant with danger to herself and the world. Mao Tze-tung would not have moved had he not believed vital Chinese interests threatened. He doubtless had military fears concerning a capitalist Korea, allied with Japan and the United States, on the Yalu line. He also feared that such a nation, taking over the power plants along the Yalu, might cut off or reduce the energy needed by Manchurian industry.

For three weeks, Americans waited to find out whether the Chinese Communists were bluffing. The United Nations troops had retreated from fifty to ninety miles, but Mao Tze-tung's Red "volunteers" did not press their attack. On November 11, the Chinese Government announced that it was dispatching a delegation to present Mao's case to the United Nations. In due course they arrived—with a demand that the United States evacuate Korea, consent to Red China's admission to the United Nations, and desist from its protection of Formosa. These terms were of course preposterous, but Moscow and Peiping indicated that they would not be reduced. On November 24, MacArthur sent his United Nations troops forward with orders to end the war. In freezing winter weather, they moved north in two great sections, one on the west, the other following the east coast of Korea.

And within three days it was evident that they had advanced into a gigantic trap.

On November 26 Chinese forces, far larger than MacArthur's defective intelligence service had supposed, poured down the mountainous center of Korea, dividing the United Nations forces into two unconnected wings. General Walter H. Walker's Eighth Army in the west was completely separated from General Edward A. Almond's X Corps on the east. A South Korean corps was so badly smashed that it all but disappeared. General MacArthur had to announce that "an entirely new war" had opened, and that the situation was one of the greatest gravity. Although the Department of Defense in Washington declared that the crisis was not "catastrophic," for a time it seemed that it might prove just that. The Eighth Army was soon in full flight, and parts of it were so badly mauled that American, British, and Turkish reserves were rushed up to assist it, only to find themselves in danger of being overwhelmed. The X Corps in the east, suffering equally fierce attacks, finally had to be evacuated from North Korea by sea and brought down to South Korean ports to resume the fighting. The Chinese moved chiefly by night, made skillful use of infiltration tactics, and employed mass assaults with total disregard of a fearful loss of life.

By the end of 1950 the United Nations troops held a precarious line between Seoul and the 38th parallel, and were still being forced southward. No unit had been cut off, though many had been decimated and some half destroyed. Lieutenant-General Matthew B. Ridgway, who had taken over the field command under MacArthur after the accidental death of Lieutenant-General Walker, had a tough fighting force of about 325,000, of whom 200,000 were Americans, about 100,000 South Koreans, and the remainder British and other United Nations men. Air and naval personnel engaged in the Korean fighting brought Walker's total command up to about 350,000. The enemy forces were estimated at nearly if not quite 500,000 men south of the Yalu River, with tremendous reserves beyond that boundary stream. The great hope of the United Nations armies lay in their vastly superior firing power and air power, giving them the ability to trade lives in battle at the rate of five to one or even ten to one, and to cripple transportation facilities.

It was still an undeclared war. The tremendous Chinese armies still posed as "volunteers" in the North Korean cause—"like Lafayette, like Rochambeau," ironically cried Vishinsky in the United Nations' debate. It was a very desperate war. When the year closed, many Americans feared that total evacuation of Korea lay just ahead. Others, better instructed, pointed out that even the Chinese would be sickened in time by the awful losses they were meeting in massed frontal attacks; that the North Korean roads and railways, poor, tortuous, and full of bridges and culverts that could easily be smashed from the air, were increasingly inadequate as supply arteries; and that as our air power (we already had between 1500 and 2000 military airplanes) grew and our armies were reinforced, we could probably bring China to a stop. But the skies of the globe had darkened, the enmity of Soviet Russia for the West had been more nakedly exposed, and the danger of a third world war seemed far more appalling than a year before.

AMERICAN REARMAMENT

The impact of the Korean war on almost every aspect of American life was instant and tremendous. One development went far toward summing it up. In December, twenty-five prominent Americans announced the formation of a Committee on the Present Danger. President James B. Conant of Harvard, Dr. Vannevar Bush, and twenty-three others proposed that the United States put under arms at least three and a half million men; that it give two years of military training to all physically fit men of eighteen; that it complement this universal service plan with a selective service scheme for special branches; that it reduce non-military expenditures drastically; and that it impose the most severe controls on credit and economic life. We have entered, said the committee, "a struggle in which our free existence is at stake, a struggle for survival."

All the armed forces immediately expanded their requirements. When the guns opened in Korea, they were basing their expenditures on Secretary Louis A. Johnson's "economy budget" of $13,300,000,000. Mr. Johnson, whose economies were dictated by President and Congress, not by his own whim, was forced out of office in September. Meanwhile, in August, the armed services had asked Congress for an additional $11,700,000,000, most of which was to be spent for guns, planes, and tanks. Congress was more than willing to take action. It was in fact ready to appropriate more than the army, navy, and air force demanded. In September it made the grand total of $25,000,000,000 (the sum of the two amounts mentioned above) available; and as the year ended it added another $16,800,000,000, about half of which was for weapons, and the remainder for personnel and overhead. This brought the whole amount appropriated up to nearly forty-two billions.

Major national agencies—the Munitions Board, the Joint Chiefs of Staff, the National Security Resources Board, and others—wasted no time in planning contracts and other commitments. Late in the year, it was estimated that $18,000,000,000 worth of contracts would have been let by March 1 ensuing. President Truman had broadcast on September 1 an announcement that the armed forces would be raised to about three million men as rapidly as possible. Military leaders assured the country that American airplanes, ordnance, bombs, guided missiles, and small arms were believed to be the best in the world; and although Russia had outstripped us in tanks, American models in that branch were being brought to the best level. Our navy remained the largest on the globe.

HELPING EUROPE REARM

But it was vital that Europe also should rearm rapidly and heavily. Russia, according to a joint report by two committees of the Senate, which was accepted in Britain as accurate, had more than five million men under arms.

She was able to mobilize rapidly about 175 divisions, while her European satellites disposed of powerful forces. The Soviet Union was credited with about 15,000 aircraft and 30,000 tanks. At sea, Russia had concentrated on snorkel submarines of great cruising range; and she had devoted great attention to guided missiles which, from her advance bases, might reach all Western Europe. As the situation stood in midsummer, Russian forces (if not deterred by fear of American atomic bombs) could rapidly have overrun all Europe up to the English Channel and Pyrenees.

Early in the year, the Council created under the North Atlantic Pact had approved plans for the integrated defense of the twelve countries included in that momentous treaty. Shortly afterward, near the end of January, the United States had formally agreed to send arms to eight of these countries. Already the money was in hand for this assistance, Congress having granted a billion dollars for the purpose. The first cargoes of arms reached Europe in April. Then came the thunder-crack of the North Korean invasion; Europe, badly frightened, clamored for more help; and in September, a month which found the defense ministers of all the North Atlantic Pact nations gathering for discussion of their problems, Congress made another $3,500,000,000 available.

The enthusiasm which Western Europe put into its rearmament program greatly heartened American observers. Far in the lead was Great Britain, which besides her powerful navy already possessed an excellent air force (including perhaps the best jet fighters in the world), strong tanks, and a growing and efficient army. She promised that by the spring of 1951 she would have nearly 700,000 men in her armed forces. The French Government had undertaken a three-year rearmament program, under which France would raise her army to twenty divisions. Belgium, Holland, Denmark, and Norway were all increasing their forces; while a military mission from the United States advised Turkey in the training of armed forces of more than 600,000. It was significant that the United States took steps during the year to strengthen their influence in Yugoslavia (which received $38,000,000 of non-military aid) and in Spain.

A NEW FISCAL ERA

A tidal wave of industrial expansion, materials shortages, wage demands, and inflation swept across the United States—and indeed, all the Western nations—in the wake of the Korean explosion. From the beginning of the year the American economy had experienced a quiet boom, obliterating all memory of the brief recession of 1949. The spring had found a spirit of confidence animating financial and business circles from Stockholm to Buenos Aires and from Capetown to Seattle. High American production and British devaluation were two stimulating factors. Then, like an automobile going into high gear, the Western economy was lifted and accelerated by the Korean war. Our government in April had spent money at the rate of $2,000,000 an hour; after June, this Federal expenditure was stepped up to ever higher levels.

The stockpiling of vital raw materials, which was rapidly developed in late summer and fall, naturally created shortages and lifted prices. Thus between June and the middle of October wool rose from $1.78 a pound to $2.50, tin from 76 cents to $1.12, and rubber from 28 cents to 61 cents. A rush of retail buying by customers anxious to supply themselves before shortages grew acute brought consumer credit to twenty-one billion dollars, a record mark, by the middle of September. Demand for steel was such that the United States again began importing from Europe. Inasmuch as American inflation outpaced that of Europe, many European wares suddenly became saleable in the United States. Before 1950 ended, the dollar gap for the world at large (though not for Europe alone) had been closed. Meanwhile, Americans suffered severely from the sharp price rise.

Once more, as Federal spending rose, all hope of a balanced budget (and even more of debt reduction) seemed to vanish. Instead, Americans looked forward to unescapable waste, higher taxes, and additions to debt. The President, in submitting his budget to Congress in January, had estimated receipts of $37,300,000,000 and expenditures of $42,400,000,000. It was then expected that with luck, receipts might prove higher, and the deficit might fall well below $5,000,000,000. But first Korea, and then China, changed the picture beyond recognition. Allowing for the great new supplemental requests in defense appropriation and for European aid, it seemed certain that national expenditures in the fiscal year 1950–51 would approach if not exceed fifty billions. To meet the national bills, Congress passed two tax measures which raised estimated revenues for the fiscal year to not less than $43,500,000,000.

So prosperous was the nation as a whole that the new tax burdens were accepted cheerfully. Nevertheless, the continuance of deficit financing gravely disturbed conservative observers. At the same time, industry was beset with problems growing out of the transition from peacetime to war production, many plants having to cope with conversion troubles at the same time that they met increased taxes. Since much of the government spending would be pushed into 1951, Federal officers and businessmen already had to plan for a still more swollen national budget in the fiscal year 1951–52.

SUCCESS OF THE MARSHALL PLAN

The dollar was a casualty of the new fiscal era—and some people spoke of dollar bills as "Truman dimes"; but the Marshall Plan was a beneficiary. By the close of 1950, indeed, the Plan—with less than three-fourths of its allotted lifetime gone—could be pronounced an unqualified success. It was fortunate that, as rearmament pushed it into a secondary position, it stood within reach of its main goals.

During the first half of 1950, the Marshall Plan countries lifted their industrial production index to a level 24 per cent above that of 1936–38. The output of the factories and farms of Western Europe reached the highest point in history, and this area seemed at last fairly certain of being able to sell the world enough goods to support a decent, stable, and improving standard of life. Studies by the Economic Commission for Europe (Geneva) showed that during 1950 most countries maintained their remarkable figure of a 7 to 9 per cent annual increase in industrial production. During the early history of the Plan, international trade had lagged behind industrial output, leading some critics to fear that recovery would be accompanied by more autarchy or self-sufficiency. During 1950, however, the solution of the payments problem by a readjustment of exchange rates, and by the work of the European Payments Union, lent a strong impulse to international commerce. Even in the first half of the year, American imports from Europe rose sharply.

The Korean crisis and American rearmament gave a spectacular stimulus to the export trade of Western Europe, Latin America, Malaya, and Japan. The European balance of payments improved so rapidly that gold and dollar reserves rose during the year by more than $1,500,-000,000. At the end of 1950, as we have said, Europe still had a certain dollar gap. But it was being narrowed in a fashion which pointed to its early elimination. Many products not ordinarily sold in the United States, such as steel shapes and industrial alcohol, were being shipped across the Atlantic in volume. Great Britain profited from the enhanced earnings of the sterling area as Australian wool, Malayan tin and rubber, and other goods flowed to America at high prices. Particularly striking was the recovery of Japan. A great boom began as American orders reached scores of Japanese factories. American expenditures in the islands reached about $175,000,000 for the year; and this meant prosperity—a prosperity that added 700,000 workers to wage rolls, and sent industrial output well above the 1932–36 level.

The great offsetting disadvantage to Western Europe and other countries was the worldwide inflation which accompanied the war boom. Raw materials became so costly that some watchers feared an undermining of Europe's still precarious economic future. Coal, copper, lead, wool, cotton, and other commodities for manufacture shot toward the zenith. Foodstuffs were higher, and wages had to be raised. Moreover, as Britain, France, and other countries shifted many factories from exportable goods to arms for home use, they lost a means of earning money. Farsighted leaders issued warnings that a temporary reduction in the standard of living was inevitable for Europe as for America. The integration of the European economy under the Schumann Plan and other measures became more exigent than ever.

At the end of the year, the new Economic Cooperation Administrator, William C. Foster, who had succeeded Paul Hoffman, called on Western Europe to meet the threat to its living scale by a vast increase in the output of goods. This region, he said, should duplicate in the next eighteen months the "near miracle of recovery" that had been achieved in the previous thirty months; that is, by the middle of 1952 it should swell its industrial and agricultural deliveries by a hundred billion dollars. Total war against Soviet Russia was not yet inevitable, he declared. "I believe that it can be prevented if Western

Europe, in continued partnership with the United States, strengthens the economic base on which effective rearmament depends. Given the proper combination of economic and military strength in Western Europe, the armies of aggression will not march."

THE EIGHTY-FIRST CONGRESS

The 81st Congress came to an end on Tuesday, January 2, 1951, when Speaker Sam Rayburn, banging his gavel, announced that the House stood adjourned. In domestic affairs it had not been a highly constructive Congress. From midsummer the international emergency had taken precedence over all minor questions. Then, too, the temper of the Congress, like that of the country, had been increasingly conservative; for an alliance of rebellious Southern Democrats and conservative Republicans had forced the Fair Deal, as a continuation of the New Deal, to put on brakes and grind toward a standstill. Distrust of President Truman as a leader had slowly grown. His ideas were distrusted, his tendency to make snap judgments was distrusted, his equipment for his complex task was distrusted. It is safe to say that Mr. Truman's prestige in Congress fell late in 1950 to a point as low as that of Taft had fallen in 1911–12, if not quite so far as that of Mr. Hoover had dropped in 1931–32.

Although the President stuck pertinaciously throughout 1950 to his main objectives, his hope of obtaining more social welfare measures and more reform legislation dwindled. Particularly in the field of race relations did the Southern bloc in the Senate stand adamant against liberal measures. The House passed a Fair Employment Practices Bill which would have created a Federal Commission with advisory powers only. But the Senate (where debate can now be ended only by vote of two-thirds of all the members) was unwilling to approve even this mild measure. The House also passed a bill outlawing poll taxes as a prerequisite to voting in any election for Federal office, but the Senate blocked action. National health insurance legislation made no progress. The deadlock over Federal aid to the States for elementary and secondary schools continued, for the Catholic demand for Federal moneys to give "auxiliary services" to parochial schools was quite unacceptable to non-Catholic elements, as a violation of the basic American principle of separation of church and state. Still another item on Mr. Truman's program, the repeal or modification of the Taft-Hartley Act, had no chance of Congressional acceptance.

Several important measures of a constructive character, however, were passed. Perhaps the most important was the Housing Act of April, 1950, which authorized the eventual use of as much as one and a half billion dollars in slum clearance and the erection of low-cost housing under the mortgage-insurance program of the Federal Housing Administration. Cooperative housing projects were to be given technical assistance as well as mortgage insurance and other aids, while the law authorized direct federal loans for housing projects at colleges and universities. Another law provided Federal aid for the building and operation of public schools in communities where government activities had increased the school population. Rent controls were extended to June 30, 1951. An interesting new law created a National Science Foundation, to devise a national program for the promotion of basic research in engineering and all the exact sciences. Another law provided $88,000,000 for a ten-year rehabilitation scheme for the Hopi and Navajo Indians.

On practically all measures for the national defense, as we have said, Congress showed more than alacrity—even eagerness—in meeting the Administration's wishes. The conviction that the nation was in sore peril and must rearm heavily was so general on Capitol Hill that even the greatest burdens were shouldered unhesitatingly. Congress on September 1 passed the Defense Production Act, conferring extraordinary defensive and economic powers upon the President. The law provided for Federal loans to industry to enlarge production; for establishing priorities and allocations in scarce materials; for the creation of a war labor board; and for establishing machinery to ration goods, control wages and prices (in conjunction), and to restrict credit to consumers.

By virtue of this act a National Production Authority was established in the Commerce Department on September 10, headed by William Henry Harrison, president of International Telephone & Telegraph. It was intended to deal with priorities and allocations. Some two weeks later an Office of Defense Manpower was set up in the Labor Department with Robert C. Goodwin as chief. Neither agency, however, had accomplished much

61

by the end of the year; they had been busy with preparatory work.

FUMBLING WITH INFLATION

The Administration was particularly slow to use the broad authority of the Defense Production Act for attacking price inflation. To be sure, an Economic Stabilization Agency was established on September 9, and Dr. Alan Valentine, former head of the University of Rochester, was named Administrator a little over a month later (October 14). But Dr. Valentine attempted little and accomplished less. His policy was one of selective price control; that is, he wished to pick out special commodities, and then ask manufacturers and dealers to keep their prices at a certain fixed level. Dissatisfaction with his work resulted in the appointment, on November 3, of Michael DiSalle of Toledo as Price Administrator, but it took time for Mr. DiSalle to establish the machinery he needed. When the year closed only one price order, rolling the prices of automobiles back to the December 1 level, had been issued.

Popular discontent with the steady rise in the cost of living meanwhile became vociferous. Prices jumped until they stood in December at the highest point in the nation's history. The familiar spiral, wages chasing prices and prices chasing wages, came into full play. The main farm products stood on artificial stilts that could be heightened but never shortened. Small wage-earners, salaried people, and fixed-income groups in general suffered dire hardship. Very belatedly, President Truman took steps to meet the situation. In mid-December, when it was plain that the war would be long, not short, he proclaimed the existence of a national emergency, announced that broad wage and price controls would soon

YOU CAN'T ESCAPE YOUR SHADOW!
From a cartoon by Kuekes in *The Cleveland Plain Dealer*

be applied, and appointed an able American industrialist, Charles E. Wilson, as chief of the Office of Defense Mobilization. This was a supervisory post for the direction and coordination of all the agencies just mentioned and of some others as well. Mr. Wilson, a self-made man who had entered the General Electric Company in 1899 and worked up rung by rung, had been president of that corporation for nearly eleven years. On December 21, he took his place in Washington.

It was by that time evident that a dispute over policy between Dr. Valentine and Mr. DiSalle, the former standing for selective price controls and the latter for sweeping price limitations, would soon be settled by Dr. Valentine's displacement. The country at large felt that stringent restrictions were long overdue. Profiteering was rife; mark-ups were renewed almost daily; and the middle classes were in danger of being squeezed to death.

THE GREAT DEBATE ON FOREIGN POLICY

Never in our history has foreign policy been more fiercely debated than it was in 1950. Everyone agreed on the necessity for large defensive measures and for helping Western Europe to arm itself. On other matters affecting our external relations, however, a violent series of quarrels shook the country. Attacks on the State Department by some Republican newspapers and many Republican leaders were continuous. Strenuous efforts were made to preserve a bipartisan front in foreign affairs; Senator Vandenberg of Michigan lent his assistance, and on April 6 John Foster Dulles, a prominent Republican close to Governor Dewey of New York, became consultant to the State Department. A considerable group of Republican Senators and Representatives remained staunchly loyal to the main Administration aims. But the bipartisan front was so badly cracked that at times it seemed about to be shattered.

The initial assault on Secretary Acheson and his department was thoroughly dishonest and discreditable. Directed by Senator Joseph McCarthy, a noisy Wisconsin politician, it presented a string of charges, some baseless and others wildly exaggerated, centering about the accusation that "the State Department is infested with Communists." In March, a Senate subcommittee under Millard E. Tydings of Maryland began an inquiry which completely exploded the McCarthy indictment. In flamboyant speeches McCarthy had variously asserted that 205, or 81, or 57 (he seemed uncertain of the number) "card-carrying Communists" or sympathizers were lodged in the department. These assertions he was totally unable to substantiate. When he charged that Ambassador-at-Large Philip C. Jessup had "an unusual affinity with Communist causes," Jessup sternly contradicted and denounced him.

McCarthy, after much floundering, finally declared that Owen Lattimore, director of the Walter Hines Page School of International Relations at Johns Hopkins University, was "the top Russian espionage agent" in Washington. At the time of this charge, Lattimore was in Afghanistan on a mission for the United Nations. During the war he had been a political adviser to Chiang Kai-shek, and after its close had accompanied the first American Reparations Commission to Japan. On examination, McCarthy's hasty accusations against Lattimore proved as irresponsible and absurd as his other major statements. The FBI handed the Senate subcommittee an abstract of its files on Lattimore, which showed that the Far Eastern expert had always been above reproach. Placed on the witness stand, Lattimore not only cleared himself but bitterly indicted McCarthy's statements and innuendoes as false and outrageous.

Although no important assertion by McCarthy was ever proved, and although most of his statements were shown to be malicious inventions, he continued to brazen out his attack. Senator Benton of Connecticut said later that his refuge when one charge was disproved was to utter some still wilder charge. On July 17, the Tydings subcommittee brought in a report which cleared the State Department of Communist taint and castigated McCarthy in blistering terms. But the sensation-mongering of the Wisconsin Senator had borne bitter fruit in poisoning many minds at home, and in raising doubts abroad as to the unity and dependability of American opinion.

Then the Korean war sharply changed the character of the foreign policy dispute.

DIFFERENCES WITH MacARTHUR

In midsummer the quarrel over foreign policy acquired a Far Eastern focus. We have seen that when fighting began the Administration ordered the Seventh Fleet to sea off Formosa, where Chiang Kai-shek had established his last stronghold; and simultaneously Washington brought pressure on Chiang to avoid any attack on the mainland. In brief, Formosa was neutralized. The United States established no bases on the island and sent no troops thither. It did, however, give Chiang limited assistance in re-equipping his forces, and lent his government technical and economic aid in harmony with the Marshall Plan and Point Four.

Naturally, the Communist regime in Peiping denounced the American course in violent terms. It was regarded with disfavor by India, which believed that Chiang had forfeited all claim to support, and with chilliness by Great Britain, which had recognized (but never approved) the Communist government in China. The British Ministry held that the status of Formosa could best be settled by a Japanese peace treaty, in the negotiation of which Peiping should have a voice. Considerable elements in the United States, too, believed that the Administration had erred in not recognizing Mao Tze-tung's Communist government, even if we did not go so far as to permit the establishment of his authority in Formosa.

A vigorous school of American opinion, on the other hand, maintained that Chiang should not merely be protected in Formosa, but assisted to renew his war against the Peiping Government. After Chinese armies entered the Korean war, these demands were redoubled. Numerous Americans of both parties argued that a Nationalist invasion of the mainland would give renewed vigor to the guerrilla warfare still raging in parts of China; would relieve the pressure on the United Nations troops in Korea; and might in the end unseat Mao Tze-tung. The main objection to this argument was obvious. Chiang's army could not possibly invade China unless an American expeditionary force invaded along with it; and since Russia was bound by treaty to help China resist any aggression, such an invasion might at once detonate the Third World War—with the United States cast in the unhappy rôle of aggressor.

In this discussion of Far Eastern policy the imperious personality and positive views of General Douglas Mac-Arthur, who declined to stick to military duties alone, became heavily involved. By midsummer it was evident that he disagreed with Administration policy and was willing to make quasi-political declarations on the subject. In August, he wrote the Veterans of Foreign Wars that Formosa was an integral part of our first line of defense against Communism in the East, a statement that came near being a flat rejection of Mr. Truman's neutralization policy. Already, on July 31, he had flown to Formosa for a much-publicized conference with Chiang Kai-shek, apparently without prior consultation with the Administration. The visit aroused much speculation, press correspondents suggesting that he and Chiang had talked over the possibility of employing Nationalist troops in Korea. The General made a reassuring statement to the effect that he had merely discussed the President's neutralization policy, but Washington was clearly worried.

President Truman at once dispatched W. Averell Harriman to Tokyo to talk with MacArthur, and (it was generally assumed) warn him to keep clear of political issues. Newspapermen and other visitors to MacArthur's headquarters reported that he was brutally frank (off the record) in condemning the Administration's position as ignorant and misguided. He wished the United States to emphasize the Far East, not Europe, in its resistance to Communism, and to follow a much more aggressive policy in the Orient, even at the risk of war. He was for a blockade of China and for use of Chiang's troops.

Rising criticism of MacArthur in United Nations circles and in the United States made doubly dramatic the unexpected air journey of the President to meet the General at Wake Island on October 15. At that date, as noted above, MacArthur's forces had totally defeated the North Koreans and were driving them northward. The United Nations Assembly on October 7 had, with some obvious doubts, authorized MacArthur to "take all appropriate steps" to end the war; that is, to use his best judgment about crossing the 38th parallel. Large elements in the United States, Britain, and other countries feared that any attempt to pursue the Red troops above the narrow waist of Korea and up to the Yalu would result in Chinese intervention. It was conjectured that the extent of MacArthur's northward thrust was a theme at Wake.

No statement was issued at the time on the nature and result of the talks. Not until much later was an official summary given the nation. Americans then learned that on October 15 MacArthur had expressed confidence in a quick victory in Korea, and had told the President that he did not believe Red China or Russia would intervene. He asserted that if the 125,000 Chinese troops along the Yalu River crossed it and tried to attack toward the North Korean capital, Pyongyang, they would be slaughtered; for they had no air cover. He declared that the Russian planes in Siberia would be no match for the

American air force. MacArthur expected to get his troops back to Japan by Christmas, leaving the reorganized Tenth Corps, along with some British and other United Nations troops, to garrison Korea. The Second Division, he declared, could be made available for service in Europe by January. Plans for rehabilitating Korea were discussed, and MacArthur recommended that about $500,-000,000 be spent during a five-year period. At one point, the General apologized to the President for embarrassing him on the Formosa question.

Altogether, MacArthur thought it safe to push to the Yalu, and took a position of excessive optimism—which the President did nothing to check.

When the Chinese invasion changed the whole face of the war, MacArthur made it plain that while he was taken by surprise, he had at no point contravened his instructions from Washington or the United Nations. He had miscalculated, but he had never been disobedient. He issued repeated statements in late November and early December denying that he had obstructed efforts to get him to stop short of the Manchurian border. He intimated that he had been entirely justified in all that he did. But he went beyond this in making clear his conviction that Washington and the United Nations were tying his hands. He specially attacked the United Nations' interdiction of air raids beyond the Korean boundary, saying that this was "an enormous handicap, without precedent in military history." The State Department thereupon issued a blunt rebuke, stating that the political issues which MacArthur had touched upon "are beyond his responsibilities as field commander" and were "being dealt with by the United Nations and by governmental consultations."

As the year closed, the differences between MacArthur and the Truman Administration were still unresolved. The General had found numerous supporters, including Senator McCarthy, the Chicago *Tribune,* and the Hearst press; but European opinion was increasingly critical of him, and the Administration, including George Marshall as Secretary of Defense and Omar N. Bradley as head of the Joint Chiefs of Staff, was increasingly resentful of his pronouncements on civil policy.

THE FALL ELECTIONS

These questions of foreign policy, with such other matters as responsibility for the painful inflation, were injected into one of the liveliest of off-year political campaigns that the country has known. So much interest was generated that in November more than 41,000,000 voters went to the polls. The result was a heavy though not decisive blow to the Democrats and to labor. Elections held midway between Presidential contests traditionally show a reaction against the party in power. Four years earlier, the Democrats had completely lost control of the incoming 80th Congress. This time, they retained a numerical lead in both houses—the new Senate would stand 49 Democrats to 47 Republicans, the new House 235 Democrats to 199 Republicans—but their actual domination was gone. A coalition of anti-Administration Southerners and Republicans would hold the reins of authority. As for labor, the A. F. of L. and C.I.O., after spending about a million dollars to win various battles, lost almost all of them.

Public attention in the fall struggle was centered upon a few specially critical or dramatic contests. In Ohio, the forces of organized labor had for two years drilled and maneuvered against Senator Robert Taft as co-author of the Taft-Hartley Act. The State contains no fewer than 1,250,000 labor union members, who were lustily besought to do their duty by voting Joseph T. Ferguson into Taft's seat. But the effort miscarried. American workingmen are notoriously independent in politics; Taft had won many admirers by his staunchly honest, if not always well-judged, course on public questions; and he carried through an exceptionally earnest, laborious canvass, going from town to town, factory to factory. Union men were for the most part enjoying good wages—"too fat to vote or vote right," said one disgusted leader. The Democratic candidate proved weakly colorless. It was no surprise that Taft's plurality exceeded 425,000 votes.

Only less interesting was the contest in Illinois, where Scott Lucas, the majority leader in the Senate, was defeated for re-election. His opponent was Everett Dirksen, a former Representative, who campaigned on a semi-isolationist program and had the hearty support of the Chicago *Tribune*. The result was widely regarded as a blow to liberalism in both domestic and foreign affairs. The Democratic whip in the Senate, Francis Myers of Pennsylvania, went down at the same time, being worsted by the able Governor of the State, James H. Duff. In a venomous struggle in Maryland, marked (as was shown later) by very discreditable tactics, the experienced Senator Millard E. Tydings was defeated by a newcomer, John M. Butler. A great deal of pressure was exerted from outside in this contest. Tydings, as chairman of the Foreign Relations subcommittee which held hearings on McCarthy's charges, had mercilessly scored the Wisconsin demagogue, and was vindictively misrepresented as a defender of Communism. Another echo of the controversy over Communism came from California, where Richard M. Nixon, a Republican Representative who had done much to bring about the conviction of Alger Hiss on a perjury charge, defeated the Democratic candidate, Helen Gahagan Douglas.

Of the gubernatorial contests, that in New York held the center of the stage. Governor Thomas E. Dewey had declared in January that he would not run for a third term. Various circumstances, however, incluuding the war crisis and his desire to promote General Eisenhower for the Presidency, brought him to a tardy change of mind. It became necessary to obtain the withdrawal of Lieutenant-Governor Joseph R. Hanley, who was supported by up-State elements for the Republican nomination. Hanley retired in Dewey's favor, taking instead the Republican nomination for Senator—a nomination worth little, inasmuch as Herbert H. Lehman, the popular Democratic incumbent, was regarded as certain of re-election. The press thereupon got hold of a letter written by Hanley, in some chagrin, to Representative W. Kingsland Macy of Long Island, in which Hanley explained

73

that he had stepped aside as a result of a bargain; stating that he had been promised by Dewey that he would be put in a position to meet some of his pressing financial obligations. The letter, which certainly did no credit either to Hanley or Dewey, provoked a brief flurry. Nevertheless, Dewey won against the Democratic candidate, Walter A. Lynch, by a plurality of approximately half a million. Lehman easily defeated Hanley, and Representative Macy was punished for his part in the affair by losing in a district ordinarily Republican.

The morale of the Republican Party was distinctly strengthened by the election. Some Republican leaders felt that it was better that they did *not* gain control of Congress; they could block the President's program without taking embarrassing responsibilities of power. They could protect the Taft-Hartley Act against repeal, and could prevent enactment of the Brannan farm price plan and of compulsory health insurance, but they would not be a target for easy missiles. The Republicans rejoiced, too, that they kept all their principal White House possibilities in the field: Dewey, Taft, and not least, Governor Earl Warren of California, who defeated James Roosevelt with the greatest ease. General Eisenhower remained the favorite for the nomination, but all these men were still potential candidates. Senator-elect Duff, too, was in the running.

While the Republican Party in general was the gainer, it could not be said that its isolationist wing had been strongly revived. The election of Dirksen in Illinois was more than offset by the victory of Dewey and Duff, both

strong internationalists. Some Republican leaders has-
tened to greet the outcome as a repudiation of Secretary
of State Acheson; but that officer announced that he had
no intention of resigning, and Truman reiterated his full
confidence in the State Department. The new Congress
could be counted upon to support the vital features of
Mr. Truman's foreign policy: vigorous prosecution of
the Korean War, unflinching support of the United Nations and generous aid to Western Europe in rearmament. It might reduce the amount of Marshall Plan assistance, but some reduction was now warranted. If the
election had any special meaning, it was probably that
the country was irritated by the high cost of living, and
had lost confidence in Truman's acumen; the voters were
certainly not turning their back on vigorous international
policies which alone could ensure national safety.

HOOVER, DEWEY, AND DULLES ON FOREIGN AFFAIRS

Just before the election, ex-President Hoover initiated
a striking debate which plainly demonstrated that the
majority of Republican leaders had forever turned their
backs on isolationist ideas. Here and there, to be sure, a
frank isolationist like Senator Kenneth S. Wherry could
be found. But the party had a much larger number
of convinced internationalists like Senator Vandenberg,
Representative Charles A. Eaton of New Jersey, Senator
Wayne Morse of Oregon, Senator Irving M. Ives of
New York, and Senator Margaret Chase Smith of Maine,
and of moderate internationalists like Senator Henry
Cabot Lodge, Jr., of Massachusetts. Even Senator Taft,

though inclined to accept MacArthur's ideas and dubious about the willingness of France, Italy, and other Continental nations to fight, supported the United Nations, a bipartisan foreign policy, the arming of Western Germany, and the stiffest possible front against Russia.

Mr. Hoover, who earlier in the year had made a series of statements on foreign policy, delivered a major address on the subject on October 18. His preliminary utterances had been notable chiefly for a proposal that the United Nations be reorganized with the Soviet Union and its satellites omitted, for these countries, he said, were using it only as a forum for outrageous falsehoods against the United States and other Western lands, and as a means of crippling peace and justice. With Russia eliminated, the United Nations might really accomplish much good. In his full-dress speech in October he astonished many Americans by declaring against any further assistance to Western Europe, whether military or economic, until "a definitely united and sufficient European army is in sight." The nations of the North Atlantic Pact, he asserted, had failed to take proper steps to resist Communism, and except for Great Britain, lacked "even the will to preparedness." These nations should be given one more chance to show whether they would really rearm. If they failed to do so, America should reconsider her whole position. The speech indicated that Mr. Hoover was edging toward isolationism.

And on December 20 the ex-President came out bluntly for American concentration on the defense of the Western Hemisphere. We should regard the Atlantic as our eastern frontier, he declared—holding Britain as our frontier outpost if she would cooperate. We should hold the Pacific as the other frontier, making Japan, Formosa, and the Philippines our outer line of defense. Thus we could maintain "a Western Hemisphere Gibraltar of Western civilization."

These ideas fell upon Europe like a thunderclap. They outraged most Democrats, and shocked great bodies of Republicans. Inside Hoover's own party, the principal opposing figure was Governor Dewey. He had repeatedly advocated a strong bipartisan foreign policy. He was wholeheartedly behind every measure for the defense of Western Europe: the Schumann plan for uniting the steel industry, plans for political unification, and, above all, powerful American aid in rearmament. He demanded not only a rapid acceleration of our own measures for war, but a steady flow of arms and men to Europe. A notable incident had advertised Mr. Dewey's intense antagonism to the Soviet Union. On September 21, speaking at a dinner at the Waldorf Hotel for delegates to the General Assembly of the United Nations, he lashed out against the labor slavery of the Russian concentration camps, where he said many millions were confined. Vishinsky and Malik at once left the room. As they departed, Dewey flung after them an assurance that he was "complimented by the withdrawal of those who plot the destruction of the world." Mr. Dewey was for cooperation with Western Europe, not abandonment of it.

From John Foster Dulles, too, supplementing the statements of Secretary Acheson, came a forcible rejection of Mr. Hoover's ideas. Mr. Acheson on December

23 said flatly: "A policy of withdrawal into our hemisphere . . . would give the Soviet Union possession of a strategic position which would be catastrophic to the United States." He pointed out that with Western Europe in Russia's hands, Africa and the remainder of Asia would quickly fall. The United States would be left besieged in the Western Hemisphere, and its final fate, confronted with overwhelming military and economic power, would be certain. Mr. Dulles took a similar position. "Any nation," he said on December 29, "which at a moment of extreme danger sheds those of its allies which are most endangered, and to whom it is bound by solemn treaty, elects a dangerous course, for solitary defense is never impregnable. . . . A United States which could be an inactive spectator while the barbarians overran and desecrated the cradle of our Christian civilization would not be the kind of United States which could defend itself." And endorsement of Dulles's stand came from Senator Wayne Morse of Oregon, who the same day assailed the "isolationism" of the "reactionaries of the Republican Party."

On one of the basic issues in the debate, the question whether Western Europe would really fight against Communism or not, the weight of evidence supported the view of Dulles, Morse, and Dewey (as of Truman and Acheson) that it would. Ever stronger assurances came from Paris, Rome, and London that the Atlantic Pact nations would effectively continue their rearmament if only they were assured of full American help, both economic and military, and of dogged American persistence once the fighting began. The apparent timidity of some groups on the Continent, informed students declared, was largely the product of a fear that the United States would give enough assistance to provoke Russia to attack, but not enough to make the defense effective. Defeatist talk in America, such as came from that perennial prophet of gloom, Joseph P. Kennedy, in an over-advertised speech of December 12, naturally produced defeatist emotions in parts of Europe. "We and our allies are moving ahead with courage and with determination to build our common strength," said Acheson. The events of the last week of the year proved him right. As it became known that General Eisenhower was about to leave for Europe to help organize the defense of the West, a wave of hope and courage swept every country from St. George's Channel to the walls of Frankfort and the shores of Sweden. News came, too, that Britain was shaping the heaviest budget for armaments in her whole peacetime history.

It was not the intention of the American Government, as one bipartisan spokesman after another declared, to lead the West in making a military effort sufficient to defeat Russia out of hand. The intention was simply to mobilize sufficient strength to deter Russia from beginning a war, to make her realize that the penalties would be greater than any possible rewards. The West did not need to train armies equal to Russia's 175 divisions. It did need, however, to train enough men, and to accumulate a sufficient stock of the latest weapons, including tanks, planes, and atomic bombs, to make an onslaught by the Russian masses too costly to be risked. "There is only one effective defense for ourselves and others," said Mr. Dulles. "That is the capacity to counterattack. That is the ultimate deterrent."

CULTURAL AND SOCIAL CHANGE

The year 1950 saw another American author, William Faulkner, added to the list of those awarded Nobel Prizes. Mr. Faulkner marked the year also by the publication of his *Collected Stories,* a 900-page volume dealing chiefly with life in his mythical Yoknapatawpha County in the Deep South. This work shared celebrity in the field of fiction with Ernest Hemingway's first book in a decade, *Across the River and Into the Trees,* which encountered a decidedly mixed reception from the critics. Two other volumes which attracted general attention were John Hersey's fictional account of the extermination of the Warsaw Jews, *The Wall,* and Robert Penn Warren's somewhat melodramatic novel of American life, *World Enough and Time.* In poetry, Carl Sandburg's *Collected Poems* and William Carlos Williams's *Collected Later Poems* shared notice with Wallace Stevens's *The Auroras of Autumn.* It is worth noting that poetry received an unusual recognition when the United States Senate paid tribute to Robert Frost on his seventy-fifth birthday, March 26.

Organized scholarship showed unusual enterprise during 1950. Yale University, in cooperation with the McGraw-Hill Book Company, issued James Boswell's *London Journal, 1762–1763,* edited by Professor Frederick

A. Pottle, this being the first of sixty projected volumes of the complete Malahide and Fettercairn Papers, which had been acquired by the enterprise of Lieutenant-Colonel Ralph H. Isham, and sold to Yale University. The book astonished everyone by becoming a best-seller. It proved that Dr. Chauncey B. Tinker was entirely right when he said that Boswell had made a life-work of "defeating the forces of oblivion," and had triumphantly succeeded. Meanwhile, the Princeton University Press issued the first of thirty projected volumes of the correspondence of Thomas Jefferson, under the editorship of Dr. Julian P. Boyd; an undertaking to which the New York *Times* helped lend financial support. And the University of California, aided by the publishing firm of Alfred A. Knopf, completed the issuance of about a hundred titles in history, memoirs, and travel in celebration of the centenary of the State of California.

In science, perhaps the greatest, and certainly the most disturbing, event of the year was the decision of the American Government, announced by President Truman, to construct a hydrogen bomb—far more horrible in its destructive potentialities than the atomic bomb. But scientists were busy in many fields of peaceful endeavor. The anti-biotic drugs were rapidly being developed. Electronic calculators were pushing back some of the boundaries of mathematical research. The electron microscopes were revealing infinitesimally small objects at the same time that the first photographs made with the aid of the new 200-inch telescope on Mount Palomar in California showed new reaches in the outer universe.

A simple blood-test for cancer was announced as a fresh triumph of medical science.

Although education prospered throughout the year, the shadow of war fell darkly upon it in the closing fall and winter months. College and university enrollment rose during the spring term to the highest level in history, a total of 2,457,000 students being registered. In the autumn, with many veterans completing their education, registration fell to approximately 2,300,000. State universities were enjoying record-breaking appropriations, and endowed institutions, severely hit by rising costs, were everywhere carrying out or planning drives for additions to their funds. The autumn decline in students presaged a further drop, which worried many university presidents. Mobilization was certain to take many students, while the low birth-rate during the depression years of the early 1930's would be responsible for a further loss of attendance. Some leaders of higher education, such as President Conant of Harvard, proposed that all young men be haled into the armed services at eighteen; others asked a general deferment for college students; and still others urged partial deferment. Advisory committees appointed by the Director of Selective Service, Major-General Lewis B. Hershey, recommended deferment for those of superior scholastic attainments. The issue was still unresolved when the year ended. Already, however, some institutions dependent on student fees were being painfully squeezed between reduced revenues and enhanced expenses.

In the elementary and secondary schools, the great

problem was that of providing for constantly growing enrollments. In 1947–48 these schools had taught 26,670,-000 pupils; in 1948–49 the number had gone above 27,-100,000; in the following year it rose above 28,100,000; and in the fall of 1950 it stood at about 29,000,000. To furnish buildings, desks, books, and teachers for this crescent army was a pressing task. In parts of the nation which had grown with special rapidity, such as Texas and the Pacific Northwest, the problem seemed almost insoluble. The teacher shortage that had followed the war had been partially met, especially in the high schools; but about 80,000 of the country's teachers had only temporary certificates, and many good teachers were quitting their positions. Living costs rose far more rapidly than salaries. With good jobs available in industry, business, and government offices, ambitious young teachers threw down their record cards. All groups of public school officers — superintendents, principals, teachers — had an average salary of but slightly over $3000 in the fall of 1950, equivalent to only $1800 in prewar dollars.

Educators during 1950 warned the country that it must gird itself for much higher expenditures in the educational field. Already the "war babies" of the last conflict were coming into the elementary grades. By 1960 the pupils in the elementary and secondary schools would reach an aggregate of about 36,000,000. The total national outlay for these schools was estimated in 1950 at just over $4,500,000,000; and it would have to go much above that figure even if the dollar remained static.

For the Negroes of the country the year was one of

unusual progress. One prominent Negro, Ralph Bunche, receiver the Nobel Prize for his contributions to world peace. A Negro woman, Edith Sampson of Chicago, was appointed an alternate delegate for the United States in the United Nations Assembly. In Korea, colored troops fought bravely, and there and in army camps at home they were with few exceptions accorded full equality of treatment. Although no new State passed fair-employment legislation, several cities, notably Cleveland, Ohio, did so. William H. Hastie, who had been governor of the Virgin Islands, was raised to a Federal circuit judgeship. Discriminations against Negroes in public-aided or public-built housing projects were under steady if not always successful attack.

Most important of all, the struggle of the Negro for equal rights in State-supported educational institutions gained new ground. The Supreme Court in two important cases, Sweatt vs. Painter (originating in Texas) and McLaurin vs. Oklahoma State Regents, reiterated the now familiar judicial doctrine that qualified Negro applicants had a right to education in State schools and universities of precisely the same grade as that given white entrants. Under the Fourteenth Amendment, a State had either to admit Negroes to its postgraduate and professional schools, or provide schools of equal equipment and standing. Negroes were duly admitted, by virtue of these decisions, to the law school and architectural courses of the University of Texas, and to graduate courses in education at the University of Oklahoma. The Negro, indeed, was at last coming into his full heritage in America. A significant token of his new status was the refusal of many newspapers to recognize—or at any rate to mention—the existence of a color differentia-

"SOME UNFINISHED BUSINESS"
From a cartoon by Summers in *The Buffalo Evening News*

tion. American citizens, to such newspapers, were no longer black or white; they were just citizens.

One of the most arresting social developments of the year was the exposé of the American underworld by the Special Senate Committee to Investigate Organized

Crime in Interstate Commerce. This body was popularly called the Kefauver Committee from its chairman, Senator Estes Kefauver of Tennessee, who was assisted by a tireless staff of investigators headed by Rudolph Halley, chief counsel. Beginning with a public hearing in Miami, Florida, on May 26, the committee moved on to New Orleans, St. Louis, Chicago, Kansas City, and other large centers. Hundreds of witnesses told a story of criminal infection of politics and society that was sordid, shocking, and at times frightening. Other witnesses, happily, described the courageous and unremitting battle of decent citizens and organizations to destroy the underworld.

It had been popularly supposed that American criminality was local and disconnected. The Kefauver Committee proved, on the contrary, that the United States had to deal with what the chairman called "a nationwide crime syndicate, loosely organized, but cohesive." This so-called crime syndicate had its origin in the murderous gangs which grew up in the larger cities, notably New York, Chicago, and Detroit, a generation ago; gangs which made profits of many millions out of illegal liquor, narcotics, prostitution, and business blackmail. Under such men as Frank Costello of New York, described by one authority as "the most influential underworld leader in America," the gangs grew more cautious and astute than they had been under thugs like Al Capone and Dutch Schultz. They allied themselves with corrupt or pliable politicians; they manipulated instead of murdering. In some cities, such as Cleveland and Reno, they specialized in gambling; in others, such as Detroit,

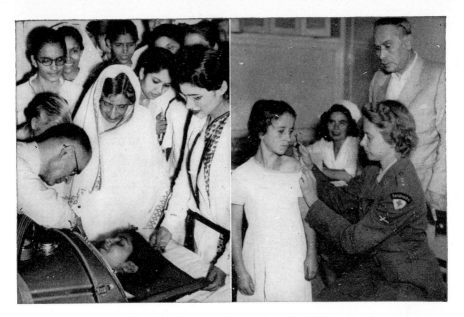

THE UNITED NATIONS IN OPERATION

Left: India's Health Minister demonstrates the operation of iron lungs, which were rushed from the United States by the United Nations World Health Organization to help India in an infantile paralysis emergency. *Right:* A child is vaccinated in anti-tuberculosis campaign in Greece.

Official United Nations Photographs

THE PERMANENT SEAT OF THE UNITED NATIONS ORGANIZATION

The General Assembly met in the open air in October to commemorate the fourth anniversary of the organization of the United Nations and to dedicate the first stone of the permanent seat.

THE HOUSING ACT OF 1949

Top: Old home of a World War II veteran who received a loan under the Farm Housing section of the Housing Act of 1949. *Bottom:* New home of the same veteran under construction. The Secretary of Agriculture is authorized under this act to extend financial assistance to farm owners to construct, improve, or repair farm housing.

SIGNING THE NORTH ATLANTIC TREATY

Vice-President Alben Barkley and President Harry S. Truman look on as Secretary of State
Dean Acheson dips a new pen before signing up for the United States on April 4, 1949.

General Lucius D. Clay, back from four years' service as the United States Military Governor of Germany, received a hero's welcome. At National Airport, he and Secretary of Defense Louis B. Johnson salute while an honor guard stands by.

The first international airing of strife-torn China's political turmoil came in the United Nations General Assembly in October after Tingfu Tsiang of China charged the U.S.S.R. with supporting Chinese Communist forces in their campaign.

Official Navy Photograph released by the Dept. of Defense.

A SALVO FROM THE GUNS OF THE USS *MISSOURI* AT CHONG JIN, KOREA, IN AN EFFORT TO CUT NORTH KOREAN COMMUNICATIONS

A wounded marine being carried from the front lines to a forward aid station and Navy underwater demolition personnel, "frogmen," clearing Wonsan of mines in preparation for an amphibious landing.

Paratroopers floating earthward from C-119 airplanes to cut off retreating Red units and captured Chinese
Communists surrendering to U. S. Marines during the fighting in the mountains of North Korea.

Official U. S. Army Photograph released by the Dept. of Defense.

ARTILLERYMEN OF THE EIGHTH ARMY FIRING AGAINST AN ENEMY POSITION NEAR SEOUL, KOREA.

in labor racketeering; in others, like Tampa, in narcotics smuggling; and in still others, such as Kansas City, in white slavery, blackmail, and Mafia violence. A close alliance was demonstrated between the Capone Syndicate in Chicago, now headed by Jake Guzik and Tony Accardo, and the Costello-Joe Adonis combination on the Atlantic Coast.

The public was horrified to learn that in nearly all the chief American cities gangs had succeeded in corrupting many policemen (in New York hundreds of them) and in forming friendly relations with sheriffs, petty magistrates, and such bosslets as Frank Clancy of Jefferson Parish in Louisiana and James Moran, one of ex-Mayor O'Dwyer's closest friends, in New York. It was pained to learn that imperfect cooperation between Federal and local authorities helped many gamblers, narcotics-peddlers, pimps, and black-market operators to escape justice. In some cities, vigilant agencies were at work. The Chicago Crime Commission under Virgil W. Peterson was a specially efficient unit of attack on the crime syndicate. The Federal Bureau of Narcotics, an enforcement agency of the Treasury Department, had a creditable record. But it was evident from the committee hearings that police departments in numerous cities needed purgation and strengthening; that magistrates courts often required overhauling; that municipal and State prosecuting officers could find many more indictments against the "mobs"; and that wherever gambling, dope-peddling, and racketeering crossed State lines, the Department of Justice could show more vigilance and energy. Help from the income-tax authorities, too, was needed.

A YEAR OF PROSPERITY—AND ANXIETY

In almost every field, 1950 had been a year of growth, prosperity, and hope. Industrial production was higher than ever before; so was employment; so was income —not merely money income, but real income. More steel was poured, more automobiles and trucks were made, more dwelling units were constructed, than ever before in our annals. The total national income reached $235,000,000,000. Although Americans complained lustily of high food prices, never had their tables been so well spread. One great new luxury, television, became distributed so widely that many people regarded it as almost a necessity. Never had literature and the arts seemed more vigorous or shown greater promise.

The one great shadow on the record of the year, as on that of all the years since the war ended, was the threat of Russian aggression. The little group who, sitting as the Politburo in the Kremlin, held despotic power over the Soviet Union and its terrorized satellites, could reach their sinister decisions in secret and execute them without fear of public opinion or parliamentary questioning. They had now made clear their intention of crippling and if possible destroying the free nations of the West; they had revealed their special and deadly enmity toward the United States. All Americans hoped that the Third World War could be avoided; but none felt safe from a sudden onslaught. It was evident that, to echo Lincoln's words, a crisis would have to be reached and passed before humanity could gain unity and peace—and nobody could guess what shape that crisis would take.

CHAPTER III

THE RECORD OF 1951

AYEAR of hot war in Korea and cold war throughout Europe and Asia; a year of titanic effort to rearm the United States and its Western allies; a year of inflation, economic strain, and general anxiety —such was 1951. As the battle lines swayed back and forth on the Korean peninsula, the world tensions remained acute. It was possible that at any time an open clash might develop between the United Nations forces and the Chinese Government, and that this would involve China's ally and supporter Russia—Russia, which was steadily supplying the North Koreans and the Chinese "volunteers" with all the implements of war. Civilization walked a field sown with hidden mines. History has shown how often, in a time of mounting tension, some chance occurrence has supplied the spark to loose a terrible explosion.

Yet as compared with 1950, the danger of a new global war did seem to diminish. Experts agreed that if the Kremlin had wished to take the chances of a world conflict, they would have had a better chance in the summer of 1950, when the Korean struggle began, than a year later. Every month added to the capacity of the North Atlantic alliance to resist a Communist onslaught; every month saw an improvement in the morale of Western Europe. Three factors accounted for the improvement. They were the rise of armament production in the United States to the point where, by December, deliveries were running at the rate of nearly two billion dollars' worth a month; the steady flow of arms across the Atlantic into European hands; and the success of European members of the North Atlantic Treaty Organization, under the guidance of General Dwight Eisenhower as supreme commander, in raising their own munitions production by about seventy per cent, and in more than doubling the combat effectiveness of their weak but growing forces.

Had Russia and her satellites attacked the West in 1950, they could have swept to the English Channel and the Pyrenees within a few weeks—though meanwhile the atomic bomb would have played havoc with their cities and communications. By the end of 1951 no such easy conquest of Western Europe was possible. Every day the deterrents to Soviet aggression were growing more formidable. Never had the ties uniting the Western democracies been so strong. Though the danger of an accidental detonation remained, it seemed unlikely that the Kremlin would now deliberately provoke war. And as Secretary Acheson constantly said, the West could negotiate out of strength, never out of weakness.

At home the year was one of high prosperity, qualified only by inflation, and of general national unity, qualified only by much petty political bickering. All economic groups—labor, farmers, businessmen, most professional people—shared in the sunshine of good times. Labor troubles were kept at a minimum; no strike occurred in any of the great basic industries, and the loss of time through stoppages fell to the lowest point since the Second World War. Gross national production rose to about $325,000,000,000, making the largest annual gain since the return of world peace. Employment was better than in the previous year, standing near the end of 1951 at 61,350,000 persons. Industrial output was one-tenth greater than in 1950. Personal income broke all records. To many people living on salaries and other fixed incomes, the rise in living costs and in taxation was a cruel (sometimes a crushing) hardship. It could not be denied, however, that a great mass of workers obtained wage increases that outran the increased expenses, or that farm income was better than at any time since the record year 1947.

The American economy, in fact, astonished many home observers and foreign Cassandras by displaying an unexpected capacity to produce both guns and butter. Indeed, the London *Economist* remarked that it furnished "not only butter but the whole cow." For example, despite the heavy defense pressure on vital materials, the automobile industry manufactured more cars, trucks, and buses than in any year before 1950, and its output was only fifteen per cent below that of 1950— about the drop that would have been caused by tapering demand, anyhow. Perhaps the most spectacular showing was that of the airplane industry. It was able not only to support the air war in Korea, and to get the mass production of new defense aircraft under way, but to maintain a thriving trade in commercial transport and utility aircraft. The steel mills supported both the normal economy and the new arms program, and did it with seeming effortlessness.

Late in the year, to be sure, some critics complained that the nation was getting too much butter and too few guns. A Senate sub-committee under Lyndon Johnson of Texas reported in December that, measured in dollars, aircraft deliveries were 34 per cent of the established goal, tanks 40 per cent, and guided missiles 70 per cent. The national economy, Johnson said in effect, should tighten its belt. But the head of the mobilization effort, Charles E. Wilson, made it plain that the government believed the defense goals could be achieved without any grave impairment of normal life and progress. "We are going to ask the most abundant economy in the world," said Mr. Wilson, "to produce in the next two or three years an extra $150,000,000,000 for defense." The object was to attain not a wartime output of arms, but simply a basis from which "we may swing rapidly into full-scale war production if a major war should come."

The experience of 1951 gave hope that this might be done. The nation, that is, might remain prosperous and lift the standard of living while bringing steel production up to 117,000,000 tons a year, increasing aluminum production by half, and otherwise strengthening industry so that any eventuality could be met with confidence. Once this program was completed in 1953, the country would be ready for all-out war, or all-out peace.

The Korean War, one of the most grueling that Americans had ever fought, was marked by a disastrous United Nations retreat, a spectacular rally, and a final stalemate, with neither side possessed of sufficient strength to strike a knockout blow. The opening of the year found the American forces suffering from MacArthur's strategic error in pushing too far and too fast toward the Yalu River. North Koreans and Chinese troops had hurled the United Nations armies back south of the 38th parallel; in a desperate manoeuvre, naval forces had removed 105,000 soldiers and 91,000 Korean refugees from their perilous northern position around the port of Hungnam; nobody knew how far down the peninsula the defenders of democracy would be driven. Matthew B. Ridgway had just taken command of the Eighth Army, succeeding Walton H. Walker, killed in a road-crash, and was striving to restore its broken morale. The outlook was darker than at any time since the early months of the war, giving rise to grave apprehensions.

Late winter and spring witnessed a succession of Communist offensives, and a grimly successful effort by the United Nations units to slow them down, choke them in blood, and finally repel them. Heavy forces of Chinese troops were employed by the Red command with a fanatical indifference to losses. Russian tanks and Russian airplanes were utilized on a lavish scale. The first onslaught of the year carried the Communists south past Seoul. Then in mid-January the United Nations forces stiffened, established a strong defensive line, and shortly opened a counter-attack. By the end of January they were approaching Seoul again. Seesaw fighting continued through February, with the United Nations troops gradually gaining ground. In March the advance swept up past Seoul, and as that month closed, Ridgway's advance forces were once more within sight of the 38th parallel. Their object was to gain a strong defensive position in the hills north of the old boundary. By mid-April the Americans and their allies had thrust a dozen miles above the parallel on the central front, and were steadily occupying the "Iron Triangle" in which the Communists had mounted their last offensive.

The Red forces had fallen back, however, only to recoil again. On April 22 their massed armies, with a terrific bombardment, began their spring assault. The Chinese and North Koreans had approximately 400,000 men on the battle line and 250,000 in immediate reserve, while the United Nations leaders could muster only about 250,000 in the front lines. At first the Communists carried all before them. Breaking through a South Korean division, they threw 130,000 troops into this gap. The Eighth Army was driven from fifteen to twenty-five miles below the parallel, leaving Seoul protected only by a thin strip of territory. Fortunately the American and British airplanes maintained an easy superiority in the air. Flying more than a thousand sorties on many days, they inflicted appalling losses on the Red armies by high explosives, machine-gun fire, and napalm bombs. Warships along the coast joined in the terrific pounding. At various points in this offensive the Communists were brought to a standstill behind high windrows of corpses. Their losses sickened even the stoical people of China.

The final Communist offensive, May 17–May 23, gained almost nothing, a mere 1100 square miles. Again the Allied air forces and warships maintained a galling bombardment. At the air strips the crews worked feverishly to get the bombers into the air to roar north, unload their missiles, and come back for fresh supplies. Some pilots flew five trips in a day. Again the United Nations troops, shielded by strong positions, mowed down their assailants in swathes. The April offensive had cost the Reds from 80,000 to 100,000 casualties, and the May attack cost them 80,000 more. On May 23, sullen with defeat, the Chinese and North Koreans began to withdraw. They were soon back in their staging area north of the parallel, relentlessly pressed by Ridgway's hardened fighters.

Observers testified that never did soldiers fight a nastier, crueler war. The fierce winter cold; the rugged terrain of hill, swamp, ravine, and unbridged streams; the ferocity of the enemy, fighting to the death without quarter to any foe; the power of the Russian tanks; the strength of the Russian-built jet planes (believed to be also Russian manned), the MIG–15s, which brought down many of the American B–29 bombers in flames; the desperate nature of many of the battles, such as that in which Heartbreak Ridge changed hands repeatedly, and that in which a British Gloucestershire regiment was virtually wiped out; fear that United Nations prisoners might get the same inhuman treatment as that which the Russians had given to German and Japanese prisoners—all this made the conflict a worse ordeal, according to experts, than either world war.

When on June 25 the first year of the Korean War ended, the Communists held 2,100 fewer square miles on the peninsula than when they began their aggression. They had lost the 38th parallel as a boundary, the United Nations line at some points reaching forty miles above it. North Korea saw her towns and cities in ruins, and her industries smashed to flinders. The United Nations had vindicated its position as a shield against wanton aggressors, and proved its ability to meet the kind of challenge that had cowed the League of Nations. The

Communist losses had reached a staggering total; according to United Nations estimates, at least 1,165,000 Reds had been killed, wounded, or taken prisoner. China, which was in a state of virtual mobilization, was feeling a heavy strain. At least one army had been added to the four previously existing, great numbers of men had been drafted into the forces, and the bill for that weak country was staggering. At the same time the Allied embargo on strategic materials, reducing China's trade with other countries than Russia to a mere trickle, was causing sore economic hardship.

On the whole, the Communist aggression in Korea had not paid. The Kremlin perhaps congratulated itself on forcing China into a closer alliance with Russia. But the Chinese were finding out that it was an intolerably costly alliance! Moreover, the war had persuaded the whole North Atlantic group of nations to rearm frenziedly against the Soviet threat, and the Western temper was such that any fresh aggression might well bring the whole world into arms against Russia. In Peking and Moscow thoughtful men must have wished that they had never started the war. The United States had paid a heavy price, for before the end of 1951 our casualties passed the 100,000 mark. The war was naturally unpopular in America. But the vast majority of citizens never doubted that the instant response of their government to the Russian challenge had been a necessity, and that the decisive action of the United Nations had postponed if not perhaps averted a much more terrible war.

With the Korean conflict at a virtual standstill by June, rumors of Russian proposals for a peace began to circulate. They were given substance when the Soviet delegate to the United Nations accepted an invitation to speak on a program which the Columbia Broadcasting System had been sending from United Nations headquarters in New York. On June 24 Mr. Malik, after flinging into the air the usual Russian diatribes against the democratic world, declared that the Soviet peoples believed that the most acute problem of the moment, the Korean War, could be solved. The Kremlin, he said, held that "as a first step, discussions should be started between the belligerents for a cease fire and an armistice providing for a mutual withdrawal of forces from the 38th parallel."

Although Malik made no mention of the former Chinese demands for Formosa and a seat in the United Nations Council—demands which the Western Powers have repeatedly said they would not grant under threat of war—his proposal was received with as much doubt as hope. It was possible that China, her armies mauled, her hospitals filled with sick and wounded, her economy sapped, really desired peace. The Mao Tse-tung regime might even be getting tired of acting as Russia's catspaw, and might be making unpleasant demands on the Kremlin. It was equally possible, however, that the proposal for a truce was delusive; that the Kremlin wished merely to gain time until Mao's shattered divisions could be re-equipped and reinforced; and that meanwhile Stalin hoped to create some division within the United Nations. By dragging out the truce negotiations, the Communists might possibly chill the ardor of Western Europe for rearmament.

Once begun, negotiations for a truce did drag out interminably. Talks between military representatives of the Communists and the United Nations began at Kaesong early in July. At first the Communist leaders demanded that the armistice line follow the Thirty-eighth parallel; but as this would have meant the surrender of valuable United Nations advantages, General Ridgway and Vice-Admiral C. Turner Joy (head of the United Nations truce delegation) made it plain that the line must follow the battle-front. The Communists spun out the talks with charge after charge of the violation of the neutrality of the Kaesong area. In the first two months the United Nations rejected ten of these charges as unfounded, admitting in only one instance a mistake by an airplane as to the area's boundaries.

Month after month the talks writhed backward and forward like a wounded snake. Sometimes a sunbeam of progress lighted up the headlines, but in general the negotiators reported nothing but Communist recriminations, hagglings, insults, disputation, and propaganda. For two whole months the parleys were stalled by an alleged bombing incident near Kaesong. Then in late October they were renewed again near Panmunjon, a town between the battle-lines. More insults, recrimina-tions, and defiances followed—and a few more comprom-ises. The Communists wished to limit the Allied rotation of troops; the United Nations refused this. The Com-munists wished to construct airfields in North Korea during the armistice; the United Nations said no. The Communists called for a bulk exchange of prisoners; the United Nations insisted that every prisoner should have the right to choose for or against his return.

By the end of the year an agreement had been reached on two important points. The armistice line had been fixed along the actual fighting front. This was done late in November. Then, just before Christmas, the two sides agreed to exchange lists of prisoners. A poignant series of events followed hard upon this second agreement.

On the afternoon of December 18, in the chilly truce-tent at Panmunjon, the Communists brusquely pushed across the table lists which they alleged to contain the names of all prisoners. These lists were hurriedly flown to Tokyo, the names were sent by radio to the Pentagon, and a rapid check was made there by a staff working all night. Then copies of the names were handed to the press, and telegrams were dispatched to the next of kin. The nation awoke next day with a gasp to the tragedy revealed. Whereas the United Nations had given the Communists a complete roster of 132,474 North Koreans and Chinese, the Communists in return had handed over only 11,502 names, of which 7,142 were South Koreans,

3,198 Americans, 919 British, and 243 Turks. Many more of the Allied forces had been captured. What had happened to them?

It was a harrowing uncertainty that the democratic nations faced. The South Koreans had about 70,000 men missing; what had become of the 63,000 unreported? The Americans had a total of 11,042 missing; what had become of the 8,000 unlisted? How many had died of wounds or disease, how many had been massacred, and how many were lost in the interior of China as the Russians had "lost" hundreds of thousands of captured German and Japanese? It was at once pointed out that the Communists had read off on their propaganda broadcasts the names of more than a thousand American prisoners not included in the lists. How many other names were they deliberately withholding? Once more General Ridgway besought the Communist commanders to let Red Cross agents visit their prison camps, and once more he met a stony refusal.

This sad page in the negotiations for an armistice emphasized the difficulty of dealing with an enemy who had no regard whatever for truth, honesty, or humanity, and who was quite capable of using cruelty to bring pressure upon the West. The United Nations delegates sharply demanded an explanation for the "wide discrepancies" in the enemy rosters, but of course got only mockery in return. Earlier, in November, the Tokyo headquarters of the United Nations had published an estimate that the Communists had slain about six thousand American prisoners in cold blood. That the atrocity totals were large there could be no doubt.

The year closed with the question whether an armistice was really possible as murky as ever. During the talks, the Communist forces had been heavily augmented. The enemy had at least 700,000 well-armed troops in North Korea, with a large reserve north of the Yalu River. Masses of artillery had been brought up. The Reds had at least five hundred Russian tanks of the T–34 type. On their airfields in Manchuria they had an estimated 1100 Russian MIG jet planes, so that the threat to United Nations domination of the air had become serious. Fortunately, these planes could not be flown beyond the Communist lines, for the Russians did not want to risk having their pilots brought down into Allied hands. Meanwhile, the United Nations forces had of course also been powerfully strengthened, and General Ridgway was confident that the existing front could be held against any assaults whatever.

The Far Eastern conflict generated political as well as military drama. On April 11 the country was taken aback by President Truman's abrupt and summary removal of General Douglas MacArthur from his various posts of command. This was one of the most dramatic assertions in our history of the supremacy of the civil arm over the armed forces. The tremendous prestige of MacArthur, his imperious temper, and his connection with strong Republican elements hostile to Truman, made his downfall doubly dramatic. One of the greatest of American generals had been treated as brusquely as Polk treated Winfield Scott, or Lincoln finally treated McClellan. At once many admirers of MacArthur stated an angry conviction that he had been humiliated unjustly. At once, too, his removal opened up for national debate several important questions of policy.

In particular, the President's action brought into the forefront of attention two issues: whether the main seat of the struggle between Communism and the West lay in Europe, or lay in the Orient; and whether the war in Korea was being waged with sufficient spirit, energy, and boldness. No sooner had MacArthur packed his bags for a quick return to the United States than a bitter discussion of these issues began in Congress and the press. It lasted all spring, and threw its shadow over the approaching presidential battle.

That MacArthur had been guilty of rank insubordination to the Administration there could be little question. As military commander, he had no right to make pronouncements on political questions. Particularly did he have no right to embarrass his government and the United Nations in their effort to work out an international adjustment. During March the fourteen governments which had troops in Korea had been trying to formulate a statement of aims which would convince Mao Tse-tung of their peaceable intentions. While they were thus busy, MacArthur late in the month made an unfortunate excursion into the political field. He issued a statement that he was ready to talk with the Chinese upon a truce, and hinted that if Mao did not want an armistice, he might carry the war to the "coastal areas and interior bases" of China. The United Nations leaders, their peace program thus rudely disrupted, were angry and humiliated. At once the Joint Chiefs of Staff had given MacArthur an urgent directive to make no political utterances whatever until he had obtained advance approval from Washington. This was a stinging but deserved rebuke.

Already, however, MacArthur had gone further in his political meddling. Representative Joseph Martin, Republican House Leader, had written him in March inquiring what he thought of using Chiang Kai-shek's Formosan army to open a second front in Asia. MacArthur on March 29 (just before the general staff directive reached him) replied in indiscreet terms. He declared that the use of the Formosan army would harmonize with his view that force ought to be met with "maximum counter-force." And he went on to attack the leaders in Europe and the United States who (like Truman, Acheson, Eisenhower, Attlee, and Schuman) gave the European theatre priority over the Asiatic.

"It seems strangely difficult for some to realize," wrote MacArthur, "that here in Asia is where the Communist conspirators have elected to make their play for global conquest, and that we have joined the issue thus raised on the battlefield; that here we fight Europe's war with arms, while the diplomats there still fight it with words. . . ."

As soon as Martin published this letter (April 5), the Truman Administration issued a tart statement that its Far Eastern policy remained unaltered. In London a Labor member of Parliament proposed a vote of no-confidence in Parliament. The French, Dutch, and Italian press made acrid comments. General Omar Bradley, chairman of the joint chiefs of staff, felt as strongly as Truman that the general had gotten out of hand. It was with his and Secretary of Defense George Marshall's concurrence that MacArthur was severed from his commands, to which General Ridgway was at once assigned. On April 15 MacArthur left Tokyo with his wife and son. On April 19 he addressed both chambers of Congress while half the nation listened to the radio.

"The issues are global," MacArthur told Congress—and that was plain. The intervention of Red China, he declared, had created a new situation which demanded "a drastic revision of strategic planning." That revision had not been forthcoming. What should be its main elements? He defined four steps which he thought should be taken at once. They were: first, an intensification of the economic blockade of China; second, a strict naval blockade of the Chinese coast; third, the dropping of restrictions on air reconnaissance over China's coastal area and Manchuria; and fourth, "removal of restrictions on the forces of the Republic of China on Formosa, with logistical support to contribute to their effective operations against the Chinese mainland." Unless these measures were taken, the stalemate in Korea would continue. But although MacArthur denied that he was a warmonger, he could of course offer no guarantee that an invasion of China by Chiang Kai-shek's troops, backed and assisted by American forces, would not result in a Chinese declaration of war against the United States—and thus in the precipitation of the third World War.

While MacArthur toured the country, receiving ovations in New York, Chicago, Milwaukee, and other cities, the Senate Armed Services and Foreign Relations Committees made preparations for joint hearings on the general's dismissal. These began early in May. For three days MacArthur testified with vigor and confidence. He wished to begin a limited war against China; he would bomb troop concentrations, railway lines, and war factories in Manchuria; he would even blockade the Russian naval base at Port Arthur. He had evidence, he said, that the Chinese were "using every ounce of power to achieve victory in Korea," and he would use every ounce of power in counter-attack. That this would bring Russia into the war he did not believe, for "the dispositions of the Soviet forces are largely defensive," and the Soviet Union lacked the capacity to launch a predatory attack from the Asiatic continent.

On the Administration side, Secretaries Acheson and Marshall, and the members of the Joint Chiefs of Staff explained at length why they remained determined to keep the war confined to Korea. To attack the Chinese mainland, said Marshall, would be to risk an open and desperate war with Russia and her satellites. All Western Europe would then be exposed to a tragic devastation by "millions of Soviet troops poised in middle and eastern Europe." General Bradley explained the military policy of the government, supporting the views of Truman and Marshall; and Secretary Acheson dealt at length with the diplomatic history of the struggle. It was clearly implied in the Administration statements that the United States, while not taking the perilous course advised by MacArthur, would be a good deal tougher in its future operations in the Far East. Pressure was at once increased on other Western nations to make the economic embargo against China more stringent.

The whole debate had been highly educational. Not since the days of the Committee on the Conduct of the War in Lincoln's time had military policy received so thorough a Congressional ventilation. To the world at large, the hearings made it plain that the intentions of the United States were fundamentally peaceable. They also made it clear that American patience was being pushed to its uttermost limits, and that the nation would fight an all-out war with Russia rather than permit any further aggression against freedom and justice.

In repeated speeches, MacArthur declared that he had "no political aspirations whatever." But he did have strong political opinions, which he several times expressed with emphasis. In an address in Cleveland, Ohio, early in September, he lashed out against the Truman Administration for a "ravenous effort to further centralize the political power" of the country in its own hands, and for its alleged suppression of individual liberties. He also let it be understood that he looked with jaundiced eye upon the movement to make General Dwight Eisenhower President, and leaned toward Senator Robert Taft's candidacy. This was natural, for Eisenhower stood for unabated aid to Western Europe, while Taft was head of the semi-isolationist wing of the Republican Party. MacArthur hinted in his Cleveland speech that Eisenhower had been partly responsible for the hasty dissipation of Allied military strength after 1946; that he had failed to foresee the gravity of the Russian menace; and that the stage had perhaps been set for the emergence of that menace in "secret and most unfortunate war conferences" in which Eisenhower had sat.

Even before MacArthur's return, the Administration had won a victory in Congress over those who wished a drastic restriction of military aid to Europe. Herbert Hoover early in the year continued to call for a complete reorientation of policy. He advocated the withdrawal of all our forces from the European continent, and the maintenance of the two Americas (with Great Britain as an advanced outpost) as a "Western Hemisphere Gibraltar." This was at the very time that Eisenhower, after a brief January tour of Western Europe, was asking that four more divisions be sent across the Atlantic to join the two divisions already stationed in Germany.

Appearing before both houses of Congress at the beginning of February, Eisenhower had made an effective plea for the defense of the North Atlantic sphere as our primary concern. "In Western Europe exists the greatest pool of skilled labor in the world, and a great industrial capacity second only to that of the United States," he pointed out. "If we take that whole complex, with its potential for military exploitation, and transfer it from our side to another side, the military balance of power will be shifted so drastically that our safety will be greatly imperiled." The real question, said Eisenhower, was not whether the United States should give aid, but whether the morale of Western Europe would rise high enough to make that aid effective. On this head he gave a reassuring answer. The general had found in some social strata of Europe a pessimism bordering on defeatism; but among the peoples as a whole he had met "a growth of determination, a spirit to resist, a spirit again to try to live the lives of free men."

The prestige of Eisenhower and the necessities of the situation swept aside most of the opposition. In the first week of April the Senate, by a vote of 69 to 21, passed resolutions hailing the North Atlantic Treaty as a major historic act, and declaring that the nation should station in Europe, for the defense of the West, "such units of our armed forces as may be necessary and appropriate to contribute our fair share." Neither Mr. Hoover nor General MacArthur shook the national commitment to the support of the Western family of nations as our first duty.

If the United States had to submit to a military stalemate in Korea, it scored a resounding success in another part of the Orient by the peace treaty with Japan. Such a treaty had become overdue. Japan was clearly entitled to a restoration of sovereignty, to an army of her own to help combat Communism, and to generous economic assistance. Late in January, John Foster Dulles reached Tokyo to conduct consultations (not negotiations). He made rapid progress. In March he completed a draft treaty, and in April the British finished one of their own. Then, in May, a British delegation arrived in Washington to smooth out differences in the two instruments. Early in July the Anglo-American draft was sent to all of the fifty-odd nations which had declared war on Japan, with a request for comments and an invitation to a final conference in San Francisco on September 4. In response to criticism from various nations, about thirty minor changes were made in the draft, but no major alterations; and the State Department announced that it expected general acceptance.

The San Francisco Conference was therefore planned as a ceremonial occasion, not a meeting for discussion. It was to last only five days at most. President Truman would be on hand to open it; Secretary Acheson and Mr. Younger would make explanatory speeches for the United States and Great Britain; and it would end in general congratulations. Neither the Mao Tse-tung nor the Chiang Kai-shek government was asked to send delegates. Of course the whole Anglo-American plan was abhorrent to Russia. Throughout the summer the Kremlin conducted a steady campaign of objection, denouncing the United States for dictating the terms of the treaty and for reviving Japanese militarism. At first it was thought (and hoped) that Russia would simply boycott the gathering. But Moscow finally announced that Andrei A. Gromyko would lead a delegation to San Francisco, and Poland and Czechoslovakia also accepted seats. It was therefore necessary to make sure that no obstruction would be possible.

The main provisions of the treaty were highly generous, and looked toward Japan's incorporation in the defensive alignment of the non-Communist nations. The instrument recognized the sovereignty of Japan, and her inherent right to self-defense. It provided for the withdrawal of all occupation troops within ninety days after the treaty became effective, but permitted the stationing of foreign forces in the islands under separate agreements. (Everyone understood that Japan would remain a United Nations base for the Korean War, furnishing ground, air, and naval facilities.) Japan agreed to accept a United Nations trusteeship for the Ryuku and Bonin Islands, to be held by the United States. She also renounced all title to Formosa, the final disposition of which was left unsettled. Inasmuch as the United States was supporting the Japanese economy by subsidies, the reparations—which in justice were due to the Philippines, Australia, and other lands—presented some difficulty. It was arranged that they should be paid not in cash, but by the manufacture of specially delivered raw materials.

The conference proved a happy event for Mr. Dulles, Secretary Acheson, and the United States Government. Meeting in the Memorial Opera House in San Francisco, it moved smoothly to its goal. The United States and Great Britain had prepared stringent rules, which limited comment on the treaty to one hour for each nation. Gromyko rose repeatedly to protest, but was silenced, and the rules were adopted without change. Then, for three days, country after country was heard in formal and mainly approbatory addresses. The Communist delegates could do little but glower. Finally, on Saturday, September 8, representatives of forty-nine nations (not including Russia, Poland, and Czechoslovakia) signed the treaty; the Japanese delegate appending his name with a contented smile.

"The Japan of today," this delegate, Mr. Yoshida, told

the conference, "is no longer the Japan of yesterday. We shall not fail your expectations of us as a new nation, dedicated to peace, democracy, and freedom." Yet what kind of Japan would actually emerge within the next ten years was a matter of grave doubt. The Filipino delegate, Carlos P. Romulo, expressed apprehension that the "aggressive, feudal, militarist" nation of yesterday was not really dead. The Allied administration had broken up big business combinations, helped provide a truly democratic constitution, and purged the chief past offenders. But it is certain that Japanese pressure for economic expansion will be tremendous, for the small island chain is already bursting with a population of eighty-four millions; and may not political expansion follow? It was evident that the United States would have to maintain a close connection with Japan, for she is the outer breastwork for the defense of the Pacific world—of the Philippines, Alaska, Australia, New Zealand, and California —against Communist encroachment. This connection would doubtless form one of the best guarantees of a truly democratic future.

As a concomitant of the peace with Japan, a mutual defense treaty embracing the United States, Australia, and New Zealand was signed, and another between the United States and the Philippine republic. This gave great comfort to the small nations involved.

Hardly had the San Francisco gathering closed, when a meeting of the Council of the North Atlantic Treaty

Organization in Ottawa claimed the headlines. Here, too, headway was being made against the Communist threat. For the NATO was irresistibly growing in strength and cohesion. Its ranks were augmented by two new members, Turkey and Greece, making fourteen in all, with an aggregate population of about 360,000,000, and with huge economic resources. Its unity was promoted by the decision to establish a committee of five to develop the extra-military phases of the great coalition.

Some of the principal statesmen of the Western world came together in the beautiful commons chamber in Ottawa. Secretary Acheson was there for the United States, Foreign Secretary Herbert Morrison for Great Britain, Foreign Minister Schuman for France, Prime Minister de Gasperi for Italy, and Prime Minister St. Laurent for Canada. To be sure, the leadership of America and Britain was evident, and the great figure of Eisenhower as supreme commander was always in the background. Some of the Continental countries had demurred to the admission of Turkey and Greece on the grounds that it meant an unwise extension of the NATO boundaries, and might result in an Eastern Mediterranean command which, operating separately from that of Western Europe, would divide authority and forces. Allied air bases would have to be established near the Russian homeland, and American arms would have to be shared with the two new countries. But the United

States and Britain believed that the Turkish army would be worth the risks involved, and they had their way.

In the discussions of the economic foundations of the NATO effort, a certain difference of opinion between Americans and Europeans was evident. The burden of the American cry was more arms, more men, more training—an enlargement of the military effort. The burden of the European response was more money, more raw materials, more attention to standards of living. America might be rich enough to have guns, butter, and the whole cow; Europe was already living on the ragged edge of want. General Eisenhower sent the meeting a message emphasizing the grim reality of the Russian peril, and reproaching some of the NATO powers (he did not specify which) for a failure to show due energy. They must start more factories and recruit more troops, he asserted; the production of arms in Western Europe in 1952 must be one-third greater than in 1951. When this was read the finance ministers of Europe wagged their heads. They declared that the United States was asking fearfully heavy sacrifices; that an economic crash might be as bad as a Russian invasion; and that they had to think of the internal peril from Communism as well as the external peril.

Just how much could Europe accomplish during 1951–53 in the economic sphere? And just how much American help would be needed? These questions no one could answer. They were handed to a special committee of twelve men, who were to weigh economic essentials against military necessities. Here the American, British, and French members would of course have special weight. Pending the committee's report, Foreign Minister Paul Van Zeeland of Belgium proposed that the free nations establish an international armament fund on which the weaker members could draw in a pinch. It was patent that European members thought that the United States might be going too fast and too far—a view strongly expressed in Britain by the fiery Aneurin Bevan. It was equally patent that American representatives thought that Europe might be too cautious and too slow —a view expressed in the United States by Senator Robert Taft. An agreement for more frequent sessions of the NATO council gave some promise of a broader future measure of coördination.

Meanwhile, Herbert Morrison took the lead in preaching the roseate doctrine of an "Atlantic Community." Tiring of the constant exhortations to a "united Europe," Morrison and others wanted a united North Atlantic world. A five member committee was appointed to mull over plans for closer social, cultural, and economic coöperation. It was Morrison's belief that in time a common citizenship, a common set of economic policies, and many common cultural institutions might be achieved; but as yet the aspiration remained but vague and misty.

Obviously, in the defense of the West a resurgent

Germany would play a key rôle. The three Western occupation powers, America, Britain, and France, had to
work out with the Bonn Government under Chancellor
Adenauer some general plan for the future of the German nation. In the week of September 9, the foreign
ministers of the Big Three, Acheson, Herbert Morrison,
and Schuman, discussed the problem in the State Department in Washington. The most urgent questions
were two. How much of a contribution to Western defense should Germany make, and just how should she
make it? And how great a degree of political and economic sovereignty should the Big Three grant to the
German people? Everyone knew that the Western alliance stood in dire need of the industrial output of the
Ruhr, the skilled manpower of that and other mill centers of Germany, and the troops that Germany could
raise. Everyone knew, too, that a revived Germany
would soon insist on political freedom. The French in
particular, however, were apprehensive of a new German
movement toward the hegemony of continental Europe.

By mid-September the three occupation Powers had
reached a decision, which they announced immediately
afterward in Ottawa. They declared that they would
immediately negotiate with Konrad Adenauer's government a new agreement to take the place of the Occupation Statute, and to restore a broad measure of German
sovereignty. At the same time, a treaty of mutual security
would be drawn up and signed. Under this security pact,

Germany would be authorized to enlist a considerable number of troops. These soldiers, however, would not constitute a national army; instead, as the French demanded, they would be incorporated into a multi-national European army composed of troops from France, Italy, Germany, Belgium, and Luxembourg. This European army would of course serve with the other forces of Western Europe (the separate national armies) under Eisenhower and his successors; but it would have its own defense minister and its own multi-national system of military justice.

As for sovereignty, the Bonn republic would in nearly all respects become quite independent. The Allies, however, would still retain control of West Berlin, and maintain the right to station troops in Germany; they would keep in their own hands all negotiations with Russia over German unification; they could veto any basic changes in foreign and commercial policy which might injure the NATO members; and they should have the right to intervene if Germany were threatened by a Communist or Fascist coup d'état.

But would Germany accept this "peace package" which was being offered her—sovereigny and limited rearmament in return for acceptance of a security pact and assent to a general European army? As the statesmen sitting at Ottawa knew, some stiff bargaining lay ahead. The spirit of German nationalism was steadily rising, and Adenauer would have to placate it. Moreover,

Russia had a counter-offer to make of which much was already being heard in the summer of 1951. If the West Germans would reject an alliance with the Atlantic Powers, and refuse any contribution to Western armaments, they might obtain the restoration of East Germany. This would be on the basis of "free elections" (a term to which the Russians were certain to give their own interpretation) and the existence of a strong Communist Party in the new Reich. The Soviet offer had manifest attractions: many West Germans liked the idea of neutrality, with its freedom from armament burdens, and all Germans passionately longed for the unification of the country. Only the general fear, distrust, and hatred of Russia and Communism kept Bonn on the Western side.

As soon as the Allied decisions respecting Germany were announced, Doctor Kurt Schumacher's Socialist Party took an attitude of outspoken opposition. "German policy must be fixed by the Germans," declared Schumacher in effect. He maintained that the West did not go far enough in the restoration of German sovereignty, which must be complete, and that the Big Three proposals for a European army simply placed the defense of West Germany in French hands. The Schuman plan for the unification of the steel and iron industries of all Western Europe was denounced as "a scheme to enrich French capitalists at the expense of the poor German workingman." Doctor Adenauer's Government had to step cautiously lest the Schumacher Socialists rally around their banner enough dissenting elements to bring down the ministry in defeat. Meanwhile the Communists of Western Germany, led by Walter Ulbricht, threatened to use strikes and sabotage against any rearmament on behalf of the North Atlantic Powers.

Adenauer was in general receptive to the Big Three proposals. His determination to keep Germany on the side of democracy and the West was unflinching. When the year closed, however, the future position of Germany remained unsettled—and it would be one of the great questions of 1952, as important to Americans as their own presidential election. As Germany regained economic vigor and moral confidence, new attitudes were naturally appearing. Even Germans who enthusiastically endorsed the Allied resistance to Russia were frequently saying: "But the Nazis were not so far wrong after all; they too waged a titanic struggle in 1941–45 against Russia." And many Germans were also saying: "You are anxious to make Western Europe a great industrial stronghold against Communist power. It is therefore logical to revive the German war plants, and to give the great Ruhr industrialists perfect freedom in restoring the coal and steel industries." For years to come, Germany would be the great psychological battleground between West and East.

Throughout the year General Eisenhower, as supreme commander of the NATO forces, was carrying on a work complex in nature and heroic in scale. Landing at Cherbourg late in February to take up his residence near Paris, he was received with quiet enthusiasm. Great reliance was placed upon his energy, grasp, buoyancy, and ability to make diverse groups work harmoniously. From his headquarters—"SHAPE"—he dealt vigorously with a situation which at first seemed highly precarious. When he began, in fact, the ground forces facing Russia were nearly zero; they could be called a myth. The best reliance of the West at the moment was upon the atomic bomb and the air squadrons to deliver it. Already ten American air bases had been established in Great Britain, and more were being built. The great B–50s at these bases were only four hours flying time from Moscow.

The problem before Eisenhower, Field Marshal Montgomery, and their aides was to create a defense system which would last a generation if necessary. Huge and costly standing armies for such a period of time were out of the question; Western Europe is too poor to support them. A large trained reserve, normally busy in civilian life but ready to rush to the colors if necessary, is the logical expedient. Eisenhower throughout the year continued to exhort the twelve governments of NATO (later fourteen) to do more to train and equip these reserve forces, "the backbone of ground defense." Ideally, Western Europe ought to have a reserve of forty to fifty well-armed divisions mobilizable within a month of the beginning of war. If heavy air support could be devel-

121

oped, and above all, if atomic artillery could be devised, the problem of defense would be greatly simplified.

By the end of the year Eisenhower's forces in the Adriatic area amounted to about four divisions, and on the main German front between the Alps and the Baltic, a line of 400 miles, to eighteen divisions. These troops scarcely balanced the twenty-four or twenty-six Red divisions immediately in front of them. The Kremlin had tremendous reserves—indeed, reserves in millions. The West had such scanty reserves that one general at SHAPE characterized them as "almost useless." Figures for air strength were kept secret, and all information upon the progress made with atomic ordnance was tightly guarded. The French still held their conscription period to eighteen months, partly because the low birth rate of the early 1930s had reduced their manpower for farming and industry, partly because of the want of equipment. Moreover, France had to devote most of her regular army to the fighting in Indo-China. Italy, with ample man-power, was crippled by lack of money and arms. The size of the new Benelux forces was also contingent on the amount of American materiel available; nobody knew how much Germany could or would supply.

Eisenhower continued to dwell upon the gravity of the Russian peril. When 1951 closed, the prospects looked brighter for the defense. Men could hope that the eighteen divisions on the German front might within the next year become twenty-four divisions, and in 1953 thirty or more divisions. If atomic shells and guided atomic missiles came into production, any defense line could be made impregnable. Even without them, thirty divisions could hold a Communist onslaught east of the Rhine until atomic bombing laid waste the Russian cities and disrupted Russian industry and railways.

In the United States the head of Defense Mobilization throughout the year was Charles E. Wilson, former head of General Electric, who aided President Truman and Congress in shaping the broad policies to be adopted. As we have said, his basic principle was the expansion of the productive capacity of industry so that the arsenals could be stocked, the air force built to formidable strength, and the navy expanded to great size, without crippling the civilian economy. Wilson's principal assistants, General Lucius D. Clay for supply and production, and Sidney Weinberg for personnel, were, like himself, men of no political ambitions. Below Wilson's office were two great agencies, the National Production Administration under William H. Harrison and the Economic Stabilization Agency under Eric Johnston. The ESA included the Office of Price Administration, whose head was the fearless former mayor of Toledo, Michael V. DiSalle, and the Wage Stabilization Board, directed by the experienced Cyrus S. Ching.

This mechanism furnished a simple and logical administration of the defense effort, very different from the complicated and ever-changing mechanisms under Franklin D. Roosevelt. It worked with little friction, and as we have seen, it was steadily if slowly bringing munitions production into high gear without disaster to the general standard of living.

One defense agency, the Atomic Energy Commission, stood quite apart from all others. Early in the year a series of atomic blasts in southern Nevada, where a great waste of desert and mountains near Las Vegas provided a good proving ground, made it evident that the Commission was testing new missiles. The prime need was for a smaller, more manageable bomb that could be used against troops in the field—a tactical bomb; and for shells and guided missiles with atomic warheads. It was hazarded that if these weapons were made available in quantity, forty NATO divisions could hold Western Europe against 150 Soviet divisions. No results of the tests were given out; but most Americans felt that great reliance could be placed on the ingenuity of our technicians and scientists.

For the fiscal year 1951–52 the Atomic Energy Commission had been given $2,300,000,000, with which it could carry out a program of the greatest magnitude at the greatest possible speed. Obviously, our national existence might depend upon its work. It was enlarging its twelve centers of production and research; building at least three new centers; buying all the uranium it could obtain and encouraging the search for more; and concentrating the best talent available on new detonating devices, atomic projectiles, and similar matters. Meanwhile, about a half billion dollars had been or was being invested in the new plant on the Savannah River near Aiken, S. C., with its surrounding tract of about 250,000 acres, for experimental work on the hydrogen bomb. If finally perfected, this "hell bomb" was expected to have an explosive force a thousand times as great as that of the atomic bomb. At the same time, the plant was being equipped to increase heavily the output of plutonium, a prime constituent of atomic bombs. Another new plant was being built at Paducah, Ky., to make uranium-235, the reactor element necessary to all kinds of nuclear operations.

All Americans devoutly hoped that in the end these costly operations could be harnessed to peacetime uses for the benefit of all humanity. Meanwhile, Chairman Gordon Dean of the Atomic Energy Commission refused to give out any information whatever. "We prefer to let people speculate," he said drily—and the Russians might well speculate.

In a world which in many respects seemed rushing forward at mad speed, Congress at times seemed as static as a 500-mule-team most of whose members had resolved to balk. In domestic legislation the first session of the 82d Congress, which ended late in October, produced nearly a complete vacuum. Not one of the domestic objects for which the Truman Administration had pleaded was achieved. The President had justly denounced the 80th Congress for doing many wrong things and few right things. But despite his amazing victory in 1948, he proved signally unable to get Congress to cooperate with him in home affairs.

The Fair Deal program, in fact, had as much vitality by the close of 1951 as a mummy of the Ptolemaic dynasty. The Taft-Hartley Act, against which the President had so loudly inveighed, stood substantially intact. One slight change had been made (union shops can now be formed without factory elections) but the vital features were unaltered. Federal legislation for civil rights was hardly mentioned during the year. Secretary Brannan's special farm plan (which Mr. Truman had cautiously refrained from endorsing) was as dead as a doornail. National health insurance, so blithely promised in 1948, made no progress whatever. Faced with an iron wall of Southern hostility, the Statehood bills for Hawaii and Alaska languished with little hope of early passage. The South did not wish four new Senators in Washington ready to support civil rights legislation. Only a few of Mr. Hoover's proposals for introducing more efficiency and economy into the federal services had been placed on the statute books.

Congress was worried about inflation, but not to such a degree as to arm the Executive with sufficient powers to repress it. Congress was still more worried about the Russian threat, but not to such a degree that it would give

Mr. Truman the immediately effective universal military training law for which he asked. Such large segments of the American people are against general military training that little less than an actual invasion of the hemisphere, apparently, would bring the country to a permanent measure of that character. When on June 19 Congress adopted Public Law 50 for U.M.T. it was with reservations which made it inoperative without further debate and action. Congress was flatly against Mr. Truman's proposed Department of Public Welfare, of which Mr. Oscar Ewing would be the probable head.

The main reason for the failure of Mr. Truman's domestic program lay in the full and joyous establishment of a hostile coalition of Republicans and Southern Democrats. After his spectacular triumph in 1948, Truman had hoped to destroy that coalition as Napoleon overthrew his Continental enemies at Austerlitz. But this time the battle was not Austerlitz but Waterloo. The Allies won! Among lesser reasons for the President's defeat were his declining prestige, especially as a mortifying amount of corruption in the Administration came to light; the growth of conservatism under the sunlight of national prosperity, with a general distrust of "reds" and fellow travellers to nourish its roots; and the imminence of the Presidential campaign, leading to a desire to shelve controversial action.

In the international field, however, the presidential program fared much better. Congressional leaders of the isolationist or semi-isolationist wing spouted and erupted, but the pressure of the world situation was too much for them. Such Senators as Wheery, Kem, Taft, Knowland, and others, made faces at foreign nations with great vigor. The unenlightened McCarthy of Wisconsin, the able but narrow Dietrich of Illinois, the ambitious and bitterly partisan Bridges of New Hampshire, followed the Chicago *Tribune* line. In the end, however, Congress voted to send more divisions to Europe, grant more military aid to the North Atlantic nations, and to extend once more the Reciprocal Trade Act which Secretary Hull had placed on the statute books in 1933.

The grimmest of the battles involved was that over the foreign aid program, intended to prime the European economic pump and strengthen the defensive front. The President asked for $8,500,000,000 as a first instalment in a three-year program of $25,000,000,000. Some cuts were made, but they did not go deep. Despite explosions of senatorial dudgeon about "paying for European Socialism," Congress finally came through with $7,300,-000,000. Only five Senators, all Republicans, voted no on the final roll-call: Capehart of Indiana, Ecton of Montana, Kem of Missouri, Langer of North Dakota, and Schoeppel of Kansas. Included in this grant was more than eighty millions for technical assistance, more than twice the amount allowed the previous year. The President was permitted in his discretion to spend as much as $100,000,000 for military aid to Spain—a very controversial item, for public opposition to any support of Franco was wide and deep.

In another foreign area Congress proved less enlightened. India in 1951 was threatened with famine. Her minimum grain requirements for the year were short by six million tons, and she lacked enough dollars to buy much more than half of this. A bill for a loan of $190,000,000 to the Indian Government for the purchase of food grains was finally passed—that sum being enough to buy two million tons. But the measure was voted only after delays which destroyed much of its moral effect in India. Some leaders in the Senate tried to attach conditions that the assistance be given full publicity in India, that the grain be distributed without discrimination as to race, creed, or political belief, and that this distribution be subject to unrestricted observation. Prime Minister Nehru indignantly declared that not even to save his people from starving would he barter away "our country's self-respect or freedom of action." The act as passed contained no stipulations. Ships loaded with grain at once began to unload in Indian ports. Had Congress acted promptly and in generous spirit, the two million tons of American grain would have far overshadowed the fifty thousand tons which the Soviet Union, with much beating of tom-toms, sold to India.

In an earlier era of the republic, say twenty years ago, the item of seven and a half billions for foreign aid would have seemed colossal. In 1951, however, it was dwarfed by the appropriations for national defense. The armed services on July 1, 1951, when the fiscal year began, still had some $37,000,000,000 of funds unspent. To this, Congress added nearly $57,000,000,000 in additional appropriations. Slightly more than ten billions of this was earmarked for the construction of 140 major new naval vessels, including another super-carrier. The remainder was for the land and air forces. This, of course, was for the fiscal year 1951–52. During the calendar year 1951 only about thirty-five billions was spent upon defense; but spending was scheduled to reach by June, 1952, an annual rate of between sixty and sixty-five billons.

To men with a conservative outlook, such a total seemed staggering. Some observers, including the able and liberal Senator Paul Douglas of Illinois, were deeply oppressed by the possibilities of corruption and waste in such tremendous sums. As recently as Benjamin Harrison's time, the country had been startled to find that its whole expenses for a year reached the then frightening amount of one billion. Senator Taft doubted if the nation's economy could stand without grave injury the expenditures which lay just ahead. Jauntier and more optimistic observers, however, declared that the tremendous outlay had to be measured against the new gross national product of about 365 billions; and they noted that even 65 billions was less than one-fifth of that amount.

The costs of defense items had risen to rather horrifying levels, none the less. In the Second World War a basic army division could be equipped completely for less than twenty million dollars; by 1951 the cost was more than ninety millions. The expense of equipping an armored division had risen from forty millions to nearly three hundred millions. In the recent war the B–29, the largest aircraft then flown, had cost about $680,000. In 1951, the cost of the largest airplane, the B–36, was $3,500,000. In other words, the equipment of one basic infantry division would suffice to establish a great University, another Yale, Columbia, or Chicago; the cost of a single bomber, which might crash on its first flight, would exceed the endowment of most such colleges as Williams, Vassar, or Knox. Costs were steadily rising, too. When the Korean War began a heavy anti-aircraft gun could be procured for $160,000; less than a year later, the same gun cost $250,000. In view of the march of inflation, it was difficult to predict how much war materiel even sixty-five billion dollars would be able to command.

Not since Civil War days had inflation loomed up as such a fearsome monster. Nearly everybody had more dollars, but the purchasing power of the dollar by the end of 1951 fell to 54.6 cents. The inflationary trend lent a stimulus to many businesses. Nevertheless, high Federal officers from President Truman down all sent out warning after warning of breakers ahead. Business, labor, and the public, they declared, must remember that, next to war, inflation was the greatest danger menacing the country.

"If runaway inflation were to take hold in America," said Chairman Charles E. Wilson of the Office of Defense Mobilization, "the nation would go bankrupt, and Stalin would realize his dreams of conquest without firing a shot."

In January, the basic price control order, which had been delayed too long, set ceilings at the highest levels reached between December 19 and January 25. The basic wage control order froze wages at the level of January 25. But both orders were subject to important exceptions.

One prime difficulty was that inflation was fixed in certain areas of the economy. Under the law, ceilings could not be placed on farm products selling below parity, the level fixed to give farmers a fair return—and most foodstuffs were actually selling below the over-generous parity rates. They therefore continued to rise in price. As for wages, many labor contracts had escalator clauses which geared the wage to living costs. Rising charges for foods and other goods therefore meant higher wages. With both A. F. of L. and C.I.O. leaders vehemently denouncing the whole wage-freeze system —they complained that "the only real stabilization is wage stabilization"—the government was under severe pressure to let many parts of the wage structure rise. As a matter of fact, Cyrus S. Ching, head of the Wage Stabilization Board, proposed early in the year that the escalators be allowed to operate for "catch up" increases until they had lifted wages as much as eight per cent above the levels of March, 1951.

Still another factor made for increases in living costs. When the freeze orders were issued, wholesale prices had risen much more rapidly than retail prices. Many retailers had ordered goods from wholesalers at costs that under the new retail ceilings would spell ruin. It was necessary for Director DiSalle to permit certain adjustments to remedy this "squeeze." Thus it was that the cost of living continued to rise. The plight of many white-collar groups, of all pensioners and the *rentier* class, and of those who had invested heavily in life insurance, was often pitiable. Politically, inflation seemed to be popular, and neither Congress nor the President battled against it with real determination or desperate energy. It was left for the future to foot the bill.

One of the methods of partially controlling inflation, an increase in taxation, was indeed called into limited play during the year. Corporate income taxes were raised from 47 per cent to 52 per cent (reckoning normal tax combined with surtax). Since the excess profits tax was fixed at 30 per cent, many corporations paid 82 per cent of their income to the government. For American industry as a whole, more than half of every dollar earned during 1951 was taken away by taxes. In this way, profits after taxes—despite the high prosperity of the year—were kept below those for the years 1948 and 1950, and dividends were held somewhat below the record 1950 disbursements.

Taxes in general, however, were not increased as much as most economists believed they should have been. The Revenue Act passed by Congress in October, after nine months of hearings and debate, fell short of the proper mark. Mr. Truman had asked for an increase of at least ten billions in the tax levy; Congress gave him only about nine billions. Much the greater part of this new burden fell upon individuals. Most American citizens found that their taxes had been raised by 11 or 12 per cent over the previous level. They paid also heavier excise taxes, levies being placed on liquors, tobacco, automobiles, and many household appliances, with other commodities, in amounts sufficient to produce an estimated $1,200,000,000.

The uneasiness of thoughtful Americans over the huge expenditures made and authorized in 1951 was accentuated by the revelation that a deep stream of corruption was flowing through the government's activities. The earlier years of the Truman Administraton had been marked by several exposures of dishonesty, the chief being the Garson-May war contracts case, and the cases of the "five per-centers" who peddled their influence in Washington. However disgusting, they were not of high importance. Certain of the numerous Congressional investigations of 1951, however—for Congress indulged in no fewer than 150 inquiries and hearings of various kinds—revealed rotten spots of a more dangerous character.

The year began with an inquiry under way into the alleged responsiveness of the directors of the Reconstruction Finance Corporation to illegitimate pressures for loans. The inquisitors, a Senate sub-committee under J. W. Fullbright of Arkansas, showed that such special pressure or influence had unquestionably been applied. One notorious offender was E. Merl Young, a former R.F.C. examiner, who was accused of offering to help the Texas Petroleum Company get a loan of more than ten millions from the R.F.C., and of offering to help the Kaiser-Frazier Corporation, which received $69,000,000 in loans from the great government agency. Both corporations rejected his aid, but other companies were not so queasy. Before the year ended, a special grand jury handed down indictments in the cases of Young, of Joseph E. Rosenbaum, a former Washington attorney, and of two associates of these men. It had been made abundantly plain that some officers of the R.F.C. were distressingly open to "influence" of a disreputable kind.

The sub-committee, reporting early in February, charged that certain men in Washington, including members of the White House circle, had used influence to get loans from the R.F.C. for friends or clients, and that three directors of the R.F.C. had been responsive. It urged that the board of directors be replaced by a single person who would be directly responsible for all R.F.C.

decisions on loans. Some indignant members of Congress wished to abolish the R.F.C. out of hand; what excuse was there, they asked, for continuing this depression agency in a time of glowing prosperity? The President in a press conference stigmatized the report of the Fullbright sub-committee as "asinine," and attempted a counter-attack by announcing that he had obtained from R.F.C. files a large number of letters from Congressmen asking special favors of the loan-agency. Thereupon the Fullbright sub-committee, thoroughly irritated, reopened its public hearings. "We intend to show that the committee was not talking through its hat," said Senator Fullbright.

A House Ways and Means sub-committee was meanwhile investigating certain malodorous scandals in the income tax administration. In the end, a series of district administrators were proved guilty of neglect of duty or downright dereliction. Especially grave charges were brought by a former Capone attorney in Chicago, Abraham Teitelbaum, against the chief counsel of the Internal Revenue Bureau, Charles Oliphant, and the Assistant Attorney-General in charge of tax prosecutions, T. Lamar Caudle. Teitelbaum, who was facing prosecution for income tax fraud, testified that he had been told that a Washington group including these two men would "fix" his case for $500,000; and that when he refused to pay, the case was accelerated. An inquiry brought out evidence that Caudle had accepted a "loan" of $10,000 in one case, a "commission" of $5,000 in another, and such "favors" as a mink coat at wholesale and a television set. Testimony was also elicited showing that Oliphant had delayed a tax-fraud case against two meat-packers until it had lapsed under the statute of limitations.

Other evidence before both the Fullbright and the Ways and Means sub-committees was equally explosive. Before Christmas, Oliphant had resigned, and Caudle had been dismissed by the President. Six collectors of internal revenue had been dismissed or had resigned, and with them nearly fifty minor employees of the internal revenue service. One of the collectors, James P. Finnegan of St. Louis, declared that when first brought under heavy criticism he had wished to resign, but that pressure from the White House had prevented him from doing so. He did finally resign in April, 1951, and was then indicted on a bribery charge.

Other revelations of the year touched the heads of both the Democratic and the Republican National Committees. It was shown that William M. Boyle, Jr., after becoming the acting head of the Democratic Committee at a salary of $25,000 a year, had exerted himself to obtain loans from the R.F.C. for the Lithofold Corporation —and the R.F.C. had actually granted that company $645,000. The St. Louis *Post-Dispatch* accused Boyle of accepting various fees and retainers from business interests after taking his high party post. This Boyle hotly denied, but he had obviously become a party liability and his resignation soon followed. Meanwhile, the Republican National Chairman, Guy Gabrielson, had also been brought under fire. He was legal counsel and president of the Carthage Hydrocol, Inc., a company which had received $18,500,000 in R.F.C. loans; and he was accused of having frequent contacts, after accepting his party office, with R.F.C. functionaries. Gabrielson denounced the "rumors and innuendo" to which he had been subjected, and asserted that his activities had been perfectly legitimate. But it was clear that he, too, had become a party liability.

Public anger over the disclosures affecting the R.F.C. and the tax administration was expressed in terms recalling the sad days of the Grant and Harding Administrations. It left the Truman regime somewhat red-faced with embarrassment and chagrin. Of the vigilance and devotion to duty of the President there was no doubt. But John W. Snyder as Secretary of the Treasury was responsible for income tax collections; J. Howard McGrath as Attorney-General, for law enforcement. The criticism of McGrath, a Rhode Island politician, reached a point where in mid-December his resignation was momentarily expected. The President had actually taken steps to find his successor when action was abruptly halted. According to current reports, high influence of a sort never properly exerted in government affairs had been called into play; and these reports intensified public indignation over this episode throughout the country.

President Truman stoutly maintained that the overwhelming majority of government officers were honest and diligent men. Late in September he sent Congress a message stating his determination to maintain the highest standards of public morality, and calling for a law which would compel the regular publication of facts and figures as to the sources of income for all the higher executive, legislative, and judical officers of the nation. All Congressmen, all generals and admirals, all public employees getting over $10,000 a year would be included; and they would have to report all loans, gifts, and commissions as well as regular earnings. Congress did not receive the proposal with favor—for many Congressmen prize the opportunity of earning large legal or other fees on the side. No action was taken. At a press conference on December 13, President Truman reiterated his antagonism to all forms of public dishonesty, declaring: "Wrongdoers have no house with me, no matter who or how big they are."

Corruption was secret; crime in the United States was all too brazen. The Senate Crime Investigating Committee, under Estes Kefauver of Tennessee, concluded its work in the spring with a final set of hearings which, placed on television, was the sensation of the season. The New York inquiry almost stopped business in the metropolis for a week while people watched the screen. Throwing a bright light on the influence which Frank

Costello and his underworld associates had for years ex-
ercised on the governmental machinery of New York
City, it left spectators dumbfounded. Underworld characters had contributed to the political funds of the
O'Dwyer Administration, and $10,000 had allegedly
gone to the ex-mayor's own political expenses. Costello
told of knowing fourteen Tammany leaders. It was
shown that the Dewey Administration had done nothing effective to halt the activities of the same underworld
crew in Saratoga gambling.

The Kefauver inquiry as a whole—it had held hearings in eleven cities from Cleveland and Miami to New
Orleans and San Francisco—had established a number
of most unpleasant conclusions. It had shown that organized crime and vice drained not merely hundreds of
millions, but actually billions, from the nation's wealth
every year. It had proved that the organized underworld,
operating from New York and Chicago as twin capitals,
had established a federation of gangs, of which the Costello group in New York and the Capone group in
Chicago were the chief. It had revealed the large-scale
operation of these gangs across State lines, in such
fashion that State and local officers attacking gambling,
prostitution, blackmail, and burglary had great difficulty
in reaching the criminals. As was to be expected when
billions were involved, many public officials were sub-
orned. Finally, it was shown that with its huge "take,"
organized crime had infiltrated many legitimate busi-

nesses. In Chicago, for example, the Capone syndicate controlled whole lines of perfectly proper enterprises.

In city after city, after the Committee's visits, the "heat" went on; law enforcement officers closed down on vice, crime, racketeering, and graft. Greater Miami's Crime Commission labored hard to wash the stain from the name of that great midwinter resort. Governor Dewey appointed a special prosecutor to probe the Saratoga situation, and also named a continuing State Crime Commission of five, empowered to cross county lines in its inquiries. Costello himself landed in jail on a charge of income tax evasion, and his confederate William Moran (a close friend of Mr. O'Dwyer) received a heavy sentence.

As the year drew to a close, all eyes were turned to the approaching Presidential battle. In mid-October Robert A. Taft of Ohio announced his candidacy for the Republican nomination. His entry into the race a good nine months before the convention date was obviously prompted by a hope to head off General Eisenhower. So many States choose delegates in connection with Presidential preference primaries that Taft, if unopposed, could obtain enough supporters to give him a strong initial lead; and it would obviously be difficult for Eisenhower, busy with his defense work abroad, to furnish any effective opposition. The willingness of Harold Stassen of Minnesota and Governor Earl Warren of California to accept a Republican nomination was generally assumed. Paul G. Hoffman of California and General Douglas MacArthur were also regarded as possibilities.

The leaders of the movement for Eisenhower were Governor Dewey of New York, Senator James Duff of Pennsylvania, and Senators Henry Cabot Lodge and Leverett Saltonstall of Massachusetts. While Taft directed his appeal in the first instance to the party officials and wheelhorses, from ward leaders up to men of national renown, Eisenhower's agents appealed rather to the rank and file of the party. Obviously, Taft represented that part of American opinion chilly toward European commitments, Eisenhower the section which believed that America and Western Europe must stand or fall together. On the Democratic side, the pivotal question was whether President Truman would seek another term. As the Republicans were divided by foreign policy and the question of the degree to which the New Deal should be accepted, the Democrats were divided by the issue of race equality in the South. If Truman should run, it was certain that a Southern ticket would again be put into the field.

CHAPTER IV

THE RECORD OF 1952

OST of the critical events of the year in the United States (and in the whole world) were in some manner related to the Korean conflict and to the cold war between the West and the Soviet Union. "Deadlock" and "stalemate" were the words most often applied to the dismal grinding conflict in the Korean hills, where both sides had built heavily fortified lines across the 155-mile front, and the frequent small battles with mortars, machine guns, high explosives, and tanks resulted in nothing more than the capture or recapture of various crests. Thirty months of fighting when 1952 ended, and eighteen months of talking about peace, had accomplished nothing decisive. Whenever the skies cleared, the United Nations aircraft hammered at areas behind the Communist lines. By the end of the year, North Korean towns and industrial establishments had been largely reduced to a shambles; more than 550 Russian-built jet aircraft had been destroyed; about 1,300 armored vehicles, of which about 900 were Russian-built tanks, had been captured or knocked to pieces; and, according to United Nations estimates, more than 800,000 casualties had been inflicted on the Chinese "volunteers." But American losses had also been heavy: nearly 130,000 men killed, wounded, or missing.

In reality, the word "stalemate" is not accurate, and Winston Churchill showed his usual insight when he described the situation as a "checkmate"—that is, the Communist aggression has been defeated by being brought to a standstill. The Korean conflict was always a limited war for limited ends, which have been achieved. For the Soviet Union, Korea was an experimental thrust; if it succeeded, other thrusts would have followed. It failed, and the Kremlin has attempted no other thrust. The Chinese timetable for conquest in Indo-China, Formosa, and the Malay Peninsula had been upset. The Western Powers, momentarily disheartened when United Nations troops were driven into the Pusan beachhead, have taken courage since the dramatic advance from Inchon, and have found time to organize and rearm. The stabilization of the Korean battle-line well north of the old boundary has meant the stabilization of the whole world front against Communism.

Having checkmated Communist aggression, the United Nations were naturally eager for peace. The economic strain of the conflict was heavy; the British Commonwealth of Nations and Turkey, as well as ourselves, had suffered painful losses in men. For every Western nation involved the war was unpopular. The West was fighting a secondary enemy on a far-off peripheral front, where no complete victory was possible unless the conflict was dangerously broadened. This distant effort impeded the North Atlantic Treaty Organization in its laborious attempt to rearm Western and Southern Europe against the main opponent, Russia. It was obvious, too, that continuance of the war did much to increase Chinese dependence upon, and friendship with, the Soviet Union. These two Powers, with their long and unstable boundary line, are in many respects natural enemies, not friends. China has already lost much territory to Russia, and is in danger of losing more. While the conflict and the blockade lasted, however, China depended on Soviet sources for military supplies, consumer goods, and to some extent food. If peace could be made in Korea and the old contacts between Western nations and China restored, much might be done to place the Chinese people on a path of development diverging sharply from Stalinism.

But the American Government and the United Nations were determined that if peace should be made, it must be a real peace. Washington and London made repeated statements that a stoppage of fighting in Korea would be worthless if it led only to an extension of fighting in Indo-China and Malaysia, where China was supporting "rebel" forces. The Russian object was seemingly to provoke her puppets in Asia to carry on a series of little wars, useful both for attrition and for propaganda, while the Kremlin continued the cold war in Europe. A settlement that did not lead to a stoppage of conflict in Southeastern Asia as well as Korea, that did not protect the West against a sudden Communist stroke in Iran, and that did not take some of the chill off the cold war, would be delusive and injurious.

Throughout the year, therefore, the United States followed with alternate hope and disillusionment (but chiefly the latter) the so-called truce talks in Korea and the discussion of peace terms in United Nations circles. Little progress was made. The negotiations defined the one crucial point of disagreement: the question whether Chinese and North Korean prisoners of war should be returned by force, if necessary, to their own countries. But all the talks left it uncertain whether the Soviet Union, which was gaining in so many ways from continuance of the struggle, would really permit the Chinese Government under any circumstances to make peace.

The principal stages in these abortive negotiations can be briefly summarized. In Korea, after a long series of meetings, the two sides agreed in February on a line to be established if an armistice was attained. This line followed the existing battle front and so preserved the strategic gains made by the United Nations. The next month partial agreement was reached on other conditions of an armistice. That is, the two sides consented to a plan for replacing front line troops by rotation at the rate of 35,-000 a month, with five points of entry for each army. When the Communists demanded that military air bases might be constructed in North Korea during the armistice, however, the United Nations sharply dissented; and the United Nations also rejected the Communist proposal that Russia be one of the five "neutrals" supervising the truce—a specially flagrant piece of Communist impudence. Nor would the United Nations permit the air base issue and the issue of Russian participation to be linked for settlement, as the North Koreans and Chinese suggested.

Then, in April, the negotiators reached the main stumbling block: the issue of prisoners of war. The 173,000 prisoners taken by the United Nations had for two reasons proved a grave embarrassment. In the first place, a hard core of Communists were determined (under orders from Russian and Chinese sources) to cause as much trouble as possible: to pin down large forces of guards and stage disturbances which might be used for Communist propaganda. In the second place, a still larger number of prisoners, fearing torture and death if returned to their own countries, rejected the idea of repatriation. They would die, they said, rather than return. The United Nations insisted that it could not and would not use compulsion on such prisoners. It would not violate an elementary rule of morality by forcing tens of thousands to exchange freedom for servitude and possible destruction. Chinese and North Korean negotiators, anxious not to lose face, demanded return in flat terms.

The dispute was intensified when the United Nations made known in April the results of a careful poll of the camps. They had found, after asking prisoners whether they would resist a return, that out of about 100,000 North

Koreans questioned, only 53,900 would consent to re-patriation; and out of about 20,000 Chinese questioned, only about 5,000 were willing to go back. A larger proportion of the North Korean civilians interned were naturally ready to go to their homes. But of the 16,000 South Koreans who had once served in the North Korean forces, only a driblet, 3,800 in all, would return. These figures were a great shock to the Communists. They at once declared they must insist on a general restoration of prisoners, and forthwith fomented a new set of disturbances in the camps.

These camps, carefully inspected by international agents, offered excellent care. Prisoners were well fed, well clothed, and housed in warm, well-constructed buildings. Originally they had been placed in large compounds, some holding more than 2,000. Riots staged in February and April led the authorities to adopt a policy of decentralization, moving the prisoners into compounds holding about 600 men each. In the April outbreaks, men in one Koje Island compound seized the camp commandant, Brigadier-General Francis T. Dodd, and refused to release him until his successor, Brigadier-General Charles T. Colson, signed an admission that prisoners had been given inhumane treatment — an admission which the United Nations command promptly repudiated. General Mark W. Clark took immediate steps to reorganize the camps.

Though the truce talks continued during spring and summer, the prisoners-of-war issue made them entirely futile, and the United Nations representatives finally broke them off on October 7 by calling an indefinite recess. As more ferocious battles and air raids ensued, the problem passed to the General Assembly, meeting early that month in its gleaming new steel and glass structure above the East River.

Here the United States and Russia at once manœuvred for position. The American representatives, supported by a score of other nations, introduced a resolution approving the principle of voluntary repatriation of prisoners, and asking the Communists to accept the United Nations proposals offered in Korea. Russia made a counter-move, introducing a resolution for an immediate cessation of fire, and the establishment of an eleven-nation commission, including North Korea and China, to deal with the entire Korean situation. As the two sides thus came into frontal collision, India undertook to mediate the dispute. V. K. Krishna Menon, the Indian delegate, proposed a long seventeen-point solution. Its essential features were that all prisoners should be released to a Repatriation Commission made up of Poland, Czechoslovakia, Sweden, and Switzerland (the four nations already tentatively selected as supervisors of an armistice) and an umpire country; that the disposition of prisoners not repatriated within ninety days should be decided by an overall Korean political conference; and that force should not be used either to prevent or effect the return of any prisoner to his homeland. Prime Minister Nehru said that the plan offered a real prospect of peace. The British accepted it. A large

Arab-Asian bloc was behind it. Most of the allies of the United States seemed likely to favor it.

Washington was placed in an embarrassing position, for the American Government disliked the vague phrasing with regard to the ultimate fate of unwilling prisoners, and believed that other Korean questions should be settled at the same time as this one. Yet the United States was reluctant to offend India and her supporters. But as it happened, Russia extricated the Western nations from the danger of a serious split. On November 24 Mr. Vishinsky seized the chair, and in his usual abusive way put India's proposals through what was known as his "meat-grinder." He denounced them as a copy of the American plan, and declared they would perpetuate war, not end it. This ended the discussion, for after Vishinsky's diatribe, China's rejection could be taken for granted. Early in December, the General Assembly voted the Indian resolutions, amended to place the ultimate responsibility for the disposition of unwilling prisoners upon the United Nations, 54 to 5—the Soviet bloc standing in the opposition. Then the Chinese Government presented its official refusal, assailing India and the West almost as bitterly as Vishinsky had done.

The year thus ended with the principal obstacle to an armistice as obdurate as ever. But by scornfully throwing out of the window a plan hailed by India and the Arab nations as fair, Russia and China had lost prestige.

Meanwhile, the North Atlantic Treaty Organization, despite serious difficulties over the German defence contribution, and great anxiety in Britain and France lest defence spending cripple the economic strength of those two nations, made some progress. N.A.T.O., it will be re-

From a cartoon by Carmack in *The Christian Science Monitor*

called, was formed in 1949 by twelve nations bound by a twenty-year treaty of mutual defence, and resolved to create a powerful force to meet Russian aggression. General Dwight D. Eisenhower remained the first Supreme Allied Commander in Europe, with headquarters

(SHAPE) near Paris, until April, when he withdrew to conduct his presidential campaign. President Truman thereupon named General Matthew B. Ridgway in his stead. A session of the N.A.T.O. Council had meanwhile been held in February in Lisbon, and had agreed on a set of goals. Arrangements were also made early in the year to fit Greece and Turkey, which have joined the group, into the defence structure.

The Lisbon conference agreed on "firm goals for 1952, provisional goals for 1953, and for 1954, goals to be used for planning purposes." It also agreed that N.A.T.O., acting through a secretary-general of eminence and prestige in Paris, would coordinate the defence policies of member governments, study the economic effects of these policies, and in general exercise a good deal of political and economic authority in the defence field. It will be able to act more rapidly and firmly than in the past. The 1952 goal was fixed at fifty divisions—half to be ready for action on the outbreak of war (D-day) and the other half within thirty days. The goal provided also for 4,000 operational aircraft, and strong naval forces. The West, it is hoped, will eventually have an army representing the European Defence Community, to which Western Germany and five other nations belong. But this will not come into real existence until both Germany and France, which take very divergent views, give wholehearted support to the Defence Community treaty.

By the last weeks of the year General Ridgway, welcoming visitors to his oak-panelled, heavily carpeted office, was able to stand before a rubber terrain-map on his wall and tell them that the "firm goal" was almost being met. For the first time, the Allied forces in West Germany were almost equal to the Russian forces in East Germany. Of course, nobody knew exactly the Soviet strength; but it was estimated to comprise twenty-two divisions and more than 500 jet aircraft. The Allied strength on November 15 was about nineteen divisions, six of them armored, and more than 700 jet aircraft. In tanks, the Allied forces were reported to be the stronger. Substantial forces in the Mediterranean area, reaching out to the Middle East, were commanded by Admiral Lord Louis Mountbatten. Independent of his command was our own powerful Sixth Fleet under Admiral Robert B. Carney; while in the Middle East, the Turks and Greeks had placed thirty well-trained divisions of fighters under the direction of Lieutenant-General Willard Wyman.

So far as manpower went, the N.A.T.O. nations by the end of 1952 could meet the first rush of a Soviet offensive. Their chief weakness was in the logistical structure behind the front lines, and in certain political elements of the situation. To keep twenty-five D-day divisions fighting in Central Europe and to rush up twenty-five more within a month would demand a strong system of roads, railways, canals, pipelines, and other modes of transport, with bases, hospitals, supply dumps, and various technical installations. The North Atlantic nations were busy building these "infra-structure" elements. The program comprehended the modernization of a number of European ports; the completion of an $800 million supply artery across France into Western Germany; the construction of more than 150 modern air bases all the way from Norway to Turkey; and the provision of fast modern highways, railroad equipment, radio and radar facilities, and warehouses. Not until 1956 can the work be finished.

Nor can the European Defence Community be placed on a strong foundation until France and Germany overcome their mutual suspicions and antagonisms. For Germany, Chancellor Adenauer has inclined to claim full equality in rearmament and full sovereignty in her military arrangements; for France, Foreign Minister Schumann is unwilling to see Germany rearm except under rigid restrictions. Both nations will have to modify their positions. The general situation, however, was far more reassuring than it was in 1951. Allied headquarters felt, as a correspondent wrote the New York *Times* of November 16, 1952, that the Soviet Union can no longer launch an unexpected attack, for any assault on the West through Germany would "have to be preceded by a telltale build-up of reserves or supplies."

At home, American rearmament was slowed down by cuts in appropriations, by a fifty-five day steel strike, and by difficulties in tooling plants and getting them into production; but the strength of the nation steadily increased. During the fiscal year ending June 30, 1952, orders placed for weapons ranging from warships to tanks and ammunition amounted to about $38 billions, and the spending continued unabated the second half of the year. By April, 1952, more than 12,000 pieces of artillery, 9,000 tanks and combat vehicles, and 800,000 rapid-fire guns and small arms had been shipped to our allies. A new medium-sized tank, the Patton 48, had been developed and put into production. Weighing 45 tons, and driven by an 810-horsepower engine, it carried a 90-millimeter gun, with a range-finding apparatus, optical and electronic, which was expected to enable it to shoot with unprecedented swiftness and accuracy. Guided missiles had also been brought to a high pitch of efficiency, and special anti-aircraft battalions were being organized to use them.

The Air Force was building up a large armament of B–47 bombers, made by the Boeing, Douglas, and Lockheed companies. This plane is capable of 600 miles an hour, and can carry ten tons of bombs, but its range of flight is only 3,000 miles. For a long-distance bomber, capable of fighting an intercontinental war, the department was still depending chiefly on the B–36, which can carry five tons of bombs for a round trip of 10,000 miles, and greater weights for shorter distances. Its speed, however, is only 450 miles an hour. The Air Force has, therefore, been developing a large all-jet bomber, the Convair YB–60, which can cover the 10,000-mile journey in much shorter time. Just how fast it can go is a secret, but the power of its engines suggests that it exceeds 600 miles an hour.

For fighter planes, the Air Force was depending mainly on the F–84 "Thunderjet" and the F–86 "Sabrejet," both of which have seen action in Korea. They are in the 600–700 miles per hour class; one "Sabrejet" model did 671 miles. If official dispatches tell the whole truth, the "Sabrejet" has had no difficulty in defeating the Russian-designed MIGs used by the Chinese forces. By an arrangement among the United States, Britain, and Canada, the Dominion is to help produce "Sabrejets" in quantity. Two other fighter planes, with elaborate electronic equipment, were announced during the year, the F–94 "Starfire" and the F–86 "Scorpion." The Navy also had its fast jet aircraft for carrier-based activities; one model, the "Savage," weighing twenty-six tons, required specially strong decks for the take-off.

The slowness with which the aircraft industry had gotten into production disturbed some observers. In 1944 the country was turning out 9,000 military aircraft a month; in 1952 it turned out only about 5,000 all told. One explanation is that the Defence Department had failed to make prompt provision for an adequate amount of machine tools. Without a full supply of drills, presses, grinders, shapers, and various jigs and fixtures, some of them elaborate, production is impossible. Once they are provided and the shops are "tooled up," production comes in a flood. But there were other reasons for the delay, which indeed affected the whole defence program.

One reason is that present-day weapons pose extremely difficult problems. In the First and Second World Wars, various segments of the industrial economy could easily be switched from peacetime to wartime uses. The automobile industry, for example, could make airplane engines about as easily as touring-car engines, tanks about as smoothly as trucks. But the government has found that jet aircraft require operations far more intricate than the old piston aircraft, and that the powerful new tanks, with their tremendous engines and complex range-finding mechanisms, are quite different from the old Sherman tanks. Machine tool designers and factory managers had to work out entirely new techniques and make strange new implements before they could approach production.

Another and greater error, as the London *Economist* pointed out, was to suppose that American labor could still be moved easily about the map. The government was anxious to decentralize industry to make it less vulnerable to attack. When new plants were erected in Kansas or South Carolina, it was thought that wage-earners would cheerfully follow. The fact is, however, that American workmen are now hardly more mobile than British or French—and for obvious reasons. Once, the ordinary mechanic had little beyond the furnishings of a rented house. Now he is likely to have title to house, garage, and car; seniority rights in his factory; claims to a company pension; and various other privileges and emoluments. He is attached to school and church, and plays a real part in community life. To move suddenly to Topeka or Spartanburg demands a sacrifice, and he hangs back, creating a manpower problem.

But one part of the defence program, the atomic energy effort, surpassed the general expectation. The closest secrecy naturally surrounded this field. We knew that the government in 1952 spent $1.7 billion on its undertakings in atomic development; we knew that the Atomic Energy Commission was responsible for about three per cent of all American construction. It was certain that a great variety of atomic weapons in a variety of shapes and sizes were being stockpiled in quantity. Really explicit facts and figures, however, were "classified" or forbidden.

In May, the Atomic Energy Commission invited officials and newspapermen to watch the explosion of the largest atomic bomb ever used in the United States; and television brought the spectacle to millions of firesides. Actually, two bombs were detonated in Nevada, one at 3,000 feet and the other lower down. A body of troops lay in entrenchments some four miles away, so that their response might be watched, and so that experts might partially determine the proper height for an explosion if soldiers were to attack the bombed enemy without danger of suffering from radioactivity. It was found that radioactivity following the loosing of the bombs was slight. So, however, was the damage to much of the "enemy position"; entrenchments and materiel were little hurt. Whether the atomic bomb would prove decisive in open field battle is doubtful.

Far more spectacular was the test of an entirely new atomic weapon at Eniewetok in the Central Pacific, early on the morning of November 1. "It was at that moment," wrote William L. Laurence of the New York *Times,* "which will surely go down as one of the great moments in man's history, that the hydrogen bomb made its first appearance on the world's stage." Secrecy surrounded the experiment; no newspapermen were allowed, and no official report was made. Members of the armed forces sent home lurid letters, however, which described a blast brighter than ten suns, a flame two miles long and a thousand feet high, and a conflagration which completely burned out a whole island. How much faith could be put in such statements nobody knew. Laurence believed, however, that a "baby" hydrogen bomb actually had been tested. What this event meant was evident from his statement on the effects of a full-sized bomb:

Such a weapon, exploding with a force equal to that of 20 million tons of TNT, could devastate an area of more than 300 square miles by blast and 1,200 square miles by fire. If encased in a shell of cobalt it could produce a radioactive cloud equal to 5 million pounds of radium, spreading death and devastation over thousands of square miles.

In June, the keel of the first atomic-powered submarine, the *Nautilus,* was laid at Groton, Connecticut, with a promise that it would be afloat in 1954. A month earlier, the Atomic Energy Commission had established an office under Dr. William L. Davidson to help administer a broad new program of "industrial participation" for peaceful use of the new force.

The foremost event of the year on the strictly domestic scene, and a more or less exciting diversion from the talk of war and defence, was the presidential election. Most people agreed early in 1952 that if Eisenhower won the

Republican nomination, his victory would be almost a foregone conclusion. For ten hectic weeks after the campaign got under way increasing doubt was thrown on this view; the Democrats seemed to have a strong fighting chance. Then, when the ballots were counted, the original opinion was seen to be correct—Eisenhower's election *had* been a foregone conclusion. Nevertheless, the battle had been full of color and suspense.

Early spring found a broad field of aspirants eyeing the great prize. On the Republican side, Harold Stassen, who had long thirsted for the nomination but never come anywhere near it, announced that he would enter nine State primaries, and began firing off speeches on every possible subject. General Douglas MacArthur seemed to entertain the belief that a tremendous wave of popular enthusiasm might suddenly arise and sweep him into the White House; at any rate, his friends thought so. Senator Robert Taft had made an early start, toiled hard and late, and built a powerful organization, which was busy enlisting delegates in the South and in conservative Northern areas. He had also, James Reston wrote in the New York *Times,* "lent his name and influence to McCarthyism with more consistency and effect than any other man in the Republican Party." Like Stassen, Taft had a burning desire to be President, and for reasons of age, this was his last chance. Above all the candidates loomed Eisenhower, who announced in February that he would take the nomination if offered. His machine was run by amateurs, his knowledge of politics was sketchy, and his ignorance of American economics and government was great; but the people had immense faith in his ability and his international experience. Governor Earl Warren of California hovered in the background, hoping that an Eisenhower-Taft deadlock would give him an opportunity.

Among the Democrats, Senator Estes Kefauver of Tennessee made the most of the national fame which sprang from his appearance on television screens in 1951 as head of the Senate Committee on Organized Crime. He was strong in rural districts, weak in the big cities. His victory in the Democratic primary in New Hampshire, in March, gave strength to his movement. Senator Richard B. Russell of Georgia came forward as the candidate of the South, aggrieved by President Truman's advanced stand on race relations. Rather belatedly, Averell Harriman announced his willingness to take the nomination; no one could doubt his great abilities, but his capacity as a vote-getter was less impressive. And both wings of the party—pro-Truman and anti-Truman, "fair deal" and conservative—showed from the outset a strong liking for Governor Adlai E. Stevenson of Illinois. He had held various government posts, had served as United Nations delegate, had proved an astonishingly successful campaigner, and had become the most efficient and popular head of his State in a generation. He was attractive, able, and eloquent. But, anxious to complete his work in Illinois, he insisted that he did not want to run as yet for higher office.

When the conventions finally met in Chicago, both proved full of drama. The Republicans gathered first, on July 7. Senator Taft, who had shown an unexpected amount of strength, stood practically even with Eisenhower. He was supported by all the old guard elements, whose philosophy was expressed by Representative Judd: "Most of the great forward steps of history were strictly negative." By steamroller tactics all too reminiscent of the course of his father's standpatters in the campaign of 1912, he tried to gain the contested delegations and make himself supreme. For several days, as General MacArthur, ex-President Hoover, and various Senators delivered rancorous speeches weighted in favor of Taft, the party seemed tearing itself to pieces. Eisenhower's staunch cohorts, marshalled by Governor Dewey of New York, had to use ruthless tactics to hold their own. In the end, wavering delegates yielded to a conviction that nobody but "Ike" could be certain of election, and the convention tumultuously named Eisenhower on the first ballot, with Senator Richard Nixon of California for Vice-President.

The Democrats were determined to maintain harmony and make the most of Republican disunity. Their only chance of winning lay in selecting a strong candidate and closing ranks behind him. The State Rights Dixiecrats, whose secession four years earlier had almost defeated Truman, were now prepared to be submissive. This was easier because the reluctant Governor Stevenson had gained overwhelming strength before the convention opened. Governor James Byrnes of South Carolina stood almost alone in his intransigence. On the first ballot Kefauver led, but everyone knew that he could not win the nomination—nor could Russell, Harriman, or the beloved but elderly Vice-President Alben Barkley. Despite pressure from President Truman, Stevenson continued to maintain that he was not a candidate. But he did not say flatly that he would not run. On the third ballot, as Harriman transferred the powerful New York delegation to him, he was nominated. This was the first time since Garfield's selection by the Republicans in 1880 that an unwilling man had been drafted. In an acceptance address of singular eloquence, Stevenson made a deep impression on the convention and on his huge television audience.

The campaign which followed was spirited—by October some newspapers spoke of it as at "white heat." It was marked by one striking episode: the disclosure in September that Richard Nixon had received more than $18,000 from private contributors in California to defray his political expenses, a procedure of dubious ethical quality. Many voices, including those of important Republican newspapers, suggested that he be dropped forthwith from the ticket; but in an impassioned and theatrical radio and television appearance, he defended himself so vigorously that General Eisenhower gave him a cordial endorsement. Both Presidential candidates made a series of long campaign tours, delivering a succession of speeches written in part by hastily-recruited staffs, and reducing themselves by November to exhaustion. The addresses of

Governor Stevenson were marked by a literary finish rare in political discourse, and characterized also by unusual candor and honesty. General Eisenhower's public appearances were highly effective; but he exposed himself to sharp criticism when, to maintain the unity of his party, he appeared in public with two men about whom there is widespread difference of opinion, Senators Joseph R. McCarthy and William E. Jenner.

At only a few points did any important difference appear between either the platforms of the two parties or the pledges made by the candidates. Except in the labor field, General Eisenhower accepted the main policies, foreign and domestic, of the Roosevelt and Truman Administrations; he stood for changes of method and emphasis but not of fundamental principle. "We are not going to turn back the clock," he said.

On election day, Eisenhower carried 39 states with a popular vote of 33,029,000 and an electoral vote of 442; while Stevenson carried 9 states with a popular vote of 26,584,344, and an electoral vote of 89. Stevenson won no Northern state, but Eisenhower swept Texas, Oklahoma, Florida, Tennessee, and Virginia into the Republican column.

Beyond question, the principal factor in Eisenhower's overwhelming victory lay in his fame, his experience, and his command of the affection and confidence of his fellow citizens. The election was a personal triumph. Two commentators, Joseph and Stewart Alsop, indeed pronounced it "a more striking personal triumph than

Roosevelt ever enjoyed." He had polled a larger popular vote (about 55 per cent of the whole) than any other candidate since Washington; and he ran ahead of the other Republican nominees in every state but three. His strength assisted in the reelection of a number of Republican candidates whose views differed sharply from his own and who were widely criticized by many of the voters: Jenner of Indiana, Malone of Nevada, and McCarthy of Wisconsin, for example. And he easily carried several states despite the handicap placed upon him by isolationist Republican candidates for the Senate whom the people defeated: Kem of Missouri, Ecton in Montana, and Cain in Washington. It was clear that the people knew, admired, and trusted "Ike."

Of the other elements responsible for the Republican victory, three stood out with special prominence: the Korean War, the corruption exposed in the national government, and the ravages of high taxes and inflation. The war, which was already the third costliest in money and casualties in our history, bore heavily on a million families whose sons had gone to the Far East, and millions more which feared that they would have to send sons there. All thoughtful observers, of course, recognized that no leader and no party could be blamed for the Korean struggle. Once the Communists attacked South Korea, any Administration would have had to act as Truman's (with bipartisan support) acted. Careful observers knew, too, that the war could not easily be stopped. As Walter Lippmann wrote, Korea was "a strategic trap, and we cannot

expect to extricate ourselves cheaply or easily from it."
But discontent with the war, and criticism of its conduct,
were nevertheless lively, and reacted against the Democrats with damaging effect.

The war issue was apparently specially potent with
the women's vote, which is larger than the men's. Numerous observers testified that women were prominent
in Eisenhower's audiences, and responded with special
fervor to his proposal that South Korean forces should
replace Americans in the front lines, and to his promise
in the last phase of the campaign that he would go personally to Korea to see what he could do to end the conflict "quickly and honorably." Neither proposal inspired
great confidence among trained analysts of the situation.
Two reasons existed why South Korean troops could not
fully replace Western front-line forces: not enough of
them had been drilled and officered, and in a United Nations war it would be manifestly improper not to have
soldiers of many nations participate. As for the President-
designate's visit to Korea, it was unquestionably valuable
in its psychological effect upon the weary troops; but it
could do nothing to end a war which would have to be
closed by diplomatic action in Washington, Moscow, and
the halls of the United Nations. The country was glad to
see General Eisenhower take the trip to Korea, but heaved
a sigh of relief when he returned.

However, the war was a cardinal factor in the Republican victory. As the Memphis *Commercial Appeal* stated:
"Women and wives plainly had a lot to do with the out-

come, and for them a big reason was wrapped up in the words, 'Peace and Korea.' "

Corruption is a story that goes back many years, and presents a number of facets. President Truman quite correctly said that nearly all government employees are honest men trying to do their duty. In the recent revelations of dishonesty, Republicans as well as Democrats were implicated; some Congressmen were guilty (in the last three years three have been convicted of illegal acts) as well as executive officials. Defenders of the Administration protested that when the government was compelled to collect such huge taxes and spend such huge sums, and when it necessarily put decisions affecting large amounts of wealth into the hands of ill-paid bureaucrats, some dishonesty was inescapable. Wars have always produced corruption; inflation and heavy appropriations breed thievery as garbage breeds maggots. It is clear, too, that moral laxity, a debasement of standards, are in the last analysis the responsibility of the whole nation, not of an Administration. When business offers bribes, the giver is just as guilty as the taker. But however complex the situation actually was, voters found it easy to simplify it as the "Truman mess" and to call for "a change."

Most of the press, which was overwhelmingly for Eisenhower, and a majority of the electorate, undoubtedly held the Administration blamable. It was felt that Truman had appointed too many mediocre men to high office, and like Harding, had stood too loyally by old friends and adherents who proved untrustworthy. Recurrent press

stories under flaring headlines, millions of words of committee testimony, damning government reports, had made
a deep impression. It was all too clear that some officers
of the Bureau of Internal Revenue had taken financial
favors for concessions to firms or persons; that the Department of Justice had certain tainted areas; that men
had sold their supposed influence with the Reconstruction
Finance Corporation; and that sporadic dishonesty had
occurred elsewhere. Most of this had been proved in 1950–
1951, but it was remembered in 1952. The head of the
General Accounting Office, Lindsay Warren, said that
many of the evils went back into the Roosevelt Administration; that his agency "has been a voice crying in the
wilderness since as far back as 1942." In vain did President Truman argue, in a speech of March 29, that no
exposures in his Administration equalled the Teapot
Dome scandal, and that the Republican Party had long
been responsible for legislation that favored "the greed
of monopoly and the trickery of Wall Street." Millions
wanted a thorough housecleaning, and voted for it.

High taxes and inflation also aroused deep irritation.
General Eisenhower carried, on his campaign train, two
pieces of lumber, one the long board purchasable for a
few dollars in the old days, the other a mere splinter that
the same sum would buy in 1952. He displayed them
with telling effect. On radio and television the Republican National Committee, appealing directly to house-
wives, made the most of the high cost of living. The
people, said the Houston *Chronicle,* "do not like our gov-

ernment's big national debt . . . they do not like the continually increasing taxes and cost of living." In the *Atlantic Monthly* for November, Paul Hoffman warned the country that so long as the cold war continued, high expenditures would endure. All the costs of general government, $7.7 billions, might be wiped out, he argued, and yet so heavy were defence expenditures that a deficit of $2 billions would still remain. But the Republicans pledged the strictest economy; Senator Taft in particular demanded hard retrenchment lest the national economy be wrecked; and on this issue Eisenhower won many votes.

One fact was clear the day after election: that in their enthusiasm for "Ike" and their urgency for a change, Americans had forgotten as never before party, sectional, and occupational lines. It had been supposed by many that labor would vote with fair unanimity for Stevenson, as nearly all labor leaders urged it to do; that turned out to be a fallacy. The vote in the big industrial centers showed a strong labor trend toward Eisenhower. It had also been supposed that the farmers and others benefiting from the New Deal and Fair Deal legislation would stand by the Democratic Party; that too was a delusion. "Well, somebody did shoot Santa Claus after all," remarked a writer in the Atlanta *Constitution*. A heavy vote for Eisenhower in districts of Virginia and Maryland near Washington showed that officeholders had forsaken the Administration. And Southern Democrats broke across the old lines as never before; in the ten States of the Lower

South, Eisenhower polled about 3.5 million votes, and came within 200,000 votes of Stevenson's total.

It was also clear after election day that never had a badly defeated candidate earned and held the esteem of the American people as Stevenson did. His candor, his refusal to promise the nation anything better than "a long, patient, costly struggle" with Russia, his refreshing humor, his hard sense, and his eloquence made admirers on every hand. One of Eisenhower's greatest achievements, said the New York *Herald Tribune,* was his ability to defeat an opponent so universally respected. "In the whole history of this country," declared the Toledo *Blade,* "so many people have never voted with greater reluctance against a candidate whom they admired so greatly."

The campaign was followed by a public revulsion against its indefensible money costs. One survey printed in the New York *Times* indicated that the parties had spent more than $32 millions. We have laws strictly limiting campaign expenditures, but they were a sorry joke. Although the National Committees were restricted to definite amounts, it was easy to create organizations standing beside and working with them, such as Volunteers for Stevenson and Citizens for Eisenhower. Individuals are forbidden to deduct campaign donations from their incomes for tax purposes; but it is easy for a man to "lend" any sum he likes to his party, and then carry it against his income tax as a bad debt. For the first time, television played a strong role in a national contest, and television time is extremely expensive. The Republicans undoubtedly enjoyed a definite advantage in their ability to buy greater use of television, as in their command of fully four-fifths of the daily newspapers of the country.

Eisenhower, anticipating his victory, had prepared to grapple instantly with the nation's problems. Within a fortnight he had resigned his presidency of Columbia University, seized a short vacation at Augusta, Georgia, conferred at length with President Truman, and named the principal members of his Cabinet. Speculation ran high over the question whether he could avoid an open breach with Senator Taft, who during the campaign had met him in the president's house at Columbia, and induced him to sign a joint statement of highly conservative tenor. As majority leader in the Senate, and a leader of unquestioned supremacy over most of his party colleagues, Taft was a formidable power. But the President-elect made it plain that he would pursue a conciliatory policy, trying to keep the national policy-makers united.

The Cabinet and sub-Cabinet appointments showed a strong inclination toward business, finance, and those branches of law allied with corporate management. For Secretary of State, General Eisenhower chose John Foster Dulles, a Wall Street attorney of 64 who combined long experience in foreign affairs with longtime business connections. As a strong advocate of a bipartisan foreign policy, he had served the Truman Administration well, attending the San Francisco Conference which completed the United Nations Charter, frequent meetings of the United Nations Assembly, several sessions of the

Council of Foreign Ministers, and other important gatherings. He had done more than anyone else to draft the Japanese peace treaty, and the treaty of mutual defence signed by Australia, New Zealand, the Philippines, and Japan. Nobody knew more about the foreign scene; and he held the confidence of both the Taft and Dewey factions of the party.

The equally important post of Secretary of Defence went to Charles E. Wilson, president of General Motors Corporation, and an industrial administrator of long experience. A brief flurry of excitement attended his appointment, for the law required him to get rid of his holdings in any corporation with which he might do business, and he was at first unwilling to surrender his large block of General Motors stock. The Defence Department is now the largest administrative unit in the world. Wilson's knowledge of industrial production for war purposes was expected to stand him in good stead. Once a bitter opponent of organized labor, he had more recently made his peace with the automobile workers. Eisenhower appointed as Secretary of the Treasury another businessman, George M. Humphrey of Cleveland, Ohio, chairman of the M. A. Hanna Company. He, like Wilson, was 62. As Attorney-General, Eisenhower named his chief political strategist, Herbert Brownell, Jr., who had managed Dewey's personal struggles to attain the Presidency in 1944 and 1948, and who at 48 was one of the best-known lawyers in New York. Douglas McKay, a former mayor of Salem, Oregon, and governor of his State, was appointed head of the Interior Department.

Among the nominations which quickly followed were those of A. E. Summerfield as Postmaster-General, Ezra T. Benson as Secretary of Agriculture, Sinclair Weeks as head of the Department of Commerce, and Martin Durkin as Secretary of Labor. Two highly important appointments, those of Federal Security Director and Mutual Security Director, went respectively to Oveta Culp Hobby, a newspaper publisher of Texas, and Harold E. Stassen, former governor of Minnesota and president of the University of Pennsylvania. Mrs. Hobby was expected soon to be given Cabinet rank. In general outlook the Cabinet was regarded as highly conservative. Nobody could possibly regard Secretaries Wilson, Humphrey, and Weeks as anything but sympathetic to big business, while Secretary McKay was an open advocate of greater State participation in the development of the natural resources of the West, and a staunch opponent of plans for developing the Columbia River Valley on T.V.A. principles. The head of Eisenhower's White House staff, Sherman Adams of New Hampshire, was also regarded as conservative. On the other hand, Secretary Dulles and Director Stassen, like the President-elect, were strong internationalists.

But we must turn back to some of the more general events and tendencies of 1952; and the economic state of the nation first demands our attention.

For the whole world, no less than for the American people, the fundamental question in every year now is:

"Will the United States remain prosperous?" The dependence of Western Europe, Japan, and Latin America on American trade, tourists, grants in aid, and other forms of spending is so crucial that even a slight American depression might mean world disaster. Every year the Soviet Union hopes for hard times in America: for unemployment, lower tax yields, and forced economy. As the flow of goods and money from the United States to less fortunate areas slackened, Communism would have its chance of exploiting confusion and misery.

But in 1952 the American republic weathered all economic storms. Higher taxes, the uncertainties of the campaign, and a 55-day steel strike were taken in the nation's stride. The year, indeed, was much like that which preceded it. Our gross national product was still rising. It had gone up by sixty billion dollars since 1947, and by one hundred and fifty billions since 1939; it went up by about another twenty billions during 1952. Since the Korean War began in 1950, tremendous sums have been spent every year in plant expansion and new equipment; they were estimated for 1952 at almost $27 billions. Savings were higher than in any year since 1945. Gross farm income, despite droughts in some areas, broke previous records, though high costs kept net income down to the 1951 mark of $14.3 billions. Altogether, it seemed to most Americans a good year economically.

No question existed, however, as to the character of the main prop of business; it was the huge expenditure for war and defence. The decision to spread this spending for "full preparedness" over four and a half years instead of three had somewhat lessened the tension and the inflationary pressures. Nevertheless, the current bills appeared to most Americans staggering. President Truman in his January budget envisaged expenditures for the fiscal year 1952–53 of well over $85 billions. Later, in his August review of the budget, he cut the estimates to $79 billions. Even this is a huge sum; and it was responsible at once for inflationary tendencies, for much of the flush national prosperity, and for mounting fears of what would happen once preparedness was achieved and military spending fell off.

The steel industry continued expanding rapidly. The government had fixed as the proper objective for the emergency a total capacity for making 120 million tons of steel a year, which would be about 20 million tons more than at the opening of the Korean conflict. During 31 weeks of the year the steel mills were working at or above capacity. As construction of new facilities went forward, leaders expected that the expansion program would be completed by the middle of 1953. The chemical industry was run at top capacity throughout the year. The rubber industry, freed in April of controls that had endured more than a decade, fell short of the high records of 1952, but did well. Aluminum production set the highest mark in history. Net corporate earnings (about $17.5 billions) were lower than in the previous year, but this was in large part because of the high federal income tax, which took about sixty per cent of corporate income.

The United States, declared the London *Economist,* was "a self-sufficient giant"; and the statistics for foreign trade proved the fact. Total merchandise exports, including military goods, were nearly $15 billions, while total imports were only 10.6 billions. During the past decade, in fact, the United States had had annual excess of exports over imports of about $6 billions. This was manifestly too high for the health of the world. The fact is that the nation is economically very nearly self-contained. Imports in recent years have ranged only from three to three and a half per cent of the national gross product. We need a better approach to a balance of trade. This was recognized by President Truman, who spoke in 1949 of a "bold new program" of foreign investment; by the National Foreign Trade Council Convention in November, which echoed the rising European demand for "trade, not aid"; and by the International Materials Conference. About half of such imports as we allowed came from Canada and Latin America, our hemispheric neighbors.

The story of the automobile industry in 1952 was particularly dramatic. Detroit had suffered heavily from the original defence program, and the decision to spread out the armament effort rescued it from a bad predicament. In the year the Korean War began, the automotive industry was booming. Its total output of vehicles reached about eight million units, a record, and unemployment fell below two per cent of the available labor force. Then the new government restrictions on steel, rubber, copper, and aluminum hit the industry hard. More and more people were thrown out of work in Southern Michigan. Many of the new defence plants were operated only on a stand-by basis, and many of them had been placed in other sections of the country. By the end of 1951 more than 120,000 people were unemployed in Detroit, and the number was expected to rise to 150,000 by the middle of 1952. The industry, the labor unions, and the city and State authorities all vigorously besought the national government to lend aid.

Then the government altered its basic defence schedule. The original plan was to allow a production of 930,-000 units in the first quarter of the year, cut the level to 800,000 units in the second, and to reduce it still further in the third. Instead, the government decided to permit the manufacture of a million cars in the second quarter, with an additional 50,000 if scarce metals were used economically, and to permit from 1,050,000 to 1,150,-000 in the third quarter. As a matter of fact, the total production of automotive units for the year, according to the Automobile Manufacturers' Association, exceeded 5,550,-000 vehicles, the fourth best annual figure in the history of the industry. Unemployment almost vanished. Profits and wages were high—and the year would have been even better but for the steel strike.

We have spoken of the part the heavy national expenditures played in the Presidential campaign, and in the seemingly exuberant prosperity of the nation. Even after Truman reduced his estimates of expenditures for 1952–1953 to $79 billions, the national deficit for that year was expected to come uncomfortably close to $10 billions. Inasmuch as the national debt on June 30, 1952, exceeded $259 billions, this increase would bring the debt near the peak point of $279.8 billions reached in the early months of 1946.

As these figures were published, a wave of anguish and protest swept over the country. Many critics thought that the financial predicament of the nation was fast becoming dangerous. David Lawrence's magazine, *United States News and World Report,* printed a succinct paragraph which was widely republished. "All Presidents through Franklin Roosevelt, in 156 years, took from the public in taxes $248 billions," it ran. "Two world wars in there. Harry Truman, in six years, took from the public $260 billions." This was unfair, for much of the $260 billions represented accumulated war costs, but it made an impression. The Baltimore *Sun* printed a diagram showing that a stack of silver dollars worth $85.4 billions would reach 153,734 miles into the sky. The Chamber of Commerce of the United States published a map presenting the whole area west of the Mississippi in black, with a legend: "The 1953 budget of 85.4 Billions is Greater Than All the Incomes of All the People West of the Mississippi." Military spending alone, declared the Chamber, equalled the incomes of all the people in a dozen States, including wealthy Texas and California.

Some of the ablest Congressional leaders of both parties declared that economy had become imperative. Senator Harry Byrd of Virginia, a conservative Democrat, offered a budget of his own which cut down spending by $8.7 billions, slashing all military estimates by five per cent. Senator Paul Douglas of Illinois, a progressive Dem-

1952, CHICAGO SUN-TIMES

Courtesy of cartoonist Burck and the Chicago *Sun-Times* Syndicate

ocrat, asserted: "One of the things Congress must do is to ride herd on the civil and military authorities, and try to make them squeeze $4 to $5 billions at the very least out of the budget." And Senator Taft declared again and again that the national economy simply could not sustain such heavy expenditures over a long period.

While our inflationary prosperity continued, labor fared well. The year would have been made eventful for organized labor, if by nothing else, by the deaths in November of President William Green of the American Federation of Labor, and President Philip Murray of the Congress of Industrial Organizations, two able veterans of labor's long struggle for power. Both had great personal prestige, and were hard to replace. Immediately after Green's death the executive council of the A. F. of L. elected George Meany, 59, a plumber by trade and one-time head of the New York State Federation, to the presidency. A man of moderate temper and liberal views, popular both within and outside the organization, Meany had shown a deep interest in the international aspects of unionism, and had heartily favored a fusion of the A. F. of L. and the C.I.O. He at once asked the leaders of both wings to renew the discussion of integration.

In the C.I.O. internal rivalries and jealousies made the choice of a new head extremely difficult. This organization contains two very powerful unions, the United Automobile Workers and the United Steelworkers, and a number of smaller bodies. Two candidates appeared. Allan S. Haywood, the vice-president, a leader long at Philip Murray's right hand, was supported by the steel men; Walter Reuther, president of the automobile workers, had their enthusiastic loyalty. This former toolmaker and Ford Company foreman had done more than anyone else to organize the automotive industry. So intense was the feeling between the two men and their factions that many leaders feared the C.I.O. might be split asunder, and the convention was postponed in an effort to reach some prior agreement. In the end, however, it chose Reuther president without dangerous friction or ill-feeling. He, like Meany, expressed himself in favor of a unification of the A. F. of L. and the C.I.O.; and both men announced their willingness to resign, if necessary, in favor of another head.

For the first time in its history, the A. F. of L. in its annual convention flatly endorsed a presidential candidate. Meeting in New York in September, it was addressed both by Eisenhower and Stevenson. The general knew that he was facing an audience that was largely unfriendly. "I have not come to bid or compete for your endorsement," he said. "My views toward labor will be the same as they have long been, regardless of the action taken." Nor did the 700 delegates get any promises from Stevenson either, except that he was in favor of the repeal of the Taft-Hartley Act and the writing of a new law, while Eisenhower wished merely a drastic revision. The A. F. of L. delegates voted to support Stevenson. Already the C.I.O. through its executive board had taken the same step.

Union membership was maintained at the same high levels (about 17,000,000, if we accept union claims) as in recent years. Strikes were more numerous than in any previous year since 1946, and cost greater loss of time; nearly 5,000 were counted. Only a few, however, were really serious. In dealing with the strike in the plant of the American Locomotive Company at Dunkirk, New York—a plant making items required in several atomic energy projects—President Truman was compelled to use an injunction under the Taft-Hartley Act against the workers. They submitted, but took a test case to the courts.

By all odds the most important strike was in the steel industry. When the year began, the union and the steel companies were at odds on wages, hours, and marginal welfare questions. President Truman assigned the dispute to the Wage Stabilization Board; and it, after public hearings, submitted a report which the steel companies indignantly rejected. This report called for substantial wage increases, a union shop, and such benefits as special pay for Sunday work. On the heels of the companies' rejection of these terms, the union called a strike. At once Mr. Truman, declining to use his emergency powers under the Taft-Hartley Act, made a technical seizure of the steel mills, and work continued in them. Practically all of industry and most of the press denounced the President's action as a highhanded invasion of the sanctity of private property. And this was the view taken by the first court to which the companies appealed. Early in May, Judge Pine of the Federal District Court in Washington handed down a decision that Truman had acted improperly.

"There is no express grant of power in the Constitution authorizing the President to direct this seizure," wrote the judge. "There is no grant of power from which it reasonably can be implied. There is no enactment of Congress authorizing it."

PARADING UNDER WASHINGTON SQUARE ARCH

After his return from Japan, General Douglas MacArthur is given a Welcome Home Parade
in New York, with more than seven million people lining Fifth Avenue.

Top: Acme Photo. Bottom: Official U. S. Army Photo released by Dept. of Defense.

Frank Costello faces the Kefauver Senate Crime Committee in New York and Army engineers
test a cable car rigged to hoist men and equipment to the top of a
thousand foot ridge in Korea.

PRODUCTION FOR PEACE AND WAR

The *Arthur M. Anderson,* a new steamer for the iron ore fleet slides down the ways
and the drawing shows a new super aircraft carrier, the *USS Forrestal.*

An artillery weapon fires the first atomic shell in history while, below, production rolls on 105 mm. shells.

Adlai Stevenson, top, waves from the rear platform of his train during his campaign and, bottom, Dwight D. Eisenhower acknowledges cheers at a Republican rally. Mrs. Eisenhower and New York's Governor Thomas E. Dewey are to the right of General Eisenhower.

Two views of the Panmunjon neutral area in Korea where United Nations and Communist representatives have been holding discussions for signing a truce. The guard at the right of the top picture is of the truce camp's Communist security patrol. At the right in the bottom picture is the conference building where the discussions have been going on.

Official U. S. Army and Navy Photographs.

A generator-powered gun, transported by specially designed trucks, is one of the Army's new weapons. Below, a group of U.N. staff officers hold a conference at Panmunjon to discuss exchanging prisoners of war.

Excited days followed. The workers walked out of the steel mills; the Court of Appeals granted a stay so that the issue could be presented in full to the Supreme Court; Philip Murray, at Mr. Truman's request, ordered his men back; and the Supreme Court agreed to review the case without delay. In the end the nation's highest tribunal substantially supported the lower court. It held that the government had no power to seize the mills, for Congress had never authorized any such action, and the President had no residual or inherent power to take so drastic a step.

Thereupon the strike at last began. It endured until July 25, the longest steel strike in the nation's history. When it ended and the smoke cleared away, observers saw that labor had won most of its contentions. The workers got substantial wage increases, a two-year contract, paid holidays, a three-weeks' vacation for those who had served fifteen years or more, and a reduction of sectional wage differentials. New employees were to be required to apply for union membership, with the right to cancel the application within thirty days; but old employees were not to be compelled to join the union. To compensate itself for these concessions, the steel mills slightly raised prices.

The most striking piece of Congressional legislation passed during the year was the controversial McCarran Act, a general revision of the immigration laws of the United States, codifying and systematizing previous legislation. Both houses accepted it in June; and when President Truman vetoed it on June 25, they promptly repassed it over his head. The act had some good features, he wrote. But they were "embedded in a mass of legislation which would perpetuate injustices of long standing against many other nations of the world, hamper the efforts we are making to rally the men of the East and the West alike to the cause of freedom, and intensify the repressive and inhumane aspects of our immigration procedures." General Eisenhower was equally vigorous in his condemnation. America had always been the land of hope to oppressed aliens, he told an audience on October 17, "yet to the Czech, the Pole, the Hungarian, who takes his life in his hand and crosses the frontier tonight . . . the ideal that beckoned him can be a mirage because of the McCarran Act."

The new law was essentially a reenactment of the quota system of 1924, based on the national origins of the American people as estimated in 1920. The strong vote for it in Congress showed that the reaction of Americans against the unlimited immigration of the period prior to the First World War was still powerful. It was evident from the Congressional debates that many people believed that mass immigration would threaten American principles and institutions; that labor groups feared that heavy immigration would reduce wages and working standards; that many thought that newcomers of alien tongues, religions, and customs were likely to prove unassimilable and to impair the national unity; and that not a few apprehended that immigration would bring us many "agitators" and "subversives," and particularly the Communist

sympathizers continuously denounced by Senator Mc-
Carthy as a fearful and pervasive menace.

Actually, nobody in or out of Congress wished to go
back to the unrestricted immigration of the nineteenth
century. But critics pointed out that so long as Great
Britain and Northern Ireland never filled their national-
origins quota of 65,700 immigrants out of a total of 154,-
000, Italy might well be allowed more than her meagre
5,800. They pointed out also that while miserable refugees
from the Baltic states, Hungary, and Greece were looking eagerly to the United States for a home, and could
offer the country good service, it was shameful that the
United States should admit only 783 Balts, 473 Austrians,
and 100 Greeks in any single year. Did we really stand
for giving men equal opportunities? At the very least,
the quota system might be made more flexible and the
general policy a little more liberal.

But the McCarran Act not merely kept the ironclad
quota system unchanged; it added some highly provoca-
tive and irritating new provisions, expressive of a fierce
distrust of the foreigner. Immigrants were no longer to
be admitted on the principle of first come, first served.
Instead, the law provided that the Attorney-General
should give preference for one-half of each quota to persons he found "urgently needed in the United States,"
and for the second half to close relatives of citizens and
resident aliens. The act also provided that no former "subversive" should be admitted unless the Attorney-General
and the consular visa officer both found his entry to be

"in the public interest." All temporary visitors were required to get a "security clearance," which meant that even the most distinguished writer or scientist had to go through an embarrassing and painful investigation. As a result of this requirement, international business conferences in the United States are gravely hampered; international scientific and cultural congresses are avoiding our shores; and distinguished Britons, Frenchmen, and others are coming to regard America as a land without freedom or courage.

Under the McCarran Act, too, all aliens residing in the United States have to be registered and fingerprinted; they must carry their registration certificates with them; they must notify the Attorney-General within ten days of any change of address; and for any of a long list of offences, they are subject to summary deportation. Any alien who leaves the country temporarily must—even if he has wife, children, and large propertied interests in the United States—meet the same tests as a new immigrant before he is allowed to return.

On another important national question Congress reached no conclusion. Enormous stores of oil (estimated by some at ten billion barrels) lie in the coastal areas of Florida, Louisiana, Texas, and California. Officers and people of these States, and the major oil interests, pressed throughout 1952 for enactment of a new Tideland Oil Bill, to give the States control over any oil to be pumped between tidemark and the three-mile limit in Louisiana and California, and in a wider area in Texas and Florida waters. It will be remembered that Texas entered the Union under a special treaty, which gave her a claim to lands up to ten and a half miles from shore. An earlier bill was vetoed by President Truman, and Congress failed to repass it over his veto. The Supreme Court, in a decision of 1947, later reaffirmed, held that the national government has paramount rights over the marginal seas beyond tidemark, but made no statement as to the powers of the government to develop the oil. Neither the States nor the federal authorities have felt free to move. The oil interests would deal with either, but prefer the States, whose officials are easier to reach (and sometimes easier to control); but they have been unable, while the uncertainty lasts, to tap this rich treasure house.

The Administration offered during 1952 to accept a compromise embodied in the O'Mahoney Bill. This would empower the federal government to sign a five-year lease for oil-drilling and pumping in the marginal seas; the States concerned to be consulted on each lease, and to get 37.5 per cent of the royalties. Senator Lister Hill of Alabama proposed that the federal government's 62.5 per cent of the royalties should be used to aid the public schools in all States. This conformed to an old American practice of allotting part of the public domain to educational purposes. But the States with coastal oil resolutely refused to consider such a compromise. During the campaign, General Eisenhower came out vigorously in favor of giving the States full rights to the tidelands area; Governor Stevenson as resolutely opposed that concession. Hoping for a favorable President and Congress, the four States involved and their supporters in the Senate preferred to wait for a whole loaf rather than accept the O'Mahoney biscuit. President Truman, just before he left office, signed an executive order reserving the disputed oil area for national defence purposes, but this could easily be set aside in favor of the legislation expected from the new Administration.

The relations of church and state continued to attract attention, generate friction, and require court definition. In May the Supreme Court, six to three, upheld the New York law which allows the release of children from the public schools for one hour a week to attend whatever religious instruction their parents designate. The court, four years earlier, in the McCollum case, had annulled an Illinois law which similarly gave the pupils "released time." In Illinois, however, the religious teachers had come into the schools and used classrooms, blackboards, and other state property; in New York the children (on written application by parents) were taught elsewhere. The Illinois system was held to violate the prohibition of any state establishment of religion, in the First and Fourteenth amendments; the New York system was held not to constitute a violation. Justice Douglas, who wrote the decision, declared that the state was not required to show hostility to religion, or refrain from recognizing it. If the school authorities had used coercion, or persuasion, the matter would be different.

The three dissenting justices, however, took the view

that the New York law was unconstitutional precisely because it opened the door to coercion. Justice Frankfurter noted that no evidence had been taken in the lower court on the question whether moral compulsion was not being used in the schools. The churches, he pointed out, preferred "released time" to "dismissed time" (the whole school closing to allow any one who likes, to take religious instruction); and this indicated a reliance on some degree of moral coercion. Justice Black was still more emphatic. New York, he said, "is manipulating its compulsory education laws to help religious sects get pupils. This is not separation but combination of church and state." About one-fifth of the school children of New York city have used "released time." The general question will doubtless recur for further judicial definition.

Among disquieting events of the year were the grave riots in the great State penitentiary at Jackson, Michigan, and two New Jersey prisons; and the exposure of a most distressing regime of violence and corruption among the longshoremen on the waterfronts of New York port.

Inquiries into subversive activities by United States citizens continued, with considerable differences of opinion expressed by the public as to the methods employed by the Congressional Committees conducting the inquiries. The most-publicized case, that of Mr. Owen Lattimore, was left undecided for future review by the proper courts.

Many items, however, might be listed on the credit side of the ledger. Education was flourishing; the country had some 6,250,000 pupils in secondary schools, and well over 2,000,000 in colleges and universities. Art continued to find munificent patrons. John D. Rockefeller, Jr., for example, gave ten millions to the Metropolitan Museum of Art, in New York, for the enlargement of its medieval collections at the Cloisters. A number of impressive works appeared in the literary field: Ernest Hemingway's short novel *The Old Man and the Sea,* Ralph Ellison's *The Invisible Man,* and Van Wyck Brooks's *The Confident Years* being among the most noteworthy. After fourteen years of labor, a group of eminent Biblical scholars brought out "The Revised Standard Version of the Holy Bible," which at once became a best seller. Two Americans were awarded Nobel prizes in physics, and one in medicine. All the main currents of American life were running forward with unabated vigor. The nation was as earnestly devoted as ever to its traditional ideals of liberty, justice, and democracy.

CHAPTER V

THE RECORD OF 1953

Nearly every great happening of 1953, at home and abroad, had to be viewed by Americans in its relation to the cold war between the Free World and the Communist World. The change in American leadership, Eisenhower replacing Truman; the shift in the Russian dictatorship, Malenkov catching up dead Stalin's sceptre; the strenuous effort of the United States to maintain its own prosperity and bolster the economies of its Allies; the armistice in Korea; the grim announcement that the Soviet Union had produced a hydrogen explosion—all these events bore directly upon the struggle between East and West, and took their main significance from it. That struggle remained in uneasy balance. The Western Powers, their armaments growing, felt safer than before. Yet no ray of hope for a sure peace appeared. Americans had to face the prospect, as President Eisenhower put it, of living not in a moment of danger, but in an era of danger—perhaps a long era.

Facing this prospect, the nation had not merely to continue mobilizing its material resources, but to summon up all its reserves of moral strength. The United States was obviously and consciously the leader of the free peoples of the world. President Eisenhower, like his two predecessors, was fully aware of that national position, and of its fateful implications. He and Secretary of State Dulles were determined to build the military strength of the United States up to a safe level, to use the Military Assistance Program to augment the defenses of the North Atlantic Treaty Organization nations, and to encourage economic and political cooperation in Western Europe. They were resolved to support the United Nations as, in Mr. Dulles's words, "an organization for world peace and justice." They acted in close harmony with other Western leaders, and particularly with Prime Minister Winston Churchill and Foreign Secretary Anthony Eden of Great Britain. But this was not enough; the United States has to be the moral as well as material leader of the Western peoples. The President, worried by demagogy and hysteria in certain quarters, repeatedly appealed for steadiness, calmness, and unity.

These appeals were needed. Some elements in the nation were impatient, abusive, or rebellious in facing the responsibilities of international leadership. The Korean armistice, for example, was welcomed by all the other countries which had contributed to the U.N. effort; it was regarded by General Omar N. Bradley, outgoing head of the Joint Chiefs of Staff, as representing a sound avoidance of "the wrong war, at the wrong time, in the wrong place." Yet it was violently attacked by prominent men and newspapers as a defeat for the Free World. The foreign aid program was brought under heavy fire, though most of such aid contributed directly to our own defense. The U.N. and even UNESCO were assailed. And strong efforts were made by some individuals, notably Senator Joseph R. McCarthy, to make anti-Communism the criterion of all policy, foreign and domestic.

On the whole, however, it was a happy year in that it found the United States and the West growing in armed power, both America and Europe making economic gains, and Russia, troubled in its own house, less likely to deliver a sudden blow. It will be logical to deal first with the new Eisenhower Administration, the new Republican Congress, and political affairs; then with the foreign scene as it affected the United States; then with the economic situation at home and abroad; and finally with certain social developments.

For the first time since the Twentieth Amendment was made part of the Constitution, a change of Presidents took place in January, and an incoming Congress of one party had to deal temporarily with an outgoing Chief Executive of another. As the year began, Mr. Truman presented his messages on the state of the Union and the budget; the Eighty-third Congress, already organized by the Republicans, marked time until the inauguration; and at a New York hotel Mr. Eisenhower, his future Cabinet members, and others, mapped out their plans. Meanwhile, Prime Minister Churchill sailed for New York to confer with the new President, saying: "We don't want to live on you; we want to earn our own living." The farewell message of Mr. Truman was notable for his warning to Russia. War today, he said, might destroy mankind. "There is something I would say to Stalin: You claim belief in Lenin's prophecy that one stage in the development of Communist society would be war between your world and ours. But Lenin was a pre-atomic man. . . . War cannot now be a stage in the development of anything save ruin for your regime and your homeland."

Mr. Truman's budget message represented a curious anomaly in our governmental system. The law requires the President to send the budget to Congress within fifteen days after it meets. This meant that Mr. Truman submitted a budget that would cover the fiscal year beginning five months after Mr. Eisenhower took office! As a matter of fact, Joseph M. Dodge, named Budget Director in the Eisenhower Administration, had been at work observing the preparation of the document since a few days after the election. And of course the fiscal committees of the Republican Congress would review it.

The budget for the fiscal year 1953–54, though it called for the heaviest spending in our history except for the Second World War years, was singularly devoid of excess fat. Of the $78.6 billions which it totalled, $57.3 billions was earmarked for national security, $6.4 billions for debt interest, $4.6 billions for veterans' benefits, and only $10.3 billions for all other governmental functions. This made it extremely hard for the incoming Administration to make notable cuts unless it sharply reduced defense expenditures. Mr. Truman reckoned that the national debt would reach the highest point in history, with a deficit of nearly $10 billions. But he did not propose any change in the tax laws. Nor, looking ahead, did he take a pessimistic view. Within ten years, he believed, the total national production would rise to $500 billions, two-fifths more than at present, and the average income of Americans would reach $2,000, half again as much as in 1953. The main question was whether such figures would be reached largely by means of inflation.

The inauguration was accompanied by a huge parade, two balls, a reception for governors and diplomats, and Republican rejoicing adequate to a party return to power. It was also accompanied by picturesque squabbles over Cabinet appointments. Farm State Senators minutely questioned Ezra Taft Benson, called to the Agricultural Department, on his opinions about price supports. Two Democratic Senators scolded John Foster Dulles for having inserted historical "distortions" into the foreign policy plank of the Republican platform. Most serious of all were the troubles encountered by Charles E. Wilson, former head of General Motors Corporation, named for Secretary of Defense. Federal law forbade the Secretary to hold an interest in or draw a profit from any business with which the Department might make a contract. It was not until Wilson agreed to sell or give away all his General Motors stock, and to consult with the President on any matter in which his former business connection might create any misunderstanding, that he was confirmed. Three other men, Robert E. Stevens, Harold E.

Talbott, and Roger M. Kyes, named respectively as Secretary of the Army, Secretary of the Air Force, and Deputy Secretary of Defense, had to take the same step.

In his inaugural address, President Eisenhower defined certain lines of foreign policy which closely paralleled those already taken by Mr. Truman. America had a mission in this "century of trial," he said; it was the mission of "world leadership"; and it would be executed "not with confusion, but with confidence." The people must not expect heavy budget cuts or sharply reduced taxes. Instead, they must be ready, individually and collectively, "to accept whatever sacrifices may be required of us." While he warned the Soviet Union that his Administration would act first of all "to develop the strength that will deter the forces of aggression," he also promised it that the United States would stand ready to help remove all causes of mutual fear, and so permit a "drastic limitation of armament." To Western Europe he pledged American aid in fields in which it was already being given. Some high-tariff Republicans winced when he said that the United States specially wished to foster trade so that overseas countries would become less dependent on aid. He also served notice on Europe that he counted on an assumption of its "full and just" share of financial burdens, on enhanced productivity, and on real progress with the European army and European economic unity.

While the inaugural address said little of importance on domestic policy—simply that our home problems are largely created by and dwarfed by the overshadowing conflict between Communism and freedom—the first long message to Congress (February 2) said a great deal. Eisenhower wished to limit bureaucratic interferences with the people, he declared, for the people disliked artificial and arbitrary controls. He would leave business, except in times of great emergency, to the natural workings of economic law. He would try, within limits, to restore the freedom of the market-place. The true role of government would be emphasized—"to stabilize the economy and encourage the free play of our people's genius for individual initiative." Taxes, he thought, should not be reduced until after the budget was balanced. Inflation should be controlled by limitations on credit, and not (save in emergencies) by ceilings on wages and prices. These were his basic general principles.

On more specific matters, he asserted that he would keep the government out of rooms in which labor and management were bargaining; at any rate, unless the national welfare was threatened by an industrial shutdown. In farm policy, he would seek full parity of income for the rural population, but inclined to the belief that flexible supports should supplant the rigid price support system when the existing law expired in 1954. In the labor field, he favored prompt amendment of the Taft-Hartley Act. As for immigration, he wished the McCarran Act overhauled to extirpate its unjust features. He proposed that social security be extended to cover several million additional persons. On the controversial question of loyalty, he remarked that the primary responsibility for keeping untrustworthy people out of the government rested with the executive branch, not the legislative.

A week after this message, the President called Republican leaders of Congress to the White House to obtain agreement on a legislative program. Already he was making it plain that he expected to gain his objects by harmonious action, not by battle. As when he headed the Allied armies, he prided himself on his powers of conciliation. Symbolically, he had walked out of the chamber where the two Houses listened to him, arm in arm with Senator Robert Taft. Now he obtained the assent of party chiefs to eleven measures. These were a renewal of the President's powers to reorganize Federal departments; a date of May 15 for House passage of appropriation bills; Hawaiian statehood; amendment of the Taft-Hartley Act; a bill giving ownership of offshore oil to the States; extension of the Reciprocal Trade Act; simplification of customs procedure; expansion of social security benefits; the increase of District of Columbia commissioners from three to five; new controls on scarce materials; and more Federal school construction in defense areas. Unhappily for Mr. Eisenhower, the assent to some measures was far from wholehearted.

It proved fortunate for the President that Robert Taft was majority leader in the Senate. At the outset many feared that the distinguished Ohioan, his ambition for the Presidency so bitterly frustrated, would impede the Administration. Instead, he proved the ablest and most loyal of its lieutenants. Applying his ability, long experience, and great influence to the tasks in hand, he did much to keep Congress at work. In both chambers the parties were closely divided; in the Senate, indeed, they stood Republicans 48, Democrats 47, and Independent (Wayne Morse of Washington) 1. Small groups on the extreme right and left of the Republican party were willing to defeat all the President's purposes. But Mr. Taft stood by him unflinchingly. The President and Senator had some differences, notably on the foreign aid bill, but in general their friendship met every test. It was a sore blow to the Administration when Taft died in early summer. His own choice for the post of majority leader, Senator Knowland of California, was at once ratified by the Republican policy committee. But while Knowland had energy and ability, he lacked the ripe wisdom, tireless intensity, and astonishing selflessness of the latter-day Taft.

The House, also closely divided, was well controlled by an astute triumvirate: Speaker Joseph W. Martin, Floor Leader Charles A. Halleck, and Party Whip Leslie C. Arends, all highly conservative. Large groups in the House chafed under Mr. Eisenhower's adoption of most of Truman's foreign policy. Special elements disliked his stand on the tariff and foreign trade, labor matters, and farm prices. But members were deterred from any outright revolt by a feeling that the party, so long out in the cold, must be on its good behavior; by recollection that Eisenhower's popularity was the greatest party asset—he had carried 297 Congressional districts (out of 435), while the Republican Congressmen had carried only 221; by fears of what would happen in the 1954 and 1956 elections if they yielded to factionalism; by the disciplinary activities of Taft, Martin, and their associates; and, not least of all, by the President's willingness to make occasional broad concessions to the Congressional leaders when bills were being hammered into shape. Right-wing isolationist intransigency, the force most feared by the Administration, was thus kept under control.

For various reasons, however, the Administration program moved slowly. One was that several great problems, notably labor, agriculture, and foreign trade, proved so complex that special agencies had to be created to study them. Another was that Congress did not feel itself facing any imminent crisis; it had time for discussing, and preferred to develop some policies cautiously. A third reason was that Eisenhower's belief in harmony and teamplay (a rather naïve belief, some observers thought) forbade him to drive Congress, no matter how impatient he became. He was not such a leader as Theodore Roosevelt or Woodrow Wilson and did not wish to be. He himself said in June that he wished to make the government (including the Presidency) "smaller rather than bigger."

The outcome was that Congress performed a few tasks, and on others did nothing. Part of its best achievement was negative. It did not, in the name of hostility to "creeping Socialism," destroy the TVA. It did not slash taxes, abolish foreign aid, drop the Reciprocal Trade Act, or cripple the State Department, as some members had urged it to do. In more constructive fashion, it did pass a small body of sound legislation. Most major measures, however, were left for the new session running into 1954.

Before Congress recessed in midsummer, it had passed a measure converting the old Federal Security Agency into a new Department of Health, Welfare, and Education, the first head of which was Mrs. Oveta Culp Hobby. It had revised the government's overseas information program. It had terminated the Reconstruction Finance Corporation created under President Hoover, and substituted a Small Business Administration authorized to lend as much as $150,000 to a single borrower. It had voted to permit the sale of twenty-eight Federally-owned synthetic rubber plants. It had simplified customs regulations as the President asked. It had enacted a limited control law governing the allocation of scarce materials. It had extended the government's farm price support program.

The President wrung out of Congress, in addition, a one-year extension of the Reciprocal Trade Agreements Act, which ever since Cordell Hull put it on the statute books has been the chief basis of the liberalization of our tariffs. Along with this extension Mr. Eisenhower obtained authority to establish a bipartisan commission to study the whole field of foreign trade, and make recommendations. The Democrats succeeded in blocking a Republican attempt to add a seventh member to the Federal Tariff Commission, a body now equally divided between the two parties. This attempt had been based on complaint that the Commission became stubbornly deadlocked on important matters. As the year progressed it became clear that although the world needs freer international trade, and the huge American excess of exports over imports creates formidable problems, certain industrial interests were making drives for higher duties. The main decisions on foreign trade policy were postponed to 1954.

One important Congressional enactment authorized the President to name a new Commission on Governmental Functions—that is, on Reorganization; and he promptly appointed ex-President Hoover to head it. The authority of this Commission was enlarged over that of the previous body under Hoover. Not only could it recommend steps to improve the efficiency of the government; it could also ferret out "non-essential services, functions, and activities" which should be discarded. But this agency, too, would not report before 1954.

Controversy raged on the foreign aid program, with the President urging generosity and right-wing neo-isolationists crying for economy. Careful observers agreed that a broad Mutual Security program was a continuing necessity; but they also agreed that economic assistance should turn gradually along new lines. American foreign investments, to stimulate the production of raw materials, foodstuffs, and manufactured goods, should be encouraged. Thus poverty would be relieved, barriers would be erected against Communism, and strength would be given to the free world. What was more, substantial American investments overseas might be made to yield adequate profits. At the same time, Point Four ought to be developed. It had initially emphasized the supply of experts to "backward" countries; it should be enlarged into a program for the exchange of experts among many countries, for the education of many corps of technical workers, and for the launching of numerous public works programs. Advocates of Point Four aid declared it had proved so useful that the United States ought not to spend less than a half-billion yearly on it, that the old Marshall Plan type of aid should give way to dynamic new patterns.

President Truman's budget had contained $7.6 billions for mutual foreign aid; President Eisenhower reduced his request to $5.8 billions, declaring that this was the absolute minimum compatible with national safety. Almost all this sum was allocated to defense materials and training ($4 billions), defense payments, chiefly Far Eastern ($1 billion), and special weapons planning ($250 millions); only $560 millions was for technical, economic, and development purposes. The House cut Mr. Eisenhower's request so sharply that he complained it went far below the "honest minimum" required. The Senate proved more reasonable. In the end $4.5 billions of new money, and $2.1 billions in uncommitted balances from previous appropriations now reappropriated, were provided. This made a total of $6.6 billions at the disposal of the Foreign Operations Administration, as the new coordinating agency under Mr. Harold Stassen, which had taken over the work of Mr. Averell Harriman's Mutual Security Agency, was called. It was not as much as the Administration had wanted, but it would do.

Still more controversial was the legislation on off-shore

oil. Congress in 1946 and 1952 had passed bills to grant this oil to the States, but President Truman had vetoed them; now President Eisenhower made the oil bill the first Republican measure in twenty years to go on the statute books. Louisiana, Texas, and California had long laid claim to the petroleum deposits on the continental shelf adjoining their shores. During the Presidential campaign Mr. Eisenhower had decisively supported this claim, thus augmenting his popularity in these three States. Attorney-General Brownell decided that the claim was properly restricted to oil within their "historic boundaries"; that is, within ten and a half miles of the Texas and Florida coastlines, and three miles of the Louisiana shore. The bill as passed therefore awarded control of the remainder of the continental shelf to the nation. Even before the measure was signed, various States were taking steps to contest it in the courts. Thus Attorney-General Tom Gentry of Arkansas invited law officers throughout the Union to join him in a challenge, since it benefited the people of three States "at the expense of the people of all the other States." The legislation called attention to a much more important matter than off-shore oil, the general question of the conservation of the immense natural resources still in United States hands.

In dealing with revenues, taxes, and appropriations, the Administration had to adjust its strong desire for economy to the immutable facts of the world situation. Although the President declared at the beginning of the year that elimination of the deficit would be the first order of business, he was wise enough not to promise it immediately. Instead, he pointed out that the national debt might soon reach the $275 billion limit set by law, hinting that he would have to ask for a higher ceiling. During February the Administration took several steps to reduce costs. It ordered departments not to fill vacancies unless urgently necessary, to postpone all but the most vital construction projects, and to submit suggestions for savings to the Budget Director. Meanwhile, various Congressional leaders were declaring that the proper course was not to fit taxes to the budget, but to cut taxes, and fit the budget to the reduced level of income. Even Senator Taft, in one of his less prudent hours, declared for a straight overall saving of $10 billions in the budget. And Representative Daniel Reed, an up-State New Yorker who by right of seniority became chairman of the Ways and Means Committee, introduced as the first bill in the new Congress a measure lowering personal income taxes on July 1, 1953.

Thus the fundamental issue of tax cuts *vs.* adequate defense was posed. President Eisenhower at his press conference on February 17 reiterated his contention that tax cuts must wait on a close examination of the nation's commitments, especially in the field of defense. While deploring high taxes, the President argued that a balanced budget must be achieved before they were cut down. Two days later the White House invited twenty-five Congressional leaders to a conference intended to teach them the hard facts of life. Among those present to describe the world situation were Allen W. Dulles, head of the Central Intelligence Agency, General Bradley, chairman of the Joint Chiefs of Staff, and Joseph M. Dodge, Director of the Budget Bureau. Still, many Representatives and Senators remained defiant; they wanted tax reductions for their voters. Mr. Daniel Reed was the most defiant of all, and declared war against the Republican leaders when they declined to let his new income tax bill be pushed forward.

In the end the Administration had to bring the country to face a disagreeable fact: that although the military program might be whittled down, it was still impossible to balance the budget or make any appreciable cut in taxation. Mr. Truman had forecast for the coming fiscal year a revenue of $68.7 billions, expenditures of $78.6 billions, and a deficit of $9.9 billions. Mr. Eisenhower, after much effort, revised the figures to read revenue $68.5 billions, expenditures $74.1 billions, and deficit $5.6 billions. The table looked a bit better, but we still had a deficit, and almost unchanged tax laws. Part of the responsibility for this rested upon the fact that the Truman Administration had scheduled defense spending so that it would reach its peak in 1954-55; more of it rested on the state of the world, with Korea and Indo-China grave danger spots.

When early in May the President's long-awaited defense and foreign aid estimates were sent to Congress, it was found that he asked $36 billions of new money for the armed services, or $5.2 billions less than Mr. Truman had estimated. He promised more defense at less cost; a bigger bang for a buck, as Adlai E. Stevenson months later put it. But because of contracts to be fulfilled in the coming year, the saving would amount to about half the sum stated. Involved in the reduction were a slash in army requests, and an ultimate, but not immediate, reduction of the spending authority of the Air Force by about $5 billions. This displeased such Republican leaders as Senator Henry Cabot Lodge, who had asked that the air force be raised to 150 wings (combat groups), and Governor Thomas E. Dewey, who had wanted an army of a hundred divisions. The budget also displeased Senators and Representatives who saw that it forbade real tax-cutting. But later in May Mr. Eisenhower effectively defended his program in his first fireside chat.

We must place defense, the President pleaded, on a level plateau. The defense burden must be one which the nation could bear for an indefinite period. "It cannot consist of sudden, blind responses to a series of fire-alarm emergencies, summoning us to amass forces and material with a speed that is heedless of cost, order, and efficiency." Still another principle involved in the defense program, as time made clear, was heavy reliance on atomic weapons. The Administration was against vast armies and navies; it was for an atomic strength which would deter any aggressor. "We put our emphasis," said Mr. Dulles, "on getting greater strength by less costly methods."

Many Congressmen for a time remained unconvinced that a deficit was unavoidable. "I believe we can convince the Administration," said John Taber, chairman of the

House Appropriations Committee, "that the budget will be balanced." Daniel Reed, after giving up his personal income tax reduction, stuck to his demand that the Excess Profits Tax be allowed to expire on July 1st. But facts were stubborn. The Administration, marshalling them, finally induced Congressional leaders to brush Mr. Reed and his stubborn Ways and Means Committee aside. That body had locked up the bill to renew the Excess Profits Tax and refused to report it for passage. Finally the Speaker and Majority Leader got the House Rules Committee to declare that the House could vote the bill even if the committee took no action—an unprecedented step; and it was passed. Even the relatively small revenue from this tax was important; for a review at the end of the year showed that the deficit for the fiscal year 1954–55 would probably be about $6 billions.

Nothing decisive was done by Congress about the Taft-Hartley Act on labor problems, though both House and Senate committees held long hearings on its possible amendment. Labor spokesmen denounced the law; representatives of management defended it. Although Mr. Eisenhower in his presidential campaign had promised to recommend amendments, the Administration took no stand. This, it later appeared, was because of serious differences in the Cabinet. Secretary of Labor Durkin, who had been head of the plumbers' and steamfitters' union of the American Federation of Labor, had gone to work with various advisers in Congress and the Administration, and hammered out by midsummer a group of nineteen amendments. He understood that the President agreed to these changes, though the White House later denied that any such understanding had been reached. Durkin also believed that Mr. Eisenhower would send a special message to Congress on July 31 urging these changes. On that day Senator Taft died; the message was delayed; and meanwhile articles reached the newspapers describing the suggested amendments. Conservative members of the Administration at once took up arms against the concessions to labor.

This conservative opposition to Secretary Durkin was led, according to press reports, by Secretary of Commerce Weeks, Vice-President Nixon, and several of the White House secretariat. One proposed amendment particularly repugnant to them involved the open-shop. A baker's dozen of States forbid the writing of union-shop contracts, under which workers, if not union members when hired, must join within a stated period. A change sponsored by Mr. Durkin would have overridden these State prohibitions by making federal law effective; union-shop contracts would be permitted everywhere, with a resultant gain in labor union strength. In any event, the split in the Cabinet deterred the President from acting. The message said to be planned for July 31 was suppressed. As a result, before the end of summer Mr. Durkin resigned, and angrily laid his case before the A. F. of L. convention which met in St. Louis on September 21. President Eisenhower, in a letter to that convention, declared that although he thought the Taft-Hartley Act a substantial contribution to sound labor-management relations, he would again ask Congress to cure its defects. The whole matter went over to the year 1954.

In the agricultural domain, as in that of labor, no new action was taken. The Administration's desire to reduce the federal controls over farming remained to be translated into law. Much doubt existed whether any such reduction would be popular. August found the wheat farmers, for the first time in more than a decade, voting on the question of continuing price supports and acreage restrictions. If they gave up the high price props (ninety per cent of parity), they could plant as much wheat as they pleased; if they kept the price aids, they could plant only 62 million acres, or about one-fifth less than the 1953 allotment. By an overwhelming vote, nearly nine to one, the farmers decided for the high price guarantees. They knew that by using fertilizers and intensive cultivation, they could grow nearly as much grain on 62 million acres as on 75 million. This vote was discouraging to Mr. Ezra Benson, Secretary of Agriculture, and others who would like to see the farmers sturdily independent in a free market; but human nature could hardly be expected to accept the drop of about a dollar a bushel (from $2.20 to $1.20) which might have followed a removal of supports.

When Congress recessed in midsummer, comment on its record was not flattering. "It certainly leaves a great deal to be desired," said the moderate New York *Times,* which had supported Eisenhower's election; it is "not impressive," said *Business Week,* which leans to the Republican side. Many observers criticized the President for failing to display the gifts with which the two Roosevelts had driven legislation through Congress. So astute an onlooker as Mr. Walter Lippmann declared that Mr. Eisenhower had taken something like the role of a constitutional monarch, with Senator Taft as prime minister; that despite Taft's devotion and skill the experiment had worked badly; and that Mr. Eisenhower would now have to comprehend the real nature and demands of the Presidency and exercise its due powers. Overseas, such able organs as the London *Economist* thought that the hesitancies of President and Congress had impaired American prestige. This was the view of Mr. Joseph Harsch, Washington correspondent of the *Christian Science Monitor,* who as Congress recessed commented on the "really appalling decline of European confidence in American leadership." Defenders of the Administration, however, declared that such problems as labor, agriculture, foreign trade, and defense were so complex that a full year of study was needed before legislation on them could be launched.

One striking feature of the governmental scene was the continuous attention paid to loyalty problems. The President's declaration in February that cardinal responsibility for excluding the disloyal and dangerous from Federal agencies rested with the Executive was sharply challenged by Senator Joseph R. McCarthy. "No one can push me out of anything," declared McCarthy in reply. "We [the Congressional committee] have complete jurisdiction of the anti-Communist fight. . . . I'm not retiring from the field of exposing Communists." The issue between him and the Administration, growing steadily more explosive, was still unresolved when the year ended.

The Executive was by no means idle. One of President Truman's last acts was an executive order creating a new procedure for testing Americans employed by the United Nations. Under this procedure, which resembled the Federal loyalty program, American workers and applicants for work at the U.N. would be investigated by the United States Government to determine whether any reasonable doubt existed as to their loyalty. Doubtful persons would be given hearings and the right of appeal. The results of the inquiry would be sent to the Secretary-General as a basis for his decisions on personnel. Mr. Trygve Lie's agreement to accept such evidence provoked much criticism in Europe, sharpened Russian antagonism to him, and thus was a factor in his resignation of the Secretary-Generalship. His successor nevertheless cooperated with the screening program.

In the State Department, Secretary Dulles no sooner took office than he demanded a "positive loyalty." Sending a letter to the 15,000 people employed in the Department and the Foreign Service, he declared that the perilous international situation demands "competence, discipline, and positive loyalty to the policies that our President and the Congress may prescribe." He added, however, that loyalty did not call for intellectual dishonesty or distortion in reporting on foreign problems or making recommendations to meet them; officers should give their best opinions, not warp them to please Red-hunters.

Secretary Dulles had reason to be specially sensitive. The State Department had long been under attack by Senators McCarthy, McCarran, Jenner and others as harboring disloyal men. Its staff of experts on the Far East had been violently disrupted. Messrs. John Carter Vincent and Edmund Clubb had been forced to resign, Mr. John Service had been dismissed, and Mr. John Paton Davies had been so violently assailed that his usefulness was greatly impaired. The same McCarthy group turned their fire on Russian experts. When President Eisenhower on March 27 nominated Charles Bohlen, an able and irreproachable career diplomat, as Ambassador to Russia, he was bitterly assailed; the Senate gave him three days of angry debate; and he was not confirmed, 73 to 14, until the full weight of Administration influence was used. Prejudice against George Kennan, former ambassador to Russia and one of the best experts on Soviet affairs, was such that the State Department dared not give him high position. Another Russian expert, Charles Thayer, brother-in-law of Mr. Bohlen, resigned rather than be publicly harassed. Meanwhile, Mr. Scott McLeod, a friend of Senator McCarthy, who was appointed personnel chief of the Department, instituted policies which a group of distinguished former diplomats attacked as doing grave injury to its morale.

When Senator McCarthy as chairman of the Permanent Senate Subcommittee on Investigations sent two agents, Roy M. Cohn and David Schine, to Europe to investigate certain aspects of State Department work, foreign criticism became acrid. These agents looked eagerly for evidence of Communist taints in the information service abroad. Mr. Theodore Kaghan, the deputy director of American information services in Germany, who had made a remarkable record of anti-Communist activity, termed the pair "junketeering gumshoes." For this Senator McCarthy had him called back to Washington, grilled him harshly for a youthful flirtation with Communism, and forced him to resign. This episode, together with the State Department's timidty in defending the overseas libraries from Mr. Carthy's attacks, led Mr. Raymond Swing, who had left a lucrative private career to lend his unusual talents and information to the Voice of America, to resign also. The Voice of America had been doing work of signal usefulness in encouraging the forces of freedom and exposing the evils of Communism. Its enemies nevertheless slashed its appropriation until it was reduced to what Mr. Swing called "relative impotence."

Particularly spectacular was the attack of senatorial Red-hunters upon the library work of the International Information Administration. The object of the libraries scattered over the world, and ably administered by experts, was to give foreign readers a picture of American achievement; to open to foreign students the treasures of American scientific and technological advance; to show other nations the best in American thought and art; and, as ex-Senator William Benton put it, to "stand as evidence of America's literacy and of its intellectual vigor and variety, as weather maps of a free intellectual climate." But Senator McCarthy alleged that the libraries were centers of Communist infection. They contained, he declared, some thirty thousand books by Communist authors. Apparently panic-stricken, the State Department between February and July issued eleven different directives on the books. It accepted Mr. McCarthy's demand that all books by writers ever tainted with Communism be banned. One library took this principle so literally that it threw out Whittaker Chamber's volume of Communist exposure, *Witness*. In various places books were actually burned. President Eisenhower, informed of this when he visited Dartmouth College in mid-June for an honorary degree, exploded against "book-burners"; but he largely destroyed the effect of this ringing utterance by several cautious press statements immediately afterward.

As the year wore on Mr. McCarthy's attacks grew more violent, and his conduct of committee inquiries more abusive. The noun "McCarthyism" gained international currency. Some of its manifestations were regrettable. For example, Scott McLeod delayed approval of Mrs. Mildred McAfee Horton, former head of the women's branch of the Navy and former president of Wellesley, as American representative at a meeting of the U.N. Social Council, until after the meeting had ended. Other manifestations were offensive. Thus a storm arose when Senator McCarthy hired as assistant a man, J. B. Matthews, who had published a statement that "the largest single group supporting the Communist apparatus in the United States is composed of Protestant clergymen"; and Matthews resigned. This episode raised the question whether Mr. McCarthy alone, as head of the Senate subcommittee, could hire and discharge its employees; and three Democratic Senators on the body, contending that he could not, indignantly abandoned it. At no time did Senator McCarthy make a genuinely important disclosure of Communist intrigue. On the contrary, some of his much-advertised cases, as when he attacked William Bundy, son-in-law of Ex-Secretary Acheson, completely blew up.

Seldom in American history has a man provoked more violent feeling for and against his activities than did Senator McCarthy. His admirers contended that, however brutal some of his methods, he had done much to alert Americans to the Communist danger. His opponents answered with Elmer Davis that he had no more done that than a man who runs about town setting off false alarms alerts people to the danger of fire. It was universally agreed abroad that temporarily at least he and his associates had done grave harm to the reputation of the American nation for sanity and justice. When the year ended it was plain that he and the Administration were approaching a complete breach.

Interest in political questions was blunted, no doubt, by the remarkable prosperity of the country. During 1953 the American economy maintained in most respects an astonishing vigor. Production reached its greatest volume in history, with goods and services valued at $367 billions.

Employment stood at the high average figure of 63,400,-
000. The flow of personal income exceeded that of any
previous year. More than a million new farm houses were
built, while non-residential construction fell but slightly
below previous records. Business spent more for plant and
equipment than ever before.

To be sure, the closing months of 1953 witnessed a
decline of economic activity. In a year-end statement,
Secretary of Commerce Weeks summarized the situation: "During the first half of the year, business activity
was accelerating too fast to be maintained indefinitely;
hence in the second half there has been some easing off
in the production peaks reached earlier. Most of the reduction has been associated with the elimination of an
exceptionally fast rate of inventory growth. Notwith-
standing the cutback in inventory accumulation, the national production in the final quarter of the year was
above the closing period of 1952." As the decline continued, an ingenious term was invented by businessmen who
wished to avoid the ominous word recession; it was a
"rolling readjustment."

The drop in business was reflected in various spheres.
Between October and November, factory employment
fell 300,000 instead of the normal 50,000. By December
20 the number of unemployed persons covered by unemployment insurance rose to 3.9 per cent of the insured
work force, compared with 2.1 per cent in the first week
of October. Railroad car-loadings were down nearly 10
per cent in November as compared with those a year

earlier, so that some railroads had to order fairly heavy layoffs of workmen. Yet, viewed in perspective, the declines were small; they had to be related to the fact that the level of economic activity in 1953 was the highest in our history. This was a happy fact not only for America but for the world. A real recession might not hurt the United States much, but would give Western Europe a painful shock.

As it was, an unprecedented volume of foreign trade indicated that the economic health of the western nations was sound. American exports reached the record figure of $16.25 billions, and our imports another record figure of $11.1 billions. Commercial exports, to be sure, continued the downward trend of the previous year, dropping about $1 billion from 1952, and about $2 billions from 1951. Military aid shipments, however, were roughly twice those of 1952, exceeding $4 billions, and more than made up the difference. The United States was now really "delivering the arms." The export of tanks, other vehicles, guns, and airplanes, which had been a mere trickle until the middle of 1952, was becoming a river. On the other side of the ledger, "offshore procurement," or the purchase by the United States of certain weapons in Europe, was making substantial contributions of dollars to Britain, France, and other nations.

The steel industry, employed largely in making arms, pushed its production up to 111,500,000 tons, or six per cent more than in its previous best year. This was in spite of the fact that steel output at the end of 1953 had fallen to less than three quarters of capacity. The automobile industry turned out 7,300,000 cars, trucks, and buses, a figure previously exceeded but once. Defense orders accounted for about one-fifth of the business. The revenues of American railroads meanwhile reached a new high level. Gross earnings came to about $11.7 billions, slightly over those of the previous year. The net earnings at the end of the year were estimated at $870 millions, or about $45 millions more than in 1952. But the railroads were making capital improvements on an impressive scale. Their expenditures for this purpose came to more than $1.3 billions, or about as much as a year earlier. For the seven years ending with 1952, the carriers could boast they had spent more than $7.8 billions on such improvements.

The general prosperity of the railroads was the more remarkable in that they suffered increasingly from the competition of inter-city trucking lines, whose tonnage reached its highest point in 1953. More efficient trucks were being built at the rate of a million a year; they were charging rates generally below those of the railroads; and for short hauls in particular they were more and more formidable competitors. Air lines were meanwhile taking a large part of railroad passenger traffic.

The industrial scene in 1953 was not marred by any major strikes. Labor was apparently resting on its recent gains, content with the general prosperity though somewhat concerned over its future prospects. Neither the American Federation of Labor nor the Congress of Industrial Organizations showed much friendliness toward the Administration. When Vice-President Nixon addressed the September convention of the A. F. of L. in St. Louis, he remarked that "there apparently was" a misunderstanding between Martin Durkin and President Eisenhower; and at this, jeering laughter rippled over the hall. At the C.I.O. convention in November, President Walter Reuther flatly charged the Administration with converting the government into a "subordinate ally of big business." This utterance sprang from the continuing bitterness of many unions over the Taft-Hartley Act. When Durkin's successor, Secretary of Labor Mitchell, asked the C.I.O. gathering to be realistic about the law, to abandon the clamor for repeal, and thus pave the way for the amendment of those sections that were "really dangerous to labor," he met with little sympathy. The convention proceeded to vote unanimously for outright repeal of the Act.

The most important development of the year in labor affairs was the significant progress toward a merger of the A. F. of L. and the C.I.O. The election of new heads in place of those oldtime rivals, William Green and Philip Murray, has lessened the jealousy between the two organizations. Recent changes in the economy have largely erased the old differences between craft unions and mass-industry unions, so that questions of structure are no longer an important obstacle to union. The A. F. of L. meat-cutters and C.I.O. packing-house workers find that they have good reasons for a merger; so do the A. F. of L. electrical employees and the C.I.O. utility hands. Some

C.I.O. unions, for factional reasons, have shown a disposition to go back into the A. F. of L. fold. It is obvious that a merger would add to the national influence of labor. Because of these considerations, the executive boards of both organizations in August approved an agreement to stop raiding each other. Next month the national A. F. of L. convention voted to end jurisdictional contests with C.I.O. unions. Altogether, hopes were bright for the emergence in the next year or two of one great American labor body.

Although labor pushed hourly wage rates slightly higher during the year, declining industrial activity late in the year reduced working schedules, and so made pay envelopes thinner. Feeling real anxiety over part-time work and layoffs, labor leaders began to talk more earnestly of a drive for guaranteed annual wages. Two big unions in the C.I.O., the Electrical Workers' Union and the United Steelworkers, served notice that they would shortly seek to gain such a guarantee.

If labor was anxious about its future rewards, the farmers were still more worried. When Mr. Eisenhower was inaugurated, farm prices had been slipping for some time. Cattlemen, the chief sufferers, were asking the Department of Agriculture to give them aid by emergency loans. But Secretary Benson, speaking to the Central Livestock Association, refused to take any such action. Lower prices, he said, would stabilize the market, and the decline would be checked by a return to orderly competition. While the Administration would continue price supports at ninety per cent of parity under the existing law, he declared that supports ought to be regarded as disaster insurance, and that they became dangerous when they produced huge unsalable surpluses. This speech evoked angry repercussions among stockmen and farmers. Parity payments at ninety per cent continued through the year, and large government-purchasing operations were maintained. Butter, for example, was bought at the rate of one to two million pounds a day and put in cold storage, while consumers ate more and more oleomargarine. More wheat was stored under government loans than ever before, and corn surpluses came close to a record high point.

Yet despite parity payments and Federal buying, farm prices continued to fall. By the middle of the year, they were 16 per cent lower than they had been two years before. At the same time, the farmer's costs for labor, fertilizers, and machinery went up. Agricultural production in other nations was increasing, and wheat exports therefore fell. The farmer began to consider himself a badly abused man. To reassure him, President Eisenhower more than once called attention to the exhaustive study of the farm problem under way by experts, the Agricultural Department, and Congress. Secretary Benson, in a September speech at Augusta, Wisconsin, asserted that the President and he were "determined to do all within our power to protect and improve the living standard of the farm people." Meanwhile, the Department did everything it could to move more farm products into the hands of users. School lunch programs were developed; allot-

ments were made for famine relief overseas. Still, however, the farmers complained. A Democratic victory in
the fall in the Ninth Wisconsin Congressional District
was regarded as an indication of their discontent. They
were not merely being hurt; they feared that the future
would hurt them more.

For the country in general, the farm year could be
called poor. Prices had fallen about 10 per cent from 1952
levels; operating charges had gone up; and the weather
had been unfavorable. Large areas of the Southwest in
particular, from Texas and Oklahoma to Nebraska and
Missouri, had been parched brown by drought. While
this was happening, consumers grumbled over the high
cost of food, and much of the government-purchased
grain and butter was deteriorating badly in storage. The
farm problem, as far as ever from a permanent solution,
had to be laid on the doorstep of 1954.

When we turn from domestic to foreign affairs, we
meet one great achievement: the stoppage of the Korean
War. All the facts considered, this was probably the
brightest single event of the year. One of the cruellest,
most wearisome, and most futile conflicts in all human
history was halted, and perhaps ended. Yet the truce produced singularly little rejoicing in America or in any
other country involved. One reason was that the war was
sadly indecisive; it had settled nothing but the great fact
that the free nations would resist Communist aggression.
The goal of Korean unity, for example, was tacitly abandoned. Everyone knew that Red aggression continued in

Indo-China. Another reason was that a weary, difficult, and perhaps futile negotiation would have to follow the unhappy war.

President Eisenhower had assured voters in November that he would halt the war, and stiff measures by Eisenhower and Dulles unquestionably contributed much to that end. Early in the year they lifted the American naval patrol which had sealed off the Chinese Nationalists on Formosa from the mainland. At the same time Secretary Dulles, visiting India, let Prime Minister Nehru know that rather than see the war continue indefinitely in a bloody deadlock, the United States would widen it by bombing Chinese supply lines. These steps unquestionably produced alarm in Peiping. Already the Chinese people were weary of the heavy costs of the struggle in blood and material. When the U.N. Assembly reconvened in New York in February, Henry Cabot Lodge, head of the American delegation, placed the blame for the maintenance of the conflict squarely on Russia. "The rulers of the Soviet Union," he declared, "can stop the war whenever they want to." The death of Stalin, and the ensuing struggle for power between Malenkov and Beria, made it important for the Kremlin to gain a respite from external difficulties. By March, with both China and Russia evincing a new and more conciliatory temper, effective action became possible.

The question whether prisoners should be forcibly returned to their own countries or allowed, if they wished, to seek asylum elsewhere, had been the great stumbling block. As recently as December the Communists had rejected India's compromise proposal in the General Assembly calling for the transfer of obstinate prisoners to a neutral commission. But prospects for a truce brightened in April when the Chinese foreign minister sent a message to the U.N. declaring: "[We] are prepared to take steps to eliminate the differences on [the entire question of prisoners] so as to bring about an armistice in Korea. . . . [We] propose that both parties repatriate immediately after cessation of hostilities all those prisoners of war in their custody who insist upon repatriation, and hand over the remaining prisoners of war to a neutral state so as to ensure a just solution." Negotiations at Panmunjom in Korea were at once resumed. Their first fruit was an agreement for the exchange of sick and wounded prisoners to begin not later than April 21. The mutilated, scarecrow Americans thus brought out of Communist hospitals had horrifying tales of brutality and massacre to tell, which sent a wave of anger across the United States; but the Panmunjom talks went on.

And at last a truce was effected. For a time in May and June the Chinese and North Korean representatives insisted on excessive demands. For a time, too, President Syngman Rhee of South Korea (a graduate of two American universities, a patriotic nation-builder, and a brave fighter, but a most stubborn old man) offered serious impediments; he would be satisfied with nothing less than the unity of all Korea under his government. Rhee was responsible for the "escape" in June of about 20,000

North Korean prisoners who wished to join the South. He declared that he would battle on alone, if necessary, for national unity. But finally on July 27 signatures were set to an armistice. Mr. Dulles immediately afterwards flew to Korea to talk with Mr. Rhee. Before leaving he made it plain that he had no intention of trading Communist China's admission to the U.N. for Korean unification or any other object.

The terms of the truce provided that troops should be withdrawn from a 2.5-mile zone along the front lines; that a repatriation commission composed of representatives of Switzerland, Sweden, Czechoslovakia, Poland, and India take charge of prisoner exchange; that prisoners willing to return home be repatriated at once; and that unwilling prisoners be placed in a special camp near Panmunjom for three months while agents of their own nations offered them "explanations" and promises. At the beginning of August the exchange of voluntary repatriates began and was concluded a month later. But the great difficulty was the disposition of about 48,000 North Koreans and Chinese who refused to go back to their own lands. A complicated machinery had to be established to deal with them. More than 4,000 Indian custodial troops arrived to guard their camp. During the "explanations" which followed, a small number of these prisoners consented to return home. But the great majority stood firm. In the end, the North Korean prisoners mingled with the South Korean population, while most of the Chinese were recruited into Chiang Kai-shek's Nationalist army on Formosa. A handful of Americans and one Briton elected to stay under the Communist banner. All in all, the desertion of so many former Communist soldiers represented a heavy blow to Red prestige.

Although one section of the truce agreement called for a political conference to begin (if possible) within ninety days, few expected such a conference to become an early reality. Throughout the year it remained a mirage. Agreement had to be reached on the participants, and on the scope of the conference; and this proved impossible. The United States wished a two-sided gathering: America, and the other U.N. countries involved in the war, on one side; North Korea, Communist China, and Russia (in some associate capacity) on the other. The Communists wished a round-table conference, with Russia participating as a neutral—a demand against which Washington stood adamant. British opinion urged the inclusion of India, another suggestion unwelcome to the United States. As for the agenda, the vital question was whether the proposed conference should deal solely with Korean problems, or should range afield to take up Red China's admission to the U.N., the relations between Communist China and Nationalist China, and the Indo-Chinese War.

It is unnecessary to follow in detail the tortuous controversy on these issues. At the end of August the General Assembly, under American pressure, declared that the conference should be two-sided, its participants limited to "belligerents" in the Korean War. South Korea and any or all of the sixteen members of the U.N. fighting against the Communists should be admitted on one side; North Korea and Red China on the other side might invite Russia if they wished. The Soviet Union at once called the Chinese and North Korean spokesmen to a conference in the Kremlin. It was made clear that nothing less than a round-table conference, with Russia seated as a neutral, would satisfy the Communist nations. Meanwhile, Prime Minister Nehru at Delhi bitterly attacked the U.N. plan for debarring all neutrals, including India. In the first week of November, the Russian Government informed the American ambassador: "The position the United States has taken in rejecting the participation of neutral countries in the Korean conference, makes the participation of the U.S.S.R. impossible." The Communists, indeed, were insisting that no fewer than five pro-Soviet "neutrals" be invited to the gathering. Utter deadlock had been reached.

At Panmunjom, where an American envoy, Arthur H. Dean, was treating with Communist representatives, tempers grew heated. In the U.N. General Assembly also the debate grew acrimonious. Early in December the Communists in the U.N. proposed that the peace conference meet at New Delhi on December 28, with Russia and four Asiatic countries participating as neutrals. The U.N. made a counter-proposal for a conference in Geneva, with Russia seated beside Communist China and North Korea. Then the inevitable happened. Communist spokesmen at Panmunjom insulted the United States, Arthur H. Dean withdrew pending an apology, and all negotiations ceased. The world had a truce, but it had no peace.

As this story indicates, relations with Russia improved but slightly during the year. The arms race continued; the main issues in Korea, Indo-China, Germany, and Austria remained unsettled. Yet a slight amelioration of the atmosphere did take place. The disappearance of Stalin, whose senility had taken the form of implacable hostility to the United States, was one factor in this; the demand of the Russian people for an improvement in living standards was another; a spasmodic revolt in East Germany in June, showing the Russians that they must not push their satellite peoples too far, was a third. A fourth element was the growing comprehension that war has now become too horrible to be tolerated. When Moscow announced late in August that it had exploded "one of a variety of hydrogen bombs," it was plain that a new conflict would really wreck civilization.

The new dictator, Malenkov, declared in March, with pointed reference to the United States, that international disputes should be peacefully settled. He told the Supreme Soviet: "There is not one disputed or undecided question that cannot be decided by peaceful means on the basis of mutual understanding between interested countries. This is our attitude toward all states, among them the United States of America." Just how much or little this meant nobody could tell. Prime Minister Churchill was optimistic. Let us be patient, he told Britons: "In my opinion, no one can measure the extent or purpose of the change that has become apparent in the Soviet mood, or even perhaps in their policy."

But President Eisenhower, replying to Moscow in a

speech in Washington on April 17, called for substantial
evidence of fairness and good will. "There can be no persuasion but by deeds," he said. What deeds? He called
for an armistice in Korea; for an end to Communist attacks upon the security of Indo-China and Malaysia; for
the unification of Germany through free elections; for a
speedy treaty with Austria; and for the restoration of full
self-government in the lands of Eastern Europe. Progress
in all these areas should be accompanied by a reduction
of armaments. He proposed a limitation of resources devoted to military purposes, a reduction of all forces, international control of atomic energy, and a prohibition of
atomic weapons, with proper international inspection.
"This Government," he promised, "is ready to ask its
people to join with all other nations in devoting a substantial percentage of any savings achieved by real disarmament . . . to develop the undeveloped areas of the world,
to stimulate profitable and fair world trade, to assist all
peoples." He held out to peaceful folk the vision of "a
golden age of freedom and peace."

The revolt of the East German workers on June 17,
which electrified the world, was at once a force for and
against peace. On the one hand it showed the Kremlin,
and its tools in the satellite states, that a volcano yawned
under their feet, and that if they provoked war it might
blow up. On the other hand it convinced the Soviet leaders that free elections in Germany and Austria would go
overwhelmingly against Communism, and so hardened
their hearts against concessions. Mr. Churchill had for
some time been urging a meeting of the great Powers.

Even if it accomplished nothing else, it would show just what possibilities of an accommodation existed. On October 18, therefore, the United States, Great Britain, and France proposed that their foreign ministers hold an early meeting with Mr. Molotov. Their invitation, specifying Germany as the chief topic, offered Russia an opportunity to discuss any aspect of the German question which it might wish to present.

The Soviet reply suggested that, in view of the East German uprising, Moscow was not ready to relax its crushing grip on Eastern Europe. A note, the first week in November, named as prerequisites to a successful conference a number of demands long since rejected by the West, including the abolition of American military bases in Europe, and the participation of Communist China in the gathering. On Germany the Soviet position was enigmatic. As quickly as possible, declared Moscow, the Powers should solve "the problems of a peace treaty with Germany and the reëstablishment of a German state on democratic and peace-loving principles." The Allied nations wished to hold free elections in all Germany, preparatory to setting up an all-German government. Russia, however, was known to insist on creating an all-German government first, the Communists of East Germany holding equal power with the people of West Germany; and then holding elections which would not be at all free. Negotiations for a Four Power meeting went forward, but little hope for a real advance toward peace was attached to them.

President Eisenhower, however, refused to lose the

initiative in the peace movement. Speaking to the United Nations in December, he offered the first important new approach to the atomic problem in seven years: a plan for a world pool of fissionable materials to develop the peaceful uses of atomic energy. He proposed that the governments principally involved, "to the extent permitted by ordinary prudence," should contribute normal uranium and fissionable metal to a joint stockpile administered by the U.N. The agency managing this stockpile should see to it that it was employed for advances in medicine, agriculture, and engineering, and to provide abundant electrical energy in the power-starved areas of the globe. Though the response in Moscow was at first chilly, Molotov soon promised to give serious attention to the proposal. And on December 19, the Soviet Union issued an official communiqué expressing its readiness to take part in discussions concerning an international atomic pool.

Meanwhile, the year 1953 had seen but slow progress made in the economic and defensive integration of Western Europe. The United States was anxious to have the Europe Defense Community Treaty, and the supplementary German Contractual Agreement, which had been signed in May, 1952, pushed forward. Unfortunately, early in 1953, the friendly French foreign minister, Robert Schuman, lost his post, and the new Premier, René Mayer, declared that he would seek a revision of the pending treaties. In West Germany, Chancellor Konrad Adenauer also wished a revision. Large elements in France feared that under E.D.C. Germany would establish her supremacy on the Continent. Many Germans feared that their nation would lose its power of unilateral action. While E.D.C. remained thus caught in a log-jam, the American Government began to display distinct irritation.

The Eisenhower Administration was ready to use what pressure it could. Secretary Dulles, during the last week in January, delivered a frank warning. The United States had made a big investment in Western Europe on the theory that unity would be achieved there, he said. If, however, disunity prevailed, and if France, Germany, and Britain went their separate ways, "then certainly it would be necessary to give a little re-thinking to America's own foreign policy in relation to Western Europe." This statement gave France a distinct jar. Some groups there resented the implied threat. Great Britain took it in better temper—though the British, as part of a world-wide Commonwealth of Nations, had always indicated that they could give E.D.C. nothing more than collaboration and coöperation. When Mr. Dulles and Mr. Harold Stassen made a fact-finding tour of European capitals in February, they renewed the American pressure. Soon afterward, the ministers of the six E.D.C. nations met in Rome to discuss a series of revisions in the proposed treaty, offered by France. These looked mainly toward a protection of France's position vis-a-vis Germany. Though no agreement was reached on these revisions, the conferring ministers did decide to work simultaneously for both revision and ratification.

But despite American pressure and European conferences, little was accomplished. In March the lower house
in Western Germany approved the E.D.C. treaty and
Contractual Agreement; but the upper chamber hung
back. Chancellor Adenauer, visiting the United States in
April, joined President Eisenhower and Secretary Dulles
in a statement declaring that nothing must beguile the
Allies to "diminish their efforts to increase unity and common strength." In San Francisco, the Chancellor made
a formal promise that no matter what bribes Russia might
offer, West Germany would never give up her place in
the European Defense Community. He returned home
to fight a great election battle in which E.D.C. was a
pivotal issue. His sweeping victory in September was
therefore a decisive victory for the idea of West European
unity. At the same time, the American Government
promised France increased military aid, which it was
hoped would encourage the French to act favorably on
E.D.C.

Secretary Dulles, appearing at the NATO Council
meeting in Paris in December, renewed the application
of American pressure. Unless France ratified the treaty,
he repeated, the United States would have to modify its
policy in relation to Western Europe. But the year ended
with France still undecided. An American agreement
with Spain on the "aid-for-bases" principle had not
pleased French labor, distrustful of Franco. The chief obstacles to the success of E.D.C., however, remained French
distrust and jealousy of Germany, and the weakness of

the French and Italian Governments. The United States was hopeful of favorable action, but it would take time.

Some of the minor happenings of the year require brief comment. A running debate in and out of Congress took place on the proposed Bricker amendment to the Constitution, which was regarded by its friends as a statesman-like effort to save the country from abuses of the Presidential treaty-making power, and by its foes as a serious invasion of the power of the Executive, and a probable source of endless confusion. The vital features of the amendment were two. It forbade use of the treaty power to permit any foreign power or international organization to control or adjudicate the rights of citizens of the United States within the country, or any other matter within the domestic jurisdiction of the United States. It further declared: "A treaty shall be effective as internal law in the United States only through the enactment of appropriate legislation by the Congress." The first of these prohibitions would estop international control of atomic power in the United States; it would perhaps even prevent participation in the work of the International Court of Justice. The second would prevent a treaty from having any internal force until it was approved by the President, two-thirds of the Senate, a majority vote of the House, and a majority vote of the Senate—a very cumbrous procedure indeed.

The amendment had strong support in certain quarters. It was popular among isolationist groups. It was favored in the South by elements which feared that

United Nations action might trench upon the sensitive race question. No action was taken on it during the year. But feeling grew that, in the words of the New York Bar Association, the amendment would "place so many impediments upon the conduct of foreign affairs as to constitute a grave threat to our chances of survival in the modern world."

Another issue which attracted much attention was that of public *vs.* private development of hydro-electric power. This was dramatized by a statement of Mr. Eisenhower's at a press conference sharply criticizing the TVA. The Administration made it clear that it was not favorable to initiating great new projects like the Bonneville Dam and the Grand Coulée undertaking. When Claude Wickard, head of the Rural Electrification Administration, was forced to resign with two years of his term still to run, it was assumed that the President meant on that front also to reduce the part played by the government in generating and distributing electricity. The Federal Power Commission, in the spring, began hearings on an application of the Idaho Power Company to build three dams on the Snake River. If this application was granted, it would frustrate a huge Federal power project which the Interior Department had planned during the Truman Administration. The new Secretary of the Interior, Mr. McKay, evinced marked hostility to what conservatives term "Federal empire-building" in the hydro-electric field. Much could be said on both sides of the issue. The year ended with no decision made on the key question whether Idaho should have three moderate-sized dams built by the Idaho Power Company, or one vast dam on Hells Canyon built by the national government.

Television continued its steady progress throughout the year. More and more telecasting stations were opened, and more and more homes installed receiving sets. Hard hit by this competition (and perhaps also by the widening use of automobiles), the motion picture industry turned desperately to three-dimensional projection to help recapture its audiences. In various forms—Natural Vision, Cinerama, and others—the three-dimensional movie proved to have decided popular appeal. Though the cost of installation was too heavy for small theatres, larger houses used the innovation effectively. Book-publishers also complained of the inroads made on their business by television, and they also turned to new devices. The various series of paper-bound books enjoyed a rising vogue. A number of publishers brought out cloth-bound and paper-bound editions of books almost if not quite simultaneously. Book-clubs meanwhile continued to multiply, and to reach out to more specialized clienteles in various fields of interest.

The most important elections of this off-year, those in New Jersey and New York City, resulted in Democratic victories. In New Jersey the chief issues between Robert L. Troast, the Republican candidate for governor, and Robert B. Meyner, his Democratic opponent, were the crime and political corruption in two counties controlled by Republicans, Atlantic and Bergen. Meyner achieved

237

a smashing plurality of 154,000, the first gubernatorial victory for the Democrats since 1940. In New York city the limp inefficiency and bungling of the Impelleteri Administration had disgusted intelligent citizens. From a three-cornered contest Robert F. Wagner, Jr., supported by Democratic regulars, emerged as the decisive winner. He found much to change. The city's finances were in deplorable shape; the schools were being neglected; the police and fire departments needed strengthening. The work of cleaning up the New York docks, a veritable jungle full of crime and extortion, needed to be pressed by the combined efforts of the mayor, the governors of New York and New Jersey, and the American Federation of Labor, which had taken the International Longshoremen's Association in hand for disciplining. Mr. Wagner initiated his labors, as the year ended, by making several admirable appointments, among them that of Dr. Luther Gulick as City Administrator.

Altogether, 1953 was a year of beginnings rather than of endings. The United States turned to a new chapter under President Eisenhower; Russia turned to what might be a happier era under Malenkov. No great question before the country or the world was settled. But a truce, at least, had been won in the Far East, and in Europe and America the forces of freedom continued to gain in strength.

CHAPTER VI

THE RECORD OF 1954

Although the year 1954 was devoid of spectacular occurrences in American affairs, and saw the international deadlock between East and West continue unbroken, the twelve months were filled with interesting events. At home the Eisenhower Administration, getting into its stride, enacted part of the program on which the President had set his heart. The Congressional and State elections proved more exciting than citizens had anticipated. In foreign affairs, the year was occupied by efforts to perfect the union of free nations against Communist aggression, and to augment their strength. To an increasing degree, Asia is now the primary arena of conflict and the region which gives Western civilization its chief anxieties. Open fighting ceased in Indo-China in mid-summer, but guerrilla warfare there continued to the end of the year; and at various points on the borders of China—Korea, Vietnam, Hong-Kong, the islands between Formosa and the mainland—the truce between East and West seemed precarious. The United States of necessity had to remain the active leader of the free nations. While Malenkov's seat in Russia as the successor of Stalin remained insecure, and an obscure struggle for power went on in that country, it was necessary to maintain a vigilant attitude. Fortunately, the United States and other free nations remained prosperous, and made continuing advances in social welfare and economic vigor.

The happiest part of our story deals with the domestic scene; the more anxious portion concerns international relations.

President Eisenhower in a broadcast at the beginning of the year promised a "dynamic and progressive" program by himself and Congress. To those citizens who were dissatisfied with the slender legislative achievements of his first twelve months he could say that the Administration had been giving the major problems—labor, agriculture, taxation, conservation, defense—elaborate study and laying the groundwork for future action. His broadcast struck some notes reminiscent of New Deal days. Thus he spoke of a government battle against slums, poor schools, and bad roads, against unemployment, ill health, and dependency in old age. It was clear that two fundamental policies would be continued: first, the administration would push hard for reduced spending and an ultimate balance of the budget; second, it would stand for a steady relaxation of controls over economic action.

With the second session of the 83rd Congress, lasting 227 days, President Eisenhower's relations were fairly amicable. He dealt with its members more firmly than in the first session, and by midsummer was prodding the leaders robustly. He was abandoning what Theodore Roosevelt had called the Buchanan-Harrison-Taft theory of the Presidency in favor of the Jackson-Lincoln-Roosevelt theory; instead of proposing measures and waiting, he was proposing and leading. His popularity with the country gave that leadership great weight. When opponents on Capital Hill were stubborn, he talked to them on the telephone, or had Sherman Adams summon them to the White House. Since many of his measures, such as foreign aid and housing assistance, had a New Deal or Fair Deal flavor, he usually commanded a solid bloc of Democratic votes. In the end, President Eisenhower was credited with fifty-three victories and only eleven failures. He could fairly claim that he had given the country some "dynamic" legislation.

The most important measure passed, by all odds, was the basic revision of the entire Federal tax structure, the first complete overhaul in seventy-five years. "This new law," wrote George M. Humphrey, Secretary of the Treasury, "will release new energies throughtout our economic system, working quietly but steadily to create new enterprises, more and better jobs, new productive efficiencies, larger payrolls, and a healthily rising standard of living." One provision reduced the double taxation of dividend income, making the first fifty dollars of dividends free from personal income tax, and allowing, within limits, a tax credit of four per cent of the dividend income above that figure. A still more noteworthy change permitted greater and more flexible tax allowances for depreciation. Industries installing new machinery in plants are allowed to write off a major part of the cost in the early years of the machine's life; more than two-thirds of the cost in the first five years of equipment with an estimated ten years' usefulness. This will encourage the scrapping of obsolescent equipment, permit purchase of new tools through short-term financing, and reduce the risks of business. Still other features of the new law give industries (particularly small units) more liberal treatment for research expenditures, and larger rewards for the development of successful inventions. In numerous minor ways the tax burden has been more equitably adjusted.

Next in importance was what President Eisenhower called the "great and sweeping victory" for flexible price supports for basic agricultural products. In carrying through this partial repeal of high rigid supports the President and his Secretary of Agriculture, Ezra Taft Benson, showed real courage. Mr. Benson had entered office declaring that his main purpose would be "to strengthen the individual integrity, freedom, and the very moral fibre of each citizen." He soon showed that this did not mean asking for 100 per cent parity payments; it meant "a vigorous re-emphasis on the principles, benefits, and values of private competitive enterprise." The Administration made it clear that it would not scale down price-supports drastically, but act in such fashion as to make the readjustment easy. It was significant that the bipartisan farm bloc split on the new policy. Apparently most of the farm population, uneasily aware of the wide gap between world market prices and government-support prices, were ready to accept the change as realistic and healthy.

Under the Agricultural Act of 1948 (which now became effective through refusal of new legislation) price supports vary from 75 to 90 per cent of parity for the so-called "basics" (cotton, wheat, corn, rice, tobacco, peanuts). Government action and the volume of supply determine the exact level. One main object of the Administration is to reduce the costly and unwieldy crop surpluses, the mere care of which has become very expensive. Another object is to encourage the farmers to prize a greater freedom, for in the long run heavy supports would mean heavy controls.

In the attack on slums, President Eisenhower got but part of what he asked. He had requested authority for constructing 140,000 housing units, over four years, for low-income families. This would have been a generous extension of the postwar program begun in 1949 with the active support of Senator Robert Taft. But strong opposition developed among Republicans in the House. The national government now pays about $40,000,000 yearly to help subsidize earlier housing projects which shelter about a million people, and many in Congress thought this enough. In the end, the two houses authorized a one-year program of 35,000 units. If that is repeated for three years, the President's goal will be attained, but the future is uncertain.

Both parties, by heavy majorities, supported the President's program for ex-"coverage" and increased benefits in social security. Old age insurance is now given to some ten million persons not previously benefited, including farm operators and (within certain limitations) clergymen. In the welfare field, Congress also passed an Administration health bill. It struck out, however, President Eisenhower's proposal for "a limited Government reinsurance service" which would "permit the private and non-profit insurance companies to offer broader protection to more of the many families who want and should have it." The President's plan was for application to health insurance of the principle of the Federal Deposit Insurance Corporation protection of bank deposits. But the American Medical Association, always suspicious of government intrusion into the medical field, opposed the undertaking.

One of the last-minute measures of Congress was a Communist Control Act which the Democrats, stung by accusations of indifference to Communist activities, rushed forward, and which Republicans dared not oppose. Its full meaning was far from clear. President Eisenhower, in signing it, declared it would "require careful study" to make sure that it did not interfere with existing laws against Communist activity and otherwise do more harm than good. Its main intent was to strip the Communist Party of all legal rights, and to apply previous anti-subversive laws in specific terms to all Communists. Party members are put under severe penalties if they do not register under the Internal Security Act already on the statute books, and Communist controlled unions are deprived of all bargaining privileges. Public opinion regarded the new law as primarily a piece of politics.

Once more Congress failed to admit either Hawaii or

Alaska to Statehood. The House passed a bill permitting Hawaii to enter the Union, but when the Senate amended it to include Alaska, it failed. The question whether these Territories are ready for admission is entangled with political considerations, for it is generally assumed that Hawaii would elect two Republicans to the Senate, Alaska two Democrats. Nor did Congress take any significant action on labor. Neither party is anxious to deal with wholesale revision of the Taft-Hartley Act, and labor itself had reasons for waiting. But Congress did take the action requested by Mr. Eisenhower for giving private enterprise (and also public power agencies) a larger share in the work of developing atomic energy. And inasmuch as the national deficit continues, Congress raised the national debt limit from $275 billions to $281 billions, a sum too large for most Americans to comprehend.

Altogether, the Administration could lay claim to genuine progress in constructive legislation under its middle-of-the-road policy. Naturally that policy did not please either aggressive radicals or stubborn conservatives; to each group it seemed to get in the way of their own road traffic. Naturally, also, the policy meant avoidance of such explosive issues as the amendment of the McCarran-Walter Immigration Act, which badly needs amendment. But it could be said that the President achieved a genuine partnership with a bipartisan majority of Congress. He himself wisely did his utmost to rise above party, and to seem a President of the whole country. He was aided by the manifest split in both party organizations—in Republican ranks between internationalists and neo-isolationists, and in Democratic ranks between Northern liberals and Southern conservatives.

No action was taken during the year on any of the various proposals for greater Federal Aid to education. Senator Lister Hill offered a bill providing that all petroleum revenues received by the national government on lands of the outer continental shelf should be given to the States for primary, secondary, and higher tuition. Another bill, introduced by Senator Cooper of Kentucky, permitted emergency assistance to the States for the erection of public schools. Neither came to a vote.

But Commissioner of Education S. M. Brownell presented a report during the year which showed that the task of education is steadily growing in magnitude and complexity. The country in 1954 had about 27,740,000 pupils in elementary schools, all but 3,500,000 of them in public systems. It had about 7,425,000 youths in secondary schools, of whom 775,000 were in private and parochial institutions. The enrollment has now risen each year for a decade. Mr. Brownell credited the country as a whole with spectacular accomplishments in meeting critical shortages of classrooms and teachers during the difficult war and postwar period. But high peaks of school and college enrollment lie ahead. By 1959–60 approximately 46,000,000 persons will be enrolled in our various educational institutions from kindergarten to the end of college. The "bulge" in population is just striking the high schools and before long will affect the universities.

Wide World Photos

"Mr. Republican and Mr. President Elect" just after Eisenhower had won the Republican nomination for President. One year later Taft died of cancer and the President said: "I have lost a wise counselor and valued friend." Below, left to right, Walter Robertson, Assistant Secretary of State, John Foster Dulles, Syngman Rhee, and Henry Cabot Lodge during a happy moment at Rhee's residence in Seoul.

PRESIDENT EISENHOWER DELIVERING HIS STATE OF THE UNION MESSAGE TO A JOINT SESSION OF CONGRESS. FIRST REPUBLI-

ted States Department of Ag-
lture Dairy Products Grader
cks part of butter stocks pur-
sed under the price support
gram.

S. D. A. Photograph by Forsythe

ndard Oil Company (N. J.) Photograph

Cattle on a ranch in Wyoming. Grand Tetons in the background.

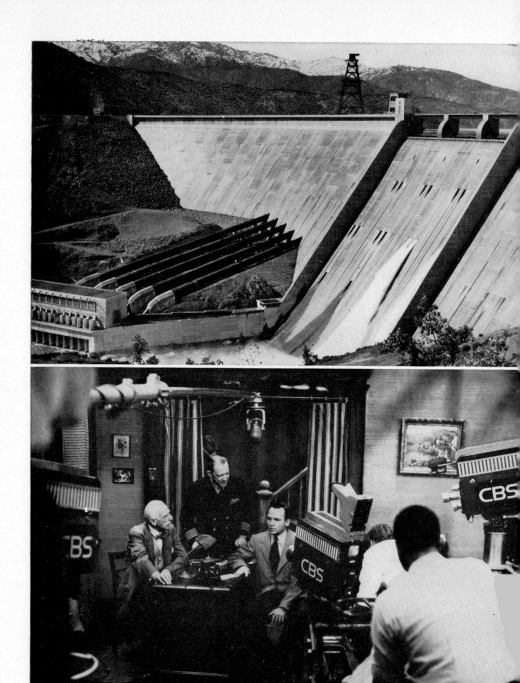

Top: Bureau of Reclamation Photograph. Bottom: Kenyon & Roberts Inc.

Shasta Dam, general view of spillway action and power plant as seen from point downstream on left abutment. Below, a scene from *The Ford Theater* production of *The Traitor* shows some of the equipment used by television cameramen to get various angles.

DISCUSSIONS IN GOVERNMENT

At a Cabinet meeting are, clockwise around the table: Persons (Pres. Aide), Hoover (State), McKay (Interior), Humphrey (Treasury), Humphrey and Brownell (Attorney General), Weeks, (Commerce), Hobby (Welfare), Young (Civil Service), Hughes (Budget), Fleming (Defence), Mitchell (Labor), Summerfield (Post Office), Dulles (State), the President, Wolson (Defence), Benson (Agriculture), Lodge (U.N.), Rabb and Adams (Pres. Aide and Assistant). Below, House Speaker Joe Martin (Rep., Mass.) points something out to Representative Sam Rayburn (Dem., Texas) and the President after a conference on the President's legislative program. Left to right in the rear are other congressional leaders: Arends, Johnson, Wilson, Short, Bridges and Clements.

TELEVISION COVERS A BIG SHOW

The nation gathered before its sets to watch the long squabble between the Army and Senator McCarthy. Left to right behind the table are Senators Potter and Dirksen, Counsel Jenkins, Senators Mundt, McClellan, Symington, and Jackson, Mr. Carr of the subcommittee staff, and Senator McCarthy.

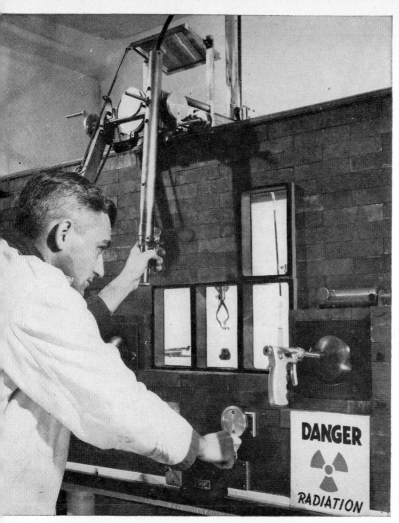

Top: Brookhaven National Laboratory. Bottom: Wide World Photo

NATIONS GROUP UNDER THE THREAT OF ATOMIC WARFARE

Behind a protective wall in the Hot Laboratory, a chemist handles radioactive liquid by remote control. Below, members of the North Atlantic Treaty Organization gather to invite Germany to join them. At the left is Pierre Mendes-France of France, signing the document is John Foster Dulles of the United States, at the right is Sir Anthony Eden of the United Kingdom.

THE OLD AND THE NEW

The Republic National Bank Building, towering above Dallas is part of the surge of modern architecture rolling across the country. Below, an era ends as the last ferry leaves Ellis Island

Top: Ulric Meisel, Dallas
Bottom: Wide World Photo

A MEMORABLE OCCASION

President and Mrs. Eisenhower smile as they leave Fitzsimmons Army Hospital in Denver, where the Chief Executive had been confined following a heart attack. *Below:* Two members of the Eisenhower Cabinet who with others, kept the machinery of government running during early phase of the President's illness; left to right: Atty. Gen. Herbert C. Brownell, Jr., Vice-President Richard Nixon, Deputy Atty. Gen. William Rogers and Assistant to the President Sherman Adams.

SINGLE GAVEL RULES LABOR

Labor leaders (left to right) George Meany and Walter Reuther share a single gavel to symbolize merger of the 16-million member AFL & CIO Labor Unions.

Associated Press Photo

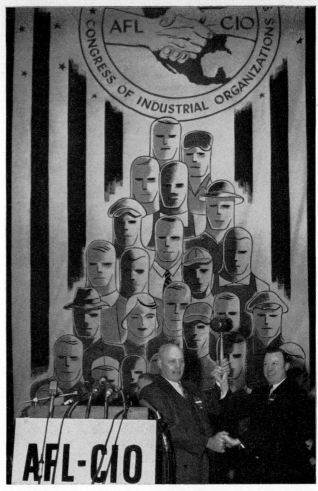

NEW AND BETTER ROADS

Under the expected rate of expenditure by nation, States and localities, the United States during the next decade will spend about $47,000,000,-000 on its roads and streets.

Ohio Department of Highways

United Press Photo

BIG FOUR PARLEY OPENS IN GENEVA

On October 27, 1955, the four foreign ministers, V. M. Molotov of Russia, Harold MacMillan of Great Britain, Antoine Pinay of France and John Foster Dulles of the United States, met in the impressive Palais des Nations, where the heads of states had gathered three months earlier.

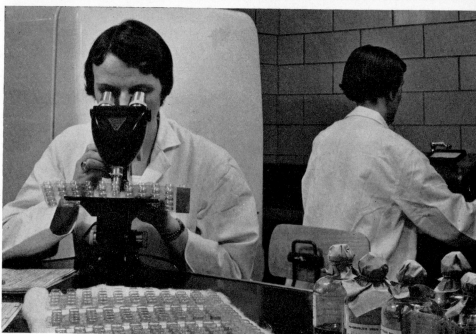

NOTABLES AT THE TABLE

First meeting of 1955 of The Commission on Reorganization of the Executive Branch of the Government: some of the members, clockwise from lower left are: Herbert C. Brownell, Jr., Sydney A. Mitchell, Herbert Hoover, Homer Ferguson, Arthur S. Fleming, Solomon Hollister and Joseph P. Kennedy. *Below:* One of the steps in testing Poliomyelitis Vaccine. On April 12, 1955, the momentous announcement was made that a vaccine measurably effective in preventing infantile paralysis (polio) had at last been developed.

"Although our communities are buildng more schools than ever before," wrote the Commissioner, "the rate of construction will have to be nearly tripled if we are to keep pace with the number of children."

One of the painful features of the educational situation is the marked disparity between rich and poor States in school facilities. The National Education Association in 1954 published figures which showed that, according to the most recent data available, New York was spending annually $324 per pupil for education, and Arkansas only $107. The average salary for a classroom teacher was $4,800 in California, and but $1,740 in Mississippi. It is partly to lessen these differences that Federal aid is urged. But the subject is complex and a wide array of arguments on each side of the issue will have to be studied. The tradition of universal free public schooling held in large parts of America, a tradition cited by advocates of Federal aid, comes into frontal collision with the traditions of economy and State responsibility, which are cited by opponents. Meanwhile, education is clearly suffering from the necessity of devoting so much of our taxation to the needs of defense.

During the spring, Senator Harry F. Byrd of Virginia forced a disclosure of scandals under the Federal Housing Administration which somehow aroused less criticism than might have been expected. It was shown that excessively liberal rules for the granting of Federal loans, and lax administration of these rules, had given builders "windfall profits" which ran into a total of hundreds of millions. On a single housing project in Brooklyn called Farragut Gardens four men who had made a combined investment of $10,000 gained windfalls of nearly $3,600,-000; on another building project at Fort Lee, New Jersey, the builders had a windfall of more than $2,425,000. One Federal official was accused of corruption, but most of the losses were attributable simply to laxity. The Administration had learned of the situation before Senator Byrd acted, and had taken corrective action. Congressional legislation was not required.

Nothing substantial was done during 1954 to amend or replace the McCarran Act governing immigration; but one incident of the year had special interest. In November, the long history of Ellis Island as a gateway for immigrants came to a close. A Norwegian seaman was the last man to use the island as a temporary haven. It had served the country for sixty-two years, had sieved, in some of these years, more than a million people into the United States, and had become part of the folklore of the nation.

Faced with the threat that Canada would build the St. Lawrence Seaway alone if the United States did not move, Congress early in May decided that the country must do its share. The Senate had acted favorably the previous fall on a bill for American participation; the House now approved the measure 241 to 158. It provided for the expenditure of $105,000,000 for the construction of two canals ,with appropriate locks and other installations, on the Yankee stretch of the waterway; Canada was expected to invest about $200,000,000 on her segment. When the seaway is completed, ocean freighters will have a minimum of twenty-five feet of water for the whole 2,200-mile stretch from the upper ports of Lake Superior to the Gulf of St. Lawrence. The upper Middle West and Europe will be made neighbors by direct water communication, while no inconsiderable amount of hydroelectric power will be generated at the dams built on the route. At long last the adverse interests—ports like New York and Boston, Charleston and New Orleans, railroads serving these ports, coal companies—which had fought the measure, had been overcome. The passage of the bill was a victory for President Eisenhower, always one of its resolute advocates.

It is almost a rule in American politics that the party which wins a Presidential election will lose ground in the next mid-term contest. Not since 1934 has that rule been broken. Inasmuch as Republican control of Congress at the beginning of the year was precarious (a majority of three in the House, and no real majority at all in the Senate), the Administration seemed likely to lose that branch of the government. Its greatest source of strength was the unquestioned personal popularity of President Eisenhower. He was ready, moreover, to do some vigorous campaigning. The principal asset of the Democrats was the economic discontent which had plainly developed among some groups of voters. Adlai E. Stevenson, who naturally has to think of 1956, was ready himself to do some energetic campaigning.

Beginning mildly, the campaign soon grew heated.

WHERE ARE ALL THOSE RICH FRIENDS?
From a cartoon by Shanks in *The Buffalo Evening News.*

Not only Congress was at stake, but 34 out of the 48 governorships, including those in the close States of New York, Pennsylvania, Connecticut, and Minnesota. The Republicans hoped to prove that, having presided over the ending of the Korean War and stopped the rise of prices, they were stronger than ever. The Democrats realized that if they lost this election their chances of winning two years later would be slender indeed. Considering that the country faced no highly divisive issues, the amount of billingsgate used on both sides was deplorable. Senator

McCarthy struck the lowest note when he said that "the label Democrat is stitched with the idiocy of a Truman, rotted by the deceit of an Acheson, corrupted by the Red slime of a White." But even Vice-President Nixon declared that the Democrats could not be trusted because of their "softness on Communism," and Irving Ives, who ran for the New York governorship against Averell Harriman, characterized his opponent as "dishonest, dumb, or stupid." The Democrats for their part assailed the Administration as "callous" about the unemployed. Mr. Eisenhower's sensible comment was that the times are too serious for such exchanges.

Most of the country paid little attention to broad national problems, concentrating on local issues and candidacies. Unemployment outside the mining and textile areas was not extensive enough to affect voting. A larger factor was the loss of overtime; two years earlier, perhaps twenty million workers got overtime pay, but in 1954, only about eleven millions. The reduction in farm income also counted. In the Northeastern States dairy income had fallen by 19 per cent in a year, and in the Middle West corn-hog-dairy income by 8 per cent. General farm income for the nation had been off three per cent. In some areas this counted against the Republicans. The question of public vs. private power was a factor in Washington, Montana, Idaho, and above all Oregon and Kentucky. Richard L. Neuberger ran for the Senate in Oregon on the contention that his Republican opponent wished to destroy the public power program; and Alben Barkley, once Vice-President, sought a Senate seat from Kentucky as an antagonist of the Dixon-Yates contract for a privately-built steam plant attached to TVA.

As the campaign reached its final stages, with a host of speakers on each side, and the President engaged to an unprecedented extent, it was clear that the result would be close. Special interest centered on the Harriman-Ives contest for the New York governorship; on the senatorial contest in Illinois between the Democratic incumbent Paul Douglas and the Republican candidate Joseph Meek; and on the effort of Homer Ferguson of Michigan (Republican), Hubert Humphrey of Minnesota, Joseph C. O'Mahoney of Wyoming, James E. Murray of Montana (Democrats all), and Leverett Saltonstall of Massachusetts (Republican) to keep their Senate seats. In New Jersey, Clifford P. Case ran for the Senate with the handicap of a factional division in his Republican following, and the probable advantage of McCarthy's enmity.

Seldom in our history have election results been closer. The widespread apathy was reflected in the fact that only about 42,000,000 people voted. In Congress, the Democrats won a clear majority of the House, 232 to 203, and a lead of one vote in the Senate—this vote being that of Wayne L. Morse of Oregon, originally a Republican, later an independent, but now on the Democratic side. Paul Douglas, O'Mahoney, Murray, Saltonstall, and Humphrey all were re-elected to the Senate, but Homer Ferguson went down in defeat. Alben Barkley came back. Of the governorships the Democrats won nineteen, the Republicans fifteen. Harriman defeated Ives by the closest of margins, only about one-tenth of one per cent of the vote. At the same time, however, the Republican candidate for attorney-general in New York, Jacob K. Javits, trounced Franklin D. Roosevelt, Jr., by the unexpected majority of 177,000. For the first time in our history, a Senator was elected by a write-in vote: J. Strom Thurmond of South Carolina, a "Dixiecrat" who had the ardent assistance of Governor James F. Byrnes.

The elections had proved nothing except three facts that the country had known to begin with: that Mr. Eisenhower is stronger than his party, that the Democrats under favorable conditions might prove their contention that they hold a "natural majority," and that many voters respond to pocketbook considerations. But even the third of these considerations could not be overstressed. In Iowa, for example, the voters rejected Guy Gillette for the Senate, though he stood for high rigid supports of farm prices; and the Democratic State Chairman had to admit that "the farmers were not as dissatisfied as we thought." President Eisenhower, like Truman, Wilson, Cleveland, and Harrison before him (not to go further back) would have to deal with an opposition majority in both chambers of Congress. But the country seemed moving in no definite direction politically—it was just swinging uneasily at anchor. Throughout his first two years Eisenhower had commanded (and usually needed) Democratic votes for his chief measures, and he would still command them for most of his policies.

During most of our political history "bipartisanship" has been but a nebulous dream. When Taft lost control of Congress in 1910, and Truman in 1946, they found themselves struggling with irreconcilable opponents. But President Eisenhower set to work in the last weeks of the year under more favorable auspices. The closeness of the election, the sense of a continuing international crisis and, above all, the resemblance of many of the President's measures to old Democratic policies, counted in his favor. In foreign affairs he could count on better support from Senator Lyndon Johnson, the incoming Democratic majority leader, than he had received from Senator William F. Knowland, the outgoing Republican majority leader. His program for reciprocal trade and for foreign economic aid had always won more Democratic than Republican backing. Then, too, Democrats remember that the recent history of bipartisanship goes back to the labors of Secretary of State Cordell Hull in wartime, when he strove to divorce the writing of the peace and the building of the United Nations from all party considerations. Debate on great measures is essential, but it need not be partisan debate.

In December President Eisenhower held conferences first with the Republican leaders of Congress, who were told what he intended to do in domestic affairs, and then with leaders of both parties, including the principal committee chairmen. It was plain that the Democrats would be cooperative on such matters as a three-year renewal of the reciprocal trade law, Federal aid to housing, and expansion of health insurance as well as on foreign policy; but they expressed sharp criticism of some of President Eisenhower's policies on power, farm aid, and taxation. Senator Johnson suggested that the President, before sending important recommendations to Congress, consult with Democratic as well as Republican leaders—with no commitment on either side. This Mr. Eisenhower and some of his principal Cabinet members agreed to do. Although the Democrats did not conceal their eagerness to find good campaign issues for 1956, the outlook for united action on a number of key measures was bright. It was but one of many indications of the fact that in recent times differences of opinion *within* each of the major parties (and we have practically no minor parties any longer) are much more important than differences of opinion *between* the two parties.

The historical fact that the Constitution evolves and grows with changing times was signally illustrated by the unanimous Supreme Court decision in May outlawing racial segregation in the field of public education. Outside the South, the country greeted the decision with a chorus of wholehearted praise. The general view was that it set the United States right with its own conscience, and with world opinion. And it was proof that the nation had moved far since the famous "separate but equal" decision of the Supreme Court in 1896—a decision which held that segregation did not violate the Fourteenth Amendment if only the facilities provided for Negroes in transportation, amusements, education, and other areas were equal to those furnished to whites. The Supreme Court in its new decision explicitly recognized that times had altered. "We cannot turn the clock back," it said in its short and emphatic opinion.

The decision established a clear basic principle: the principle that the Constitution, as Justice Harlan had said in a dissenting opinion in 1896, is color-blind. But the Court left the implementing of this principle to the future, declaring that it would hold further hearings before deciding how it would be applied. A number of defiant voices were raised in the South. Governor Herman Talmadge of Georgia rumbled: "We are not going to secede from the Union, but the people of Georgia will not comply with the decision of the Court." Governor James Byrnes of South Carolina spoke in the same vein. The general view was that some years of difficult litigation would be required before the decision was made generally effective, and Justice Jackson spoke of perhaps a "generation" of legal manoeuvring. But it was also the general view that when a little time had been given to work out the transition, the American tradition of obedience to law would triumph. In the Border States many communities moved toward immediate acceptance.

The fact is that the steady advancement of the Negro race, the industrialization of the South, the part played by Negroes in two World Wars, and the growing sensitiveness of world opinion to color bars, has made segregation more and more untenable. In Reconstruction days the 14th and 15th amendments, giving the Negroes citizenship, equal protection under the law, and the ballot, seemed to many Americans premature. By "grandfather clauses" and literacy tests many Southern States deprived the Negro of the ballot; by segregation they deprived him of equal rights. The "separate but equal doctrine" reconciled the Fourteenth Amendment to segregation, but it could do so only temporarily. The courts grew steadily stricter in insisting that equality had to be real and complete. With this end in view they ruled that segregation could not be practiced on trains and buses in interstate commerce; that segregated postgraduate schools in State universities could not be permitted; and that all-white primaries were unconstitutional. The time had come in 1954 for the broadest step of all.

According to the Supreme Court, segregation in the public schools on the basis of race alone, no matter how good the facilities provided, is inherently discriminatory against the minority group. "To separate them from others of similar age and qualifications solely because of their race generates a feeling of inferiority as to their status in the community that may affect their hearts and minds in a way unlikely ever to be undone." Seventeen States and the District of Columbia, with a population of about 40,500,000 whites and 10,500,000 Negroes, required segregation; four other States (Arizona, New Mexico, Kansas, and Wyoming) permitted it. Segregation had been legal in more than 10,000 school districts. No wonder that one Negro newspaper called the decision the greatest Negro victory since the Emancipation Proclamation! In some areas, such as Kentucky, the change promised to confer an immediate economic benefit upon many poor communities which could not afford two school systems side by side. In other areas segregation was expected to survive for some time by a careful drawing of school district lines so as to separate white residential zones from Negro zones. But everywhere, even in the Deep South, the decision was certain before long to have a tremendous influence in reducing the spirit of racial intolerance. Such intolerance is weaker among school children than among any other elements in the population, and a single generation will wipe it out in many communities.

As race discrimination is broken down, the way will be opened for a more energetic assault upon an equally fundamental problem, the general poverty of educational systems in large parts of the South. In the past, much of the Southern opposition to Federal aid stemmed from a fear that it would bring anti-segregation influences with it. Now this ground for distruct has been removed, and the South may give greater support to Federal aid legislation.

The sudden death of Associate Justice Robert K. Jackson of the Supreme Court left a vacancy which President Eisenhower announced on October 27 he would fill by the appointment of John M. Harlan of New York. Only fifty-five, and thus younger than any other justice except Tom C. Clark of Texas, Mr. Harlan was a judge of the Second Federal Court of Appeals. He is a grandson of a former justice of the Supreme Court who left a notably liberal record, John M. Harlan. The bar of the country has frequently criticized Presidents for not placing in the highest court more men with previous judicial experience. Of the eight judges at the time Mr. Harlan was nominated, only one, Sherman Minton of Indiana, had ever sat on the bench, and he had been best known as a Senator. Judge Harlan had been Assistant Federal Attorney in New York, Assistant State Attorney-General, and chief counsel to the State Crime Commission before he joined the Court of Appeals. He would raise to three the number of justices who counted as Republicans.

The complicated story of Senator McCarthy of Wisconsin and his activities held public attention during half the year and almost monopolized it for weeks together. As 1954 opened Mr. McCarthy was chairman of the Permanent Senate Subcommittee on Investigations, a leader of considerable power in the Republican Party, and symbol of one of the most explosive issues in recent American history. When the year closed he had been censured by the Senate, largely discredited before the nation, and cast into outer darkness by the Administration. He was about to lose his chairmanship and his power. In the months between, Americans had watched one of the most extraordinary—and disturbing—dramas in our entire political history.

The story began in February, when Senator McCarthy questioned Brigadier-General Ralph W. Zwicker about the honorable discharge from the Army of Major Irving

Peress, a dentist who when charged with Communist leanings had pleaded the Fifth Amendment as ground for not replying. General Zwicker made it clear that he had simply obeyed orders, and that he was forbidden under a Presidential directive to discuss details of loyalty inquiries. McCarthy grew insulting. "I cannot help but question either your honesty or your intelligence," he snapped; he intimated that Zwicker did not have "the brains of a five-year-old child"; and he ended by declaring that the general was "not fit to wear that uniform." He ordered Zwicker to appear again for more questioning. At this, the Secretary of the Army, Robert T. Stevens, interposed. He directed the general *not* to appear, and said he would himself take the stand. It seemed that the Eisenhower Administration and Mr. McCarthy were coming into direct conflict. The Senator insisted that his subcommittee had the right to get all relevant facts; the Secretary asserted his right to protect an honorable officer from "abuse and humiliation." A battle royal was in prospect.

The battle came, but not without a great deal of preliminary action. First, under heavy pressure from McCarthy and other Senators, Secretary Stevens issued a statement which was universally interpreted as a surrender. Zwicker and others *would* appear before the subcommittee, he said, and the inquiry into the Peress case would be completed as rapidly as possible. Headlines all over the nation bore the words "Stevens Retreats" or "Stevens Capitulates." The deepest dismay was felt by tens of millions. Already the Administration, men said, had retreated before McCarthy on the question of the information libraries; on that of the Greek ships; on that of Stassen's criticism of the Senator. Now it had retreated again. The Washington *Post* declared that the "disgraceful cave-in" was not really Stevens's, but "goes back to the President." The New York *Herald-Tribune* asserted that McCarthy's assault on Stevens offered "a supreme test" of the leaders of the Administration, and "they have failed to meet that test." Thus far President Eisenhower had kept personally aloof from the combat, although plainly indicating his dislike of McCarthy. Now this was no longer possible. Under White House prodding, Stevens issued a defiant new statement; McCarthy made an insolent reply; and a greater battle than ever began.

This battle centered in a set of new charges and countercharges between Secretary Stevens and Senator McCarthy. The Secretary sent to McCarthy's own subcommittee a 34-page memorandum alleging that McCarthy and his counsel, Roy M. Cohn, had taken highly improper steps on behalf of G. David Schine, a friend of Cohn's, who had acted as consultant to the subcommittee. He accused the Senator and Cohn of trying to get Schine a commission for which he was unfit. When they failed at that, declared Stevens, they had attempted to get him assigned to duty not at any army camp, but in New York. It was implied that McCarthy's long investigation of the Army had really been an effort to punish it for not granting Schine special privileges. McCarthy for his part charged that Secretary Stevens and Army Counsel John Adams had used improper means to try to get McCarthy to call off his investigation. They had attempted, he declared, to divert his inquiry to the Navy and the Air Force; they had begged him to let up. The Army charges, said McCarthy, were "blackmail."

To sift the charges and countercharges, the Senate's Permanent Sub-Committee on Investigations, under Karl Mundt of South Dakota, opened hearings late in March in the largest committee room in Washington. Half the nation watched through television sets. The deeper question was not between the Senator and the Army. It lay between McCarthy and President Eisenhower. It was not a question of misconduct on the part of Mr. Stevens or Mr. Cohn; it was the question whether an irresponsible exploitation of fear of Communism, and a flagrant invasion of civil liberties, should be checked or permitted to continue. As the inquiry began a "Joe Must Go" movement was launched in Wisconsin to try to recall Mr. McCarthy from the Senate; Bishop Sheil of the Catholic Church in Chicago attacked McCarthy as "a pitifully ineffective anti-Communist"; and the Gallup polls showed that he was fast losing much of his old support.

Much of McCarthy's political prestige had been built on a belief that he possessed such strength with one segment of the voters that he would be able to defeat any man who crossed his path. Senator Tydings of Maryland in 1950 had poured contempt on Mr. McCarthy's original charge that 205 "members of the Communist Party," or any real number at all, infested the State Department; and that autumn, after a disgracefully abusive campaign in which Mr. McCarthy participated, Tydings was defeated for re-election to the Senate. Senator Benton of Connecticut had frequently denounced McCarthy, challenging his truth and honesty; and in 1952 Benton was beaten for re-election. (Actually he polled more votes than Adlai E. Stevenson.) But while the committee inquiry continued, McCarthy lost a significant contest in Maine. He had opposed Senator Margaret Chase, one of his critics, and had brought forward a rival candidate in the Republican primary; but Mrs. Smith won by more than five to one. The Republican National Committee made it clear that it did not wish Mr. McCarthy to participate in the fall campaign; and Republican candidates in Michigan and Minnesota specially asked him to stay away.

The Army-McCarthy hearings resulted in a sharp castigation of Messrs. Cohn and Schine and Senator McCarthy by the Democratic members of the Mundt Committee, coupled with a milder rebuke of Secretary Stevens; some muted faultfinding with the principals by most of the Republican members; and a separate report by Senator Potter of Michigan, who believed that witnesses on both sides had committed perjury. But the reports counted for little, for the public, watching the thirty-six days of televised proceedings, had made up its own mind. It had been able to take the complete measure of McCarthy's abusiveness and Stevens's well-meaning clumsiness. It was outraged by the fact that a nation facing the heavy responsibilities of a dangerous world situation should have to waste its time and energies in such a spectacle. President Eisenhower expressed the general sense of disgust. But before the reports were submitted, a new act in the McCarthy drama had opened.

Early in August, Senator Flanders of Vermont, Republican, had presented a motion: "Resolved, that the conduct of the Senator from Wisconsin, Mr. McCarthy, is unbecoming a member of the United States Senate, is contrary to senatorial traditions, and tends to bring the Senate into disrepute, and such conduct is hereby condemned." This motion had been hotly debated. During the discussion Senators Flanders, J. W. Fullbright of Arkansas, and Wayne Morse of Oregon had brought forward nearly fifty specific charges against McCarthy. A special committee of three Republicans and three Democrats, under Arthur V. Watkins of Utah, sifted out the thirteen most important specifications, and arranged them in five categories. On August 31 this committee opened its sittings in the Senate Caucus Room in Washington.

One charge against McCarthy was that he had shown contempt of the Senate in 1952 by repeatedly refusing to appear before a Subcommittee on Privileges and Elections which was inquiring into certain intricate financial transactions of his. Another charge was that he had encouraged Federal employees to violate their oaths of office and to defy executive orders; for during the Army-McCarthy hearings the Senator had urged Federal workers to disregard a Presidential directive forbidding them to give papers or facts from security files to members of Congress. A third charge was that he had possibly transgressed the Espionage Act by receiving secret security information which it was not within his province to take, and by divulging it to a newspaper "columnist" and others. A fourth set of charges dealt with Senator McCarthy's slanderous language; for he had called Senator Hendrickson of New Jersey "a living miracle without brains or guts," and Senator Flanders "senile." Finally, he was charged with defaming and abusing General Zwicker during the hearings on Major Irving Peress.

The Watkins Committee followed a course refreshingly different from that of the Mundt Committee. Neither radio nor television was permitted. Strict judicial rules of evidence were followed. While McCarthy or his counsel were allowed to cross-examine witnesses, irrelevant interruptions were sharply gavelled down. Comparatively little oral testimony was needed, for ample documentary evidence existed on all the charges. The committee dispatched its work with a promptness and efficiency which won it express commendation from the President.

At the beginning of November the Senate met in extraordinary session to consider the committee report. This report recommended censure of McCarthy on two main counts. First, declared the Watkins Committee, he had shown contempt for the Senate both by refusing to appear before a subcommittee which was investigating his finances, and by using opprobrious terms respecting it and its members. In the second place, he had employed "reprehensible" language in attacking General Zwicker. McCarthy was quick to issue a characteristic reply to the committee. The Communist Party, he declared, "has now extended its tentacles" into the Senate, and "has made a committee of the Senate its unwitting handmaiden." This, like some of McCarthy's attacks on President Eisenhower, further incensed his opponents. A confused debate in the open Senate followed. Democratic members, who could not forget McCarthy's assertion that they were guilty of "twenty years of treason," lined up unanimously against him; so did a large part of the Republican membership. At the end, McCarthy was censured by a vote of more than three to one.

This was actually a vote of censure for all that was summed up in the word "McCarthyism": for the Senator's invasions of civil liberty, his arrogant investigative methods, his intemperate language, his exaggerated charges, his harsh retaliations against all who criticized him, and his open defiance of President Eisenhower and his sphere of authority. Beyond question the President had referred to him when he declared at a Columbia University bicentennial dinner that "we will drive from the temple of freedom all who seek to establish over us thought control—whether they be agents of a foreign state or demagogues thirsty for personal power and public notice."

As the Democrats took control of the Senate, McCarthy lost his subcommittee chairmanship. He was definitely relegated to an obscure role. In the four and a half years since he had made his famous speech at Wheeling, West Virginia, declaring that "I have here in my hands a list of 205 names" of members of the Communist Party "who nevertheless are still working and shaping policy in the State Department," McCarthy had played a great and disruptive part in American political affairs. He had heavily impeded the constructive work of the Eisenhower Administration. He had done enormous damage to American prestige abroad. By future historians his four years on the public stage will doubtless be regarded as one of the most extraordinary (and most unfortunate) episodes in all our recent political history.

Throughout 1954 anxious attention had to be given to questions of security, and their relation to civil liberties. One noted case, that of Dr. Owen Lattimore, the Far Eastern expert connected with Johns Hopkins University, reached no conclusion. Since Senator McCarthy first pointed to him as "top Soviet espionage agent in the United States" (a charge so patently false that it was soon abandoned) he had had to meet a prosecution that often looked like persecution. His indictment on perjury charges was weakened during the year when the Court of Appeals sustained Judge Youngdahl in dismissing the principal count against him: the charge that he had falsified in assuring a Senate committee that he had never been a "sympathizer and promoter of Communism." This, said Judge Youngdahl, was too vague to be worth examining. The other charges deal chiefly with what might be regarded as ordinary lapses of memory in a long grilling by examiners. Nevertheless, the Department of Justice made it plain that it would continue the prosecution. Another Far Eastern expert, a veteran member of the diplomatic service, John Paton Davies, was dismissed by the State Department after repeated clearance by loyalty boards, and without any proof of dereliction. Press comment on this dismissal was scathing.

The fact is that "loyalty," "subversion," and "security" in 1954 were sensitive and hazy terms, in danger of becoming political footballs. The rule in the Truman Administration was that no Federal employee could be dismissed as disloyal except on "reasonable grounds," which had to be established by evidence. The Eisenhower Administration established a rule that no employee was entitled to keep his position unless this was "clearly consistent with the interests of national security." Various types of behavior were defined as inconsistent. They included not only what would ordinarily be called disloyal activity, but "any criminal, infamous, dishonest, immoral, or notoriously disgraceful conduct," including habitual intoxication, drug addiction, or sexual perversion. When the Administration gave out large figures (first 1,456, later 2,200) for dismissal on security grounds, friends of dismissed workers protested that this was unfair, and Democrats declared it mere politics; a man whose fault might have been too frequent indulgence in a social glass incurred the stigma of "disloyalty," or of being a "subversive." Actually cases of clear disloyalty were few.

Dr. Robert Oppenheimer, an eminent nuclear physi-
cist and one of the principal creators of the atomic bomb,
was subjected during the spring to a special investigation.
A Personal Security Board conducted six weeks of secret
hearings and took almost a thousand pages of testimony.
It reached the conclusion that Dr. Oppenheimer had been
loyal and vigilant in dealing with atomic secrets; but it
threw doubts on his judgment and on some aspects of his
character, and by a vote of two to one decided that it
would be inconsistent with the security of the nation to
restore his access to confidential information. The Atomic
Energy Commission under Admiral Lewis Strauss accepted this verdict. It was clear that the board, headed by
President Gordon Gray of the University of North Carolina, had acted on the basis of hard, conscientious research. But public opinion at once became passionately
divided, both on the question whether Dr. Oppenheimer
had been wronged, and the still larger question whether
the national security system was outrageously defective.
Behind these issues lay the largest problem of all: How
can science and technology, now vital to American safety,
be screened without impairment of morale?—how can
they be harnessed to the nation's needs and yet be policed?

Vehement articles and books quickly appeared and debated these issues. A volume called *The Hydrogen Bomb*,
by James Shepley and Clay Blair, Jr., assailed Dr. Oppenheimer as a man who had tried to obstruct development
of the bomb, and lauded the scientist Dr. Edward Teller
and Admiral Strauss as heroes who had insisted that the

United States must possess it. Opposing arguments were marshalled by Joseph and Stewart Alsop in a magazine essay, later expanded into a book, entitled *We Accuse*. Its thesis was that Dr. Oppenheimer had brilliantly served the public, while Admiral Strauss had deliberately tried to ruin him. Other articles raised the question whether a security system which brought such a violent controversy into the open without settling it did not do more harm than good. Loyalty and integrity are difficult traits to define, and security boards have to make decisions on evidence which is both slippery and subjective. It was difficult for many people to understand how the Gray Board could find Dr. Oppenheimer loyal and discreet, and yet find him unfit for security clearance. "Oh," one newspaper humorist remarked, "Dr. Oppenheimer's a perfectly loyal scientist, but he's too radioactive."

Dr. Edward U. Condon, director of the Bureau of Standards 1945–51, and more recently head of the research and development division of the Corning Glass Works, had at first been given government clearance on secret (classified) projects assigned to these works; then his clearance was revoked; then a Navy board gave him limited clearance again; and finally Secretary of the Navy Charles S. Thomas suspended his clearance once more. At this point, in December, Dr. Condon announced that he would drop his efforts to obtain final and full clearance, and would resign from his Corning position. Denying under oath that he had ever participated in any "un-American" activities, he protested his complete innocence.

He received the sympathy of various scientific bodies, while a group of atomic physicists declared that his case illustrated once more the "political abuse of the nation's security system."

Another security dispute involved Wolf Ladejinsky, who has successively been a Far Eastern farm specialist of the Department of Agriculture, and agricultural attaché in the American embassy in Tokyo. He has been credited with playing an important part in the land-reform program instituted in Japan since the war. But late in the year the Agricultural Department rejected his application for re-transfer (as required by a new law) to its jurisdiction; he did not meet the technical requirements, it said, and his record (he was Russian-born, and in 1931 briefly acted as interpreter for the Russian trade office in New York called Amtorg) forbade security clearance. An indignant outcry ensued. The State Department sharply contested the decision of the Agricultural Department. It seemed certain that the Ladejinsky affair would be taken into Congress and kept before the public unless means were found to keep him in Federal employ.

Indeed, a growing list of private organizations, scientific and professional, demanded during the year that the government revise its security program, with more emphasis on positive aspects and less attention to negative barriers. One branch of the Ford Foundation, the Fund for the Republic, granted $100,000 to the Bar Association of New York for a study of security procedures, leading to recommendations for their revision.

World tension showed no abatement during the year, and the four primary world problems—disarmament, the unification of Germany, the liberation of Austria, and the restoration of friendly relations between China and the Western Powers—remained at the close of 1954 as far from settlement as ever. American diplomacy had to meet a succession of crises. For a time, early in the year, it seemed that the dikes against a Communist advance in Southeast Asia had broken down, and that Russo-Chinese power would rapidly pour over Burma, Thailand, and Malaya as well as over what had been French Indo-China. Secretary of State John Foster Dulles had to make a desperate emergency effort to repair the breached dam, and erect new barriers against Red aggression. Before he succeeded in this, the defences of Western Europe were in danger, and he had to turn to that quarter. Anglo-American effort has been concentrated upon the establishment of a European Defence Community, including a rearmed Germany. But the political instability of France suddenly destroyed E.D.C., and made necessary the hurried improvisation of a substitute. When the year ended the successful establishment of that substitute, though probable, was not a certainty.

On the whole, the international history of the year could be called not merely disappointing but unhappy. When 1954 began, hopes were high that the new regime in Moscow under Malenkov might come part way to meet the West in terminating the global conflict. When it ended, the West had lost ground in Asia, and gained

FOUNDATION STONES FOR THE WALL
From a cartoon by Ray in *The Kansas City Star*.

nothing in Europe. Communist intentions were as enigmatic and threatening as ever, and in both Eastern Europe and the Orient the outlook was disturbing.

Early in the year the first Four Power meeting of foreign ministers in five years was held in Berlin with inconclusive results. For twenty-five days, beginning in late January, Secretary Dulles and Foreign Minister Anthony

Eden of Britain, Georges Bidault of France, and Vyacheslav Molotov of Russia conferred, partly in open sessions, partly in secret. On European affairs they reached no agreement. Russia was as yet totally unwilling to see free and fair elections held for the unification of Germany; her government knew all too well that in East Germany such elections would go heavily anti-Communist, in West Germany almost unanimously so. Nor was Russia willing to agree to the evacuation of troops from Austria; to do so would remove her main excuse for keeping large forces in the satellite states. As for disarmament, the Soviet Government remained quite unwilling to permit of adequate systems of inspection to enforce an interdict upon atomic weapons.

On Far Eastern matters, Dulles and the foreign ministers reached an agreement for a supplementary conference to be held in Geneva on April 26 to discuss means of settling the Korean question and restoring peace in Indo-China. At this meeting not only the four leading powers but the Chinese Communist Republic and other interested states were to be represented. The admission of Red China to the gathering constituted a distinct concession by the United States, which ever since Chinese aggression in Korea began has regarded the Peking Government as unfit for membership in the world community. A number of Western nations, however, believed their interests in Asia would be better secured if some agreement were reached with China. France in particular, weary of the long strain of the war in Indo-China, was anxious for a peace which Peking would obviously have to help guarantee.

When the Berlin Conference ended, Western opinion was divided on the results. In Germany, Chancellor Konrad Adenauer congratulated Dulles, Eden, and Bidault on their insistence that a new all-German Government be based on absolutely free secret balloting. He was delighted by their "iron resistance to temptation." But leftist groups in Western Europe thought that a less inflexible stand might have been more profitable. Secretary Dulles professed to be pleased with the terms laid down for the Geneva conference. They "are one hundred per cent what we wanted," he said. But some members of Congress were uneasy. They talked gloomily of appeasement, and saw dangers ahead. The event proved that the dangers were all too real.

Before the Geneva meeting took place, the world was electrified by the announcement that the United States had exploded a hydrogen bomb on March 1 at Bikini in the Pacific. The Russians had asserted their possession of such a bomb the previous August, no doubt truly; but nothing was known of its character. Washington was candid in describing the terrible destructive power of the new weapon. Its force was equal to at least ten million tons of T.N.T. It would totally destroy everything within an area of fifty square miles; the blast would seriously damage everything within an area of two hundred square miles; the blast would less seriously damage everything within about six hundred miles; and the bomb would be

"DON'T CROWD ME, H-BOY"
From a cartoon by Little in *The Nashville Tennessean*.

likely to destroy by fire everything within eight hundred square miles. News soon crept out indicating that the injurious effects of the bomb extended over a wider region than had been anticipated. A Japanese fishing boat well outside the supposed radius of peril reached port with more than twenty of its crew so badly burned that they had to be sent to a hospital, and one subsequently died. Fish

276

caught over a wide area were so dangerously radioactive that they had to be destroyed. When it was announced that much larger bombs could be made, and that radioactive ash particles could be scattered by winds over whole nations, men realized for the first time what Mr. Eisenhower had called "the awful arithmetic" of nuclear weapons.

Bertrand Russell, declaring that weapons would soon be developed capable of obliterating all animal life on the globe, warned that some agreement on their prohibition was indispensable to the future of mankind. Prime Minister Churchill showed the keenest concern. Prime Minister Nehru stirred the Indian Parliament with a demand that the making and testing of such instruments of destruction be halted by a standstill agreement. How much the Russian people were allowed to learn of the latest developments is not known. But in the United States thoughtful citizens were deeply perturbed by the statement of Admiral Lewis Strauss, head of the Atomic Energy Commission, that a hydrogen bomb could be made large enough to "take out" a city like New York. What he meant by "take out" was revealed by reports that the Bikini bomb had completely destroyed an island a half-mile long and dug a deep hole in the ocean bottom twice that length. It was clear, however, that total prohibition of H-bombs was impossible until East and West developed a real and lasting trust in each other.

The Geneva Conference began at an unhappy moment for France, which was fighting a losing battle in Indo-

China. Her army heads had unwisely chosen to create a fortress at Dienbienphu, an exposed point 180 miles northwest of Hanoi. Here, in a circle of entrenchments and concrete walls, they had committed more than 10,000 of the best troops under the French flag. This garrison had been surrounded in February by 30,000 or 40,000 Communist fighters, who began a series of desperate assaults. Though at first these attacks were repulsed, the enemy gradually overran French outposts, blew up the outer fortifications, and with total disregard of losses forced themselves within a mile of the central citadel. It became difficult to supply the beleaguered troops by air. In itself Dienbienphu was of no great importance, but the moral effect of a Communist victory there would be immense—and it was plain that the Communists wished to time its fall with the final stages of the bargaining in Geneva. The French people, they realized, would be too depressed by such a defeat to wish to fight longer.

American attitudes toward the Geneva Conference were at first highly confused. On the eve of its commencement in late April, Secretary Dulles went to London and Paris in an evident effort to stiffen British and French policy. The American stake in Southeast Asia was real and important. The National Security Council regarded Indo-China as the keystone in a defensive arch formed by all the nations of the area and the islands beyond. If the Communists once seized the natural resources from Burma and Thailand to Celebes—oil, tin, rubber—the economic balance of the world would be decisively shifted in their favor. Mr. Dulles therefore at first proposed a "united declaration" by the Western nations to stop the Communist advance, and spoke of taking "united action" to protect Indo-China. Vice-President Nixon said flatly that the United States might have to send troops to that area. Even President Eisenhower spoke of Indo-China as representing a "transcendent interest" of the United States. National opinion, however, dissented vigorously from any policy likely to lead to the use of American forces.

This dissent was based on various grounds. French colonial rule in Indo-China had been bad, and most Americans dislike colonialism even when it is fairly good. French promises of independence for Indo-China had been belated, and their sincerity was questioned. It seemed poor military strategy to place American troops on the Asiatic mainland: the wrong war at the wrong time in the wrong place. Memories of the bloodshed in Korea and of the ultimate stalemate there were still keen. Moreover, Americans asked whether the problem of halting the Communists in Southeast Asia could not be solved by other means. Would not India, Pakistan, and Burma awake in time to the need of defending themselves and their weak neighbors such as Thailand? Could not a Pacific Pact be arranged similar to the North American Treaty Organization? Secretary Dulles finally turned to the latter expedient, and the British and French Governments agreed to discuss it.

When the fall of Dienbienphu came on May 7, French

anxiety to make peace in Indo-China greatly increased. Foreign Secretary Bidault, negotiating face to face with Chinese leaders in Geneva, felt that he had little choice. Mr. Dulles, who took care not to attend, had little power to affect the ultimate decision. This decision was to halt the war by a temporary partition of the contested area. Northern Vietnam would pass into Vietminh or Communist hands; Southern Vietnam would become for the time being an independent state; free elections would ultimately decide the character of both. Laos and Cambodia were to be granted complete independence. What the future of the region would be nobody knew. It was certain that twelve million people of Northern Indo-China were already lost to the Communists. Prophets of gloom predicted that the three new states would soon also pass under the Red yoke, paving the way for a conquest of the whole peninsula down to Singapore. More optimistic observers believed that Laos, Cambodia, and Southern Vietnam might make a successful stand against subversion. Their prospects would be particularly hopeful, it was said, if the United States furnished them capital, military assistance, and technical aid. By 1956, the date set for the Vietnam elections, the West might hope for victory at the polls.

The Geneva Conference completely failed to settle the Korean question. The armistice there continues unbroken, and American forces were sharply reduced during the year; but a treaty of peace was found impossible. While both sides stand for the unification of the country,

Communist leaders are totally unwilling to base this union on free elections in both North and South Korea.

Secretary Dulles at once set himself to the creation of a Southeast Asia Treaty Organization, called SEATO for short, to parallel the now sturdy NATO which he had inherited from the Truman Administration. In this he had the enthusiastic support of Australia, which felt itself in a position of special danger. But while he was at work on his bold plan, a grave crisis developed in the affairs of the European Defence Community. It resulted from a sudden demonstration that France would simply not ratify the E.D.C. treaty, even though France had been its main author.

Since the initiation of the treaty in the spring of 1952 by representatives of France, West Germany, Italy, Luxembourg, Belgium, and Holland, parliaments of all these nations except France and Italy had ratified it. Italy was sure to agree in time, but French hesitations were more serious. The idea of merging the military forces of the six nations into one defence force offended some French nationalists; the idea that West Germany should arm twelve new divisions alarmed many people. Frenchmen also objected that the promises of support which Great Britain and the United States had made in parallel treaties were too vague. Among French parties the Socialists and DeGaullists in particular feared that, once the European Community was created, Germany would quickly assert her dominance. Such fears have grown since West Germany has become prosperous and vigorous, and they made it impossible for the groups favoring ratification, led by the Popular Republican Party, to obtain action. When, in June, M. Mendes-France became premier, and gained prestige by helping to end the war in Indo-China, prospects momentarily brightened for ratification. Then hope completely collapsed.

This collapse took place late in August, when M. Mendes-France himself turned against the treaty. On August 30 the National Assembly voted it down. The defeat was a severe shock to the American Government. The State Department had become enthusiastically eager for the birth of the European Defence Community. Such a community, Mr. Dulles believed, would achieve two great objects: the creation of a strong army, multi-national in character, as a first line of defence against Russia, and the obliteration of the age-old hostility between Germany and France. President Eisenhower called the rejection of the treaty "a major setback" to our policy. The fact that the Soviet Government was desperately anxious to smash E.D.C. added to the American chagrin over the action of Mendes-France and the French Assembly. Coming on the heels of American humiliation over French defeat in Indo-China, the shock was especially severe. "And so having lashed ourselves to the mast," wrote Walter Lippmann in the New York *Herald-Tribune,* "we have gone down twice with a sinking ship."

Happily, the reverse was but temporary. Before the end of September, representatives of nine nations were sitting in London to construct a substitute for E.D.C.

Among them three men were particularly influential: Secretary Dulles, Foreign Minister Anthony Eden of Britain, and Foreign Minister Henri Spaak of Belgium. At a critical point Mr. Eden uttered a momentous sentence: "I have a new proposal to put to my colleagues."

This proposal was that if a scheme of European Union came into existence as a substitute for E.D.C., Great Britain would maintain indefinitely on the Continent the equivalent of her military forces now there: four divisions and an air force. She would pledge herself not to withdraw these forces without the consent of a majority of the other nations of the Union unless she faced an "acute overseas emergency." Thus Britain reassured France by throwing her weight into the European balance against Germany, and by promising to shoulder a large share of the defence burden. Secretary Dulles went as far on the same path as constitutional limitations permitted. He promised military support for the new substitute organization, but could not make the promise indefinite without Congressional sanction. At any rate, France could now feel sure that Anglo-American forces would not withdraw, leaving her to deal alone with a strong and perhaps aggressive Germany.

Agreement was then rapidly reached on the creation of a body to be called the Western European Union. The final negotiations were complicated, but on October 23, in Paris, ministers of fifteen nations concluded their work. Four main points had to be settled. The United States, Britain, and France agreed to give West Germany all but complete sovereignty. Practical arrangements for West German rearmament under the control of the Union were devised. All the nations of the North Atlantic Treaty Organization joined in inviting West Germany into that body. And finally, France and Germany came to a somewhat hazy, but it was hoped workable, agreement on the future of the Saar.

If the Western European Union succeeds, it will greatly strengthen the defences of the free nations. West Germany will have the right to raise 500,000 troops, to be under the command of the supreme NATO commander. These divisions, with those of the United States and Britain on the Continent, will constitute a formidable army. The success of the Union should do much to erase needless Franco-German antagonisms. That the substitute plan was regarded with apprehension and hostility in Russia at once became plain. Moscow immediately proposed a conference of Four-Power ministers on the unification of West and East Germany; but when inquiry was made as to her intentions with regard to free elections, it became plain that the proposed meeting would be merely a delaying tactic, and the West rejected the invitation. For that matter, the West prefers to negotiate from strength. A North Atlantic Community of 350,000,-000 free people, well armed, will give Western diplomatists the strength they need.

The central question when the year ended was whether France, even with the new British and American guarantees, could be brought to ratify the changed arrangement. Her political instability made prediction impossible. The National Assembly in the closing days of 1954 approved the four treaties by narrow margins, but the Senate still had to act. In Germany, too, ratification—despite the strong leadership of Chancellor Adenauer—was not wholly certain. Secretary Dulles could take pride, however, in the fact that his unwearied efforts had done much to keep a strong Western coalition together, and to maintain the idea of a great European Union transcending national lines.

Meanwhile, his leadership was mainly responsible for bringing into existence the Southeast Asia Treaty Organization, devoted to checking Communist expansion in that part of the globe. Washington sent out invitations. The eight nations which comprise SEATO (the United States, Britain, France, Australia, New Zealand, the Philippine Republic, Thailand, Pakistan) leagued themselves together, at a conference held in Manila, to combat armed aggression and subversive propaganda, and to raise the standard of living among Asiatics. In connection with this last objective, Premier Yoshida of Japan in November proposed a four-billion-dollar Marshall Plan for Asia. India and Burma held aloof, preferring a neutral status.

Tension between China and the United States increased as the year neared its end. The Chinese Government announced November 23 that eleven American aviators had been imprisoned for varying terms as spies. As a chorus of popular denunciation broke forth in America, the United Nations adopted a resolution condemn-

CLOSE QUARTERS
From a cartoon by Lewis in *The Milwaukee Journal*.

ing the Chinese for this violation of the Korean armistice
stipulation that all prisoners be returned. The Secretary-
General, Dag Hammarskjold, who was entrusted by the
resolution to make unremitting efforts to obtain the release of the prisoners, at once asked and received permission to visit Peiping. The Chinese Prime Minister, Chou
En-lai, made it evident in his reply (which spoke of "questions pertinent to the relaxation of international tension") that he wished to discuss a broader range of issues.
Communist China will never be satisfied, he said, until

she obtains Formosa, and a seat in the U.N.; but the American Government is totally unwilling to discuss either demand. Mr. Hammarskjold therefore left for the Orient with a gloomy prospect for achieving any immediate gain.

American support of the United Nations remained strong throughout the year, for it was a cardinal policy of the Eisenhower Administration as it had been of Mr. Truman's. In the major international settlements of 1954 (those of the questions centering in Iranian oil, the Suez Canal, the Trieste boundary, and the future of Indo-China) the U.N. played no direct part. It was sympathetic, and it rejoiced in the progress toward concord in these troubled areas; but it was not a participant. Nevertheless, the Assembly remains an indispensable forum of international debate, where great issues can be threshed out in view of all mankind, and where Communist hypocrisies have been more clearly exposed than anywhere else.

During the year it became necessary to face the fact that the North Atlantic Treaty Organization had failed to make the desired gains in military strength, and that to meet the constant Soviet threat it must be prepared to use atomic power. The program drafted by its Council at Lisbon in 1951 called for 96 divisions ready for immediate service, and an equal number in reserve, a well-organized European army under NATO control, and the rearmament of West Germany. This was to be achieved by the end of 1954. But that date found West Germany still unarmed, no European army, and only half the proposed number of divisions ready and in reserve. Against fewer than a hundred divisions all told possessed by the NATO Powers, Russia and her East European satellites had at least 235 ready for combat, and another 150 subject to mobilization within a month. Obviously some action had to be taken to meet this disparity of strength.

It was duly taken by the NATO Council which met at Paris in December. This body, which included fourteen foreign ministers and seventeen defence and treasury ministers, adopted as a basis for defence a plan by its military committee which assumed the use of nuclear weapons. Such weapons were to be kept in readiness; but the member governments would alone hold the right to decide on their use. This was in accordance with the statement of Marshal Montgomery, Deputy Supreme Commander, that atomic power "will be used if we are attacked." It is obvious that the decision to employ such weapons may have to be made in a hurry, and may have to be made by a few leaders. "If an atomic bomb knocks out the telephone," said Foreign Minister Spaak of Belgium, "I don't think we can wait for the service to be re-established before we make a decision." President Eisenhower was at pains to make it clear that the United States would not imperil its allies by rash action. We would take their interests and convictions into consideration in any crisis, he told a press conference, and would "negotiate it out."

Western Europe is understandably much more nervous

about an atomic war than the United States. It is in the front line; a single hydrogen bomb would practically destroy Holland, and three or four might completely paralyze France or Britain. But even if the twelve new divisions expected from West Germany become a reality in the near future, NATO will be too weak in ground forces to cope with the Communists. The new atomic energy legislation passed by Congress permits the President to give our Allies a certain amount of atomic information; and as Britain has valuable information of her own, the NATO decision meant a considerable pooling of data on both the use of such weapons, and the best defence against them.

Public attention has naturally been centered on the atom bomb and the hydrogen bomb; the United States has unquestionably a larger stock of both than any other power, while Britain is steadily stockpiling atomic bombs. But by 1954 the United States also had a wide range of lesser nuclear weapons. In Germany, according to Hanson Baldwin in the New York *Times,* the American forces had at least thirty cannon equipped to fire both conventional and atomic shells. Our army in Europe also had a number of pilotless planes (Matadors) able to carry atomic warheads at high speeds as far as five hundred miles; guided rockets bearing atomic explosives which can travel a hundred miles at supersonic speed; and short-range artillery rockets which can be equipped with atomic warheads. The Russian arsenal supposedly includes weapons of equal power, though fewer and less varied. The appalling possibilities of the new warfare gave many people in America, as in other lands, a fatalistic outlook. To thoughtful men and women, the fact that atomic war would now be absolutely suicidal, the victor perishing with the vanquished, seemed to offer a modicum of hope; no rational leader of any nation, no matter how great the passion of the moment, would resort to such a conflict. The unhappy fact, however, is that we cannot be sure that the leaders of some nations will always behave rationally.

Once more, a cardinal feature of the nation's history was the high level of economic well-being. When the year began, a certain slackening of prosperity was evident. Some called it a "rolling readjustment," some an "inventory recession," but at any rate it was real. It provoked one economist, Alvin Hansen of Harvard, to suggest that the government do more to assure the country that it would "employ all its powers to promote maximum employment, production, and purchasing power." The government did in various ways try to stimulate economic activity. Revision of the tax structure lightened the load on corporations. The Federal Reserve Board adopted an easy money policy, which gave business credit at low rates. Perhaps it was not an unhealthy fact that the nation made a "descent from overtime," for the economy in 1953 had been on a rather artificial level. The most troublesome element in the economic picture as a whole was a fairly high level of unemployment. In midsummer, union leaders were pointing to the fact that about three

million people were out of work, as against about 1,500,-
000 the year before, and that 800,000 had used up their
unemployment compensation.

Some industries were in difficulties. One was the textile industry in the North and even in parts of the Southeast; the New England mills have been hard pressed by
new factories in the South, while the movement of cotton
production away from the coastal States to Texas and
Oklahoma has injured some Carolina industry. The coal
industry continues to suffer from the competition of oil
and natural gas. As the railroads have adopted Diesel
engines, oil has supplanted coal as their motive power.
The drop in farm income affected farm-implement factories adversely, and so did the prolonged Southwestern
drought, the over-mechanization of some Middle Western farms, and the uncertainty as to future price supports.
The intense competition in the automobile field was a
source of some uneasiness. General Motors and Ford held
so much of the market that even Chrysler seemed threatened, and smaller automobile companies, like Studebaker and Packard, were forced to amalgamate to escape
extinction. Steel production for 1954 fell 21 per cent below that for 1953; it was 88,200,000 tons as against 110,-
600,000.

Nevertheless, most of the indices of prosperity remained
high. The Federal Reserve Board as the year ended estimated that gross national product for the year would
reach $356 billions, only 2.5 per cent below the high rec-
ord set in 1953. Building construction reached an un-

precedented level. According to the Department of Agriculture, the volume of the country's crops in 1954 was the fifth greatest in our history. Foreign trade remained in a healthy condition. Its total value came to about 25.5 billions; and if this was a decline of about 1.25 billions from the previous year, this drop was almost wholly accounted for by the reduction in military aid to foreign nations.

In agriculture, the year showed some very mixed results. Wheat farmers, dairy farmers, and to some extent cattle and hog growers suffered from reduced returns, while farmers with diversified crops did fairly well outside the drought areas. Beef prices, low early in the year, rose as it drew near its close; pork prices showed an opposite tendency, falling as the year advanced. After a succession of good years, farmers in general are in a strong position. Mortgage debt has been paid off, farm equipment has been accumulated, and homes have been modernized. The size of farm units has risen markedly since pre-war days, and the number of farms has fallen by about a million since 1935. With more acres and more machinery, the efficiency of the average farmer has greatly increased, and is still increasing. Today, this farmer is growing enough food and fibre for sixteen people.

Apart from the unemployment already noted, labor too had a good year. Strikes were few and comparatively unimportant, the most spectacular being a walkout of longshoremen in New York which hit that port hard. Negotiations for a merger of the American Federation of

Labor and the Congress of Industrial Organizations were steadily pressed. Labor leaders meanwhile continued to agitate the question of a guaranteed annual wage in place of the weekly pay-check, and the United Automobile Workers were plainly girding themselves to attain that goal.

For the American economy as a whole, the vital question was whether, with all its vigor, resourcefulness, and general stability, it could be kept dynamic enough to lift production, wages, consumption, and international trade. Its leadership and flexibility will have to meet constant tests. New industries such as electronics, television, and air-conditioning have grown with remarkable energy. The movement of factories and population into the Southwest and Far West proves that our economy still possesses remarkable mobility. A loss of momentum might be disastrous not only for the United States but for the whole free world; for it is still true that when America sneezes, Western Europe is in danger of pneumonia.

During 1954 the country heard more of the possible use of atomic energy in private industry than ever before. It is important that the government retain ownership of all fissionable materials, but the Atomic Energy Commission and the Administration are both anxious to develop the leasing of these materials to corporations. The fundamental idea is that companies would be permitted to own and run atomic piles or nuclear reactors, and to sell the energy they generate to public utilities or other licensed customers. As yet many mysteries surround nuclear power. The Atomic Energy Commission has therefore been eager to promote experimentation. During 1954 work was got under way on one large-scale nuclear reactor, which is expected to measure just how safe, how dependable, and how long-lived an atomic-energy plant can be. Four smaller pilot operations will test various other types of reactors. One is the "fast-breeder" type, which yields as much fissionable material as it consumes, or more.

The contract for building the large-scale plant was awarded to the Duquesne Light Company of Pittsburgh, which was willing to expend very large sums with but slight assurance of any sizable return. Its object was presumably to acquire technical knowledge of this novel field, to obtain such patent rights as a pioneer might find, and to keep the use of nuclear power for generating electricity in private hands. Meanwhile, various other corporations—notably the Dow Chemical and Detroit Edison companies—have undertaken research in the use of atomic energy. Between twenty-five and thirty associated firms have appropriated more than two million dollars for such work. Federal authorities do not encourage any supposition that highly economical power can be obtained from nuclear reactors for many years to come. But if experimentation is vigorously pushed, plants may be developed which will operate about as cheaply as steam or even hydroelectric plants; and this will enable States far distant from rich coal fields or waterfalls to share in the general growth of industry. By-products, such as radio-active isotopes, may also be highly useful.

ONCE more the United States had a year of prosperous and serene development at home, where the standard of living and the level of general culture both steadily rose. Once more its anxieties over the world scene and the unabated antagonism of East and West kept it harassed and uneasy. The year 1955 will go down in history as that of a great and on the whole beneficent boom; it will also go down as the year in which it became plain that the death of Stalin had by no means freed the globe from the tensions and terrors associated with his regime.

The most arresting event of the year in home affairs was the sudden illness of President Eisenhower. His health ever since he entered office had seemed excellent. At all times he had kept the country conscious of his age by his own frequent references to it (he was sixty-five on October 14th); for he repeatedly noted that if he accepted a second term, he would be older at its termination than any previous President had been. But when he went to Colorado for a vacation soon after Congress recessed, he seemed in robust physical condition. His remark at a breakfast in Denver to the forty-eight Republican State chairmen that "Humans are frail—and they are mortal," was accepted as having no special significance. He divided his time between work in his Denver office, and vigorous fishing and golfing.

Then, in the early hours of September 24, he was seized by a heart attack. When he was awakened by severe chest pains, his physician General Howard M. Snyder at once diagnosed the seizure as a coronary thrombosis. For two or three days the nation was badly frightened. But Dr. Paul D. White, a specialist summoned from Washington, diagnosed the attack as moderate and announced that many men survive such attacks for years. For a time the President was kept under an oxygen tent. But his recovery, though gradual, proved to be steady. It proved unnecessary to make any formal delegation of his powers. Vice-President Richard Nixon, Sherman Adams the Assistant to the President, Attorney-General Herbert C. Brownell and others kept the machinery of government running. Even in the first week the President initialled some papers; in the fourth week of his illness he held conferences with individual Cabinet members; and in November he returned to the East, dividing his time between the White House and his Gettysburg farm.

It was fortunate for the country that the President's temporary and partial disability occurred at a time when no vital domestic or foreign problems demanded an immediate solution. Had this not been so, a constitutional crisis might have occurred akin to that which arose in 1919-20, when Woodrow Wilson was stricken by a paralytic stroke in the midst of the battle over the League of Nations. As it was, only routine questions had to be considered. Soon after he returned to Gettysburg, on November 17-18, Secretary Dulles reported to him on the conference the foreign ministers had just held in Geneva; but that report dealt only with Russian obstruction.

The President's illness changed the political scene as a sudden shift of weather changes a landscape. For Republicans it was as if a heavy cloud had passed over the sun. The party had counted on persuading Mr. Eisenhower to run again, and on winning an easy victory at the polls in 1956. He had united all factions of his party to an unusual degree. Every poll showed that his following had greatly increased since he won about 34 million votes in 1952. Now it was at once assumed that he might withdraw himself from the race. He was believed to desire, after years of strain and turmoil, a return to private life; he had repeatedly urged the party not to depend on one man; and he might well shrink from letting his health become a topic of campaign debate even if he felt well enough to run again. But to whom could the Republicans turn? Chief Justice Earl Warren possessed great ability, experience, and personal popularity; but to leave his high post to run for political office would create a most unhappy precedent, and he had flatly said, not once but twice, that he would not run. Attention turned to other men—to Vice-President Nixon, to Harold Stassen, to William Knowland, and to Governor Thomas E. Dewey.

297

"APPEARS TO BE A HERD OF DARK HORSES IN THE WILDERNESS"
From a cartoon by Green in *The Providence Journal*

For the Democrats it was as if a cloud had rolled away from the sun after a period of gloom. They had looked forward to the campaign of 1956 with dread. No Democrat really wanted the nomination if Eisenhower were to be his opponent, for defeat would be practically certain. Adlai E. Stevenson had been ready to accept the honor, but as a duty rather than as an opportunity. Now, since most experts believe that the country is really Democratic, the prize of the Presidency seemed to swing within reach. Stevenson on November 15 announced his candidacy, and was quickly followed by Senator Kefauver of Tennessee, whose coonskin cap had played such a part in the pre-convention struggles of 1952. At the outset Stevenson seemed to possess a long lead.

298

This, however, might diminish as various States brought forward their "favorite sons"—New York, Governor Averell Harriman; Ohio, Governor Lausche; Missouri, Senator Stuart Symington; and Michigan, Governor Mennen Williams.

The fall elections gave the Democratic Party renewed encouragement. All over the country they swept their municipal candidates into office; in Indiana, for example, they won nearly three fourths of the city and town contests, and in Philadelphia they maintained a Democratic Administration. In Kentucky, A. B. ("Happy") Chandler was returned to the governorship with the largest majority in the State's history. But whether these results pointed to a continuing trend was matter for debate.

Whatever happened in the next campaign, the earnest desire of the whole country was that President Eisenhower should recover sufficiently to give the nation the same wise, moderate leadership that he had offered during his first three years. His illness evoked a moving display of popular affection. Said the Democratic St. Louis *Post-Dispatch:* "May his fourth year in the office of Washington and Jefferson, of Lincoln and Cleveland, of Wilson and Roosevelt, be his best year yet!" He could not at once disclose his intentions with respect to a second term, even if he had made up his mind (and he said he had not) on the subject. So long as he was a possible candidate, he would be able not only to exercise a strong influence over Congress, but to dictate his own terms to his party, demanding that it effectively purge itself of reactionaries and demagogues, and move forward to the positions demanded by the times. It was in the national interest that he should make no early decision. The year ended with the President working on his state-of-the-union message to the second session of the Eighty-fourth Congress.

One result of the illness was that various proposals were made for lightening the load of detail laid on all Presidents' shoulders. Of these the suggestion of ex-President Hoover that an Executive Vice-President be elected or appointed to deal with routine administrative matters attracted the most attention; but ex-President Truman opposed it, and members of the Eisenhower Administration were chilly toward it. Beyond doubt the President should be relieved of part of his work of seeing callers and signing papers. But the heaviest strain upon him, that of making incessant decisions, cannot be reduced; and nobody thinks that the White House will ever become a vacation resort.

The first session of the Eighty-fourth Congress, sitting during the first half of the year, could not be called very fruitful. President Eisenhower during the last Congressional campaign had prophesied that if the Democrats won control, little of his program would be made law, and the blame for inaction would be hard to fix. This prediction proved correct in both parts. But with the country more acutely interested in foreign affairs than home problems—for we face grave foreign dangers, while the domestic scene is prosperous—public sentiment was not much worried by the postponement of important bills.

Congress organized in January under a benignly conservative group of Southern gentlemen. In the Senate, where the decision of Wayne Morse of Oregon to vote with the Democrats gave them a narrow majority, Lyndon Johnson of Texas was floor leader, while Walter George of Georgia, the able dean of the body, gave Johnson effective support and after Johnson became ill filled his place. In the House, Sam Rayburn of Texas, a sagacious and much-beloved chieftain, entered on his eighth term as Speaker. Other Southerners filled important committee chairmanships. For obvious reasons Southerners are more likely than Northerners to sit for long periods, and seniority gives them an advantage. On the Republican side William Knowland of California, who held views on Far Eastern issues very different from those of the Administration, was minority leader in the Senate, and former Speaker Joseph Martin of Massachusetts was minority leader in the House.

The moderate Southern leaders got on amiably with the moderate President. While Eisenhower termed himself "a dynamic conservative," Lyndon Johnson said he wished to see the issues presented in such a way "that the true middle of the road character of the Democratic Party could assert itself." But this all-around moderation meant that the session lacked thrust and drive. The Northern Democrats are obviously more liberal on many subjects, such as social welfare, than the Southerners or the old-fashioned Republicans, like Styles Bridges of New Hampshire (chairman of the Republican Policy Committee), and they pulled angrily at the traces. What legislation was passed, outside the foreign field, the country owed chiefly to them and to the President's enormous prestige.

Naturally legislation concerned with foreign relations took precedence. The United States is the main pillar of the free world, and cannot evade its responsibilities. The President gave priority to a "modest, gradual, and reciprocal program" for developing foreign trade, to appropriations for foreign aid, and to military measures. All three measures were carried, though not in the untouched form which Mr. Eisenhower wished.

The bill for a three-year extension of the Reciprocal Trade Agreements Act, the historic legislation which began under Secretary Cordell Hull, went on the Congressional calendar as H.R. 1, at the head of the list. Both Democratic and Republican leaders endorsed it. It gave the President power to reduce tariffs five percent a year for three years in return for foreign concessions, to cut down any duties that are more than fifty percent ad valorem, and to reduce by half the rates on articles imported in negligible amounts. The President on January 10 sent a message pleading for the bill. The nation, he wrote, must give the world the encouragement of free competitive markets. "Our own self-interest requires such a program because (1) economic strength among our allies is essential to our security; (2) economic growth in under-developed areas is necessary to lessen international instability . . . ; and (3) an increasing volume of world production and trade will help assure our own economic growth." The Cabinet stood squarely behind this program for emphasizing "trade not aid." The two great labor organizations, A.F. of L. and C.I.O., the Farm Bureau Federation, and other powerful organizations supported it. What opposition existed came from textile, coal, and oil interests. At first it seemed slight, but in the end a hard fight was needed.

The bill passed the House on February 18 by a vote of 295 to 110; it went through the Senate a little later 75 to 13. But it had been modified to permit domestic industries to appeal to the government for higher tariffs whenever they felt that they would be injured by imports. Moreover, the Administration's hope that it could obtain ratification of entry into the international body known as the Organization for Trade Cooperation was doomed to frustration. The Senate, led by Byrd of Virginia, balked. Many members thought it improper for Congress to delegate powers to the President which the President might then delegate to an international body. The United States has come a long way since the folly of the high Smoot-Hawley Tariff of 1930, and indeed now occupies a more liberal position on tariffs than numerous other nations. Our economic position is so strong, however, that the area in which industry needs high tariffs constantly shrinks, and we should go still further in cutting down duties and encouraging other countries to do likewise.

303

In foreign aid, Congress voted by overwhelming majorities to continue the present program, which now bears the label Mutual Security. But whereas President Eisenhower asked $3,530 millions for MSA, Congress gave him only $2,704 millions. On the final vote the Democrats lent the President better support than the Republicans, one group of whom tend constantly to revert to the isolationism of Coolidge days. A large body of public sentiment unfortunately regards Mutual Security Aid as a "give-away" scheme to help lazy, ungrateful foreigners, whereas it is actually a hardheaded program for welding and strengthening the free world to resist aggression. Every penny of it counts at least as much for our defense as similar sums spent on airplanes and carriers.

Nor was Congress liberal with the cooperative technical assistance program of the United Nations. The President requested a grant of $8,000,000 for this program; Congress, after much reluctant scrimmaging, voted $6,500,000. This was less than half what Congress had appropriated in 1954.

Yet no program has been, within its limits, more farsighted and beneficial. The UN has sent about two thousand experts of many different nations to various countries to assist in improving economic and social conditions. The nations asking for the help have contributed more to the general work than the nations which sent the experts. Results have been out of all proportion to the meagre sums spent. The whole cost of the UN program in 1954 was only about $23,000,000, and American aid should rise, not fall.

The President has progressively reduced the standing military forces. To keep the country properly safeguarded, he asked for legislation which, by compulsory provisions, would create a trained military reserve of 2,900,000 men. But Congress would not go nearly so far. Rejecting the idea that every man now or previously in service should hereafter be subject to compulsory reserve training, it made the program applicable only to those who are newly brought into the army. These veterans, after reentering civil life, will be subject to recall in any national crisis. The traditional sentiment of Americans against "universal military training" remains powerful; mothers in particular object to it; and every proposed step in that direction meets stubborn resistance.

Federal aid for housing, for education, for highway construction, and for public health represented the most progressive side of President Eisenhower's "dynamic conservatism." On all four the Democrats took a rather more liberal attitude than did the Republicans. Indeed, in public housing they went quite beyond the President's own program. Mr. Eisenhower had asked for authority to build 35,000 public housing units a year for two years. In the Senate the Democrats seized the initiative, approving a plan for a maximum program of 135,000 annual units, and a minimum program of 50,000 annual units, for four years—the size of the program to be left to the President. In the House the Republicans were against this bill. To defeat it they refused at first to authorize any public housing at all, hoping that they could force a compromise. The manoeuver succeeded, for finally the two chambers agreed on a bill for but 45,000 units, and for a single year only. This could not be called much of a victory for either public housing or the President.

As for education, Congress in this field accomplished nothing specific. Action was postponed until 1956. But the President did get an important program for Federal aid in school construction placed before Congress in a special message and embodied in a bill introduced by Senator H. Alexander Smith of New Jersey. Under this bill, the national government would provide a stimulant; the local taxpayers would pay most of the costs. It was a partial gain to obtain some public discussion of a constructive plan.

Thousands of school buildings in the United States are disgraceful. They are wretched makeshifts because the local districts are too impoverished to pay for better ones. The national government, under the President's plan, would take three steps to help them. It would buy the school bonds of poor districts, unable now to sell them at reasonable interest-rates, up to a total of $750,000,000. It would provide $150,000,000, to be matched by States, to establish State funds for erecting and renting buildings in needy districts. And it would grant as much as $200,000,000 outright (again to be matched by States) to help the most impoverished communities in school-building. This program was much debated in and out of Congress during the year. Along-side it, were other measures to help education—for example, Senator Lister Hill's proposal to appropriate $500,000,000 for two years in emergency assistance to the States "in the construction of urgently needed public elementary and secondary school facilities, and for other purposes." None came to a vote, but the need is so great that some action will have to be taken in the near future.

Roads also drew the President's attention; and, with the automobile industry pouring out more than 9,000,000 motor vehicles during the year, well they might. The country has about three and a third million miles of roads and streets to be maintained and extended. It has about 40,000 miles of main interstate trunk highways, which carry—it is said by experts—about one-third of the nation's traffic. Under the expected rate of expenditure by nation, States, and localities, the United States during the next decade will spend about $47,000,000,000 on its roads and streets. It seems a huge sum but it is far from enough. At least as much again is needed if the roads are to meet the additional traffic burden expected by 1956. President Eisenhower proposed a program for finding this additional fifty billions, the nation to contribute roughly forty millions.

Everybody is in favor of the new and better roads; but where shall we find the money? Many States are already eager to get their hands on the Federal tax of two cents a gallon on gasoline. Some States are now taxing gasoline themselves to an extent which brings cries of indignation from car-owners. The President proposed the creation of a Federal Highway Authority to sell its own bonds, pay the interest and principal from the national gasoline taxes, and assist the States to market their bonds for highway improvement. Various objections were at once made. Was this system of ear-marking special Federal revenues for special purposes wise? Could the States really sell such huge quantities of bonds as to raise about 25 billions in ten years? Was it right that drivers of motor vehicles should pay all the costs of new and improved highways, when real estate interests, for example, would reap much of the benefit?

Congress adjourned without taking any action; this subject, too, went over to 1956. The Senate adopted a Democratic substitute bill for combined Federal-State expenditures of nearly $18,000,000 over the next five years, the national government to contribute about $12,500,000 of the whole, and to take the money out of its general tax receipts. But in the House, by over-whelming vote, both plans were killed.

As inheritors of the traditions of Franklin D. Roosevelt, the Democrats were consistently ready to go further in social legislation than was the Administration. Thus when Eisenhower suggested that the minimum wage floor be raised from 75 cents an hour to 90 cents, the Democrats brought it up to $1—though the final vote in the House, 362 to 54, included many Republicans in the affirmative. (No vote was recorded in the Senate.) The Democrats in the House, against Administration opposition, also carried a bill to liberalize the social security benefits paid to women and disabled persons. This, however, died in the Senate. After the President had suggested a rise in the pay of postal employees averaging 7.5 percent, the Democrats carried a bill providing for an 8.2 percent increase. If Democratic House leaders had been given their way, they would have passed legislation to reduce income taxes by $20 a person, to the special benefit of the low income groups. Speaker Rayburn exerted his great influence to carry it through the House. But in the Senate the reduction failed.

Once more a variety of much-discussed (and in general praiseworthy) measures were lost in the Congressional hurlyburly. Inasmuch as the Administration wishes Statehood for Hawaii alone (presumably Republican) and the Democrats insisted that Alaska (presumably Democratic) must also come in, both were kept waiting on the doorstep. The oft-renewed, often-blocked effort to liberalize the immigration laws again failed. Everyone agrees that the present statutes contain what Senator Irving M. Ives of New York called "serious inequities," but the forces of inertia are strong. Once more President Eisenhower (like Truman before him) declared that the country should do far more for the nation's health. "Many of our fellow Americans cannot afford to pay the costs of medical care when it is most needed, and they are not protected by adequate health insurance." One of his proposals was to provide Federal guarantees for voluntary health insurance schemes; another was to use Federal money, on a State-matching basis, for the medical care of the aged, the totally disabled, the blind, and the orphaned. But once more the opposition, backed by a singularly violent propaganda, defeated these proposals.

One of the measures dearest to Eisenhower's heart was his project for an atomic "peace ship" to carry, from port to port around the world, an exhibit illustrating the peaceful use of atomic energy. It would, he believed, do much to demonstrate, in Asiatic and European countries where much misunderstanding exists, the peaceable temper and policy of the American people. The Democrats, however, while approving the object, thought that the method was faulty. By the close vote of 42 to 41, on strict party lines, the Administration failed to get the $21,000,000 it asked for such a vessel.

In foreign affairs, the cold war experienced a July thaw only to grow as cold as ever after an autumn frost. A conference "at the summit" took President Eisenhower to Geneva early in the summer to join the British and French Prime Ministers in conferring with the two principal Russian leaders, Bulganin and Khrushchev. A jovial, optimistic week of meetings, dinners, toasts, and friendly exchanges followed. Never, the world agreed, had the President appeared to better advantage. But when October brought the foreign ministers of the United States, Britain, France, and Russia together in the same city, the atmosphere quickly grew frigid. On the principal questions between West and East, disagreement was found to be as bitter and implacable as ever.

It was Winston Churchill who had first suggested a

parley of the very highest officers of government. If only, he had urged in the spring of 1953, Mr. Eisenhower, Stalin, and himself could sit down at a table and quietly discuss their problems, they might clear away at least part of their differences. The conception was long distasteful to the United States, which felt that Presidents Wilson and Roosevelt had not scored brilliant successes when they left the country to visit Paris and Yalta respectively, and which doubted that Stalin would budge an inch. But after Stalin's death, and still more after the removal of Malenkov placed the seemingly more reasonable Marshal Bulganin and Nikita Khrushchev in power, the one as prime minister, the other as head of the Communist Party, American sentiment changed. Millions of people believed that the Soviet attitude might have altered. If a change of heart had taken place, clearly the United States should encourage it. The President therefore left for the Big Four conference in mid-July amid general public approval.

The event seemed to justify his decision. So amiable was the gathering that, said the New York *Times,* it seemed to "call up vistas of Tennyson's 'fair meadows crowned with summer seas'." On the first day President Eisenhower declared that none of the problems dividing East and West was "inherently insoluble"; Marshal Bulganin rejoined that he saw no "natural differences" between the American and Russian peoples. Throughout the week of talks the President dominated the conference by his obvious honesty, earnestness, and ability. He made a tremendous impression on all the participants and on the public sentiment of Europe. His main object, he had said before leaving, was to "change the spirit" of such meetings, and he did so. His prestige as a world figure reached its apex when he proposed that the United States and Russia should each permit a continuing aerial inspection of all their military facilities, and should exchange the blueprints of their armed establishments. When he returned he could well say: "We cannot afford to be negligent or complacent, but we must be hopeful."

The assemblage for a few days really achieved that "intimate contact" of world leaders for which Churchill had longed. Mr. Eisenhower's good will was infectious. The most dramatic moment of the conference came when, after the Soviet spokesmen had questioned whether the North Atlantic Treaty Organization (NATO) did not harbor aggressive purposes, the President turned impulsively to Marshal Bulganin and said: "The United States will never take part in an aggressive war." To this Bulganin replied: "We believe the statement." For a brief time a new spirit, which men called "the Geneva spirit," actually seemed to come into existence. People hoped that "the new look" in Moscow would make it permanent.

Yet of concrete accomplishments the conference was singularly destitute. The Western Powers took to the Swiss city a number of constructive proposals; the Russian leaders gently rejected them without making any really substantial counter-suggestions. The most important practical object to be gained, in the view of President Eisenhower, Prime Minister Anthony Eden, and Premier Faure, was the reunification of Germany. They recognized that this must be accomplished in a way that would not threaten either Russia or France—for German power will soon again be tremendous. Eden therefore suggested unification with three safeguards: a five-power mutual defense pact, an agreement as to the total level of forces and armaments in Germany, and a demilitarized zone between East and West. But the Russian leaders would not hear of this plan. They did not wish to discuss German unification at all; that could wait. To provide for general security, they suggested an all-European treaty of mutual defense, with China and the United States acting as "observers." This, of course, would be a way of ejecting the United States and its forces from Western Europe. And the Russians turned a very cold shoulder to the President's suggestions for the control of armaments by an international system of air inspection and by exchange of plans.

In the end, the conference broke up with a directive to the foreign ministers of the Big Four to work upon "European security and Germany," subjects which had a "close link," and upon "a progressive elimination of barriers which interfere with free communications." Disarmament was turned over to a United Nations subcommittee. The great question was whether the so-called "Geneva spirit" would assist the foreign ministers and United Nations delegates to solve these harsh difficulties. President Eisenhower attached to his words of optimism, when he returned, a cautious warning: "We must never be deluded into believing that one week of friendly, even fruitful, negotiations can wholly eliminate a problem arising out of the wide gulf that separates East and West." Americans felt pride that for a brief interlude, at least, their leadership of the world had apparently been reestablished. But they wanted to see good words followed by good works.

A suspicion at once grew up that the Soviet Government was trying to beguile world sentiment while it deliberately obstructed German unification. It had known well, since the East German uprising, that free elections would result in the overwhelming defeat of Communism. It knew also that the liberation of East Germany would inspire in the breasts of countless Poles, Czechoslovakians, Hungarians, and Rumanians a wild hope that their nations too might be liberated from the Communist yoke. It would therefore be natural for the Soviet Government to postpone any move toward a changed status for Germany until, by education, propaganda, and concessions, they might alter the sentiment of the East Germans—perhaps until a new generation grew up there which had never known any but a Soviet regime. Meanwhile, the aged Dr. Adenauer would have died. The new leaders of the West German Government might then be willing to negotiate for unification on a basis favorable to Russia. At the very least, they would surrender rearmament and a place in NATO for the privilege of unification.

The acid test at Geneva, said President Eisenhower, would come when in October the foreign ministers met to discuss practical questions. During the interim the Russians made a series of moves planned to strengthen their position. They brought Dr. Adenauer, Chancellor of West Germany, to Moscow in September for negotiations. The aging Chancellor hoped he could make some progress toward unification, and obtain the return of an estimated 100,000 German war prisoners still kept in Russia; the Soviet leaders hoped to detach West Germany from the Western alliance, which she had joined in May. It was the Russians who gained most. They declared that they held only 9,626 prisoners, all "war criminals," and as a price for releasing them they insisted on a resumption of diplomatic relations with West Germany. This gave Moscow a means of bypassing the United States, Britain, and France in dealing with German questions. Immediately afterward, Moscow gave East Germany her "sovereignty" (though it remained in every way a satellite state), with control over her own boundaries. The Russians could now play the East German dictatorship against the West German democracy in all discussions of unification. Though East Germany has only 40,725 square miles and about 17,000,000 people as against 94,500 square miles and some 50,000,000 people in West Germany, and is economically backward and depressed, Moscow could call it an equal state.

The Russians also made the most of frictions in the Middle East and of the grievances of the Arab populations against Western powers. They continuously assailed "colonialism," and paraded their sympathy with those rebellious Arab elements in Algeria and Morocco which were carrying on a bitter struggle against the French. Through its satellite, Czechoslovakia, the Soviet Union also began shipping arms to Egypt in exchange for cotton and rice. As Israel and Egypt have repeatedly clashed along the boundaries of the Gaza strip, a narrow tongue of land which Egypt holds on the Mediterranean side of the new Jewish state, the Israelis feared that such shipments would encourage their Arab neighbors to undertake a war of conquest. Soviet troublemaking in the Near East was like throwing lighted firecrackers into a room full of petroleum fumes; a terrible explosion might occur at any time.

The "Geneva spirit" had therefore been largely dissipated when in the last week of October the four foreign ministers, V. M. Molotov of Russia, Harold MacMillan of Great Britain, Antoine Pinay of France, and John Foster Dulles of the United States, met in the same room in the impressive Palais des Nations where the heads of state had gathered three months earlier. That same week MIG-15 fighter planes from the Soviet bloc were being uncrated at Port Said by Egyptian workmen; Egyptian officers were unpacking and distributing several large cargoes of Communist arms. The foreign ministers had three main subjects to discuss: first, German unification and European security; second, disarmament; and third, the strengthening of communications between East and West. At once both sides brought forward concrete proposals.

The West insisted that Germany should be unified on the basis of free elections, and that it should keep the place in NATO which West Germany already held. To reassure Russia, it proposed that nine powers should adopt a treaty by which they renounced the use of force and agreed to take unified action against aggressors: the nine being the United States, Germany, Britain, France, Russia, Poland, and Czechoslovakia. The West also proposed that a demilitarized zone, stretching from the North Sea to Austria, be established along the boundary between Germany on the west, and Poland and Czechoslovakia on the east. In this zone, from 100 to 150 miles wide, radar warning systems should be built; the Russians to man the installations on German territory, the Western Powers those on Polish and Czechoslovakian ground. This, said Mr. Dulles, was "a momentous and historic proposal." It should give the Communist nations "a true sense of security."

Russia, in her counter-proposals, held that German reunification could wait. Before it could take place, declared Molotov, a feeling of confidence and harmony must be created between East and West Germans. Moreover, the great "gains" that "democracy" had made in East Germany must be safeguarded. He proposed that pending the establishment of a "united, peace-loving, democratic German state," the United States and all the European nations should sign a fifteen-point treaty. They would agree not to take part in any alliance or grouping of the NATO type. They would pledge themselves to refrain from the use of force and to defend each other against attack. After the signing of the treaty all foreign (that is, American) troops would be with-

317

drawn from Europe. It was at once plain that the Russian terms meant surrendering Germany to Communism, and laying all Western Europe open to Communist pressures and invasions. Dulles told Molotov flatly that he had violated the directive of July.

On the two remaining sections of the agenda, East and West were equally far apart. The Russians were unwilling to accept President Eisenhower's suggestions regarding disarmament. Molotov called attention to the fact that the Soviet Union had reduced its armed forces by 640,000 men (which still left them far above the Western level), and had given up its naval base on the Finnish coast (which it should never have seized in the first place). But he would not accept the American proposals on inspection except as part of a broad disarmament scheme, which must include a flat and final renunciation of atomic weapons—that is, of the one type of arms on which the West relies to deter Russia from aggression. Nor would he even discuss stopping Communist arms shipments to Egypt. No progress was made toward lessening the arms burden which is now almost crushing the world. Even after this failure, some men still hoped that something could be done to open wider the door for cultural and commercial relationships between the Communist and free nations. Already the United States and Russia had agreed on a freer exchange of books and periodicals. But here too hope faded before Russian intransigence. Molotov announced that he would give no privileges to "Western scum."

Looking back on the international events of the year,

Americans had reason to feel disillusioned and pessimistic. The Russians had made absolutely no concessions to promote world peace. At Geneva in July their smiles, bows, and honeyed words had poorly hidden the fact that they had yielded nothing, and had made demands which if granted would have left Western Europe defenseless. They had then retired to Moscow to test fresh nuclear weapons, including a bomb which they proclaimed the most terrible yet known; to foment mischief in the Near East by the sale of munitions; to use their German prisoners to extort cruel terms from the helpless Dr. Adenauer; to accelerate the arming of East Germany; and to carry on a ceaseless propaganda against the West. They had come back to Geneva in October to renew their demand that Western Europe give up all its defenses, that the United States return to isolation, and that the German people accept Communism as the price of unification. Then, as 1955 drew to a close, Bulganin and Khrushchev made a noisy tour of India and Burma, delivering diatribes against the Western Powers, and even accusing Britain and America of inspiring Hitler's attack on Russia in 1941! The cold war was as severe a blizzard as in the worst years of Stalin.

The one gain of the year was that at the first Geneva meeting both sides, clearly though tacitly, had agreed that a great new war, which would inevitably involve nuclear weapons, would be intolerable and almost unthinkable. It would ruin everyone. Militarily, East and West had come to a stalemate. This fact transferred the

319

contest between them, throughout much of Asia and Africa, to a new sphere: Russia and the free world would compete with economic and cultural weapons, using money, technicians, trade, books, and ideas to gain the ascendency. The victory would go to the side which showed the most intellectual enterprise, economic vigor, and crusading zeal. This was a kind of contest in which the great democracies—if they exerted themselves—had a manifest advantage.

The Far Eastern scene throughout the year remained troubled and uneasy. Early in the year the Secretary-General of the United Nations went to China in an effort to bring the Peiping leaders to a friendlier position and to obtain the release of eleven American airmen whom they still held. His mission ended in failure. Tension between Communist China and the United States increased as evidence appeared that Chinese forces were being massed for an attack on the Tachens and other coastal islands, and on Formosa. On January 24 President Eisenhower sent a message to the Congress declaring that the situation in the Formosa Straits "seriously imperils" the United States, and asking for an approval in advance of the use of armed force in protecting Formosa and "closely related" territories. Congress at once assented. To lessen the danger of a collision, the Seventh Fleet in February evacuated American forces from the Tachens, which lie close to the Chinese coast; the focus of attention then became Quemoy and Matsu, two islands still under American protection.

Gradually, however, the tension over these positions relaxed.

Meanwhile, the nations bound by the Southeast Asia Treaty Organization (SEATO) held a meeting at Bangkok, Thailand, during February; and they began to organize machinery for cooperative defense. Throughout the year the United States assisted the government of South Vietnam with economic aid and expert advisers.

From beginning to end, 1955 was the year of a great boom. As the richest spending Christmas in the nation's history closed, the New York *Times,* reviewing the economic history of the twelve months, printed a series of exuberant headlines: "Los Angeles Area Bursting Seams"; "Industry Zooms in Philadelphia"; "Sights Set High by New England"; "U. S. Trade Abroad Surges to Record." The prosperity was built on many factors. Some of them, such as the continued heavy spending for defense, the slight but real inflationary movement, the tremendous use of installment-buying and other forms of credit, and the extraordinary stock market boom, were of a character to arouse doubts. Nevertheless, for the most part American prosperity seemed well-based.

Two principal elements in the boom were the record-breaking production of cars and trucks, and the continued expansion of the building industry. The automobile companies, and especially the Big Three, General Motors, Ford, and Chrysler, had the best year of their history. Their production was 40 percent above that of

1954; it was greater by a million motor vehicles than the record set in the previous highest year, 1950. Of the grand total of units built, 7,795,000 were passenger cars. The total wholesale value of the automobiles, trucks, and buses built was placed by the Automobile Manufacturers Association at fourteen billion dollars. Once more the Ford and Chevrolet cars raced neck and neck. The most interesting aspect of the year, however, was the dramatic recovery of the Chrysler Company, which after an unhappy experience the previous year, pushed forward in 1955 to claim 17 percent of all sales.

For the tenth year in succession, the volume of building broke all previous marks. It represented more than one-seventh of the gross national product of the United States and provided more than one-seventh of the employment. The number of new houses begun was computed at 1,300,000. This building boom reflected some interesting changes in American society. One was the rapid growth of suburbs all over the country, with a simultaneous creation of suburban shopping centers. Another was the rapid increase in population, the product of an increased birth-rate; new families were multiplying, and they now wanted three or four children where once they had been content with two. Then, too, the Great Depression, the Second World War, and the Korean conflict had all prevented or delayed construction, so that a marked vacuum existed. This had to be filled with houses, schools, hospitals, stores, and other facilities. Finally, the modernization of homes—new styles in architecture, new demands for convenience,

light, air, economical heating arrangements, and so on—
meant the demolition of old houses, and their replace-
ment by revolutionized designs. Never before have styles
in housing shown so marked a shift as between 1935
and 1955.

It was expected as the year closed that the gross national product would reach $387 billions, a figure suffi-
ciently close to the $400 billion mark to lead many ob-
servers to predict that this impressive total would soon
be reached. Personal income for 1955 certainly exceeded
$300 billions. More steel was poured than in any pre-
vious year. The demand was such that even century-old
furnaces and aged and obsolete coke ovens were called
into service. Consumption of goods of all kinds was at
unsurpassed figures. It was estimated at the end of the
year that retail buying had reached $185 billions, a sum
sufficient to keep merchants highly prosperous. Net
earnings of corporations reached $44.6 billions before
Federal income taxes, and $22.3 billions after their de-
duction—the biggest profits in our business history.

Industry was taking on entirely new shapes in the
United States. Never before had so much attention been
given to automation, which one writer defined as "machines telling other machines what to do and when to
do it." Perhaps the simplest and most comprehensible
forms of automation are the devices used to control the
heating of homes and the air-conditioning of homes
and offices. They have become so common, that about a
million of them are now telling furnaces when to go on
or go off, and air-conditioning machinery when to start

and to stop. Some great automobile plants, like the assembly plant of Ford near Cleveland and the Chrysler plant in Detroit, have introduced automatic controls to an extent that has permitted them to discharge a quarter or more of the old working force. The effect of automation on the worker is much debated. Some experts fear it will lead to much unemployment; others say that it will help diversify industry to a point where it requires more men, freeing the individual worker from much manual drudgery.

Another marked tendency of the new industrial era is toward the ever greater use of research experts. All the great industries have large staffs of highly-trained scientists. Such corporations as Du Pont, General Electric, and Westinghouse have research buildings and equipment that would make many a great university envious. According to the New York *Times,* well over four billion dollars was spent in 1955 by private industry and the government in laboratory and field research. Some five thousand privately owned industries employed a total of about 300,000 scientists. One of the officers of the National Science Foundation pointed out that a definite connection existed between the fact that the United States gave a higher percentage of its national income to research and development than any other country, and the fact that the United States probably had the highest rate of economic growth among the world's highly industrialized countries.

Increasing attention, too, was given during the year to one query of world-wide interest: How great a role would atomic energy play in the industrial activity of the next decade, or the next quarter century? Many scientists and many industrialists believed that the rate of its application to the peaceful work of the world might astonish humanity. A great international conference on peaceful use of such energy was held in Geneva, Switzerland, under United Nations auspices, in August. Here, on August 8, just ten years and one day after American airmen dropped the bomb on Hiroshima, the president of the conference, Homi J. Bhabba of India, made a momentous prediction. He declared that it might not be long before the power of the hydrogen bomb, the thermo-nuclear fusion reaction, would revolutionize all industry. This power would be released in a controlled manner, not by explosion. "I venture to predict that a method will be found for liberating fusion energy in a controlled manner within the next two decades. When that happens the energy problems of the world will truly have been solved forever, for the fuel will be as plentiful as the heavy hydrogen of the oceans."

This statement prompted spokesmen for the British, American, and Russian governments to declare that they were all working hard on the problem of a controlled release of thermo-nuclear power. The winning of this race—and it may be won by 1975 or even earlier —will truly usher in a completely new age of human development.

Foreign trade during the year continued at a high and indeed previously untouched level. The American boom was almost matched by the boom in Western

Europe. Naturally, commerce responded. Canada, too, was developing at a tremendous pace, and both exporting and importing larger quantities than ever before. On the basis of figures for the first ten months of the year, it appeared that imports from abroad would reach about $11,500 millions, and that exports, meanwhile, would stand at $14,500 millions for the year.

No item of business history attracted so much attention as did the announcement early in the autumn that a large block of the Ford Motor Company stock would at last be sold to the public. That huge corporation, founded in 1903 by Henry Ford, had long been under complete family control. Henry Ford had bought out most of the original partners in 1907 and the remainder in 1921. His domination of the company, highly liberal in some respects, and very illiberal in others, had been autocratic. On his retirement in 1945, two years before his death, control had passed to his grandsons, chief among them the able Henry Ford II. But while the Ford family had continued to own all of the voting stock, ownership of about 88 percent of the corporation was vested in the Ford Foundation—by far the richest foundation on the globe. Its trustees recognized that they should diversify their investments. While income from the Ford Motor Company was large (for the first nine months of 1955 the company made a net profit after taxes of nearly $350 millions), it was subject to all the fluctuations of the automobile business. At the same time, Henry Ford II, his associate Ernest Breech (chairman of the board), and other company officers realized that widespread stock ownership would mean widespread good will.

The Foundation decided to permit seven large brokerage houses to handle the sale of about one-sixth of their stock holdings; the Ford family announcing that it would give up at least sixty percent of its voting rights. Control would still remain with Henry Ford II and his brothers, for they would hold a compact block of votes sufficiently large to safeguard it. Measures were taken during the autumn to guarantee that the stock would be scattered all over the country, and that small buyers would receive equitable attention. Nobody knew what price would be set on the stock, but the general guess was that the seven million shares would go for about $450 millions. It is safe to say that no sale of stock in American annals created so much excitement among investment houses and so much interest among investors as this.

Labor had one of the happiest years in its history. Only one great strike occurred, that in the plants of the Westinghouse Electric Company, which when the year ended was still unsettled. Elsewhere, when labor stoppages were threatened, employers took advantage of the boom and willingness of customers to pay higher prices for goods, and increased wages and other benefits—sometimes in a sweeping fashion.

Particularly striking—and a long step toward committing industry to support a welfare system even when workers were unemployed—was the decision of the two greatest motor companies, in June, to pay what was called "a guaranteed wage." For two months the Ford Motor Company and the United Automobile Workers under Walter Reuther discussed wages, hours, and fringe benefits, but always with the question of a long-term guarantee foremost in their talks. The union knew that it had the Ford Motor Company on the hip. For one reason, Mr. Reuther had built up a strike fund of $25 millions. For another, the rivalry of Ford and Chevrolet was so close that Ford simply could not permit a strike and a consequent loss of ground; in the great national race, the Ford cars had just pulled ahead. For still another reason, young Henry Ford II is anxious to establish his position as a liberal and progressive leader, with a broad social vision.

The automobile industry has always been one of the best paid in America—while it was running. But it has also been an industry subject to sharp fluctuations. Production is often high in the first eight or nine months, and then tapers away as the plants are retooled to bring out new models. If demand slumps, large numbers of men are laid off for long periods. Unemployment insurance does not meet the full need of hands out of work. It rises little above the subsistence level, and it is usually confined to a half-year (26 weeks). A Ford worker getting, on the average, $85 or $90 a week, feels sharply a drop to the Michigan unemployment pay of $30 or $35. The United Automobile Workers therefore demanded that the company, if it laid off employees, should guarantee them a total income (counting unemployment insurance compensation) of eight percent of their full annual wage. It wished Ford to create a huge special fund, $130 millions within three years, to assure this.

Naturally the company balked at so huge a commitment. It offered a counter scheme which included the sale of its stock to employees at half price. In the end, as walkouts began all over the country—for many Ford workers wished to go fishing—the union won the greater part of its demands. President Reuther obtained from Mr. Ford a three-year contract under which the employee, when laid off, would get 65 percent of his net weekly wage for the first four weeks, and 60 percent for the next twenty-two. The company refused to accept any liability beyond a half-year. At the same time, the company gave a straight wage advance of six cents an hour, with new pension and insurance benefits. Ford could say that the wage was neither guaranteed, nor was it annual. Reuther could say that it was practically guaranteed, and that semi-annual was good enough. He had won his battle in essence and principle.

At once General Motors, which had just established new production levels, and was as much averse to a strike as Ford, followed its rival's example. It too gave what was practically a guaranteed semi-annual wage. And at the beginning of July the 600,000 United Steel workers threatened to stop the steel mills, which were running full blast with a great backlog of orders, if they were not given a high wage increase. Here there was no question of a guaranteed annual wage. It was only the rate of pay that was in question. The steel industry had to pause and think. Every cent added to wages meant forty cents added to the price of a ton of steel, and it would be easy to raise prices to a point where customers would turn to substitute metals or plastics. But in the end the steel workers gained most of what they wanted.

The response of industry and the general public to these advances was mixed. Nobody wanted the great boom then in progress stopped short. At the same time, the wage increases did give an accelerating push to inflation. Steel went up at once, and when the new automobile models were brought forward at the end of the year, they bore higher price tags. The farmers of the nation, with falling incomes, were bound to regard these wage gains with a jealous eye. So were the unorganized majority of workers, and in particular two groups suffering from depression, the millhands of the cotton textile industry, and the coal miners in both the anthracite and bituminous fields.

But by far the greatest development of 1955 for labor was the merger of the Congress of Industrial Organizations and the American Federation of Labor into one group of some fifteen million members. The head of the colossal new body was a one-time plumber's assistant in the Bronx, George Meany. He and the much younger, more spectacular, Walter P. Reuther had been the principal agents in bringing the conservative Federation and the progressive Congress together in general harmony. The marriage had been agreed upon in principle in February; a new charter was hammered out during the spring and summer; in August the union leaders announced that all negotiations had been completed; and in the first week of December the merger was completed. It was significant that the new name was "AFL and CIO," neither partner being willing to give up its identity. It was also significant that Mr. Meany used the magazine section of the New York *Times* to announce that he wished to cooperate with industry in a "live and let live" spirit.

Under the charter of the consolidated union, craft organizations and industrial organizations have equal rank. Neither racial nor religious lines are hereafter to be tolerated. The two large railroad brotherhoods still maintain racial barriers, but they are independent. If Mr. Meany succeeds in his dream of bringing them within the fold, they will have to give up their color prejudices. It seems clear that the huge new group, once it gets rid of some duplications and jealousies, will exercise far more power than its predecessors. It has large money resources, which will be used in an effort to organize the chemical industry (especially the Du Pont empire), retail trades, and business office forces. The invasion of the South, heretofore always poor ground for the unions, will be carried further. Nor will the AFL and CIO neglect politics; some of the leaders have expressed discontent with the recent record of Congress, and have said that at coming elections union men will act vigorously to support the party groups and candidates which promise to favor labor policies. But the day of a Labor Party in the United States is still happily far distant.

The greatest of all the unsolved problems of the nation, beyond all question, is the farm problem. Its perplexities during the year reminded many people of the bitter disputation in the 1920s over the McNary-Haugen Bill and other suggested remedies for rural depression. The situation in 1955, though not nearly so grave, was alarming. On one side lay the stubborn fact of chronic overproduction in basic farm crops, and a Federal investment, down to the end of the year, of approximately $7,500 millions in price-supporting operations. During the fiscal year 1954-55 the government lost the record sum of $800 millions in these operations—a very pretty penny. On the other side is the conceded hardship of many farmers, and particularly hundreds of thousands of them who own family-size farms. From the autumn of 1951 to the autumn of 1955, under Truman and Eisenhower, net farm income dropped by twenty-five percent. This drop, which began under high rigid crop-supports, was for a time equally divided between the two administrations, but 10 percent of it took place in 1955. It really pinched badly many farm people all over the Middle West. Taxes, costs of farm implements, and labor charges remained high; when income sank, hardship was certain. The farmers felt this the more keenly when they saw that wages and dividends were higher than ever.

Secretary Benson, in 1955 as in previous years, pursued a courageous course. Under his leadership, the Administration tried to persuade farmers to dispense with high rigid crop-support payments. He had carried legislation in 1954 authorizing lower supports, and in 1955 he used it. His object was to reduce the tremendous weight of accumulated stocks. The Administration severely restricted wheat and cotton acreage, at the same time making the farm situation more flexible by allowing farmers a free hand in growing what they liked on the land thus thrown open. To cut down the stocks now held in government warehouses, the Administration accelerated the sale of food abroad, and used it freely for school lunch and relief programs.

Stung by the rural distress, Congressional leaders brought forward a variety of programs for alleviating it. One group wished to restore the 90 percent price supports on the five basic crops (wheat, corn, rice, cotton, peanuts)—growers of these crops in return accepting marketing quotas. Representative H. D. Cooley introduced a bill for this purpose. Another school of thought favored the Federal leasing of land to be held out of cultivation for these staples. Still another body of opinion favored direct Federal subsidies or "compensatory payments" to growers of certain crops, on the principle the government has already followed in making payments to wool-growers. Senator John J. Sparkman of Alabama introduced a Family Farm Development Bill, the purpose being to "strengthen the nation by preserving the family-sized farm." It provided for special programs in five hundred small-farm counties. Here the farmers would be given technical assistance and the grant of low-cost credit, to increase the productivity of their holdings or to enlarge the area of the unit farmed in order to make it truly economic.

All these proposals were open to certain objections,

and none was translated into law on the nation's statute books. This problem, like so many others, went over to 1956. It is clear that the country has more farmers who make a bare subsistence, even in the fertile Middle Western States, than we had supposed, and that their distress has become a danger-signal. It is also clear that we cannot afford to lessen our farm population without grave loss, for rural life is in many ways the best school of character that we possess.

The corn-hog section of the farm economy was particularly hard hit. Many farmers in Iowa and other corn-growing States west of the Mississippi were injured by a drought; the Iowa corn crop fell twelve percent below that of 1954 and eight percent below the ten-year average. Nevertheless, the drought failed to send prices upward. For one reason, Iowa alone had 437 million bushels of corn in storage; and the corn crop for the nation as a whole was seven percent above the 1954 mark. Corn prices dropped. Even worse was the fall in the price of pork. "At this time," wrote an agricultural expert from Des Moines as the year ended, "hogs are eating considerably more than they are worth." The cost of producing a hundred pounds of pork ranged from $13.50 to $15.35 in Iowa and Nebraska; but at small towns in those States farmers were being paid only $10.50 a hundred pounds. The price of soy beans (on which Secretary Benson lowered support prices for 1955 to 70 percent of parity), alas, dropped; it was $2.08 a bushel in the fall as compared with $2.54 a year earlier.

The position of the wheat-growers had some aspects

of special interest. Year by year the surplus of wheat has grown. It has been necessary to store great quantities of it in surplus war shipping. To see whole fleets of unused vessels riding in the Hudson or on the waters of Puget Sound full of unused grain is to have a sense of puzzlement that a hungry world (for populous nations *are* hungry) should also be so wasteful a world. Yet if the United States government began dumping this grain at low prices on the world market, the wheat farmers of France and Argentina, Canada and Australia, would be in arms against a step so unjust to them. Because of this huge American surplus, it is necessary for the government to place stringent controls on seeding, and to lower its support prices to the lowest figure legally permissible.

In June the wheat-farmers had to make a choice of policies. They had to vote on whether they should again keep wheat-planting down to a very low level with fairly high crop supports ($1.81 a bushel, or perhaps a little more), or should plant as much as they liked for a free market in which wheat might fall as low as $1.20. By an overwhelming majority, the wheat farmers chose a restriction on acreage. They realized that a free market could be very dangerous. The government was undoubtedly pleased by the choice they had made. If they had voted against price-supports, wheat would have fallen to unprofitable levels, other grains would have dropped in sympathy, and Congressional pressure for radical farm-relief measures would have become troublesome. But the problem of a billion-bushel wheat carry-over, almost wholly in government hands, remains. What can be

335

done with it? More gifts to poor countries, more free school lunches, more low-priced sales to families on relief, may help a little, but not much.

On all farm crops, the wide spread in prices between producer and consumer remained a disturbing element. The Kansas farmer who in September got $1.97 a bushel for wheat at his small-town elevator was told by investigators that this bushel made 67 loaves of bread which sold at retail in Chicago or New York for $12.73; the flour mill having meanwhile sold byproducts for 35 cents. In short, a bushel of wheat which paid the grower less than $2 became worth more than $13 before it reached the final buyer. Is such a wide margin necessary? Secretary of Agriculture Benson thought not. Speaking to the American Bakers' Association early in October he used such stinging words as "inefficient" and "excessively profitable," and told them bluntly that until they got costs down they were doing an injustice to farmers and bread-buyers.

The financial position of the government improved so steadily during the boom year that long before it closed the Republican leaders were declaring that they would be able to balance the budget in the fiscal year 1955-56. At the beginning of the calendar year, in January, 1955, President Eisenhower estimated in his budget that the expenditures would exceed receipts by about $2,400,000,000. Then in August this estimate was cut down to 1.7 billions; and by December the Treasury officials were confident that the fiscal year (which begins July 1 and ends June 30) would wind up with a small surplus. Of course nobody will know until the final columns are added. A slump in prosperity, a fall in corporate revenues, would wither all these happy prophecies as a wintry wind blasts orange blossoms. But the hope of a surplus with which the calendar year ended was a pleasant change from the expectation of a deficit with which it began.

Because of this change, it was unnecessary for the Administration to ask for a rise in the debt limit. The legal ceiling on our debt has stood at 281 billion, which Senator Byrd of Virginia, the Congressional watchdog on finances, is unwilling to disturb. Secretary of the Treasury Humphrey agreed with Congressional leaders to extend the existing limit for another year. It is of course true that a deficit in the national budget acts as an inflationary force, while a surplus will (if it appears) be deflationary. But some economists think that in a national economy which stood, during the calendar year 1955, at about $385 billions, and was rapidly approaching $400 billions, a few billions in the budget one way or the other would not influence the business trend as much as was once supposed.

Late in the spring the Supreme Court took its first step toward translating its decision of 1954 against segregation into action. It ordered the lower courts to require local school boards to "make a prompt and reasonable start toward full compliance." This drove a path midway between Negroes who were demanding a fixed date for the end of segregation, and Southern whites who wanted an indefinite term allowed for compliance.

Local authorities in all States are now required to establish non-segregated schools "with all deliberate speed." Just what that phrase means is anybody's guess. Obviously the Supreme Court is giving the Southern States plenty of room to change from resistance to reluctant obedience; it does not want to precipitate a crisis in Federal State relations.

For the South is recalcitrant. The States of Mississippi, Georgia, South Carolina, Louisiana, before the end of 1954, had taken steps to abolish the existing public school systems, and make it possible to vote direct payments to children, who would go to private and segregated schools. Meanwhile, some of these States would act to so improve educational facilities for Negroes as to make them physically equal to those for whites; in the hope that the Negroes would then give up their opposition to segregation. Before the end of 1955 Virginia followed the other four States along this road. Nobody supposed that the Supreme Court would permit this evasion of its decree to succeed. Test cases would certainly be brought, and the new State legislation would certainly be declared invalid. But the delaying tactics would consume time.

The year closed with the outlook uncertain, and with reports of a dangerous rise in race tensions in the South. In the long run Federal law and Federal courts cannot be defied. But much litigation may have to be decided, and some severe crises may have to be passed, before non-segregated schools prevail throughout the United States.

338

But the outlook steadily grows more hopeful. When the Supreme Court in its original school decision held that "separate but equal" is a contradiction in terms, and that separate facilities for a minority are psychologically unequal even if physically superior, it laid down a principle which could be widely applied. In November, the Court took a further step forward. It passed on cases from Maryland and Georgia which involved discrimination in public recreation facilities. Quietly but emphatically, the justices ruled that segregation of Negroes in public parks and playgrounds, on public beaches and golf-courses, as in any other tax-supported amusement places, is unconstitutional. Most of the nation heartily approved of the decision. The border States from Maryland to Oklahoma at once made it clear that they would accept the new order. In the Lower South, however, the same resentful defiance reared its head as in the educational sphere. Once more it seemed likely that evasive and delaying tactics would be used, and that public beaches and golf-courses would be turned into private holdings in an effort to defeat the Supreme Court.

It is now supposed that at least three million Negroes may be expected to vote in the South, as against only 750,000 in the election of 1948. They have become a great political power. Even in the five States which still require payment of a poll tax they are becoming formidable. If their rights are seriously infringed, they may—with the support of sympathetic whites—rally to elect men who will defend their privileges. As important as this new voting strength are some other novel elements in Southern life. One is the growing industrialization of the region, so that in State after State manufacturing is now more important than agriculture; the Negro wage-earner in mills and factories is in an advantageous position to move toward full equality. The rise of scientific mechanized agriculture in the South, and the growth of large cities and towns there, also assist progress toward that goal. It may be added that many members of the younger generation in the South take a very different attitude toward segregation from that of their elders.

Civil liberties remained a matter of deep concern throughout the year, but the emotional tension which surrounded the subject was sensibly relaxed. One reason for this was that the whole international situation relaxed a bit following the first Geneva Conference in June. As anxiety over the possibility of active hostilities with Russia and China abated, internal suspicions and fears lessened, and the temptation to infringe the basic rights of citizens was reduced. Another explanation of the calmer state of mind in America was the decline of Senator McCarthy's prestige. Throughout the year his influence on national affairs was virtually zero. His one important gesture was an effort in June to tie President Eisenhower's hands at the Geneva Conference unless he obtained in advance the agreement of Russia to discuss the position of her satellite states; and the Senate voted his resolution down by the overwhelming majority of 77 to 4.

Discussion of the security program of the government, however, never ceased, and feeling grew that the existing Federal security system would have to be overhauled and repaired. Many Democrats still recalled with indignation the charge made by Republicans in the last Congressional election that they had been "soft on treason," and the "numbers game" that had followed the Administration's early announcement that nearly 1,500 people had been dismissed from office as "security risks"—a statement widely misinterpreted to mean that many people had been subversives. Many Republicans were also discontented with the security regulations. They touch directly about two million officeholders and their families; indirectly they affect the attitudes of State and local officers and industrial executives charged with maintaining safety rules. As John B. Oakes expressed it, they were criticized as neither safeguarding freedom nor providing adequate security.

In June the Senate almost without debate passed a bill to create a bipartisan commission of twelve to review the government's standards of loyalty and security, and to report to Congress by March, 1956, whatever reforms it thought proper. The President had told Congress early in his administration that security was the concern of the executive, not Congress. However, he acquiesced in this measure. Four members of the commission were to be named by the President, four by the Vice-President, and four by the Speaker; six were to be government officers, six private citizens. President Eisenhower meanwhile said that the executive branch was itself constantly reviewing its security procedures and making whatever changes were necessary. But Washington was full of scores of men dismissed on totally inadequate grounds, or (if they chose to fight) kept waiting for months before hearings were concluded and judgment was given. The upshot might be, as in the case of Wolf Ladjesinsky, a complete clearance, but in the interim the man accused had suffered heavily.

The return to national sanity on security issues was illustrated by a variety of events besides the passage of the Senate bill. One was a decision in June by the Federal Court of Appeals that the State Department had no right to withhold a passport for foreign travel from a citizen who belonged to a small Trotskyite group. Another was the activity of the Senate's Internal Security Sub-committee, under Senator Johnson of South Carolina, in studying the question, and in questioning the Attorney-General's list of subversive organizations. Still another was the work of the Fund for the Republic, created by the Ford Foundation, in supporting special studies of case histories of persons accused of being security risks, of postoffice censorship of publications, and of intimidation of teachers. Adam Yarmolinsky, after making a careful inquiry into more than 400 case histories of persons assailed, concluded that a majority of the charges were absurdly silly.

Early in the year one witness, Harvey Matusow, who had testified against some 280 persons in public investigations of Communism, declared that he had perjured himself. Later on the Department of Justice dropped its effort of two and a half years to try Owen Lattimore for perjury. The charges against him, characterized as "formless and obscure" by Judge Luther Youngdahl (whose objections to them were twice sustained by the Court of Appeals), had been inspired by those who thought the victory of Communism in China owed something to alleged treason by Far Eastern experts.

One incident of the year carried a reminder of the sad old-time days of lynching and one-sided Southern justice. For a few days in September all eyes were turned on Sumner, Mississippi, where two white men were on trial for the alleged murder of a Negro boy. This fourteen-year-old lad, Emmett Till of Chicago, had been visiting relatives in the neighborhood; he had been accused of whistling at the pretty wife of one of the defendants; he had disappeared; and his supposed body had been found in the Tallahatchie River on August 31. Sumner, center of a rich cotton-growing county, was thrown into a turmoil. Northern reporters, Negro observers led by a Detroit Congressman, and representatives of radio and television stations thronged the place. It was evident that Mississippi herself was at the bar along with the defendants.

In the end the two men were acquitted. But the prosecution failed because the body was never clearly identified, not because Tallahatchie County rigged the trial. Both Judge Curtis M. Swango, who presided, and the prosecuting attorney were clearly anxious that exact and impartial justice be done. The failure lay with the law enforcement machinery. The sheriff was a political officer, the public prosecutor lacked funds for a proper investigation, and prejudiced local agencies impeded the

State authorities. Under all the circumstances, the indictment of the two men was creditable to Mississippi, and the insistence of the judge that Negroes be allowed to testify fully showed that a new era was dawning. Later the two defendants were put on trial for kidnapping. Even in the Deep South flagrant crimes can no longer be committed against Negroes with impunity.

The tenth anniversary of Franklin D. Roosevelt's death, April 12, was chosen for a momentous announcement: a vaccine measurably effective in preventing infantile paralysis (poliomyelitis) had at last been developed. The really creative work in making this possible had been done by various American scientists, two of whom had earlier received the Nobel prize; they had isolated the virus responsible. The final step of creating a vaccine from the killed virus was assigned to Dr. Jonas Salk of the University of Pittsburgh. The National Foundation for Infantile Paralysis, which had collected funds for scientific research as well as curative work, could justly boast a great victory. Careful trials had been made; nearly half a million children in forty-four States had been given doses of the vaccine, while parallel groups had received only dummy inoculations. The results conclusively proved the utility of the treatment.

The initial announcement was followed by a period of confusion and partial disappointment. Stocks of the vaccine were so inadequate that much heartburning was felt over their distribution; standards for testing the vaccine were at first poor, with the result that one drug firm released a dangerous type. Both the National Foundation and the Federal Government were criticized for premature and unguarded action. These difficulties, however, were but temporary. By August the National Foundation was able to declare that rigid testing standards had been instituted, that more than five million safe doses of the vaccine had been released, and that free treatment was being given to all first and second grade children throughout the nation. A Congressional medal was voted to Dr. Salk.

The country decided during the year that there was nothing mirthful about "comic books." Before 1955 was half over, thirteen States had passed laws to restrain their depiction of crime, sex, and scenes of horror; a dozen other States had debated such legislation; and two States had appointed committees to study the "comic books" and report on the problems they posed. It is obviously difficult to frame laws in this field without infringing upon legitimate rights of publication. The courts are justly sensitive to restrictions which might outlaw parts of the Bible and Shakespeare. At the same time, the presentation of violence and immorality in certain American picture books had reached a point which aroused indignation not only in this country but in other English-speaking lands to which they were exported. A storm over them raged in England.

A much larger problem, that of juvenile delinquency, is involved. This is of late a subject of the keenest concern to many Americans. It was reported during the year that statistics for juvenile delinquency showed a rise of forty-five percent between 1948 and 1953; and a Senate sub-committee under Estes Kefauver carried on an investigation. The FBI presented figures indicating that in 1953 half the burglaries and car thefts had been committed by teen-agers, nearly one-sixth of the rapes, and even one-twenty-fifth of the homicides. What are the causes? Numerous factors have been suggested, including the great wartime and postwar shifts of population, increasing use of the automobile, growth of big cities and of slum areas within them, the sale of narcotics and drink, and the currency of bad motion pictures and unwholesome television shows. At any rate, Senator Kefauver was justified in declaring: "The causes of delinquency are as complex as our society."

It is assuredly deplorable that the number of youngsters brought into juvenile courts should have risen from 300,000 in 1948 to 435,000 in 1953. Some of the remedies lie in the domain of general community improvement. Better housing, so that children may escape the overcrowding of the slums, with their low standards of living; better schools, so that teachers may exercise a direct influence upon youngsters; better recreational facilities, so that the gang will lose its appeal—these are certain of the broader needs. Juvenile courts, which have increased steadily in number since the first one was established in Chicago in 1899, may be very useful if officered by professionally trained appointees instead of political hacks. An improvement in the police forces of the cities will also help. Senator Kefauver has proposed Congressional legislation for grants to assist the States in formulating programs for the control of juvenile offences, and for training staff workers.

That youngsters are ready to respond to a very different kind of stimulation from that afforded by the comics was shown by the Davy Crockett craze that swept the country in the first half of 1955. Walt Disney's celebration of the "Legend of Davy Crockett" on the screen started a movement which was developed by song, story, and all sorts of appurtenances. Hundreds of thousands of youngsters began wearing coonskin caps, and when the raccoon population of the country showed alarming symptoms of decline, various substitutes for the real fur were found. Even overseas the craze attracted attention. "The King of the Wild Frontier," commented the London *Economist,* "aged from 3 to 12, who stalk the streets of American cities, are all agreed . . . on one point—the need for wearing, like their hero, a coonskin cap with the tail hanging down the back, and, if possible, for toting a 'b'ar-killing' flintlock rifle on their trips with mother to the supermarket and other outlying territory." All this was a reminder that the Boy Scouts and Girl Guides, among other outdoor organizations, were helping to give proper guidance to that vast majority of American children which never came within miles of delinquency.

During the summer Mr. Herbert Hoover completed his labors as chairman of the Commission on Reorganization of the executive branch, and after some forty years of public service, retired to private life. The Hoover Commission had accomplished a remarkable service.

Established just after the war (1947) by President Truman to recommend steps for making the government more efficient and economical, it did two years of fruitful work; nearly three-quarters of its proposals were ultimately adopted. Under Truman its membership was equally divided between Democrats and Republicans, and it concerned itself with the governmental machinery alone, paying no attention to policy. Then in 1953 President Eisenhower reestablished the body on a different basis. It was given a Republican majority, and empowered to examine the functions of government as well as its mechanism. Under Mr. Hoover's guidance, it took a distinctly conservative attitude, particularly in all affairs which suggested that the government might be indulging in "undue interference with free enterprise."

During the year the Commission made report after report which showed a sharp party division, or sometimes a conservative-liberal division, and the majority findings were often criticized for a tendency to look backwards. Nearly 250 distinct recommendations came from the Republican majority. Those it made on the waterpower resources of the country, urging less Federal activity and more reliance on private initiative, provoked special controversy. It was clear that these policy recommendations would encounter more opposition than the earlier and simpler proposals for improving the governmental mechanism. But the country nevertheless expressed its warm gratitude to Mr. Hoover for his devoted and valuable labors.

The controversy over public vs. private power had

several foci during the year. One was the Dixon-Yates contract; another was the Hell's Canyon question.

The meaning of Dixon-Yates was simple: The Administration was trying to introduce into the TVA, a great public-power system, an arrangement for a little privately generated power. The TVA, whose facilities have been taxed by atomic undertakings in the region as well as by growing industrial needs, required more power if it were to serve the Memphis area. Under the Dixon-Yates contract a group of private power interests would build a steam-generating plant in West Memphis, Ark., and the TVA would transmit the 600,000 kilowatt hours of power thus produced. To President Eisenhower this was a sensible step toward the partnership of national, municipal, and private enterprise in the power field which he has always advocated. To public-power enthusiasts it was the head of the camel which was soon to tear down the whole TVA tent. Many Democrats raised a cry of "Nixon, Dixon and Yates." But in June the House astounded observers by voting against a proposal to give TVA $6,500,000 for a new steam-generating plant at Fulton, Tenn., as a substitute for the Administration plan.

Then came the sudden action of Memphis, Tenn., in voting to build its own municipal steam-power station. This made the Dixon-Yates plant unnecessary. The Administration, already embarrassed by the political storm it had raised, immediately terminated the contract just as work was beginning under it. Who had won the battle? The Eisenhower Administration declared that it

349

had won by calling forth local initiative. The defenders of the TVA asserted that they had won by keeping their great power system uncontaminated with private enterprise. What was certain was that Tennessee was pleased, and Arkansas disgruntled.

Hell's Canyon, too, became a symbol. It is a gorge in the Snake River about a hundred miles below Weiser, Idaho. During the Truman Administration government officers recommended that a high Federal dam be built here. The Eisenhower Administration, however, left it to the Federal Power Commission to decide between one high Federal dam and the building of three small dams by the Idaho Power Company. The Commission after long public hearing awarded a license to the company. In this decision it had the support of Senator Herman Welker of Idaho, and of Governor Robert E. Smylie, who told a Senate sub-committee that three-fourths of the people of Idaho were in favor of private development of the waterpower. While Idaho Power went ahead with construction plans, its opponents promised that the struggle would be taken to the courts, and to the polls in the next political campaign.

Unquestionably the Northwest is suffering from a serious shortage of power to meet the needs of industrial expansion and of the fast rising population. It will need all the power that both public and private interests can furnish.

INDEX, Volume VII*

* For other references to subjects see indices in Volumes V and VI.

351

INDEX

Bricker Amendment, 235

Bridges, Senator Styles, 128, 302

Brownell, Herbert, Jr., Attorney-General, 172, 204, 296

Budget, balancing of, 5, 55, 194-195, 336

Bulganin, Marshal Nikolai A., 310-312, 319

Bunche, Ralph, 84

Byrd, Senator Harry F., 178, 247, 303, 337

Byrnes, James, 162, 253

Case, Representative Clifford, 252

Caudle, T. Lamar, 136, 137

Celler Bill, for increasing number of displaced persons admitted to country, 19

Chambers, Whittaker, 8, 215

Chiang Kai-shek, 20, 21; Formosan government, 37, 66, 104, 111

China, Communist, victory over Nationalists, 19-22; declaration of People's Republic of China, 20; treaty with Soviet Union, 36; question of recognition, 36, 67; intervention in Korea, 47-51; losses in Korean war, 97; dependence on Russia, 145; question of admittance to U. N., 226; tension with United States, 285 f.; attack on Tachen islands, 320

Ching, Cyrus S., Director of Wage Stabilization Board, 123, 132

Chou En-lai, Prime Minister, Communist China, 45, 286

Churchill, Winston, 46, 192, 193, 229, 230, 277, 310, 312

C.I.O., 132, 180, 181, 220, 221, 292, 330, 331

Clark, General Mark W., 148

Clay, General Lucius D., 123

Cold war, 1, 33, et passim

Commission on the Organization of the Executive Branch of the Government, 31, 347 f.

Commodity Credit Corporation, The, 14

Communist Party, 9; Communist Control Act, to strip Communist Party of all legal rights, 244; trials of Communists, 6; Harold Medina, Presiding Judge, 7, 8-10

Conant, James B., President of Harvard University, 51, 82

Condon, Dr. Edward U., Director of the Bureau of Standards, 270

Conference of foreign ministers, 22-23, 273 f., 297, 315

Congress, 1949 appropriations a peacetime record, 4; Eighty-first "streamlined Congress," 11; passed Housing Act, 11, 60; increased minimum wage, 12, 13-19; appropriates funds for defense, 52, 53; passed Defense Production Act, 61; extended Rent Control, 61; addressed by General MacArthur, 105-108; Eighty-second, 125-129; additional billions appropriated for defense, 130, 131, 132, 133, 134; passed McCarran Act over President's veto, 184-186; Eighty-third, 199-202, 203; grants off-shore oil rights to States, 204, 205-211, 235, 240; passed measure for revision of Federal Tax structure, 241, 242, 243; enacted Communist Control Act, 244, 245-249; Eighty-fourth, 300 f.; extended Reciprocal Trade Agreements Act, 302-303, 304-308, 341

Consumer credit, 55

Coplon, Judith, trial as Russian agent, 7, 8

Corruption, Truman Administration, 134-139

Crime investigations, 85-87, 139, 140, 141

Cripps, Sir Stafford, British Chancellor of the Exchequer, 29

Davy Crockett, legend appeals to youth, 347

Dean, Arthur H., American envoy to Korean truce talks, 228

Dean, Gordon, Chairman of Atomic Energy Commission, 125

Defense Production Act, 61, 62

Department of Health, Welfare, and Education, creation of, 201

Dewey, Thomas E., 64, 73-74; advocation of bipartisan foreign policy, 77; 140; support of Eisenhower, 142, 162; 172, 207

Dirksen, Senator Everett, 72

DiSalle, Michael, Price Administrator, 62, 64, 123

Disarmament, 313, 318

Dixon-Yates contract, 252, 349 f.

Dodge, Joseph M., Budget Director, 194, 206

Douglas, Senator Paul, 130, 179, 252

352

INDEX

Dulles, Allen W., head of Central Intelligence Agency, 206

Dulles, John Foster, 30, 32, 64, 77; stand on bipartisan policy, 78, 80; consultations concerning Japanese peace treaty, 110; chosen as Secretary of State, 171, 173; 192, 195, 212, 213, 224, 226, 233, 234, 273, 275, 278, 280, 281, 283, 297, 316-318, et passim

Durkin, Martin, Secretary of Labor, 173, 208; designs, 209, 220

Economic Commission for Europe, 57

Economic Cooperation Administration, 29, 30, 58

Economic Stabilization Agency, 62

Eden, Anthony, 192, 274, 275, 283, 313

Education, Federal aid measure stirs controversy, 15, 16, 17; Boswell's *London Journal* issued by Yale University, 80; correspondence of Thomas Jefferson issued by Princeton University Press, 81; growing enrollment and teacher shortage, 83, 189-190; growing problems, 246, 247, 305; Federal aid to, 15-17, 60, 61, 246; Education and Labor, Committee on, 16

Eisenhower, Dwight D., as possible candidate, 73, 74; 79, 90; appearance before Congress, 1951, 109; 114; message to NATO council meeting, 1951, 115; supreme commander of NATO forces, 120-123; 142, 151, 159, 160; nomination for President, 162; elected as President, 164-171; selection of members of Cabinet, 172-173; trip to Korea, 166; 184, 187, 191; inauguration, 195, 196; 197-199; 204, 220, 222, 224, 229, 231, 232, 240, 249, 253, 254, 277, 279; illness, 295 f.; speculation on second term, 300; 302, 307, 309, 310-314; aerial inspection plan, 312; 318, 320, et passim

Eisler, Gerhard, German communist, 9

Elections, 31, 32, 71-75; many aspirants for Presidential nominations, 160, 161, 162; 237, 249 f.

Ellis Island, closed as immigration headquarters, 248

Ellison, Ralph, author, 190

Employment, 2, 3, 91, 217, 218, 219

Europe, Western, 4; economic problems, 28-31; enthusiasm toward rearmament program, 53, 54; export trade, 57, 78; improvement in morale, 90, 192; 234, 288, 293, 325 f.

European Defense Community, 152, 154, 232 f., 272, 281 f.

European Payments Union, 57

European Recovery Bill, 30

Excess Profits Tax, renewal, 208

Exports, 4, 6, 218

Fair Deal, 10, 17, 59, 126, 169, 241

Fair Employment Practices Commission, 19

Fair Employment Practices Bill, 60

Fair Labor Standards Act, amendment to, 12

Family Farm Development Bill, 333

Farm Bureau Federation, 303

Farmers, conditions, 3, 4; opposition to Brannan Plan, 13; farm legislation, 13-14; farm problems, 210, 221, 292; flexible price supports, 242 f., 331-335

Faulkner, William, 80

Faure, Edgar, French Premier, 313

Federal Highway Authority, 308

Federal Housing Administration scandal, 247

Federal Power Commission, 236, 350

Flanders, Senator Ralph E., resolution to censure McCarthy, 264

Ford Foundation, 271, 326, 327, 342

Ford Motor Company, sale of stock, 326-327

Foreign aid, 52-54; battle over, 128-129, 193, 202, 203; 304

Foreign Ministers, Berlin meeting 1954, 273-275; Geneva meeting, 277-280, 313, 314; Geneva meeting October 1955, 316-319

Foreign Operations Administration, agency in charge of foreign aid, 203

Foreign trade, 218, 292, 325 f.

Foreign Trade Council Convention, advocation of "trade, not aid," 176

Formosa, neutralization of, 66

Foster, William C., Economic Cooperation Administrator, 58

France, fails to ratify EDC treaty, 282

French Indo-Chinese war, 277 f.

Frost, Robert, 80

Fulbright, Senator J. W., 264

353

INDEX

Garson-May contracts case, 134

Geneva Conference, 277 f.; "At the Summit" meeting, 310-314; Foreign Minister meeting, 316-318, 340

George, Senator Walter, 301

Germany, revolt in eastern, 229 f.; offered sovereignty and limited rearmament, 116-120; proposal for unification of, 313, 314, 316

Government spending, 4, 54, 55, 128-131, 206

Great Britain, devaluation of the pound, 28, 29

Gromyko, Andrei A., Russian delegate to San Francisco Conference, 111

Groves, Lieutenant-General Leslie R., 23

Guided missiles, 155

Halleck, Charles A., Republican Senate Floor Leader, 199

Hammarskjöld, Dag, 285; visit to China, 320

Harlan, John M., appointed to Supreme Court, 258

Harriman, Averell, 23, 68, 161, 163, 203, 252, 253, 299

Hemingway, Ernest, 80, 190

Hersey, John, author, 80

Hill, Senator Lister, 246, 307

Hiss, Alger, trial of, 6, 8

Hobby, Oveta Culp, 173; made head of Department of Health, Welfare and Education, 201

Hoffman, Paul G., 142, 169

Hoover, Herbert, 75; speech on foreign aid, 76; 108, 126, 162, 201, 202, 300, 347

Hoover Commission, 31, 202, 347 f.

Housing, 243, 305, et passim

Housing Acts, 11, 12; aid to city housing agencies, 60

Hull, Cordell, 254, 302

Humphrey, George M., chosen as Secretary of the Treasury, 172, 173, 241, 337

Hydrogen bomb, American government decides to construct a hydrogen bomb, 81, 125, 159; first explosion by Soviet Union, 229; first American explosion, 275 f., 289

Inflation, 55, 58, 62-64, 131-134, 175

Income tax administration scandal, 136, 137

India, aided by United States, 129

Installment buying, 4, 321, et passim

International Information Administration, 214

"Inventory recession," 2

Ives, Senator Irving, 75, 252, 253, 309

Japan, peace treaty with, 110-113; mutual defense treaty with, 113

Javits, Jacob K., elected Attorney-General of New York, 253

Jenner, Senator William E., 164, 165, 213

Johnson, Rev. Hewlett, refused entry into United States, 7

Johnson, Secretary Louis A., 51

Johnson, Senator Lyndon, 92, 254, 301, 342

Johnston, Eric, head of Economic Stabilization Agency, 123

Joy, Vice-Admiral C. Turner, 99

Juvenile delinquency, 345

Kefauver, Senator Estes, 86, 139, 161, 163, 298, 346

Kennedy Bill, for Federal Aid to Education, 17

Khrushchev, Nikita, 310, 311, 319

Knowland, William, 128; made Senate Majority Leader, 199, 254, 297, 301

Korean War, background, 35-39; North Korean attack, 39; American troops ordered to battle front, 40; establishment of Unified Command for U. N. forces, 41; initial retreat, 42; counterattack, 43-47; crossing of 38th parallel by U. N. troops, 45; Chinese intervention, 47-51; Russian equipment used by North Korean troops, 89, 96; U. N. retreat and rally and a final stalemate, 93, 94; U. N. and Chinese losses, 95, 97; conflict at a standstill in June, 1951, 98; long-drawn-out truce negotiations, 99-102; lists of prisoners exchanged, 100; continued stalemate, 143 f.; compound outbreaks, 148; Indian proposal, 149 f.; American sick and wounded prisoners tell of enemy's brutality, 225; "escape" of 20,000 North Korean prisoners, 225-226; truce terms, 226

354

INDEX

Parnell, Thomas, Chairman, House Un-American Activities Committee, 10
Peress, Irving, 259
Pinay, Antoine, 316
Point Four, 202-203
Price control, 62, 64

Quemoy island, 320

Rankin, John, excluded from House Un-American Activities Committee, 10
Rayburn, Sam, 307
Reciprocal Trade Agreements Bill, 11
Reciprocal Trade Act, 128, 198, 201, 202, 302
Reconstruction Finance Corporation inquiry, 135-136
Reconstruction Finance Corporation, termination of, 201
Reed, Representative Daniel, 205, 206, 208
Rent-control, extension of, 15, 61
Reuther, Walter, 180, 181, 220, 328, 329, 330
Revenue Act, increasing taxes, 134
Rhee, Syngman, 43, 44; "escape" of North Korean prisoners, 225, 226
Ridgway, General Matthew B., 49, 93, 99, 101, 105, 152
Riots, State penitentiaries, 189
Road construction, Federal aid to, 307, et passim
Rockefeller, John D., Jr., gift to Metropolitan Museum of Art, 190
Roosevelt, Mrs. Franklin D., 17
Roosevelt, Franklin D., Jr., defeated in election, 253
Russell, Senator Richard B., 161, 163
Russell, Bertrand, 277

St. Lawrence Seaway, 248
Salk, Dr. Jonas, 345
Saltonstall, Senator Leverett, 142, 252
Sampson, Edith, Negro, appointed alternate delegate for U. S. in United Nations Assembly, 84
Sandburg, Carl, 80
San Francisco Conference, for Japanese peace treaty, 11, 171 f.

Sawyer, Secretary of Commerce, 3
Schuman, Robert, French Foreign Minister, 117, 154, 232
Schuman Plan, for unification of iron and steel industries of Western Europe, 77, 119
Southeast Asia Treaty Organization (SEATO), 281, 285, 321
Security regulations, 267 f., 340 f., et passim
Segregation, 84, 85; Supreme Court decision outlawing, 255 f.; 337 f.
Senate Committee on Organized Crime, exposé of American underworld by special committee, 85, 86, 87, 161
Senate Crime Investigating Committee, 139-140
SHAPE, North Atlantic Treaty Organization Headquarters, 121, 122, 152
Small Business Administration, substitute for Reconstruction Finance Corporation, 201
Smith Act, 6-8
Smith, Senator H. Alexander, 306
Smith, Senator Margaret Chase, 75, 263
Snyder, Howard M., 296
Social security, 243
Southeast Asia Treaty Organization, 283
Soviet Union, growth in strength, 20, 53; plan for curtailing of atomic power, 25; boycott of U. N., 37; explosion of hydrogen bomb, 191, 229; relations with the United States, 229 f.; granting of East German sovereignty, 315; make most of friction in Middle East, 316; shipment of arms to Egypt, 316, et passim
Spaak, Henri, Foreign Minister of Belgium, 283, 288
Sparkman, Senator John J., 333
Spellman, Cardinal Francis J., 17
Stassen, Harold, 160, 173, 203, 233, 297
State Department, 6, 8; issuance of "White Paper," 21; attacks on, 64, 65, 75, 110; Secretary Dulles demands "positive loyalty" from personnel, 212, 213; attack by McCarthy, 213; 342, et passim
Statehood bills, Hawaii and Alaska, 126, 198, 244, 245, 309
Stevens, Robert, Secretary of the Air Force, 195, 260-262

356

INDEX

Stevens, Wallace, 80

Stevenson, Adlai E., 161, 162; nomination for President, 163; 170, 181, 187, 249, 298

Strauss, Admiral Lewis, Head of Atomic Energy Commission, 269, 270, 277

Summerfield, A. E., Postmaster-General, 173

Supreme Court, 8, 84, 188-189; decision outlawing racial segregation, 255 f., 337 f., et passim

Symington, Senator Stuart, 299

Taber, John, Chairman of House Appropriations Committee, 207

Taft, Senator Robert A., 15, 18, 72, 74, 75, 116; view on nation's economy, 130; announcement of candidacy for Republican nomination for President, 141, 160, 161; 169, 171, 179; cooperation with Eisenhower, 198; death, 199, 200

Taft-Hartley Act, 19, 60, 74, 126, 182, 197, 198, 208, 245

Talbott, Harold E., Secretary of the Air Force, 196

Tax structure, revision of, 241, 242

Television, growth of, 237

Thurmond, J. Strom, 253

Tideland Oil Bill, 186, 187

Till, Emmett, 343

Truman, Harry S., announcement of first atomic bomb explosion in Russia, 1; 5, 17, 37; announcement of sending American forces to Korea, 40; announcement of increase in armed forces, 52; loss in prestige, 59; 62; disagreement with MacArthur in policy, 68; meeting with General MacArthur at Wake Island, 69; removal of MacArthur, 102; opening of San Francisco Conference, 111; 126; decline in prestige, 127; 131, 134, 139, 142, 163, 167, 171, 176, 182, 188, 191, 193; farewell message, 194; 196, 204, 212, 348, et passim

TVA, expansion of principle, 18, et passim

Tydings, Senator Millard E., 65, 73, 263

UNESCO, 193

United Nations, 22, 34, 35; boycott by Russia, 37, 38; Security Council asks for action in Korea, 40-41, 46; loyalty checks on American workers and applicants, 212; American support of, 287, et passim

Universal military training, 305, et passim

United States, "inventory recession," 2; economic stability, 2-6; policy towards China, 21 f.; signed North Atlantic Pact, 25-27, 28, 29, 30; outbreak of Korean conflict, 34; rearmament, 89-90; signs peace treaty with Japan, 110-113, 123; problem of combating crime, 130-141; faced with stalemate in Korean war, 143-147; truce talks, 148-150, 174; called a "self-sufficient giant," 176-179; 191, 192, 193, 218, 228, 229, 232, 235, 248; tension in relations with Red China, 285-287; produces new nuclear weapons, 289-290; concern over President Eisenhower's illness, 295, 296; 1955 a year of great boom, 321-324; problem to establish non-segregated schools, 337-340

Vandenberg, Senator Arthur H., 64, 75

Voice of America, 214

Wage Stabilization Board, 123, 132

Walker, General W. H., 49, 50, 93

Warren, Earl, 74, 161, 297, et passim

Warren, Robert Penn, author, 80

Watkins, Arthur V., head of committee on the censure of McCarthy, 264

Weeks, Sinclair, Secretary of Commerce, 173, 209, 217

Weinberg, Sidney, assistant to Secretary Wilson, 123

Western European Union, 283, 284

Westinghouse Electric Company strike, 327

White Paper, issued by State Department to excuse and explain loss of China to Communists, 21

White, Dr. Paul D., 296

Williams, Governor Mennen, 299

Williams, William Carlos, 80

Wilson, Charles E., 63, 92, 123, 132; chosen as Secretary of Defense, 172, 173; confirmed for cabinet post, 195

Youngdahl, Judge Luther, 267, 343

Zwicker, General Ralph W., 259, 260, 265

357